Retiree Health Benefits: What Is the Promise?

AN EBRI-ERF POLICY FORUM

EMPLOYEE BENEFIT RESEARCH INSTITUTE

© 1989 Employee Benefit Research Institute
Education and Research Fund
2121 K Street, NW, Suite 600
Washington, DC 20037-2121
(202) 659-0670

Material in Appendix B copyright by Financial Accounting Standards Board, 401 Merritt 7, P.O. Box 5116, Norwalk, Connecticut, 06856-5116, U.S.A. Reprinted with permission. Copies of the complete document are available from the FASB.

Library of Congress Cataloging-in-Publication Data

EBRI-ERF Policy Forum (1989: Washington, D.C.)
    Retiree health benefits, what is the promise? / an EBRI-ERF Policy Forum.

The forum was held October 1988 in Washington, D.C.

Includes index.
ISBN 0-86643-064-4

    1. Insurance, Health—United States. 2. Insurance, Health—United States—Accounting. 3. Postemployment benefits—United States. 4. Postemployment benefits—United States—Accounting. I. Employee Benefit Research Institute (Washington, D C.). Education and Research Fund. II. Title.
HG9396.E27   1989   331'.25'5—dc19   89-1289

Printed in the United States of America

                                                            CIP

Table of Contents

PART TWO
LEGAL ISSUES AND ACCOUNTING REQUIREMENTS

PART THREE
THE RESPONSE OF EMPLOYERS AND UNIONS

PART FOUR
PUBLIC POLICY CONCERNS

List of Tables and Charts

Foreword

Until the early 1980s, many employers provided their retirees with health insurance coverage without giving much attention to costs. Retirees represented only a small proportion of the entire work force and were typically included in the active-worker health insurance plan, with no assessment of age-related costs. As well, many employers presumed they could end the benefit at any time.

The combination of escalating health care costs, growing numbers of retirees, and legal precedent establishing employee entitlement to retiree health insurance now confronts many employers, who face huge unfunded liabilities for these benefits. In addition, employers now face a rule proposed by the Financial Accounting Standards Board (FASB) that would require them to determine the cost and value of benefits promised to retirees and include the amounts on their corporate income statements (1992) and balance sheets (1997).

The costs involved are substantial. The Employee Benefit Research Institute (EBRI) estimates the present value of private employers' liability for retiree health insurance obligations to be between $169 billion and $250 billion, depending on the ultimate value of Medicare. To cope with these challenges, many employers are reconsidering the nature and implications of their retiree health care benefit commitments. They are restructuring plans, developing new strategies to manage costs, attempting to limit legal liabilities, and seeking appropriate prefunding vehicles.

In 1987, the Education and Research Fund of EBRI published a policy study, *Measuring and Funding Corporate Liabilities for Retiree Health Benefits*, which focused on how employers might deal with the issue through funding, and how much alternative approaches might cost. In October 1988, an EBRI policy forum comprehensively explored the issue, which provides the basis for this book. Participants in the day-long forum discussed employer initiatives under way and possible future strategies, as well as relevant legal and legislative issues. The forum brought together corporate executives, government officials, and representatives from labor and the legal profession, each of whom brought a unique perspective to the discussion.

Retiree Health Benefits: What Is the Promise? integrates the papers and proceedings of the policy forum with additional supplemental material, including the exposure draft of FASB's proposed standard, "Employers' Accounting for Postretirement Benefits Other Than Pensions." The book is organized into four parts, dealing with the benefit "promise" and its cost, legal issues and accounting requirements, the response of employers and unions, and public policy concerns. EBRI's intent in developing this volume is to give corporate planners, benefit experts, policymakers, the news media, and the public a fuller understanding of the importance and complexity of the retiree health benefit issue, and clarify the reasons for the increasing attention it is given. EBRI's Education and Research Fund will publish a second major study on retiree health financing in late 1989 that builds upon this book.

On behalf of EBRI and its Education and Research Fund, I wish to thank the policy forum speakers and participants for their substantial contributions to this book. Special thanks are due to Laura Bos, Nancy Newman, and Shannon Braymen for planning the policy forum; to Deborah Holmes for compiling, editing, and producing this book; and to Christine Dolan for preparing the index.

The views expressed in this book are solely those of the authors and the forum participants. They should not be attributed to the officers, trustees, members of EBRI, its staff, or its Education and Research Fund.

DALLAS L. SALISBURY
President
Employee Benefit Research Institute

May 1989

About the Authors

DEBORAH J. CHOLLET

Dr. Chollet is senior research associate at the Employee Benefit Research Institute (EBRI) in Washington, DC, where she conducts research related to private health insurance and public health care financing. Before joining EBRI, Dr. Chollet was a research fellow at the National Center for Health Services Research, U.S. Department of Health and Human Services, and served on the economics faculty of Temple University in Philadelphia. Dr. Chollet has written and lectured extensively in the area of private and public health insurance and employee and retiree benefit plans. Her current research includes health care financing for the elderly and for the uninsured population in the United States.

JOSEPH W. DUVA

Mr. Duva is corporate director of employee benefits at Allied-Signal, Inc., in Morristown, New Jersey. He is responsible for planning and directing the company's employee benefit programs worldwide. He was previously director of employee benefits and compensation at SCM Corporation in New York. Mr. Duva is a member of the National Association of Manufacturers subcommittee on health care and a member of the Pew Corporate Fellowship, which is held in conjunction with Boston University's Health Policy Institute. He writes a regular column for *Business Insurance* and has made many presentations on health care costs and written numerous articles on human resource subjects.

ALAIN C. ENTHOVEN

Dr. Enthoven is a professor of public and private management and health care economics at Stanford University. Before joining Stanford in 1973, he held positions at The RAND Corporation, the U.S. Department of Defense, and Litton Industries. He has held teaching and consulting positions at numerous institutions, including the Massachusetts Institute of Technology, the University of Washington, the Brookings Institution, and the health care studies unit of the Mayo Clinic. Dr. Enthoven has written and lectured extensively on a variety of subjects.

KEVIN P. FLATLEY

Mr. Flatley, vice president, employee benefits, at American Express Company, is responsible for the coordination and planning of the company's worldwide benefit programs. Mr. Flatley is a member of the executive committee of the board of directors of the Association of Private Pension and Welfare Plans. Before joining American Express, he was director of employee benefits for Emhart Corporation, a multinational manufacturing firm headquartered in Farmington, Connecticut. Prior to that, he was a consultant for Coopers and Lybrand.

GARY HENDRICKS

Mr. Hendricks is chief economist and director of the Office of Research and Economic Analysis in the Pension and Welfare Benefits Administration (PWBA) of the U.S. Department of Labor (DOL). Previously, he was associate director of office policy and legislative analysis within PWBA and worked within the office of the secretary as an advisor on pension and Social Security matters to the assistant secretary for policy. Before joining DOL, Mr. Hendricks spent nine years at the Urban Institute as a researcher and policy analyst in the area of income security and retirement policy. For the six years prior to coming to Washington, he was a member of the teaching staff and an associate project director at the University of Michigan's Survey Research Center.

CHARLES N. KAHN

Mr. Kahn is the minority health counsel to the House Committee on Ways and Means. Before joining the Committee's minority staff, he was the senior health policy advisor to Sen. Dave Durenberger (R-MN), while Sen. Durenberger served as chairman, Health Subcommittee of the Senate Finance Committee. Mr. Kahn also served as legislative assistant for health to Sen. Dan Quayle (R-IN). From 1980 to 1983 he served as director of the Office of Financial Management Education at the Association of University Programs in Health Administration (AUPHA). Before going to AUPHA, he completed an administrative residency with the Teaching Hospital Department of the Association of American Medical Colleges.

PATRICK F. KILLEEN

Mr. Killeen is assistant director of the Social Security department of the United Auto Workers (UAW). This department comprises employee benefits consultants, actuaries, and health care specialists who assist with the development and negotiation of UAW employee benefit plans. The department is also centrally involved in UAW public policy activities relating to Social Security, health care, and regulation of employee benefit plans. Mr. Killeen is a member of the Health Alliance Plan of Michigan, the Health Security Action Council, the National Association of Health Data Organizations, and the American Public Health Association.

BURMA H. KLEIN

Ms. Klein is assistant director of the Pension Equity Group of the U.S. General Accounting Office (GAO). The division has issued numerous reports and testimony on pension integration, top-heavy rules, and pension portability. Ms. Klein is currently involved with the GAO project to assess corporate liabilities for retiree health benefits. Before joining GAO eight years ago, she worked for the U.S. Department of Education as an evaluator of education programs.

DAVID MOSSO

Mr. Mosso became assistant director of research and technical activities of the Financial Accounting Standards Board (FASB) in January of 1988. He joined FASB in 1978 as a member of the board. In 1986 he was appointed its vice chairman, serving in that position until the completion of his second five-year term. Before joining the board, Mr. Mosso was fiscal assistant secretary of the U.S. Department of the Treasury. He joined the Treasury Department in 1955 and served in various capacities, including commissioner of accounts.

THOMAS G. NELSON

Mr. Nelson is an associate member with the Chicago office of Milliman & Robertson, Inc. A fellow of the Society of Actuaries and member of the American Academy of Actuaries, he has been active in each of these organizations, as well as in the Chicago Actuarial Association. He has served on the Academy's committees on health and on relations with accountants and on its task force on national health care issues. He is chairman of the committee on health and welfare plans. Nelson has written articles and made presentations on a number of topics related to group health care programs, such as postretirement benefits and the implications of recent legal and accounting actions.

K. PETER SCHMIDT

Mr. Schmidt is a partner in the Washington, DC, law firm of Arnold & Porter, specializing in tax and employee benefit matters, particularly as they affect multiemployer plans. He has written and spoken extensively in the benefits area, including papers and seminars for American Law Institute/American Bar Association, the Practicing Law Institute, New York University, the Institute on Labor, *New York Law Journal*, and Warren, Gorham & Lamont. He also writes a regular column on benefits litigation for EBRI's *Employee Benefit Notes*.

PART ONE
RELATING THE PROMISE TO THE COST

The security of retiree health benefits has become a prominent public policy issue affecting employers, policymakers, and labor unions and other organizations that represent millions of active and retired workers. Part One of *Retiree Health Benefits: What Is the Promise?* examines the legal nature and prevalence of this commitment and the relation of the expense involved to the larger issue of general health care cost inflation.

Our most important challenge, according to Alain C. Enthoven in chapter I, is not coping with the new Financial Accounting Standards Board (FASB) rule on the reporting of retiree medical benefits, but rather to come to terms with "the awesome total of health care costs for elders and the growing number of elders per working aged person."

There is a need for fundamental, long-term efforts to slow the growth of health care spending and bring it roughly into line with the growth in the Gross National Product (GNP), according to Enthoven. He proposes that consumers be offered incentives to reward provider organizations for the delivery of high-quality, cost-effective health care. In addition, he says, there is a great need to increase savings to the extent that each generation saves enough during its working years to pay for its own retirement.

Enthoven supports tax-sheltered savings opportunities for all workers and not merely for long-service employees retiring from large corporations or for middle- and high-income retirees. He discusses the possibility of a system of compulsory saving and points to the need for universal health insurance.

In chapter II, Deborah J. Chollet describes the prevalence of retiree health insurance as an employee benefit and the prevalence and distribution of this benefit among early retirees (aged 55 to 64) and retirees aged 65 and older. She estimates the present value of private employers' liability for retiree health insurance obligations to be approximately $169 billion, of which nearly $101 billion is associated with current workers and slightly more than $68 billion with current retirees.

Chollet reviews FASB documents that address the appropriate accounting practice for corporate-sponsored retiree health and life in-

1

surance benefits, and describes various legislative proposals aimed at encouraging employers to advance-fund retiree health insurance obligations. The legislative debate will be a long one, she suggests, and the result may be measures that are less favorable to employers than comparable pension legislation has been.

In chapter III, participants reflect on a number of questions related to retiree health benefits and health care costs in general. They discuss whether individual saving is an appropriate answer to the problem of escalating health care costs, and whether some system of compulsory saving should be considered.

Participants also discuss the effectiveness of health maintenance organizations and similar group practices in managing costs, and explore policy issues surrounding the provision of tax-sheltered employer-provided health benefits. Looking ahead, they attempt to estimate future medical care inflation in terms of the GNP.

I. Retiree Health Benefits as a Public Policy Issue

PAPER BY ALAIN C. ENTHOVEN

Putting the Problem into Perspective

Start with the Grand Total—In 1982, the Financial Accounting Standards Board (FASB) proposed that the cost of retirees' health care be accrued during the service lives of employees who are expected to receive these benefits. The pay-as-you-go method of funding would no longer be acceptable in accrual basis financial statements. In 1986, the Department of Labor estimated that the present value of the liability of private-sector employers for postretirement health benefits was about $100 billion in 1983 (U.S. Department of Labor, 1986). Subsequently, the Employee Benefit Research Institute (EBRI) has developed estimates for total unfunded employer liability, including the public sector, of about $280 billion (Chollet, 1988). This figure includes the accumulated liability for workers who have not yet retired. The private sector's share is estimated to be about $169 billion. The U.S. General Accounting Office (GAO) has recently estimated the private sector's liability at $221 billion, not adjusted for this year's changes in Medicare (Klein, 1988). In July 1986, LTV Corporation filed for reorganization under bankruptcy and terminated the health benefits of 78,000 retirees. These events and others like them have attracted much attention. What is the problem? And how big is it?

Employers' liability is a piece of a much larger problem. To gain perspective, we should start with the total magnitude of the retiree health cost problem. I arbitrarily pick 40 as the age at which savings for retirement should begin. What is the present value of post-age-64 health care expenditures for all people now aged 40 and over? A precise calculation would take each annual cohort, factor in a life table, retirement rates, age-specific health care spending, and growth rates— all discounted to a present value. The task exceeds my resources, but there is a simple way to get a rough figure.

Personal health care expenditures for people aged 65 and over were estimated at $4,202 per elderly individual in 1984 (Waldo and Lazenby, 1984). That would be approximately $5,600 in 1988. There are about 60 million Americans aged 40 to 64 today. The average person reaching age 65 in the year 2000 will have a remaining life expectancy of 17.9

3

years (Wade, 1988). Real health care spending per capita has been growing about 4.6 percent per year in this decade. What is the real long-term interest rate? That is a very complex issue, but I believe that a reasonable answer would be in the range of 4 percent to 5 percent; for convenience, call it 4.6 percent. The present value of each of these people's post-age-64 health care costs is 17.9 times $5,600 in 1988 dollars or around $100,000. Of the 60 million, approximately 90 percent will reach age 65. Therefore, the present value of their post-age-64 health care costs is $5.4 trillion. A similar calculation for people now aged 65 and over adds another $1.3 trillion, for a total of $6.7 trillion. This is about three times the national debt. This number is, of course, extremely sensitive to some very uncertain assumptions. In particular, it is difficult to believe that real health care spending per capita can continue to grow at anything like 4.6 percent per year.

Among other considerations, this calculation suggests that the "iceberg" is the future cost for people still working; the costs for present retirees are the tip.

It is difficult to deal with such a huge number, so I will express the same problem another way.

The $4,202 per elder in 1984 multiplied by 28.33 million elders equals $119 billion, or 3.2 percent of Gross National Product (GNP). Let us extrapolate these figures to the year 2020. Real GNP per capita grew 1.8 percent per year in the 1980s, more than during the 1970s and about the same amount as during the 1960s. The 1.8 percent consisted of 0.8 percent growth in real GNP per worker, 0.8 percent in workers per working age population, and 0.2 percent working age population as a share of the total (U.S. President, 1988). By 1984, 79.3 percent of the working age population was in the work force, so there is not much room for further growth in that ratio. Assume this figure tops out at 90 percent in the year 2020. That is 0.35 percent per year growth. Working age population as a share of the total will be flat. Therefore, 1.15 percent per year growth in GNP per working age person looks like a reasonable baseline case. How fast will real costs per elder grow? As noted earlier, real expenditures per capita have been growing about 4.6 percent per year in this decade. However, a recent Health Care Financing Administration (HCFA) analysis projects that from 1986 to the year 2026, a changing age/sex structure alone will account for a 0.58 percent per year increase in real per capita expenditures.[1] Thus, an age-specific expenditure growth rate might be

---

[1] See U.S. Department of Health and Human Services, Health Care Financing Admin-

closer to 4.0 percent. If we project the growth of a particular age group, it would be more accurate to use age-specific rates. However, there will be aging within the elder group. If we assume, respectively, that real health care expenditures per elder grow 4.0, 3.0, or 1.15 percent per year, elder care as a share of GNP will be 13.1, 9.2, or 4.8 percent. The higher numbers are staggering amounts. I believe that spending 13 percent of GNP on the health care of elders simply cannot happen. Some corrective forces are bound to come into play. Nevertheless, this calculation helps define a very serious problem.

The reaction of many people to the proposed FASB ruling, the hundreds of billions of dollars in employer liability for retiree medical benefits, and the LTV bankruptcy has been to focus attention on how bookkeepers are going to present this information, who will pay for employers' past promises, and how to secure retirees' rights to promised benefits. These questions are secondary; they are like arguing over deck-chair rights on the Titanic. The big problems are the awesome total of health care costs for elders and the growing number of elders per working aged person.

The Need for Fundamental Long-Term Solutions—It is important to get away from the musical chairs approach in which everyone tries to make someone else pay. As a nation, we must focus on fundamental long-term solutions. I see two broad avenues of approach.

First, we must slow the growth of health care spending, bringing it roughly into line with growth in GNP. This will not be easy. A number of industrialized democracies have done it by having their governments assume responsibility for health care financing and placing it under firm prospective global budgets. Obviously, this is not painless. In Great Britain and Sweden it has resulted in queues and rationing of care.

Some slowing of the growth in health care spending for elders might be achieved by a change in social priorities and medical ethics. Former governor of Colorado Richard Lamm and others have questioned the appropriateness of spending large amounts of money for costly medical technology to achieve small gains in the health status of frail elderly persons near the end of their lives. Others have questioned the medical appropriateness of much of the care they do receive (Winslow, Solomon, Chassin et al., 1988, and Winslow, Kosecoff, Chassin, 1988).

---

istration, Division of National Cost Estimates, "National Health Expenditures, 1986–2000," *Health Care Financing Review* (Summer 1987). Per capita expenditures are deflated by the GNP implicit deflator.

I have proposed that we try to get spending under control by a concerted strategy of managed competition in which sponsors—the large group purchasers—use cost-conscious consumer choice as a way of transforming our health care system into efficient delivery organizations. The idea is to manage the incentives consumers have to reward provider organizations for delivering high-quality, cost-effective care (Enthoven, 1988a and 1988b). It is a complicated strategy, which may be too complex for most employers to manage. However we do it, I cannot overemphasize the importance of getting this spending under control soon. Continued growth at even 3 percent per year would impose an enormous burden on taxpayers and elders.

Next, we must greatly increase savings. Each generation ought to save enough during its working years to pay for its own retirement, including health care. It seems unjust for each generation to impose these costs on the next. The custom of each generation relying on younger generations seemed reasonable in the past. But by the year 2020 there will be only 3.3 working aged people for each elder, or 2.1 workers per beneficiary in the Social Security system. The present generation of frail elderly can complain that they did not know how costly their care would be. But people now in their forties and fifties should be warned. Public policy should warn people and require savings. As each person reaches age 65, he or she or society should have saved about $100,000 for his or her future health care costs (adjusted for cost growth and post-age-65 earnings on assets). This would be roughly $50,000 net of Medicare. I am not now prepared to make specific recommendations, but we ought to be thinking in terms of strong medicine, such as compulsory individual medical accounts. I appreciate that the suggestion of compulsory savings will seem unpalatable in our free society. However, if elderly persons reach retirement age without adequate savings, the rest of society will be forced to pay for their care. As a society, we are simply not going to let them suffer and die without care.

To encourage adequate savings, we should reconsider normal retirement age, not to mention policies favoring early retirement. At present, many policies are biased in favor of early retirement. For example, Social Security beneficiaries in effect are taxed at 50 percent on their post-age-64 earnings.* It would be easier for people to save

---

*Editor's note: Currently, there is a Social Security earnings test limiting the amount that can be earned before Social Security benefits are partially or fully reduced. In 1989, a 65-year-old person with $8,800 or less in earnings can continue to work and receive all of the Social Security benefits; those who retire early are permitted to

for their postretirement incomes and health care if they worked longer. Thus we need to reconsider the concept of retirement, to make it a process rather than an event. We need to change the incentives, to let people get the full actuarial benefit of working longer, and to restructure careers so that people can work full or part time after age 65. As we consider alternative policies for securing postretirement health benefits, we should avoid creating more incentives for early retirement.

Who Shall Pay?

Who should pay for these costs?

Medicare and Medicaid—HCFA actuaries estimated that in 1984 two-thirds of the personal health care costs of the elderly (or $2,823 per elderly person) were paid by Medicare, Medicaid, or other government programs and, therefore, largely by working taxpayers (Waldo and Lazenby, 1984). Medicare's share will increase as a result of the passage of the Medicare Catastrophic Coverage Act of 1988, although the additional costs will be borne by beneficiaries.

How much should Medicare and Medicaid pay? We are caught in a bind. One the one hand, Medicare and Medicaid ought to assure every elderly person access to what we can tolerate as a decent minimum of health care. On the other hand, we must not transfer more of the burden from retirees to workers. In 1988 approximately 37 percent of federal outlays went to incomes and health care for the aged and disabled, about $100 billion more than was spent for national defense. More increases will be produced as current programs interact with demographic trends. Reluctance to transfer more of the burden to workers was reflected in Congress' decision to fund Medicare catastrophic coverage with higher premiums and taxes on beneficiaries. More tax increases on workers to support health care for the elderly would probably result in higher marginal tax rates, a drag on economic growth, and incentives to avoid payment of taxes.

Of the $6.7 trillion liability for postretirement benefits, approximately one-third, or $2.2 trillion, is the liability of individuals and firms in the private sector. Apparently roughly $170 billion to $221 billion of that is the liability of private-sector employers (Chollet,

---

earn up to $6,480 (these figures are adjusted annually). For every two dollars in earnings above the limit, Social Security will withhold one dollar of benefits. Beginning at age 70, however, there is no limit on the amount that can be earned without penalty. Beginning in 1990, one benefit dollar will be withheld for every three dollars in earnings above the limit for those 65 and older.

7

1988, and Klein, 1988). One way or another, most of the private sector's cost for postretirement health care will be borne by retirees.

What looks large to employers is a small part of the total problem.

Financial Accounting Standards Board

What issues are raised by the FASB proposal to require corporations to report the liabilities and accrued expenses of postretirement health care benefits on their financial statements? Contrary to what some company spokespersons appear to be saying, this requirement would not "raise their postretirement benefit costs by tens of millions of dollars" (Berton, 1988). It would merely require the accurate reporting (if such a term can be used in connection with such uncertain amounts) of costs and liabilities that already exist. It is simply a matter of truth in financial reporting. What justification could there be for concealing these liabilities from interested readers of financial statements? Would it not make sense for all public- and private-sector organizations to have to report such accruals in full? For one thing, this would force current recognition of benefit accruals in wage determination. Some public-sector officials and private-sector managers want to reconcile the conflicting pressures they experience by reporting a balanced budget or a profit while buying labor peace with promises that will not become due until later, on someone else's watch. Surely public policy should discourage this practice.

I have heard expressions of concern that the FASB standard will hurt stock prices, raise the cost of capital, put executives' options "under water," and increase the danger of unfriendly takeovers. I sympathize with the executives. I know what it feels like to have one's stock options deep under water. At first I was inclined not to believe that the FASB standard would affect stock prices. After all, reporting the accruals does not change cash flows. I believed that there was some truth in the view that the market processes and discounts all available information and that the growing costs of health care for retirees had received so much attention that by the late 1980s they could not come as a big surprise. Then I heard EBRI President Dallas Salisbury say that EBRI had questioned 25 securities analysts and found that none of them knew anything about the liability for postretirement health benefits. Apparently the analysts have not been doing their jobs and have missed liabilities by the billions. Booking these liabilities will change important debt-equity ratios that might affect indentures, loan agreements, and the like. On the other hand, analysts may have figured that what the United Automobile Workers and United Steelworkers receive in health care they will not receive in wages, so it does not matter. In any case, the cat is out of the bag now. Surely it would be a Pyrrhic victory for management to win a big battle with FASB on this issue and not be required to report accrued costs and liabilities. The battle itself would call attention to the problem. Analysts will find out and factor these costs into their evaluations. The credibility of financial statements would not be helped by an attempt to cover up these liabilities.

The Roles of Employers, Stockholders, and Workers

Promises, Promises—Employers and stockholders obtained the services of some employees by promising them postretirement health benefits. It seems reasonable for the courts to take the view that they should have to fulfill these promises, although it may not be wise for the "creditors" to insist on full payment.

I am not aware that any stockholders are asking for taxpayers to relieve them of this obligation, but if they were, it would be difficult to see any justification for it. However, the new discovery of the burden of postretirement health benefits—much of which is for pre-Medicare retirees—may create some new converts to publicly financed universal health insurance.

There are some serious problems inherent in the way the issue of promises is being resolved. One is the dynamic aspect of health benefits and the consequent need for flexibility. This point is argued cogently by Willis Goldbeck, who points out that, in response to changing conditions in recent years, major socially responsible employers have made benefit design changes that improve retirees' medical plans (U.S. Congress, 1986). These changes include the addition of hospice services, second surgical opinion, outpatient surgery, prescription drugs, prevention programs, outpatient mental health and substance abuse treatment, preadmission testing and certification, concurrent utilization review, home health care, case management, health maintenance organizations (HMOs), and organ transplants. It makes no sense to say that employers can add but they cannot subtract. Restructuring for cost containment is essential. We certainly would not want to force employers to say "we will pay only for technology that was available the year you retired," or to force them to drop benefits altogether.

When one reflects on the rapid and continuing changes in the technology and organization of medicine, one must realize that it is unclear precisely what was promised to retirees. Certainly it cannot be exactly the coverage and standard of care they had in their final years as active employees. Too many things change every year. Congress enacts catastrophic coverage. Employers replace indemnity coverage with HMOs and preferred provider organizations. It would not make sense for the courts to say that employers are obligated to continue the same indemnity coverage with the same deductibles. What about coverage for new drugs and procedures introduced years after retirement? I doubt that health care of retirees is good material for a long-term contract. For example, try to write down exactly what you are promising today's workers for their coverage in the year 2001. You will find that it is a nearly impossible task.

Congress changes Medicare every year: there are increased deductibles, changes in coverage and premiums, and changes in the payment system. This is accepted because the process is democratic and nobody gets hurt too badly. People think of the private sector as more flexible than government, but this may not be the case if the courts freeze retiree health care coverage. Perhaps a public social insurance model will prove to be a more adaptable way to finance retiree health care.

Death Spiral for Mature Employers?—One can imagine some grim scenarios for mature industrial companies and their retirees resulting from the burden of unfunded postretirement health benefits. What I say here is speculative, and I hope it is wrong. However, people should be thinking about this issue now while there is time to do something.

The health care cost per automobile for a mature American producer is likely to exceed by a significant amount that for a new manufacturer, for instance, a foreign company that produces automobiles in the United States. The mature American company will have an older work force, more health care costs for active employees and retirees, and more retirees per active worker. I doubt that the amount can be quantified on the basis of public information. But some available information can help give us a rough idea. The Ford Motor Co. reported 1987 outlays for postretirement health benefits for U.S. and Canadian employees of $341 million (Ford Motor Company, 1987). Because there are a larger number of U.S. workers and Canada has universal publicly financed health insurance, I estimate that 95 percent of this cost is for U.S. workers. U.S. factory sales of cars, trucks, and tractors came to 3.7 million units year. This would amount to approximately $88 per unit. GAO estimates that, on average, employers' 1988 accruals would be about

3.5 times current cash outlays for retiree health care (Klein, 1988). Thus, we may be seeing costs of $300 or more per car. Of course, the foreign companies have postretirement benefit costs, too. I am assuming that their workers are younger, so they have a longer time during which to reserve funds for retirement. Also, their benefits may be less generous. It seems reasonable to guess that the difference might be at least $100 per car now, and may possibly be several times that in a decade—enough to become a significant competitive factor. The same circumstances would apply to mature steel companies competing with new mini-mills and to other manufacturing companies, unless their managements succeed in reducing retiree benefits.

If the mature companies adjust their prices to cover these costs, one can imagine that this competitive disadvantage would cause them to lose market share to the younger companies. As they do, the problem would become worse. The ratio of retirees to active workers would rise, and eventually the companies would go into a "death spiral" and join LTV. They could not pay the high retiree health care and other costs and price their products competitively.

How serious are the consequences? Does this scenario require public intervention?

The bankruptcy of the mature steel and auto companies would not mean an end to steel and auto production in the United States. It would mean that the production of mature companies would be replaced by that of newer companies with lower costs. If the United States remains a good place to make these products, they will be made here.

What impact will this have on retirees? Those aged 65 and over would be eligible for Medicare and, if necessary, Medicaid. So their out-of-pocket costs for medical care would be limited, although possibly substantial. These people would remain protected by what our society considers to be an acceptable level of social insurance.

Retirees under age 65 and their dependents would present a different problem. They would not be covered by Medicare. They would have depended on our employment-based system of health insurance and been failed by it. They would join millions of other uncovered early retirees and others unprotected by our system. In fact, roughly 37 million Americans have no coverage at all. The plight of the retirees of bankrupt companies is especially poignant because they had reason to believe they had made prudent provision for their health care. But their problem is essentially the same as that of the rest of the 37 million. There is an urgent need for public policies that assure access to affordable health care coverage for everyone.

Some would argue that these workers bargained for overly generous compensation, at a level that could not be sustained. The rest of society is likely to resist accepting the burden of maintaining their high levels of benefits if their former employers cannot pay.

The main losers from this process would be the workers who did not get the benefits they were expecting and the stockholders and managements of these companies. This is essentially a private matter among them. What should they do? All these parties have an interest in the survival of their companies and would be better off making some concessions to preserve their viability. The following is one scenario they might consider.

The unions and management would negotiate a large reduction in benefits, especially in the area of health benefits for early retirees. Workers would accept reduced benefits and substantial employee contributions. Perhaps they would accept a health plan limited to efficient HMOs, where available. They would make concessions designed to give companies real leverage in controlling costs by directing employees and retirees to efficient providers. These "give backs" could cut the present value of the liability substantially. In exchange, management would prefund the obligation for past service on an agreed-upon schedule, with the funds going to a trust fund to pay future benefits. Future liabilities would be fully funded as accrued. Wage levels would be adjusted to keep the companies competitive. As a part of the scenario, unions might agree to defined contribution as opposed to defined benefit plans. All parties might agree to some form of worker/retiree participation in decisions about plan redesign intended to keep the plan viable under changing conditions as an alternative to an inflexible contractual arrangement.

One lesson for workers in this scenario is that promises of future benefits may be illusory if they are not fully funded in a secure trust fund. A lesson for employers is that they should be careful, definite, and precise about promises of future benefits and they should factor the present values of future costs into present decisions about wages. FASB is trying to help them do the right thing. Both management and labor leaders have been under powerful pressure to take a short-run view. Retiree health benefits were a bargaining prize that apparently could be won or granted with no

12

present sacrifice in wages or profits. Now the long-run consequences are becoming apparent.

Public Policy

What are the implications for public policy? Here are a few.

Encourage Savings, Discourage Borrowing from the Future—Public policy must encourage savings. The goal should be to encourage enough savings to enable each generation to support itself in retirement, including health care. It is difficult or impossible for individuals to save without tax-sheltered vehicles because of the interaction of inflation and taxes. Therefore, tax-sheltered arrangements must be designed. This must be done with care, however. For one thing, it can be costly to the U.S. Treasury. If corporations were allowed to deduct $34 billion instead of $10 billion a year, as suggested by the GAO numbers, the annual federal deficit would increase by about $8 billion, not counting the revenue lost on untaxed interest. It is far from obvious that this is the most urgent use of $8 billion.

Other important public policy objectives are also involved. One is "horizontal equity": for example, tax-sheltered savings opportunities should be equally available to all, not only to those who happen to be long-service employees retiring from large companies. Another objective is "vertical equity." Employer-provided postretirement health benefits are much more prevalent among middle- and high-income retirees than among those with low incomes (U.S. Senate, 1988). It does not make sense to spend scarce forgone tax revenues to help the most financially secure individuals to improve their positions while doing nothing to assist those who are less well off. In such circumstances, the latter suffer and some become a charge on public support. An additional public policy objective should be to encourage cost-consciousness and economic responsibility for choices. From this point of view, it is counterproductive to offer open-ended tax shelters for open-ended benefits. The well-to-do with employer-provided coverage are already receiving a substantial tax-free benefit as well as costing Medicare more than beneficiaries who have no private coverage. Public policy should also encourage job mobility, or at least avoid creating artificial barriers to it. For economic efficiency, workers should be able to move to jobs best suited to their skills. From this point of view, tax-favored savings plans should include instant full vesting and complete portability.

Large open-ended tax breaks for large employers to prefund health benefits for long-service employees would not score well according to any of these criteria.

In fact, a capped individual medical account (IMA) appears to meet these criteria much better. Let everyone shelter from taxes, say, 10 percent of earnings up to the wage base in an account that would be available for postretirement health benefits. There is much to recommend this in terms of equity, portability, and cost consciousness.

IMAs have some features that make them particularly interesting for financing long-term care. Long-term care financing is filled with conundrums. For one, for every disabled elderly person in a nursing home there are two living in the community with similar disabilities who are making do with help from family, friends, and hired help. If we create a social insurance program for nursing home care, with no provision for home help, we create a powerful incentive for families to give up the struggle and put their elders in nursing homes. We reward those who give up the struggle and do nothing for those who continue to support their elders at home. This creates a powerful argument for a home health aide benefit. Here the problem is that many of the services that can keep the disabled elderly out of nursing homes are indistinguishable from domestic help. Every elderly person would like to have a maid. It is very hard to define need and to manage such a benefit at a low cost. Another conundrum is the lack of reward for savings in the present Medicaid system. One elderly person works hard, saves her money, and is able to pay her nursing home bill for a year before spending down into poverty and receiving assistance from Medicaid. Her less frugal sister has no savings, goes to the same nursing home, and is immediately covered by Medicaid. So the frugal sister saves the taxpayers money and receives no reward for her frugality. That is a very counterproductive policy in a society that needs to save more.

If people entered their disabled elderly phase with a substantial fund of savings—their own money that they could spend or leave to their heirs—they would have an incentive to use it economically on home health aides. Or they could pay their own first year or two in a nursing home. Social insurance for nursing home care, with a large front-end deductible, could back this up.

But there are problems with the IMA. Individual retirement accounts (IRAs) were criticized for creating a tax break for the well-to-do without increasing their savings while not motivating much savings by people less well off. Alice Rivlin and Joshua Wiener have concluded that the IMA would not save taxpayers money (Rivlin and Wiener, 1988). The well-to-do who use it would not go on Medicaid anyway. People with modest incomes who might end up on Medicaid will not use it. However, IMAs could be structured differently from IRAs to reduce these problems.

Another problem is that one needs to tie into a sponsored group to be able to buy affordable health care coverage, or perhaps any coverage. This would not be the case for individuals eligible for Medicare, who could buy individual Medicare-supplemental coverage. But it would be a serious issue for those who retire early. Therefore, some compromises are needed.

In 1987, Rep. Rod Chandler (R-WA) proposed a voluntary retiree health plan (VRHP) which would enable employers to prefund retiree health care and long-term care benefits (Chandler, 1987). Contributions and interest would be tax deductible. Annual contributions would be capped. Employees would be vested on a schedule similar to that used for pensions. Once vested, the employee could take his or her account to a new employer who also funds a VRHP. At retirement, the employee and his or her spouse would receive coverage from the employer who currently maintains the employee's account. Beneficiaries would not be able to cash in the benefit, even in the case of death.

This concept encourages savings, ties savings to specific employees with some portability, and caps the benefit and spreads it widely. The reasons for tying this account to employers are to increase the likelihood the benefits will be funded and to tie the retiring employee into a sponsored group. Employers are now obligated to pay the postretirement benefits, so it is they who need the tax-sheltered vehicle.

One might consider extending Rep. Chandler's idea in various ways, such as faster vesting, portability to an insurance company if an employee with a VRHP account moves to an employer without postretirement health benefits, and permitting accumulations in IMAs in the case of employees or others who do not have employer-sponsored postretirement health benefits.

Another radical idea would be a compulsory savings scheme, requiring perhaps 10 percent of earnings to be deposited in a tax-sheltered fund up to a maximum annual contribution, adjusted annually for inflation. These accumulations might be used at retirement to buy postretirement coverage, with some funds available to individuals for noncovered health care goods and services. This would be a way of assuring that most people reach retirement with substantial savings to help cover health and long-term care expenses.

The savings issue and accrual accounting are related. Public policy ought to support full accrual accounting, disclosure, and funding of all employer-provided compensation and benefits for all employees, public sector and private. The present value of accruals for pensions and postretirement health benefits for all public employees should be disclosed. To the great extent we have not done this, we have created anti-savings incentives. We have reduced employees' incentives to save by promising them future benefits, but we have not required employers to make the offsetting savings.

Tax Treatment of Employer-Paid Benefits—The tax treatment of employer-paid postretirement health benefits is a public policy issue, as is the tax treatment of employer-paid health benefits in general. Aside from the size and growth of the drain on the budget, there are two key issues: efficiency and equity. If we want our decentralized market system of health insurance to seek efficiency, tax-induced cost-unconsciousness must be considered contrary to public policy. And it seems inequitable to use scarce tax dollars to subsidize more generous coverage for those who are already well protected by employer-paid plans while doing nothing for millions of others who lack coverage.

What would seem appropriate would be a cap on the annual value of tax-free employer-provided coverage and tax deductibility for individual purchases of coverage up to that level.

The Need for Universal Health Insurance—We have discussed the problem of early retirees left without coverage. They are only one example of the many ways that 37 million Americans are excluded from health care coverage by our employment-based system, and this problem is only one of several important shortcomings of this employment-based system. Another problem is the difficulty of writing a suitably flexible long-term contract for postretirement health benefits. Congress "breaks its promises" and restructures some aspect of Medicare almost every year. This is considered acceptable because Congress is constrained by the democratic process.

All of these considerations point to the need for a universal health insurance program with a socially acceptable process for modifying benefits as conditions require.

Chrysler-Type Bailout?—If, and as, mature industrial companies are driven toward bankruptcy, pressures for a bailout by the taxpayers will arise. People will confuse the prospective demise of large and famous companies with the demise of the whole industry. Will such

16

bailouts be appropriate public policy? In the case of Chrysler, bailout proponents argued that the company's troubles were temporary and that it could be returned to viability if the government would guarantee its loans.

A key feature of the Chrysler bailout was the principle that all who had a stake in the company would have to make concessions. The problem of retiree health care cannot be solved without major concessions by labor and stockholders. Any promises of bailouts would send the wrong message: that these people, who ought to be economically self-sufficient and managing for long-term economic viability, can be bailed out if they act irresponsibly.

Protectionism—Finally, some may suggest that protection against imports is needed to solve the problem of companies threatened with bankruptcy. But protectionism does not solve problems of competitiveness. Protection of steel, for example, would mean American manufacturers using steel in their products would become less competitive against, say, Korean manufacturers using Korean steel. In any case, the scenario I described was predicated on competition for the mature companies from other companies manufacturing in the United States.

In general, we should resist Band-Aids and the usual musical chairs approach. The real problem is not bookkeeping. The real problems are uncontrolled and rapid growth in the costs of health care for retirees, the fact that we have not been saving enough money to support ourselves in retirement at the standards to which we are accustomed, and the fact that roughly 37 million Americans lack any health care coverage.

References

Berton, Lee. "FASB Plan Would Make Firms Deduct Billions for Potential Retiree Benefits." *Wall Street Journal*, 17 August 1988.

Chandler, Rod. "Pursuing Funding for Retiree Benefits," *Business and Health* (December 1987): 21–25.

Chollet, Deborah J. "Retiree Health Insurance Benefits: Trends and Issues." In *Retiree Health Benefits: What Is the Promise?* Washington, DC: Employee Benefit Research Institute, 1989.

Enthoven, Alain C. "Managed Competition: An Agenda for Action." *Health Affairs* (Summer 1988a): 25–47.

_____. *Theory and Practice of Managed Competition in Health Care Finance*. Amsterdam: North Holland Publishing Company, 1988b.

Ford Motor Company. *1987 Annual Report*. Dearborn, MI: Ford Motor Company, 1987.

Klein, Burma H. "Future Security of Retiree Health Benefits in Question." In *Retiree Health Benefits: What Is the Promise?* Washington, DC: Employee Benefit Research Institute, 1989.

Rivlin, Alice, and Joshua M. Wiener. *Caring for the Disabled Elderly.* Washington, DC: Brookings Institution, 1988.

U.S. Department of Labor. Pension and Welfare Benefits Administration. *Employer-Sponsored Retiree Health Insurance.* Washington, DC: U.S. Government Printing Office, 1986.

U.S. Congress. Senate. Joint Committee on Taxation. *Overview of Present Law, Proposals, and Issues Relating to Employer-Provided Retiree Health Insurance.* Committee Print. Washington, DC: U.S. Government Printing Office, 1988.

————. Senate. Special Committee on Aging. "Retiree Medical Benefits, Issues and Trends." Testimony by Willis Goldbeck, 7 August 1986.

U.S. President. Council of Economic Advisors. *Annual Report, 1988.* Washington, DC: U.S. Government Printing Office, 1988.

Wade, Alice H. "Social Security Area Population Projections: 1987." *Social Security Bulletin* (February 1988): 3–30.

Waldo, David R., and Helen C. Lazenby. "Demographic Characteristics and Health Care Use and Expenditures by the Aged in the United States: 1977–1984." *Health Care Financing Review* (Fall 1984): 1–29.

Winslow, Constance M., Jacqueline B. Kosecoff, Mark R. Chassin et al. "The Appropriateness of Performing Coronary Artery Bypass Surgery." *Journal of the American Medical Association* (July 22–29, 1988): 505–509.

Winslow, Constance M., David H. Solomon, Mark R. Chassin et al. "The Appropriateness of Carotid Endarterectomy." *New England Journal of Medicine* (March 24, 1988): 721–727.

II. Retiree Health Insurance Benefits: Trends and Issues

PAPER BY DEBORAH J. CHOLLET*

Introduction

Retiree health insurance—its cost, funding, and future—has become a focus of concern and controversy among employers and public policymakers. An emerging history of court decisions upholding contractual retiree rights to continued benefits when employers have sought to terminate retiree plans or modify benefits has made employers cautious about the way they represent retiree rights to both workers and retirees.

New accounting rules from the independent Financial Accounting Standards Board (FASB) are expected to force employers to phase in recognition of unfunded liability for retiree health benefits promises as an offset to corporate income in 1992.[1] Employers may be required to fully recognize the present value of unfunded liability by 1997, for both current retirees and workers eligible to retire. Furthermore, FASB's forthcoming rules may not recognize employer funds held to offset liability if those funds are held in the tax-preferred trusts that, under current law, are the most likely avenues for funding health and/or retirement benefits (that is, 501(c)(9) trusts and 401(h) trusts), since the law does not prohibit other uses of funds held in these trusts.

In any case, employers with retiree health plans have generally claimed that funding these benefits during active workers' careers in order to assure benefits after retirement (the way that pensions are funded under current law) would pose a substantial expense both absolutely and in relation to current spending for health benefits.

---

*Editor's note: The tabulations of data from the Survey of Income and Program Participation (U.S. Department of Commerce, Bureau of the Census) in this chapter are preliminary and may change in future Employee Benefit Research Institute publications.

[1] On February 14, 1989, FASB released an exposure draft of a proposed accounting standard that would require companies to recognize postretirement health care and insurance benefits as a form of deferred compensation and to report these obligations on their balance sheets. Selections from the exposure draft, *Proposed Statement of Financial Accounting Standards: Employers' Accounting for Postretirement Benefits Other Than Pensions*, are included in Appendix B.

Although Congress has been concerned that retirees who expect these benefits may have no real claim to benefits in the event of a plan termination or sponsor bankruptcy, the prospect of tax revenue losses will probably impede enactment of legislation allowing tax preferences to encourage employer funding.

This chapter describes the prevalence of retiree health insurance as an employee benefit and the prevalence and distribution of retiree health insurance benefits among early retirees (aged 55 to 64) and retirees aged 65 or older. The discussion generally distinguishes between retirees who receive benefits from a private employer plan and those who receive benefits from past employment in federal, state, or local government. It includes estimates of the current value of both private and public employer liability for retiree health insurance benefits, distinguishing between liability for benefits being provided to current retirees and expected liability for active workers.

Finally, the discussion summarizes the legislative environment of retiree health insurance benefits and reviews the implicit involvement of pension benefit guarantees as, in effect, an insurance system for retiree health benefits in cases of plan sponsor bankruptcy. Corporate funding ability and federal budget structures are likely to constrain the future of health insurance benefits for tomorrow's retirees, reducing the proportion of the elderly population with benefits from an employer plan and changing retirees' own cost for the benefit. Corporations' obligations to current retirees, however, are likely to pose an increasing financial burden on them. Their wish for legislative assistance providing greater tax preferences for retiree health benefits raises difficult public policy questions related to federal budget priorities and retirement policy.

Retiree Health Insurance as an Employee Benefit

Continuation of health insurance benefits after retirement is a common feature of both private and public employer plans. In 1986, three-quarters (75 percent) of full-time workers in medium-sized and large private-sector establishments participated in health insurance plans that continued coverage after early retirement (before age 65); more than two-thirds (68 percent) participated in plans that continued coverage after retirement at age 65 (U.S. Department of Labor, 1987).

Most plans that continue coverage after retirement also provide for an employer (or sponsor) contribution to the cost of coverage. In 1986, 64 percent of full-time workers under age 65 in medium-sized or large private-sector establishments had plans that continued coverage after early retirement, with the plan sponsor paying all or part of the plan cost; 58 percent had plans with fully or partly sponsor-financed coverage after retirement at age 65 (table II.1). An estimated 41 percent of workers in larger private-sector establishments had health insurance plans for which the plan sponsor paid the full cost of coverage after either early or normal retirement.

Fully or partly employer-paid retiree coverage is less common among public-sector workers (state and local government employees) than among private-sector workers in larger establishments. In 1987, nearly one-half (47 percent) of full-time state or local government workers with employer-based health insurance had plans that would continue with an employer contribution after retirement; 44 percent had coverage that would continue with an employer contribution after retirement at age 65. About one-half of state and local employees who participated in plans to which the employer contributed had the full cost of coverage after retirement paid by the employer.

Employer plans that continue coverage typically continue benefits at the same level as that provided to workers before retirement; that is, the scope of services covered and retirees' cost-sharing under the plan are maintained at preretirement levels. However, retiree plans typically integrate Medicare coverage into plan benefits. That is, Medicare is first-payer for services covered by both Medicare and the retiree plan.[2] Because Medicare integration substantially reduces plan costs, it has probably encouraged the growth of health insurance as a retiree benefit.

Since 1981, the number of workers with health insurance plans that continue coverage after retirement has grown substantially. Between 1981 and 1985, the number of private-sector workers with plans that provide benefits after early retirement grew by more than 14 percent (table II.2); the number of private-sector workers with plans that continue after age 65 grew 18 percent. The most rapid growth of retiree benefits apparently occurred among workers in manufacturing establishments and those in very large establishments (establishments with 2,500 or more workers). The number of workers in medium-sized and large manufacturing establishments with plans that continue benefits after retirement at age 65 grew nearly 20 per-

---

[2]Alternative methods of Medicare integration are described in Deborah J. Chollet and Robert B. Friedland, "Employer-Paid Retiree Health Insurance: History and Prospects for Growth," in Frank B. McArdle, ed., *The Changing Health Care Market* (Washington, DC: Employee Benefit Research Institute, 1987).

21

TABLE II.1

Percentage of Private and Public Employer Health Insurance Plan Participants with an Employer Contribution to Coverage after Retirement, by Selected Benefit Provisions and Age of Retiree, 1986–1987

Benefit Provision	Medium-Sized and Large Private Employer Plans[a]		State and Local Employer Plans[b]	
	Retirees under 65	Retirees 65 or older	Retirees under 65	Retirees 65 or older
With Retiree Coverage	64%	59%	47%	44%
Effect of Retirement on Benefit Level				
No change	50	46	45	41
Reduced coverage	12	10	3	3
Increased coverage	1	1	c	c
Retiree Share of Cost				
Partial cost	23	17	24	23
No cost	41	41	24	24
No Retiree Coverage[d]	32	38	48	52
Provision Not Determinable	2	2	2	2
Retiree Policy Not Established	1	1	e	e
Other[f]	1	1	e	e

Source: Estimated from U.S. Department of Labor, Bureau of Labor Statistics, *Employee Benefits in Medium and Large Firms, 1986* (Washington, DC: U.S. Government Printing Office, 1987), tables 29 and 30; and U.S. Department of Labor, Bureau of Labor Statistics, *Employee Benefits in State and Local Governments, 1987* (Washington, DC: U.S. Government Printing Office, 1988), tables 48 and 49.

Note: Data reflect benefits provided to full-time permanent employees. Detail may not add to totals because of rounding or because the specific provision was indeterminable.

[a]Data are for 1986. Estimates assume that specific benefit provisions are proportionately distributed among plans to which the employer contributes.
[b]Data are for 1987. Data on the number of participants with retiree plans to which the employer does not contribute are unavailable.
[c]Less than 0.05 percent.
[d]Includes participants in plans that continue access to coverage after retirement other than that required by federal law (the Consolidated Omnibus Budget Reconciliation Act of 1985), but to which the employer does not contribute. These workers represent 11 percent of all plan participants.
[e]No plan participants in this category.
[f] Includes employees who participate only in the employer's dental insurance plan and for whom health insurance coverage and provisions are unknown.

cent between 1981 and 1985. The number of workers in very large establishments with this type of benefit increased 41 percent.[3]

Retirees with Employer-Sponsored Coverage

Employer-sponsored plans are an important source of health insurance among retirees. In 1984 (the most recent year for which data are available), at least 11.3 million retirees aged 55 or older had health insurance from an employer-sponsored plan (table II.3). Of these, 7.6 million were aged 65 or older. In 1984, at least 29 percent of all elderly persons reported having health insurance coverage from a past employer.

The evolution of retiree coverage as a feature of employer health plans is reflected in higher rates of retiree coverage among recent retirees. In 1984, nearly one-third of the elderly aged 65–69 (33 percent) reported having insurance coverage from a past employer, compared with just over one-quarter (26 percent) of elderly persons aged 75 or older.

Employer-sponsored retiree health insurance plans represent a substantial share of the elderly's Medigap insurance (table II.4). Among all people aged 65 or older with private insurance to supplement Medicare (62 percent of the elderly in 1984), about one-half—47 percent—had all or part of that coverage provided by an employer-sponsored retiree health insurance plan. Nearly 60 percent of elderly workers and retirees with private coverage to supplement Medicare derived all or part of that coverage from an employer plan.

Most retirees who report having health insurance from a past employer live in low- and middle-income families. Consequently, health insurance benefits represent an important real income supplement for most of the retirees who have them. In 1984, more than one-half of the elderly with retiree health insurance (56 percent) had family income of less than $20,000; 79 percent had family income of less than $30,000 (table II.5). Retirees under age 65 with health insurance from a past employer report slightly higher, but generally comparable, levels of family income. In 1984, 47 percent of early retirees with employer-sponsored health insurance reported family income of less than $20,000; 76 percent reported family income of less than $30,000.

Available data do not directly indicate whether the health insurance benefits that retirees are now receiving are sponsored by a private or

---

[3]These data from the Bureau of Labor Statistics are not strictly reliable in firm-size and industry disaggregation. Nevertheless, the tabulations presented here probably provide reasonable estimates of general magnitudes.

TABLE II.2

Number and Percentage of Workers in Health Insurance Plans with an Employer Contribution to Coverage after Retirement: Medium-Sized and Large Private Establishments, by Establishment Size and Industry Group, 1981–1985

Establishment Size/ Industry Group	1981 Number (in millions)	1981 Percent- age	1985 Number (in millions)	1985 Percent- age	Percentage Increase 1981–1985
		early retirement[a]			
Participants with Employer Contribution	11.2	61.1%	12.8	63.9%	14.3%
Establishment size					
100–249	0.8	39.3	1.1	46.2	37.5
250–499	1.6	45.7	1.6	40.6	[b]
500–999	2.4	61.3	2.2	63.4	−8.3
1,000–2,499	2.4	64.8	2.8	72.5	16.7
2,500+	3.7	80.4	5.0	80.7	35.1
Industry group					
manufacturing	6.3	59.7	7.3	64.4	15.9
nonmanufacturing	4.8	63.2	5.4	63.3	12.5
		retirement at age 65[c]			
Participants with Employer Contribution	10.0	55.0	11.8	58.9	18.0
Establishment size					
100–249	0.8	39.3	1.0	42.6	12.5
250–499	1.3	37.1	1.5	36.4	15.4
500–999	2.2	55.5	1.9	54.2	−13.6
1,000–2,499	2.2	58.7	2.6	67.3	18.2
2,500+	3.4	72.9	4.8	76.8	41.2
Industry group					
manufacturing	5.6	52.4	6.7	59.1	19.6
nonmanufacturing	4.5	58.6	5.0	58.6	11.1

Source: Michael A. Morrisey and Gail A. Jensen, "Employer-Sponsored Post-Retirement Health Benefits: The State of Knowledge and Some Unresolved Issues," Working Paper, Birmingham, AL: University of Alabama (September 1988); and Gail A. Jensen, unpublished tabulations of the U.S. Department of Labor Employee Benefit Survey, 1981 and 1985.

Note: Detail may not add to totals becuase of rounding. Data are not strictly reliable in firm size and industry disaggregation.

[a]Data include workers with coverage that continues at least until age 65; workers with some other limited period of continuation are not included.
[b]No measurable change.
[c]Data include only workers with coverage that continues indefinitely; workers with a limited period of continuation are not included.

TABLE II.3

Number and Percentage of People Aged 55 or Older with Retiree Health Insurance, by Age, 1984

Retiree Age	Number[a] (in millions)	Percentage within Age Group	Percentage of All People Reporting Retiree Health Insurance
Total	11.3	23.6%	100.0%
55–59	1.2	10.2	10.2
60–64	2.6	24.4	23.1
65–69	2.9	32.9	25.2
70–74	2.1	30.0	18.8
75+	2.6	26.3	22.6
Summary			
Under 65	3.8	17.1	33.4
65 or older	7.6	29.6	66.6

Source: Preliminary Employee Benefit Research Institute tabulations of the Survey of Income and Program Participation, matched waves 2 through 5 (U.S. Department of Commerce, Bureau of the Census).

Note: Data omit individuals living in households that were not interviewed at any time during the calendar year. Items may not add to totals because of rounding.

[a]Includes primary-insured retirees and people with dependents' coverage.

public employer. Nevertheless, most retirees' health plan sponsors can be inferred from available data about their pension plan sponsors. From these data, we estimate that at least one-half of all retirees with health insurance from a past employer receive coverage from a private employer plan; that is, the retiree also receives income from a private pension plan (table II.6). While 20 percent of retirees with health insurance from a past employer report no current pension income, most of these individuals probably receive their health insurance benefits from a private plan sponsor. At least 30 percent of retirees now receiving health insurance from a past employer have coverage as retirees from public employment—federal, state, or local government.

The relatively high rate of private employer-sponsored coverage reported among recent retirees corroborates industry survey data showing that private employer plans that provide retiree benefits have become increasingly common. Similarly, the relatively low proportion of retirees of any age with public plan benefits indicates that retiree coverage as a feature of public plans matured relatively early. Among covered retirees aged 75 or older in 1984, 44 percent had

TABLE II.4

Percentage of People Aged 65 or Older with Private Health Insurance from Selected Sources, by Age, 1984

Source of Coverage	Total, Age 65 +	Age 65–69	Age 70–74	Age 75 +
Active Worker Coverage from a Current Employer	8.5%	16.4%	7.2%	2.5%
Direct[b]	5.6	10.4	5.1	a
Dependents' coverage[c]	2.9	6.0	2.1	a
Retiree Coverage from a Past Employer	29.6	32.9	30.0	26.3
Direct[b]	23.7	24.7	23.6	22.9
Dependents' coverage[c]	5.9	8.2	6.4	3.4
Other Private Insurance	54.8	48.6	58.2	57.9
No Private Insurance	38.1	31.7	36.3	45.1

Source: Preliminary Employee Benefit Research Institute tabulations of the Survey of Income and Program Participation, matched waves 2 through 5 (U.S. Department of Commerce, Bureau of the Census).

Note: Data omit individuals living in households that were not interviewed at any time during the calendar year. Items may not add to totals because of rounding.

[a]Statistically insignificant.
[b]Includes people with survivors' coverage and those who report both direct and dependents' coverage of the same type.
[c]Excludes people with both direct and dependents' coverage of the same type.

coverage sponsored by a private employer, and 31 percent had coverage from a public employer plan. By comparison, among younger retirees (aged 65–69) with coverage from a past employer, at least 55 percent were covered by a private employer plan and 28 percent had public plan coverage.

While most retirees receive some contribution to the cost of their plan (a characteristic of private and public plans that is clear from the Department of Labor data on active workers' plans described earlier), a significant minority report that they pay the full cost of coverage themselves, with no sponsor contribution. In 1984, nearly 22 percent of all retirees paid the full cost of the coverage without a sponsor contribution; among retirees aged 65 or older, 23 percent paid the full cost of coverage (table II.7). Conversely, for nearly 39 percent of retirees with health insurance from a past employer, the employer paid the full cost of coverage.

TABLE II.5
**Number and Distribution of People with Retiree Health Insurance,
by Family Income and Age, 1984**

Family Income	Recipients under Age 65		Recipients Aged 65 or Older	
	Total[a] (in millions)	Cumulative Percentage of Beneficiaries	Total[a] (in millions)	Cumulative Percentage of Beneficiaries
Less than $10,000	0.5	11.7%	1.2	14.8%
$10,000–$14,999	0.7	29.2	1.5	35.2
$15,000–$19,999	0.7	46.7	1.6	55.8
$20,000–$24,999	0.4	63.8	1.2	70.2
$25,000–$29,999	0.5	76.2	0.7	79.4
$30,000–$39,999	0.5	88.3	0.8	89.7
$40,000 or more	0.5	100.0	0.8	100.0

Source: Preliminary Employee Benefit Research Institute tabulations of the Survey of Income and Program Participation, matched waves 2 through 5 (U.S. Department of Commerce, Bureau of the Census).

Note: Data omit individuals living in households that were not interviewed at any time during the calendar year. Items may not add to totals because of rounding.

[a]Includes only retirees aged 55–64.

The likelihood that the plan sponsor contributes all or part of the cost of coverage is substantially higher among retirees with coverage from a private plan than among those with public plan coverage, an observation also consistent with the reported features of active worker plans. Among both early retirees (aged 55 to 64) and retirees aged 65 or older with private plan coverage, approximately one-half (49 percent and 51 percent, respectively) had their coverage fully paid by the plan sponsor.[4] By comparison, about one-quarter of retirees with coverage from a public employer (23 percent) had the full cost of coverage paid by the plan sponsor.

Employer Liability for Retiree Benefits

Since 1979, the Financial Accounting Standards Board (FASB) has issued a series of documents that address appropriate accounting practice for corporate-sponsored retiree health and life insurance ben-

---

[4]Because retirees in plans whose sponsor was indeterminable are excluded, the percentage of retirees in private plans with coverage fully paid by the plan sponsor may be slightly biased upward.

TABLE II.6
Number and Percentage of People Aged 55 or Older
with Retiree Health Insurance, by Type of Pension Plan Sponsor[a]
and Recipient Age, 1984

Recipient Age	Total with Retiree Health Coverage (in millions)	Percentage with Pension Income			Percentage with No Pension Income
		Total[b]	Private pension	Public pension[c]	
Total	11.3	79.8%	50.2%	29.7%	20.2%
55–59	1.2	78.7	44.7	34.1	21.3
60–64	2.6	82.3	54.5	27.8	17.7
65–69	2.9	82.1	54.0	28.1	17.9
70–74	2.1	79.2	49.6	29.6	20.8
75+	2.6	75.8	44.4	31.4	24.2
Summary					
55–64	3.8	81.2	51.4	29.7	18.8
65+	7.6	79.1	49.5	29.6	20.9

Source: Preliminary Employee Benefit Research Institute tabulations of the Survey of Income and Program Participation, matched waves 2 through 5 (U.S. Department of Commerce, Bureau of the Census).

Note: Data omit individuals living in households that were not interviewed at any time during the calendar year. Items may not add to totals because of rounding.

[a]For people with only dependents' coverage from a spouse's plan, the spouse's pension plan sponsor is reported.

[b]Also includes military pensions and other pensions from unspecified sources.

[c]Federal, state, or local government employee plan. Category excludes military pensions.

efits.[5] In 1984 these documents culminated with FASB Statement No. 81, which required employers to disclose either the current cost of retiree welfare benefits or the accrued unfunded liability for them as a footnote to the corporation's balance sheet, if the amounts were

---

[5]The following FASB publications are concerned with retiree welfare benefits: *Disclosure of Pension and Other Post-retirement Benefit Information* (July 12, 1979); *Employers' Accounting for Pensions and Other Postemployment Benefits*, discussion memorandum (February 19, 1981); *Preliminary Views on Major Issues Related to Employers' Accounting for Pensions and Other Postemployment Benefits* (November 1982); *Employers' Accounting for Pensions and Other Postemployment Benefits*, discussion memorandum (April 19, 1983); *Disclosure of Post-retirement Health Care and Life Insurance Benefits*, exposure draft (July 3, 1984); and Statement No. 81, *Disclosure of Post-retirement Health Care and Life Insurance Benefits* (November 1984).

TABLE II.7

People Aged 55 or Older with Retiree Health Insurance by Level of Retiree Contribution to Coverage, Type of Pension Plan Sponsor, and Retiree Age, 1984

Retiree Age and Pension Sponsor	Number of Retirees with Benefit (in millions)	Share of Plan Cost Paid by Retiree		
		All	Part	None
		(percentage of participants)		
All Retirees	11.3	21.9%	39.3%	38.8%
Age 55–64				
Total	3.8	19.3	42.2	38.5
Pension sponsor				
private	2.0	14.3	36.4	49.3
public	1.1	19.1	60.2	20.7
not reported	0.8	33.4	29.6	37.1
Age 65 +				
Total	7.6	23.2	37.9	38.9
Pension sponsor				
private	3.9	14.8	34.0	51.2
public	2.2	22.4	54.4	23.3
not reported	1.7	44.3	23.8	31.9

Source: Preliminary Employee Benefit Research Institute tabulations of the Survey of Income and Program Participation, matched waves 2 through 5 (U.S. Department of Commerce, Bureau of the Census).

Note: Data omit individuals living in households that were not interviewed at any time during the calendar year. Items may not add to totals because of rounding.

distinguishable from benefits costs for active workers. Although most corporations apparently now disclose the current cost or unfunded liability for retiree welfare benefits, many do not.[6] Statement No. 81 offers no guidance on how employers should measure or amortize

---

[6]A survey of 100 corporate annual reports for 1987 indicates that nearly 90 percent of corporations with retiree benefits disclose costs. Of these, 8 percent reported costs to be immaterial, 18 percent did not distinguish between costs for retirees and active employees, and 74 percent provided separate cost figures for retirees. See Charles D. Spencer and Associates, Inc., "What Retiree Health Coverage and Life Insurance Cost 100 Major Firms Revealed in Spencer Survey," news release, 17 June 1988 (Chicago, IL: Charles D. Spencer and Associates).

TABLE II.8
Private and Public Employer Liability for Retiree Health Insurance Benefits: Preliminary Intermediate Estimate, Discounted Present Value, 1988

Worker/Retiree Status	Private Employers	Public Employers	Total
	(in billions)		
Current Retirees	$ 68.2	$ 23.0	$ 91.2
Current Workers	100.5	87.7	188.2
Total, retirees and current workers	168.7	110.7	279.4

Source: Deborah J. Chollet, *Financing the Elderly's Health Care* (Washington, DC: Employee Benefit Research Institute, forthcoming).
Note: Estimates include reductions in plan cost as a result of recent legislation expanding Medicare benefits. On average, corporate and public employer liabilities are estimated to decline by approximately 30 percent as a result of new Medicare benefits.

accrued unfunded liability, and it specifically does not apply to multiemployer plans.

Subsequent to issuing Statement No. 81, FASB has been considering appropriate standards for mandatory measurement and disclosure of accrued unfunded liability for retiree welfare benefits. Anticipating new accounting rules for retiree health benefits, employers have begun to focus on the amount of unfunded liability that they will be required to disclose as an offset to corporate income, directly reducing reported profit.

Table II.8 provides estimates of both private and public employer liability for retiree health insurance benefits. Although private employer and public employer estimates are reported together, they are of public policy interest for different reasons. Specifically, the new FASB rules would apply only to private employers. Amounts of unfunded liability for retiree health benefits are probably distributed very unevenly among employers that sponsor retiree plans. If, as seems likely, equity markets have not fully anticipated individual corporations' unfunded liability for retiree health benefits, disclosure of the liability will probably produce an adjustment in the relative value of corporate stocks.

The issues associated with public employer liability for retiree health insurance are different. Public employer liabilities represent a claim against future tax dollars. The current cost of state and local government

30

obligations for retiree health benefits directly affects their operating budgets and poses an increasing strain on fiscal management. Most states and municipalities are required to balance their budgets annually.

We estimate the present value of private employers' liability for retiree health insurance obligations to be approximately $169 billion. Most of this liability, nearly $101 billion, is associated with current workers. The present value of corporate liability for current retirees is slightly more than $68 billion. These estimates are low compared with those recently reported by the General Accounting Office (U.S. Congress, 1988), in part because they include a downward adjustment for recent legislation expanding Medicare benefits.

The value of the new Medicare benefits to plan sponsors can vary radically from plan to plan, depending on the plan provisions and the Medicare assignment rate among physicians in the areas where retirees live. The new Medicare benefits, phased in over a five-year period, are likely to greatly reduce liability for many employers for benefits provided to retirees aged 65 and over. Much of this saving is likely to occur as a consequence of Medicare's coverage of prescription drugs during the last two years of the phase-in period. The estimates presented here assume that the new Medicare coverage will reduce employer plan costs by 10 percent in 1990, 40 percent in 1991, 45 percent in 1992, and 50 percent in subsequent years. This assumption, applied to both private and public plans, reduces estimated liability by approximately 30 percent. Without this adjustment, the current value of private, corporate liability for retiree health benefits would be $247 billion: $98 billion for current retirees and $149 billion for current workers.

A second major assumption implicit in these estimates is the projected rate of inflation in health care services. The estimates assume that health care cost inflation will continue to exceed general inflation, but that the difference between the rates will decline incrementally over the next 25 years. The rates of inflation are assumed to converge (at 3.5 percent) in the year 2013, when aggregate spending for health care services reaches 22 percent of Gross National Product (GNP); real per capita GNP is assumed to grow at a rate of 1.5 percent per year, resulting in assumed annual per capita health care spending increases of 5 percent after the year 2013.[7]

---

[7]These economic assumptions are also used by Phyllis A. Doran, Kenneth D. MacBain, and William A. Reimert in *Measuring and Funding Corporate Liabilities for Retiree Health Benefits* (Washington, DC: Employee Benefit Research Institute, 1987).

Employers' annual cost to amortize these obligations is likely to be substantial. Based on a survey of 76 retiree medical plans conducted by one benefits consulting firm, the annual cost of retiree health insurance benefits would total about 12 percent of payroll (about 10 times more than the current pay-as-you go system) if it were calculated on a basis comparable to that used for pension plans (*Investor's Daily*, 1988).

Legislative Activity and Proposals

The loss of health insurance by retirees when a plan sponsor declares bankruptcy has captured congressional attention and generated legislation to protect retirees. The LTV Corporation's Chapter 11 bankruptcy reorganization in 1986, in particular, became a catalyst for congressional action. The Omnibus Budget Reconciliation Act of 1986 made a firm's initiation of Chapter 11 bankruptcy reorganization a qualifying event under the coverage continuation provisions of the Consolidated Omnibus Budget Reconciliation Act of 1985 (COBRA). COBRA requires employers to offer continued health insurance benefits to workers and/or their dependents in various circumstances that might otherwise lead to benefit termination. Under COBRA's amended continuation provisions, retirees may purchase continued postretirement medical benefits from the plan until they die or obtain coverage from another source. The retiree's surviving spouse can purchase continued coverage for an additional 36 months. As with other continuation provisions in COBRA, the plan may require retirees to pay premiums of as much as 102 percent of the plan's average (per participant) cost.

In 1986, Congress also issued House Joint Resolution 738, requiring any company paying postretirement medical benefits as of October 2, 1986, that had not had reorganization plans confirmed by a bankruptcy court, as well as companies filing for Chapter 11 reorganization after that date, to continue paying benefits until May 15, 1987.

Subsequently, Congress passed, and President Reagan signed into law, the Retiree Benefits Bankruptcy Protection Act of 1988 (P.L. 100-334). This law prevents an employer from unilaterally canceling retiree coverages on filing for Chapter 11 protection in bankruptcy; it also prevents the plan sponsor or administrator from attempting to collect from individual retirees repayment of plan expenses incurred before the filing. P.L. 100-334 allows retirees to claim creditor status in Chapter 11 bankruptcy proceedings and to be represented by a court-designated representative or committee. The law requires the plan sponsor to continue retiree benefits pending agreement to modification by the retirees' representative or a decision by the bankruptcy court to modify or terminate benefits. As a formal creditor in bankruptcy proceedings, retirees may increasingly compete with the Pension Benefit Guaranty Corporation (PBGC) as a principal claimant to employer assets. If PBGC is able to recover less of its insurance loss because of unfunded retiree health claims against employer assets, it in effect becomes an insurer of retiree health benefits. Lower recoveries by PBGC would presumably force higher employer premiums to ensure defined benefit pension obligations.[8]

Various legislative proposals have been forwarded to encourage employers to fund retiree health insurance obligations by allowing them to use excess pension assets to fund retiree health benefits and/or allowing tax-free contributions to a designated trust fund. One proposal (H.R. 5309) sponsored by Rep. Rod Chandler (R-WA) in the 100th Congress would allow employers with defined benefit or defined contribution pension plans to make tax-deductible contributions toward future retiree health care and long-term care expenses. The bill would allow employers to deduct funding for plans that provide annual retiree health benefits worth $2,500 per retiree and, additionally, long-term care plans that provide average annual benefits worth $2,500. Annual contribution limits would be set at $825 for retiree health benefits and an equal amount for long-term care benefits; both contributions would count against the pension contribution limits now imposed under section 415 of the tax code. Plan investment earnings would be tax exempt. H.R. 5309 would also allow employers to transfer excess pension assets (above 125 percent of plan liability) to a separate trust for the purpose of funding retiree health benefits or long-term care benefits.

A similar proposal, circulated in 1988 by the Senate Special Committee on Aging as a draft bill, would authorize tax-deductible employer contributions to retiree health insurance but limit the value of a qualified plan to $1,200 per retiree per year. Tax-deductible employer contributions would not be counted against section 415 limits, but the proposal would apply pension vesting, funding, and participation standards to the retiree health insurance plan. In addition, the proposal would require employers to provide health ben-

---

[8] In May 1988, PBGC filed an objection in the U.S. Bankruptcy Court of the District of Colorado related to the Kaiser Steel Corporation bankruptcy reorganization proceedings (*In re Kaiser Steel Corporation et al.*, May 27, 1988), protesting the way that retiree health insurance liabilities (estimated at $400 million) were calculated in the firm's disclosure statement. PBGC has since settled its claims in this case.

efits to spouses of deceased employees, if the deceased employee had been eligible for benefits. This proposal was not introduced.

The Prospect for Retiree Health Benefits

The history of retiree health insurance benefits is probably a poor predictor of the future. The relatively low current cost of retiree health benefits and their usefulness as an early retirement incentive contributed to the expansion of these benefits even during the 1980s, when it has been clear that the courts would strictly enforce employers' implied or stated promises to retirees and that a ruling from FASB on accounting standards for retiree health benefits was virtually inevitable. Possibly the best explanations for such short-sighted corporate behavior include the 1982 economic recession, which put great pressure on employers to reduce their work forces through early retirement rather than layoffs, and pressure from older workers and senior management who anticipated retirement with high and fast-growing out-of-pocket health care costs under Medicare.

While the Employee Retirement Income Security Act of 1974 (ERISA) establishes vesting and funding rules for private pension plans, there is no current law governing vesting and funding for retiree health benefits. Employers have generally regarded retiree health benefits as a year-to-year promise, and have financed benefits as part of the same health plan provided to active workers. Very few employers have funded future retiree health benefit obligations at all, and none have funded them fully.

The legislative proposals that are likely to emerge in the 101st Congress will present employers with some difficult choices. No legislation is likely to come without a "price": a benefits-related provision in the legislation that would make new tax incentives budget-neutral and perhaps also include funding and vesting rules for retiree health benefits. Employers are likely to find reaching a consensus on a benefits "sacrifice" difficult but necessary, given the prospect of reporting unfunded liability and the possibility that FASB will not recognize funds held in current-law tax-advantaged trusts as an offset to liability. As a result, employers may badly need new legislation establishing tax-advantaged trusts exclusively for retiree health benefits, but the price may discourage further expansion of retiree health benefit promises and lead employers to terminate plans for future retirees.

A microsimulation analysis of the effect of vesting rules on future benefit recipiency offers some idea of the impact such rules might

have on employer costs.[9] Currently, workers who terminate employment before they are eligible to retire generally retain no right to
retiree health benefits when they do retire. That is, retiree health
insurance plans generally do not allow benefit deferral, even if the
terminating employee is vested in the employer's pension plan.

If, however, employers were required to vest employees in their
health plans, using the employer's 1985 pension vesting standard
(before tax reform), benefit receipt among future retirees would rise
significantly. Among the cohort of workers projected to retire between
the years 2000 and 2009, the projected rate of recipiency would rise
44 percent: from about 25 percent of workers retiring with benefits
to more than 36 percent. Among workers projected to retire between
2010 and 2019, the rate of recipiency would rise 58 percent: from 25
percent to 39 percent.

If employers were required to vest employees using the five-year pension vesting standard effective in 1989 under the Tax Reform Act of
1986, benefit recipiency among future cohorts of retirees would rise
even more dramatically. Assuming a five-year vesting standard, but no
benefit deferral, benefit recipiency among workers projected to retire
between the years 2000 and 2009 would rise 55 percent: 39 percent of
workers in this cohort would retire with benefits. Among workers projected to retire between the years 2010 and 2019, benefit recipiency
would rise 72 percent, with 42 percent of workers retiring with benefits.

These results suggest that the coming legislative debate over retiree
benefits will be particularly difficult. As in past benefits debates, the
U.S. Department of the Treasury may want vesting rules to ensure
that retirees ultimately benefit from current tax expenditures. However, by raising benefit recipiency rates among future retirees, vesting
rules will raise both employer costs and the federal revenue cost of
tax incentives to fund benefit promises. This conundrum is likely to
delay legislation, maximizing incentives for employers to terminate
their retiree health plans for future retirees or to substantially modify
the benefit.

Employers are now widely discussing conversion of their benefits
for future retirees to a "defined contribution" benefit, instead of
the service benefit that is now virtually universal. Such a benefit
would transfer much or all of the risk of continuing health care

---

[9]These results are based on a rebenchmarked, enhanced version of the pension and
retirement income simulation model (PRISM). A description of the model and complete results are reported in Deborah J. Chollet, *Financing the Elderly's Health Care*
(Washington, DC: Employee Benefit Research Institute, forthcoming).

cost inflation and rising benefits costs to the future retiree and enable employers to graduate the value of the benefit for longer-service workers.

In summary, it seems unlikely that future retirees will enjoy the kind of health benefits that we see among today's retirees. Confronting huge financial liabilities for retiree benefits, many employers are likely either to terminate their health plans or substantially alter the benefit promise to reduce projected corporate cost. The budget and philosophical constraints on legislation that would assist employers in funding benefit obligations suggest that the legislative debate will be a long one, and that the ultimate legislation may be less favorable to employers than comparable pension legislation has been.

Unlike pensions, retiree health insurance benefits may not be a congressional priority. Congress recently expanded Medicare benefits and will probably be asked to consider controls on physician charges in the next session. That these controls will include price regulation seems inevitable; they may also include mandatory Medicare assignment. A Congress that completes such an agenda may perceive supplemental coverage—including corporate-sponsored retiree benefits—to be largely unnecessary, particularly since Medicaid is already required to pay Part B premiums and Medicare cost-sharing for most elderly in poverty. Having addressed the acute health care financing needs of the elderly, Congress may be willing to take further revenue losses only for health care issues related to other needs or populations: specifically, financing care for the uninsured and financing long-term care. Employers may gain more tax concessions related to these issues than concessions to their standing obligations to finance acute health care benefits for retirees.

References

"Retiree Health Benefits Total 12% of Payroll." *Investor's Daily.* 2 February 1988, p. 9.

U.S. Department of Labor. Bureau of Labor Statistics. *Employee Benefits in Medium and Large Firms, 1986.* Washington, DC: U.S. Government Printing Office, 1987, tables 29 and 30.

U.S. Congress. House. Committee on Ways and Means. Subcommittee on Oversight. Statement of Lawrence H. Thompson, U.S. General Accounting Office, 15 September 1988.

III. Part One Discussion

An Institutional or an Individual Responsibility?

MR. PAUL: One of the issues that has surfaced in this discussion is that of institutional versus individual solutions. We now have an expanded Medicare program that includes catastrophic coverage and that, according to Deborah Chollet's figures, provides slightly larger benefits for eligible persons—those over age 65, in general. Mr. Enthoven, you argue that savings through an employer for additional health care for retirees is not the best public policy. On the other hand, you urge that there be some kind of individual portable accounts. In your judgment, should they be tax sheltered during the accumulation period? And how do you encourage people to use these accounts if they are totally voluntary?

MR. ENTHOVEN: Your questions are a good ones. I am going to say something that will sound absolutely wild and off the wall, but it is something I think we have to think about. A student of mine from Singapore said to me after class one day, "I want to explain to you the social insurance system in Singapore." According to his description, for every $100 that an employer pays an employee, they each must contribute $25 to a compulsory savings fund. That fund is available for retirement and also for ordinary medical expenses incurred by the employee and his or her immediate family members. People with conditions that would involve catastrophic medical expenses are treated free of charge in teaching hospitals. Thus, savings are high in Singapore, he said, and national income per capita has increased very rapidly.

I know that compulsory savings brings to mind Big Brother, but I think we need to think about it. We have other forms of compulsion in this society, including a kind of moral compulsion. If a person is badly injured in an automobile accident, my whole life, upbringing, and cultural conditioning tell me that I have no choice as a decent human being but to see that he or she is given care. We do not let people die because they cannot pay for medical care. Once we realize that we are tied together by a fabric of mutual responsibility and moral obligations, we say that everyone should have to provide for their old age, because if they do not and they are poor, the rest of us will be imposed on to provide for them. Therefore, I have no problem with the idea that we ought to think about some requirement to ensure adequate savings.

The Question of Savings

MR. BALL: I liked so many points in Mr. Enthoven's paper, in fact, almost all of them, that it seems all the more important to pick up on one omission. We do have a compulsory savings system. The Social Security program is currently producing annual excesses of approximately $40 billion. In 1990, that will be approximately $100 billion a year. To make that a major contribution to an increase in national savings requires bringing the non-Social Security budget of the government much more into balance. When that is done, we will have a real opportunity. Three Brookings Institution analysts have estimated that if the Social Security surpluses already legislated are saved, national income will rise about as much as retirement benefits will go up because of the population bulge.* I do not want you to overlook that. Your idea is already there.

MR. ENTHOVEN: I certainly agree that we ought to bring the rest of the government budget into balance. Your point is a good one.

Ms. YOUNG: I do not know much about Singapore, but in most of the world outside the United States the governments take care of other major expenses, such as university education, in addition to medical expenses. They are very different societies. You talk about starting to put money away. Most people over age 40 who are in a position to do so are paying universities for the education of their children. I do not know how you can get around that point.

Another point concerns the 37 million people who are uninsured and do not have any means of paying for their health care. Are you going to tell the middle class—who are perhaps struggling to get by since the government is not providing catastrophic health care or education for their children or many other services—that they are going to be compelled to save more and that they must also pay for the 37 million uninsured who cannot afford health care? What is you solution to this problem?

MR. ENTHOVEN: On the first point that you raised, since three of my six children are in private colleges today, the other three having

---

*Editor's note: See Henry J. Aaron, Barry P. Bosworth, and Gary Burtless, *Can America Afford to Grow Old? Paying for Social Security* (Washington, DC: The Brookings Institution, 1989).

completed Harvard and Stanford, I am aware of the problem parents face. I am not saying that I have an easy solution. I am merely trying to pose the problem and saying that I think we have a major problem of undersavings in our society, and that we must move toward the ideal that each generation must save for its own needs.

I think a lot of middle-class struggling is competitive—keeping up with the Joneses. If these people put 6 percent or 8 percent of their income into a retirement account, they would probably still be struggling about as much, but they would have savings. I am not saying there is an easy solution. I think Robert Ball's point is very well taken.

In fact, if I could come back to his question about institutional versus individual solutions, I think that a lot of this does have to be accomplished through collective institutions. As a way of motivating people to save, I think that if some of the savings were more clearly tied to individual benefits, that might increase the incentive.

Ms. YOUNG: How do you view the people who basically cannot afford to save?

MR. ENTHOVEN: You have to make some judgment about the point at which people are too poor to save.

Payment System Reform

MR. WELLER: Your reference to the Titanic hit a very important point. I think what I heard you say is that talking about financing and accounting issues is like rearranging the deck chairs. Isn't the real issue how we change the Titanic's direction? A central part of changing the direction is the payment system. How do we pay doctors and hospitals for medical care? Obviously, the future scenario is gloomy for those of us on the Titanic who will need to have health benefits in the future, if we do not change the direction. My question is, how far have we come toward that fundamental change in the payment system for doctors and hospitals, and is there still a significant opportunity that might, indeed, change the direction?

MR. ENTHOVEN: That is a very good question. I feel quite pessimistic and quite disappointed about what has been accomplished so far. There is a great flurry of creation of service organizations, such as individual practice associations (IPAs) and preferred provider insurance plans, that fly under the banner of health maintenance organizations (HMOs). Ten years ago, I felt some optimism that these organizations would function as transition mechanisms and that they would become more cohesive and more cost-effective organized medical care systems.

What we see today is that prepaid group practices, such as the Harvard Community Health Plan, Kaiser-Permanente, and similar organizations, continue to exceed the rest of the system in terms of efficiency and cost effectiveness, and they demonstrate that cost-effective quality health care is possible. Many individual practice associations (IPAs) that started in the 1970s as physician groups or doctors in individual practice used the organization as a vehicle with which to compete against Kaiser Permanente and the Harvard Community Health Plan while at the same time offering their patients cost-contained, high-quality care. Many IPAs have been bought by insurance companies, or for one reason or another have become separated from local control and from the commitment of the doctors, who now perceive them as "just one more damned insurance company that is trying to rip us off."

One thing that makes Harvard Community Health Plan and Kaiser Permanente Plan different is that they can control the number of doctors by specialty in relation to the number of patients. I think that is fundamental, because busy doctors are a key to economy and quality in health care. In other situations there are too many doctors, and they are looking for new ways to make themselves useful, driving up costs.

We really have not come very far in payment system reform. We have not accomplished much in the last 10 years. Preferred provider insurance is helping by providing discounts. But again the fee-for-service doctors have figured out how to beat that, and so we are seeing health care costs go up faster than ever.

Should Health Care Benefits Be Tax Sheltered?

MR. JACKSON: I would like to comment on the need to mandate savings and why Americans may be saving too little. When you have inflation, why should you prefund anything? For example, after World War I the French totally lost faith in stocks and bonds, which had become worthless paper, and adopted a system for their long-range promises that was not based on investment. I was surprised to read a reference to this event in an article concerned with placing more confidence in trust funds. When the stock market took a little blip in October 1987, everyone was upset. The market could well go down to 10 cents on the dollar, if history is any example, and then I wonder what will happen to all the wonderful programs like the Teachers

Insurance and Annuity Association-College Retirement Equities Fund (TIAA/CREF) program.*

I read recently that 60 percent of the increase in corporate profit during the period from 1986 to 1987 was due to lower pension costs. That was done by adopting the Financial Accounting Standards Board (FASB) standard no. 87 and using projected unit credit with higher interest to lower the cost, combined with the rise in the market. It was sort of a one-time occurrence, and with FASB waiting in the wings in 1992 to require the reporting of retiree health benefit liabilities, you wonder what happens to a market that is largely grounded on earnings.

Another thing mentioned in the debate over pension legislation that concerns me is the reference to the big tax break that occurs when an employer purchases a health plan and workers do not pay income tax on it. That is the reason usually given for the creation of some huge governmental program that government benefits design experts conclude that everyone ought to have. For my part, I would prefer to drop the tax break entirely. Let the individual citizen spend his or her own money. Let employers pay their employees and let the employees do as they wish with their money. It seems to me that we now have employers buying health insurance with the employees' money, and then, because of the loss of tax revenues resulting from this tax-free benefit, we say that the government ought to take more of the employees' earnings and make them save that. My answer is, why not drop both of them and go back to ground zero?

MR. ENTHOVEN: I have been proposing for a long time that we limit the tax break both for reasons of fairness and as an incentive for economy. The federal budget loses between $40 billion and $50 billion a year because of the nontaxation of employer-provided health benefits, and most of that money goes to upper-income people, giving them an incentive to buy a more costly, rather than less costly, health plan. I have a certain sympathy with what you are saying: if we eliminated employer-provided health benefits and gave employees the money, they would probably spend it more carefully, and be motivated to ask their doctors whether certain tests were really necessary.

---

*Editor's note: TIAA is a nonprofit, legal reserve life insurance and annuity company that was established for the benefit of educational institutions and their faculty and staff. CREF is a separate, nonprofit corporation companion to TIAA that was established to provide a common-stock-based annuity component for the TIAA-CREF retirement system.

I think one reason for not going all the way, though, is that it is not possible to have a workable market for health insurance at the individual level. It simply does not work. The market gets torn apart by a process of adverse risk selection and "free riders." That is why there are 37 million uninsured Americans and why it is impossible for many people to buy health insurance. The insurers fear that the unhealthy people want to buy insurance, but the healthy do not want to buy it because they do not need it. And so a spiral of adverse selection takes place that increases premiums.

This process has, in fact, destroyed most of the nongroup market for health insurance. Therefore, I am afraid we do need some kind of collective compulsory arrangement that finances everyone's serious medical expenses.

Another reason we need a compulsory arrangement is the one I commented on earlier, which is the moral imperative to care for the sick. If you did not save enough money to afford a car in retirement and I saw you walking around, I would not feel a moral imperative to do anything about that. But if you are sitting on the doorstep in pain and suffering for lack of medical care, I would feel that that is intolerable and I must do something about it. And I think you should not be able to take a free ride on me. You have to have some kind of health care coverage, and so we need some kind of collective arrangement, and tax subsidies for group health insurance are just such an arrangement. It is a way of socializing health care expenses by giving even the healthy a powerful incentive to participate in health insurance. So I would go part way with you, but definitely not all the way.

Government's Role

MR. FLATLEY: Mr. Enthoven, I agree with your general thrust that each generation ought to fund its own retirement, but I would urge a word of caution as you look outside the United States for role models. The central provident fund in Singapore that you mentioned has run into some significant funding problems over the past 10 years because, like most government-provided social welfare programs, it is not prefunded but is a current transfer scheme. It has run into severe liquidity problems, as did our own social welfare programs in the late 1970s.

I am concerned when massive amounts of capital are accumulated under government auspices. I question whether it will be there beyond the next budgetary year. I think that is a real concern with compulsory programs under government auspices. The government's ability to save that money until the bills come due is a problem for many countries, including the United States. So it is important to be careful as you talk about compulsory government-sponsored schemes funded by employees and employers under a government-controlled payout. I do not know of any system that has been able to defuse the demographic time bomb, including Singapore's current transfer scheme or any other government-provided programs.

MR. ENTHOVEN: I am not advocating compulsory savings, I am merely throwing it out for consideration. The idea was that workers would have to put 10 percent of their pay into accounts with their names on them and it would be their money to use in retirement. One argument for trying to do this on an individual basis is that the money is in the employees' names, and congressmen are not free to take it and spend it.

When I spoke of Singapore, what I had in mind was that *kind* of system. I did not realize that there was a large element of current transfers. I grant you that the problem with the kind of arrangement that Robert Ball was talking about is that we are all afraid that when Congress sees that money they are going to think of all kinds of good projects in their districts that ought to be funded with it.

Group Medical Practices

MR. KILLEEN: I agree that the record fairly strongly indicates that the old prepaid group practices and other HMOs of that model represent the one part of the health care system that has maintained quality and is cost effective. I am a member of the board of directors of Michigan's Health Alliance Plan, which is the seventh largest HMO in the country and is based on a prepaid group practice model. I would take issue with the point made about cutting benefits, reducing benefit packages, or putting individuals more at risk. It seems that where there are system controls and certain financial arrangements are instituted to make a medical care system function appropriately, prepaid group practices are not only working efficiently but tend to offer the broadest benefits with the least amount of out-of-pocket cost sharing.

MR. ENTHOVEN: Prepaid group practices have generally done best in those situations in which the employee is cost conscious, such as the Federal Employees Health Benefits Program or Stanford University's health care plan. In the latter, the employer makes a fixed dollar contribution that is less than the premium of any of the plans; the employee chooses between the prepaid group practice and a much more expensive fee-for-service arrangement, keeping the savings if he or she joins the more cost-effective health care plan.

For many years the United Auto Workers and the auto companies have agreed on a formula that pays for coverage up to the cost of Blue Cross and Blue Shield and an HMO. In California one year the auto companies paid approximately $80 a month for employees who joined Kaiser Permanente and $110 a month for those who joined Blue Cross and Blue Shield. In other words, the workers were making the auto companies subsidize fee-for-service medical practice against prepaid group practice. That is very perverse economics and I cannot understand why such an irrational, counterproductive arrangement would be tolerated. The answer is that union officials like to get reelected, too.

Horizontal and Vertical Equity

MR. KILLEEN: I agree with Mr. Enthoven's analysis of horizontal and vertical equity. However, our society seems to approach problems one part at a time. In collective bargaining we build up benefit programs a piece at a time, starting with active workers and then including retirees to broaden the package. The government has also tended to take one piece at a time, with the exception of Medicare, which was one big program it created in a single step. As a practical matter, the step-by-step approach is the way our society seems to solve problems. What is wrong with addressing retiree health benefits at this time if, for whatever reason, FASB has decided that this is the time to consider the problem?

MR. ENTHOVEN: Why not solve this problem now and work on the others later? That is probably the way we will end up doing it, because the people who are going to benefit from tax-sheltered prefunding of health care benefits are articulate and relatively well organized. I am just speaking up for the poor and downtrodden and saying we have a $165 billion annual deficit and are short on funds. The $8 billion or $10 billion a year we would add to the deficit if tax-sheltered prefunding were allowed is real money. Before we spend a nickel of that on making health benefits better for those who are already well protected, we ought to get serious about the 37 million Americans who do not have health insurance and cut them in on the same kind of tax subsidies that we employed people receive.

Why not now? Because we are short on money, and the situation of the uninsured represents a pressing need.

MR. McMahon: I would like to take exception to your comment that there is no horizontal equity. I think medical benefits are the most egalitarian benefit corporate America provides. When you and others go to Congress and say what you have said—that there is no horizontal equity—we wind up with section 89.* Now section 89 is probably going to give you the other thing you want, taxation of the medical benefits of almost 80 percent of the people in this room.

Let me go through the entire scenario. Corporate America gets taxed for its benefits, so Paul Jackson's theory says, "Well, let us give everyone a benefit. Let us give them the income, not just the top level people like myself who can afford the $5,000 it costs me as an individual in California, but also the keypunch operators, so that they will receive another $5,000 in income. State and local taxes in California will cost them $1,250. They will not be able to get the same medical benefits for $3,750, and they will not buy the insurance. Providing them that benefit is forced savings. If they have the money in their pockets, they will not use it for the intended purpose. You will see not 37 million people uncovered but probably 50 million or 60 million as a result of that kind of approach.

That, coupled with the FASB standard that is coming, is going to make it much easier to give people income than to go through the section 89 tests. There will be more tax revenue, but there will also be more people who are not covered.

MR. ENTHOVEN: I am not saying that there is no horizontal equity in the system. I certainly have not favored section 89, which seems to me was an answer to a nonexistent problem. I grant you that, generally speaking, among most large employers health benefits are provided fairly equitably. I was merely raising the question of horizontal equity here with respect to the question of retiree health benefits. If we add $8 billion to the deficit by allowing tax-sheltered prefunding by employers who provide retiree benefits, then we are helping those employees and those companies while doing nothing for the larger number of people who are not long-service employees and who do not receive these benefits. Many of the latter are worse off than the former and are more likely to end up on Medicaid if we do not help them to help themselves.

I think we could devise a way to provide medical benefits that would not involve anything like section 89 but that would make the

---

*Editor's note: Section 89 refers to the section of the Internal Revenue Code created by the Tax Reform Act of 1986 that requires employers to subject their employee welfare benefit plans to qualification and nondiscrimination tests.

money available for that tax break, or subsidy, on a more equitable basis and would include all income groups and both short- and long-service employees. Why should we have a policy that gives this benefit to long-service employees but not to workers who happen to move from one job to another or do not work for a large employer? The people who are best off in our society tend to be long-service employees of large employers. We ought to understand that most of the people who are hurting are ones who are not in that category.

I do not agree that this would wipe out health insurance. I am not talking about just giving them the money. I think that any subsidies that are made available should be in a form usable only as a premium contribution to a group health insurance scheme.

Social Responsibility and Public Policy

Ms. YOUNG: I want to challenge one of your basic premises—that our society and our worries have not changed and that we would not leave someone who needs medical care on the street. What is happening is the opposite. People without health insurance, most of which is employer provided, do not get treated at hospitals. Many of the people discussed in the Employee Benefit Research Institute data on the uninsured are children whose parents probably have coverage, but who are not covered because their parents have not paid the little extra amount to cover them. Child abuse statistics indicate that we have a lot of children at risk. We did not force the system to cover them. We have many people in this country who have no way of providing for themselves, and they are children under the age of 18.

MR. ENTHOVEN: I am personally in favor of a public policy that is, in effect, universal, based on mandatory health insurance. I have written on that and am a well-known advocate of universal health insurance. So if there is any doubt about that, let me make it clear. I think we ought to support universal coverage, and I think it takes public policies to do it: tax subsidies, incentives. It has to be compulsory. You have to pay for it whether you take it or not.

With respect to the other point, I will grant you that we are all sinners in this world, in this country, and that we often depart from our moral standards and that at times we find circumlocutions and ways of looking the other way. But I do think that the moral standards shared by most people in our society are such that it is considered wrong to let people suffer and die for lack of medical care because they cannot pay for it. That sort of thing happens in hospitals that dump and transfer patients; then Congress passes laws against this practice and we read editorials condemning it. I am referring to a standard of behavior that I think is accepted by the great majority of American people. I realize we do not live up to that standard every day, but at least we acknowledge that is the way we ought to live. I believe we ought to create a health care financing system that is consistent with our American values of fairness and compassion.

Ms. YOUNG: I guess my response to that is that there are a lot of children who, instead of being treated for strep throat, would wind up with rheumatic fever or scarlet fever when finally treated.

Health Care Cost Inflation

MR. DUVA: Ms. Chollet, is the 15 or 25 percent increase in health care costs that you mentioned an annual increase? Would it be on top of the costs that we have today?

Ms. CHOLLET: The costs would increase the average corporate budget by about 23 percent a year.

MR. DUVA: One thing that is very important is the freedom to redesign the retiree medical programs. They have been poorly structured over the years: the plan for active workers was passed on to the retirees. I think that the ability to change these plans to meet a new environment would go a long way to help solve the problem. I think some of the current legal constraints make it very difficult.

Ms. CHOLLET: I agree. I think that there is going to be a lot of pressure on corporations to decide how they would like those legal impediments removed and on Congress and the administration to figure out how they can afford to remove them.

MR. WYMAN: I have the impression from your paper that the difference between the General Accounting Office estimate and yours may well be that you applied that discount for prescriptions to the cost of the postretirement coverage for people who are under age 65. Is that possible?

Ms. CHOLLET: No. Only for those aged 65 or over.

MR. WYMAN: Perfect technique.

Ms. CHOLLET: The reduction in cost that we expect from Medicare prescription drug coverage is huge. I produced these estimates with Phyllis Doran of Milliman & Robertson. The staff at Milliman & Robertson have evaluated quite a few retiree health insurance plans over the last year or so. I had the opportunity to look at a range of cost reductions associated with the Medicare Catastrophic Coverage Act of 1988. Their estimates of cost reductions associated with the new Medicare coverage varied across the board. They ranged from trivial amounts to huge reductions. Two major factors were involved in the magnitude of the adjustment. One, obviously, was the coverage the employer already offered. If the employer was covering only limited physician care but a lot of catastrophic hospital care and prescription drugs, the new Medicare coverage basically supplanted almost all the coverage provided by those plans and produced a huge decrease in employer liability.

The other critical variable was whether or not the retirees were in a market area where physicians largely accepted Medicare assignment. If they were in markets where Medicare assignment was prevalent, the employer liability was relatively small and the fact that the new Medicare benefits do not pick up physician services made no difference in terms of impact on employer plan cost. For example, in many of the western states, where the rate of physician assignment is relatively low, the fact that the new Medicare legislation did not address physician care made physician cost and plan cost very stable. In those plans, most cost is associated with physician care, and the Medicare legislation had little effect on plan cost. Basically, in order to come up with reasonable assumptions about the average impact of Medicare, we aimed for the middle of the range of cost impacts estimated for actual plans. In the out-years, we assumed that the new Medicare coverage will reduce employer cost by 50 percent for Medicare beneficiaries.

We do know that employer plans are very volatile with respect to Medicare benefits. Changes in Medicare benefits and administration can change employer costs a lot. Employers have generally claimed that small changes in Medicare benefits generate disproportionately large changes in their plan cost.

MR. MIKKELSEN: In calculating the liabilities, how did you account for the so-called maintenance-of-effort rule under the catastrophic bill?

MS. CHOLLET: We assumed that during the first year employer costs did not change and during the second year they were reduced 10 percent. It was not until the out-years, when prescription drug benefits begin, that we projected real drops. We assumed that the maintenance-of-effort rules held employer liability approximately constant.

MR. PETERTIL: You indicated that there will be 20 percent to 30 percent increases in employee benefit health care costs on an annual basis. To what extent was that type of inflation trend put into your long-term projections? Another way of putting this is, in your long-term projection what percentage of Gross National Product (GNP) did you see ultimately going to health care?

Ms. CHOLLET: That is the major difference among the estimates that have been made: what is assumed about inflation in the long-term. What is a realistic economic distribution between health care and all other goods and services produced in the economy? The estimates that I presented in my paper assumed a declining margin between general inflation and health care cost inflation. When the total cost of health care services reached 22 percent of GNP, we inflated health care costs at the rate of general inflation and maintained health care services spending at 22 percent of GNP. That happened in about 12 years. But the assumed rate of health service cost growth is the primary reason that the estimates vary—that and whether the discount rate you use to produce a present value figure is eventually allowed to exceed the rate of assumed growth in health care services prices. Our estimates did allow that. Other analysts are more reluctant to allow the discount rate to exceed assumed inflation. My position is, that is a relatively unorthodox thing to do. I have never seen a present value calculation that forced the discount rate and inflation rate somehow to relate to one another in that way. But one can produce extremely large estimates if one never allows the discount rates to exceed the rate of inflation.

MR. WELLER: Ms. Young's and Mr. Enthoven's comments about efficient delivery systems underscored my preexisting bias concerning the central significance of payment system reform. It has been estimated by a number of people that the waste and ineffectiveness—in terms of services that do not improve outcomes or have marginal impact on them—account for approximately 20 percent of health care costs, or $100 billion. Assuming we are smart enough and have the political will to change that payment system (which I liken to drinking wine out of leaden chalices in the sense that it is wasting the wine of our health benefits), what would health care spending and unfunded liability look like? It is obviously a very unorthodox approach, but I think it might be an interesting number.

Ms. CHOLLET: It would be, but it would be virtually impossible to estimate. That may be why we have policies that effect marginal change: we are not very good at estimating nonmarginal effects. I cannot tell you what the effect of comprehensive payment reform would be. Certainly there is an entire provider group that would like to see it make absolutely no difference at all. And they might be successful.

MR. KILLEEN: The point that you made about estimating future medical care inflation is really the key one. We were involved in this as early as 1982 in the White Motor bankruptcy. It was a real problem. It was going to determine how much money we received to provide a medical program for people. We had an excellent dialogue with Dan McCarthy of Milliman & Robertson, who said that health care costs could not continue to increase. Society would not tolerate it. But we have 30 years of data to show that that happened. While I admit that it could not consume 100 percent of GNP, because people still need clothing, food, and housing, there is no magic reason to say that it is going to stop at 12 percent or 15 percent.

MS. CHOLLET: I agree. I personally have a lot of hope that it would stop at 22 percent.

PART TWO
LEGAL ISSUES AND ACCOUNTING
REQUIREMENTS

In chapter IV, K. Peter Schmidt views retiree health benefits from a legal perspective. He points out that the Employee Retirement Income Security Act of 1974 (ERISA) established few substantive benchmarks with regard to welfare benefit plans as distinct from pension plans. Because ERISA contains no vesting or other rules for these plans, difficult legal questions arise concerning the nature of current workers' and retirees' entitlement to future benefits.

The courts have responded by creating a body of federal law, largely through the adoption of generally applicable contract principles. Schmidt describes how the courts have used contract law to provide a general framework for resolving retiree entitlement questions.

In chapter V, David Mosso gives the history of the Financial Accounting Standards Board's (FASB) retiree health accounting project from the time these benefits were first addressed in 1979 to the present. He reviews FASB's decision on the vexing question of whether these benefits should be accrued over an employee's entire working life or only to the point at which he or she becomes fully eligible for them. Mosso also discusses the board's deliberations concerning how employers should account for already-accrued liability at the time they adopt FASB's accounting change.

In chapter VI, Thomas G. Nelson points out that a lack of information prevented many employers from realizing the extent of the liability they were incurring when they formulated their retiree health benefit plans. Long-term projections of employers' retiree health insurance costs are consistently larger than expected, regardless of plan design. The accounting profession, through its standards-setting process, has been instrumental in pointing out the existence and extent of this problem, he maintains. Employers may soon be faced with requirements to begin accrual accounting and to establish vesting, funding, and participation provisions for their plans, according to Nelson, who believes employers will need sound management, legal, and financial information if they are to formulate cost-effective strategies.

In chapter VII, participants continue to explore the legal issues involved in the interpretation of retiree medical plan documents as put forth by K. Peter Schmidt. They also ask David Mosso to clarify FASB's position on the amortization of liability for retiree health benefits. Participants discuss the nature of the transition obligation and possible funding vehicles, such as 501(c)(9) trusts. They also exchange ideas on whether plan assets should be placed into irrevocable trusts, raise questions about FASB guidance in estimating the inflation rate, and debate the issue of vesting.

IV. Retiree Health Benefits: An Illusory Promise?

PAPER BY K. PETER SCHMIDT

Introduction

Life, health, and other coverage for retired workers and their families are sometimes among the benefits promised by employers. For a variety of reasons, including tax and legal considerations,[1] a funded trust arrangement is generally not involved, and such retiree benefits are therefore dependent on a continuing stream of employer contributions or payments. Where the employer encounters financial difficulty or, for other reasons, wishes to curtail benefit payments, a thorny legal question arises as to its right to do so.

Statutory Framework

ERISA—The Employee Retirement Income Security Act of 1974 (ERISA) was meant by Congress as a "comprehensive and reticulated statute"[2] governing employee benefit plans. It established disclosure and reporting requirements, trust and fiduciary responsibility requirements, and enforcement rights in participants, administrative agencies, and fuduciaries. It established the Pension Benefit Guaranty Corporation and its pension insurance program, and, with respect to most *pension* benefit plans, minimum participation, vesting, and funding standards. With respect to welfare benefit plans, however,

---

[1]The Employee Retirement Income Security Act of 1974 (ERISA) and the Internal Revenue Code (IRC) require the prefunding of pension, but not welfare, benefits. Moreover, contributions for such pension prefunding are tax deductible, whereas contributions to prefund retiree health benefits are generally deductible only to the extent of the amount necessary to fund nondiscriminatory medical benefits (determined on the basis of current medical costs) on a level basis over the working lives of covered employees. Compare IRC section 404 with IRC section 419A. Retiree medical benefits prefunded in this fashion must be provided, in the case of "key employees" (certain owners and officers), through separate accounts, contributions to which reduce the maximum contributions that may be made to a pension plan (IRC section 419A(d)). In addition, a welfare benefit trust may be subject to tax on its income to the extent of amounts set aside to prefund retiree medical benefits (IRC section 512(a)(3)(E)).
[2]*Nachman Corp. v. Pension Benefit Guaranty Corporation*, 446 U.S. 359, 361 (1980).

particularly retiree welfare benefit plans, ERISA established few substantive benchmarks.

Lack of Substantive Welfare Plan Standards—The U.S. Supreme Court recently contrasted ERISA's treatment of pension plans with that of welfare plans, as follows:

> ERISA imposes on pension plans a variety of substantive requirements relating to participation, funding, and vesting. . . . It does not regulate the substantive content of welfare-benefit plans.[3]

Because of these substantive requirements relating to vesting, funding, and benefit guarantees, the entitlement/curtailment issue described above with respect to retiree welfare benefits does not arise in the pension context. ERISA section 203 and section 411 of the Internal Revenue Code (IRC) require that, on attainment of specified minimum levels of service, pension benefits become "vested," i.e., nonforfeitable. Moreover, through its funding and pension insurance provisions, ERISA helps assure not only that workers will have a legal right to their pensions but also that the resources with which to pay such pensions will actually exist when they retire. These vesting and funding requirements are established by statute and are thus independent of the contractual undertakings and respective intents of the employer, the workers, and their collective bargaining representative.

If ERISA contained vesting requirements for welfare as well as pension benefits, there would be no difficult legal question concerning entitlement thereto. ERISA specifically provides, however, that its minimum standards provisions, including those relating to vesting, apply only to plans "other than an employee welfare benefit plan."[4] Similarly, the regulations under IRC section 411(d)(6), which prohibits retroactive reductions of a participant's accrued benefit, state that ancillary life insurance protection and accident or health insurance benefits are not among the benefits so protected.[5]

ERISA Preemption—Notwithstanding its failure to provide substantive vesting or other rules regarding retiree welfare benefits, the sweeping preemptive effect of ERISA section 514 dictates that principles of federal law are the only ones applicable in this area:

> ERISA's broad preemption provision makes it clear that Congress intended to establish employee benefit plan regulation as an exclusive

---

[3] *Metropolitan Life Insurance Co. v. Massachusetts*, 471 U.S. 724, 732 (1985).
[4] ERISA section 201(1).
[5] Treasury Regulation sections 1.411(d)–4(d)(1), (2) (1986).

federal concern, with federal law to apply exclusively, even where ERISA itself furnishes no answer.[6]

Thus, courts faced with this issue have had to create a body of federal common law. As described below, this has been done to date largely through the adoption of generally applicable contract principles.

Judicial Contract Law Analysis

Freedom to Contract under ERISA—The courts have generally agreed that, while ERISA does not require vesting of retiree welfare benefit rights, neither does it forbid it:

> The exemption from ERISA's vesting requirements does not prohibit an employer from extending benefits beyond the expiration of the collective bargaining agreement. Rather, the exemption allows the parties to determine the duration of the welfare benefits. Thus, the issue is "simply one of contract interpretation."[7]

Yard-Man—The most frequently cited retiree benefits entitlement decision is the Sixth Circuit's landmark, *International Union, United Automobile, Aerospace and Agricultural Implement Workers of America v. Yard-Man.*[8] In adopting a contract law analysis, the court noted that contracts are controlled by the intent of the parties and went on to catalog a variety of relevant contract interpretation principles:

> Many of the basic principles of contractual interpretation are fully appropriate for discerning the parties' intent in collective bargaining agreements. For example, the court should first look to the explicit language of the collective bargaining agreement for clear manifestations of intent. The intended meaning of even the most explicit language can, of course, only be understood in light of the context which gave rise to its inclusion. The court should also interpret each provision in question as part of the integrated whole. If possible, each provision should be construed consistently with the entire document and the relative positions and purposes of the parties. As in all contracts, the collective bargaining agreement's terms must be construed so as to render none nugatory and avoid illusory promises.[9]

---

[6]*In re White Farm Equipment Co.*, 788 F.2d 1186, 1191 (6th Cir. 1986); see also *Metropolitan Life, supra.*

[7]*Anderson v. Alpha Portland Industries, Inc.*, 836 F.2d 1512, 1516 (8th Cir. 1988); see also *DeGeare v. Alpha Portland Industries, Inc.*, 837 F.2d 812 (8th Cir. 1988) (related case involving salaried, nonunion workers); *in re White Farm, supra; International Union, United Automobile, Aerospace and Agricultural Implement Workers of America v. Yard-Man*, 716 F2d 1476 (6th Cir. 1983), *cert. denied*, 465 U.S. 1007 (1984).

[8]716 F.2d 1476 (1983), *cert. denied* 465 U.S. 1007 (1984).

[9]716 F.2d at 1479–80 (citations omitted).

Unambiguous Contract Terms—As in any question of contract interpretation, and as stated by the *Yard-Man* panel to be appropriate here, the courts begin their analysis with the terms of the contract itself. If retirees are or were covered by collective bargaining agreement, that agreement is thus the starting point for analysis. Where, however, the employees in question have not been so covered, there may be no written plan or other agreement, and the very "contract" to be analyzed must first be implied or derived. In these contexts, courts have had to consider such evidence as summary booklets and testimony regarding oral statements or promises. (As discussed later, similar evidence is adduced where there is a written contract, but its terms are regarded as ambiguous.)

Occasionally this starting point, the terms of the relevant agreement, does in fact end the analysis. In *Policy v. Powell Pressed Steel Co.*,[10] for example, the court interpreted "the collective bargaining agreement to unambiguously grant lifetime health insurance benefits to certain retirees. . . ." No additional analysis was required. Similarly, albeit with opposite result, the court in *Moore* vs. *Metropolitan Life Insurance Company*,[11] held that the employer had unambiguously reserved the right to amend (or terminate) the program at issue there.

The *Moore* decision rejected the participants' argument that the "contract" had to be derived from the totality of the employer's communications to the employees. The participants and their representatives had introduced evidence of communications that were allegedly less than complete, or even misleading, since they did not describe the possibility that this benefit might be modified in the future. The participants argued that the totality of these communications had to be looked to as the relevant contract, which would then be interpreted to determine the employer's obligation.

In the court's view, however, Congress intended that official plan documents and summary plan descriptions exclusively govern an employer's obligations under ERISA plans. It held that these documents contained, in the case before it, the unambiguous reservation described above.

---

[10]770 F.2d 609, 611 (6th Cir. 1985), *cert. denied*, 475 U.S. 1017 (1986) (*"Despite anything to the contrary herein contained*, present pensioners who have, prior to August 31, 1976, elected and maintained hospitalization and surgical coverage, and those who retire subsequent to that date will, *subject to the conditions hereinafter set forth*, receive Medicare complementary coverage on their hospitalization and surgical benefits for the pensioner and his spouse, if any, *during the life of the pensioner* at no cost to the pensioner.") (Emphasis supplied by the court.)
[11]856 F.2d 488 (2d Cir. 1988).

56

Thus, courts have regarded some benefit contracts as unambiguous, but have then gone on to decide the cases in both directions.

Interpreting Ambiguous Language—More often, however, the controlling terms of the contract (whether there is a written agreement or not) are seen as ambiguous, and the courts look to inferences drawn from other contract terms and from extrinsic evidence of the parties' intent. The *Yard-Man* court summarized this approach as follows:

> Where ambiguities exist, the court may look to other words and phrases in the collective bargaining agreement for guidance. Variations in language used in other durational provisions of the agreement may, for example, provide inferences of intent useful in clarifying a provision whose intended duration is ambiguous.[12]

Courts examining extrinsic evidences of intent have looked to the following: summary plan descriptions, other benefit summary booklets, or personnel material;[13] oral statements to employees from personnel managers or others, *e.g.*, in application or exit interviews;[14] specific durational clauses in other parts of the contract, *e.g.*, where the contract specifically provides for termination of the insurance benefits of active employees but has no such limitation with respect to retirees;[15] and the conduct of the parties, *e.g.*, continuation of benefits past the expiration of the collective bargaining agreement (implying that continued entitlement is not a function of current agreements) or prior curtailment of retiree benefits without complaint from the retirees (implying that retirees did not have vested rights).[16] As might be expected, the parties often disagree fundamentally on the basic facts and draw widely differing inferences from the facts on which they do agree, leading to judicial resolutions that are not wholly predictable.

Shortcomings of Contract Law Analysis—Applying contract law analysis to these questions has drawn criticism on several fronts. One commentator, for example, argues that past behavior and employment agreements have generally been premised on the later-shown-to-be-inaccurate assumption that the business would continue in-

---

[12]716 F.2d at 1480.

[13]*Bower v. Bunker Hill Co.*, 725 F.2d 1221, 1224 (9th Cir. 1984); *Eardman v. Bethlehem Steel Corp. Employee Wel. Ben.*, 607 F. Supp. 196, 209 (E.D.N.Y. 1984).

[14]*International Union, UAW v. Cadillac Malleable Iron*, 728 F.2d 807, 809 (6th Cir. 1984); *Eardman, supra* at 199–200.

[15]*Yard-Man, supra*, at 1481.

[16]*Local Union No. 150-A United Food v. Dubuque Packing*, 756 F.2d 66, 69 (8th Cir. 1985); *Cadillac Malleable, supra* at 808–09.

definitely. In these circumstances, neither the terms of such agreements nor the prior conduct of the parties are particularly relevant to the parties' expectation. This commentator cites with approval the following language from a 1973 arbitration decision:

> The difficulty here is that the parties had no intent one way or the other on the specific issue when they negotiated the agreement, or any of those which preceded it. No one at any time even broached the question of what would happen if the Company went out of business. There is no evidence that such a possibility even crossed either party's mind .... It is not surprising, therefore, that the words of the Agreement provide no clear guide; if they seemed to, it would only be an illusion, an unintended result .... When confronted by such a problem of interpretation, little is gained by dissecting the words of the contract or searching for intent on a matter which no one considered. Whatever intent is found will not be one which was in the mind of the parties but one which was constructed by the interpretation.[17]

Another commentator has criticized the lack of certainty, and the resulting costs and delay, inherent in applying a contractual analysis in this context.[18] (This commentator also believes that social policy considerations militate against the creation of minimum standards.)

To date, however, neither the courts nor Congress has established any generally applicable, substantive rules in this area.

Judicial Attempts at Further Guidance—Theoretically at least, the role of courts is not to make substantive law. As noted previously, however, the sweeping effect of ERISA preemption has required courts to create a body of federal common law in this area, since ERISA itself provides no answer. With one notable exception, the courts' response has been the contract law analysis previously described. The exception itself was short-lived, as it involved a district court opinion that was subsequently reversed.

• *White Farm.* In Re White Farm Equipment Co.[19] is a Sixth Circuit decision involving a manufacturer that ceased operations and filed a bankruptcy petition in 1980. The manufacturing operations were then purchased by another entity, which soon had its own financial problems. As a result, retirees covered by a noncollectively bargained insurance plan were notified that the plan would be discontinued.

---

[17] Donald T. Weckstein, "The Problematic Provision and Protection of Health and Welfare Benefits for Retirees," *San Diego Law Review* 101 (1987): 123–124.

[18] John T. McNeil, "The Failure of Free Contract in the Context of Employer-Sponsored Retiree Welfare Benefits: Moving Towards a Solution," *Harvard Journal on Legislation* 213 (1988).

[19] 788 F.2d 1186 (1986).

Their response was to sue their former employer for recovery of lost benefits and reinstatement of the plan.

Initially the bankruptcy court entered summary judgment for the employer, relying on its view that "the plain language of the various insurance coverage description booklets . . . does not admit of a construction other than that [the employer] retained the unqualified power to terminate or amend" the plan.[20] However, the bankruptcy court was reversed by the district court, which in turn entered summary judgment for retirees.

The district court felt required to fashion a federal common law principle applicable to the case before it, and therefore looked to analogous state law decisions. The court first noted "[a]n older line of cases" that permitted amendment or termination, pursuant to a reserved power. The court went on, however, to adopt what it characterized as the "modern view," namely vesting at retirement:

> During the past 30 years, however, more and more courts have accepted "the modern view that the promise of a pension constitutes an offer which, upon performance of the required service by the employee[,] becomes a binding obligation."[21]

The court saw *dicta* from *Yard-Man* as "an important further endorsement of the modern view that welfare benefits vest upon retirement."[22]

Applying this view, the district court held that the retirees must prevail whether or not the employer had otherwise properly reserved termination rights:

> Assuming *arguendo* that the undisputed facts prove the existence of a termination clause in the formal documents . . . , at the time the retirees completed their employment with White Farm they nonetheless acquired a vested contractual right to continued coverage . . . .[23]

The Sixth Circuit, however, rejected establishment of a common law, vesting-at-retirement principle and reversed this aspect of the district court's opinion:

> In the absence of clear precedent, we find that the statutory scheme of ERISA, though silent on this issue, counsels against the imposition by

---

[20]*In re White Farm Equipment Co.*, 42 B.R. 1005, 1010–11 (N.D. Ohio 1984), *rev'd*, 788 F.2d 1186 (6th Cir. 1986).
[21]42 B.R. at 1017.
[22]42 B.R. at 1018.
[23]42 B.R. at 1019.

this court of an absolute rule effectively requiring mandatory vesting at retirement . . . . We conclude, moreover, that the parties may themselves set out by agreement or by private design, as set out in plan documents, whether retiree welfare benefits vest, or whether they may be terminated.[24]

Although it reversed on the point discussed above, the Sixth Circuit underscored its agreement with the lower court "that no leap of logic transforms Congress' exclusion of welfare benefit plans from various ERISA requirements into an express endorsement of unfettered unilateral termination of such plans."[25] In other words, neither ERISA itself nor common law developed thereunder provides a universally applicable answer, and relevant contract principles must be applied on a case-by-case basis.

• Status Benefit Inference. Several courts have, however, added an important gloss to contract law analysis of these issues. In examining the context in which benefits were negotiated, and the nature of the benefits themselves, the *Yard-Man* court saw a lifetime benefit "inference" that could be thought to exist in every case of this kind:

> If [workers] forego [sic] wages now in expectation of retiree benefits, they would want assurance that once they retire they will continue to receive such benefits regardless of the bargain reached in subsequent agreements. . . . Further, retiree benefits are in a sense "status" benefits which, as such, carry with them an inference that they continue so long as the prerequisite status is maintained. Thus, when the parties contract for benefits which accrue upon achievement of retiree status, there is an inference that the parties likely intended those benefits to continue as long as the beneficiary remains a retiree.[26]

The court indicated that this "inference" was not controlling but rather was one of the factors to be taken into account with all other indications of the parties' intent.

In a subsequent decision, *International Union, UAW v. Cadillac Malleable Iron,*[27] the Sixth Circuit made clear that this inference was not a "presumption," that is, it did not shift the burden of proof to the employer to prove that the benefits were not meant to last the retiree's lifetime. The *Cadillac* district court had found for the retirees,

---

[24]788 F.2d at 1192–93.
[25]*Id.* at 1192. Ultimately the case was remanded for further proceedings in the bankruptcy court, since the Sixth Circuit also agreed that the allegedly unrestricted reservation of termination rights was in fact ambiguous, precluding entry of summary judgment for the employer on that basis.
[26]716 F.2d at 1482.
[27]728 F.2d 807 (1984).

based on a contract law analysis of the factors outlined previously. It had, however, gone on to find that " 'the inherent duration of the retirement status beyond any particular contract' supported its conclusion. . . ."[28] The Sixth Circuit made the following comments in upholding the lower court decision:

> While we agree with [the employer] that there is no legal presumption based on the status of retired employees, we do not believe that this leads to a conclusion that the district court erred in its determination.[29]

In *Anderson v. Alpha Portland Industries, Inc., supra,* however, the Eighth Circuit took an entirely different tack:

> [W]e disagree with *Yard-Man* to the extent that it recognizes an inference of intent to vest. Congress explicitly exempted welfare benefits from ERISA's vesting requirements. It, therefore, seems illogical to infer an intent to vest welfare benefits in every situation where an employee is eligible to receive them on the day he retires. The Court in *Yard-Man* recognized that no federal labor policy presumptively favors vesting. Because Congress has taken a neutral position on this issue "traditional rules for contractual interpretation are applied as long as their application is consistent with federal labor policies.". . . We believe that it is not at all inconsistent with labor policy to require plaintiffs to prove their case without the aid of gratuitous inferences.[30]

The existence or nonexistence of this inference may prove an important factor in the outcome of these cases. Given the leeway possible in drawing inferences from the factors that all courts see as relevant, however, it may be that this point is actually of little moment.

Bankruptcy Interaction—Attempts at benefit curtailment by employers who have filed for bankruptcy pose a separate set of issues. On one level, at least, the analysis described above may not be affected. The initial question likely remains one of contract analysis: has the employer contractually committed itself to continue the program? If the answer is no, that is, the employer has effectively re-

---

[28] *Id.* at 808.

[29] *Id.; cf. Policy v. Powell Pressed Steel Co., supra* at 613 ("the *Yard-Man* court recognized that 'retiree benefits are in a sense "status" benefits which, as such, carry with them an inference that they continue so long as the prerequisite status is maintained.' ").

[30] 836 F.2d at 1517; the court went on to explain the consistency of its holding with its own prior decision, *Local Union No. 150-A United Food v. Dubuque Packing,* 756 F.2d 66, 70 (1985), which had seemed to adopt the *Yard-Man* view on this point. ("The right to receive health and welfare benefits arises from the retiree's status as a past employee. It is not dependent on a continued or current relationship with the Company. The status of a retiree cannot be affected by future negotiations or agreements between the Company and the Union; neither can act on behalf of retirees.")

served the right to make the contemplated change, the analysis presumably stops there.[31] Assuming, however, that the court does find an ongoing contractual obligation—an obligation that would determine the issue in nonbankruptcy contexts—bankruptcy situations may require further analysis.

In general, the federal Bankruptcy Code permits an employer that has filed a bankruptcy petition to reject an executory contract under which it would otherwise be obligated.[32] If retiree benefits are seen as nothing more than executory contract obligations, this aspect of the Bankruptcy Code might be regarded as authorizing curtailment by an employer that would not be so permitted in the absence of a bankruptcy petition filing.

In response to this possibility, and to the reality of the LTV bankruptcy and LTV's attempts to terminate its retiree benefit programs, Congress enacted in 1986 a stopgap measure requiring continuation of retiree health and other coverages in certain instances, "[n]otwithstanding any provision of [the Bankruptcy Code]."[33] The legislation precluded, until May 15, 1987, curtailment of such programs by employers that either commenced bankruptcy cases after October 2, 1986, or were still paying benefits on such date, notwithstanding prior commencement of a bankruptcy proceeding. The Retiree Benefits Bankruptcy Protection Act of 1988 extended this legislation through the enactment of such act, and precluded retiree benefit curtailment thereafter except where procedures similar to those now required for rejection of a collective bargaining agreement have been followed.[34]

---

[31] The Retiree Benefits Bankruptcy Protection Act of 1988 and its predecessor (discussed in this chapter) do not appear intended to change this result. As Sen. Howard Metzenbaum (D-OH), the legislation's principal sponsor, stated on the floor of the Senate:

"This measure sends a strong and powerful message to companies which make promises to their workers—you cannot expect to use the bankruptcy courts *as a way of reneging on retiree promises.*" *Congressional Record* 26 May 1988, pp. S. 6824–6825 (emphasis added).

Thus, the legislation seems clearly aimed at preventing the use of the bankruptcy laws to curtail retiree benefit programs that could not otherwise be curtailed. Nonetheless, the literal language of such legislation could be read to preclude unilateral curtailment by bankrupt employers even where a clear contractual right to do so exists quite apart from bankruptcy. Even if the law were so interpreted, it would presumably have no effect on an employer's exercise of such right on the eve of bankruptcy.

[32] 11 U.S.C. section 365(a) (1982).

[33] Continuing Appropriations for Fiscal Year 1987, P.L. No. 99-591, 100 Stat. 3341–74 (1986).

[34] Retiree Benefits Bankruptcy Protection Act of 1988, P.L. No. 100-334, 102 Stat. 613 (1988).

Bankruptcy situations present a further twist where the benefits in question are provided pursuant to collective bargaining. In its *Bildisco*[35] decision in 1984, the U.S. Supreme Court held that the contract rejection right described above extended freely to collective bargaining agreements and an employer's obligations thereunder. Congress responded with an amendment to the Bankruptcy Code providing that collective bargaining agreements can be rejected only with the approval of the bankruptcy court and only after a specified showing has been made and specified procedures followed.[36]

Since then, at least one employer has argued unsuccessfully that this Bankruptcy Code amendment and its required proceedings do not apply to those provisions of a collective bargaining agreement that pertain to retirees, or, alternatively, that they apply only to those situations covered by the "stopgap" anticurtailment legislation discussed earlier.[37]

Conclusion

As evidenced by the foregoing discussion, entitlement to retiree benefits is an issue at the intersection of a number of different, and sometimes conflicting, policies—policies relating, for example, to taxation,[38] retirement, bankruptcy, financial accounting, and labor

---

[35] *NLRB v. Bildisco & Bildisco*, 465 U.S. 513.

[36] 11 U.S.C. section 1113 (1982).

[37] *In re Unimet Corp.*, 842 F.2d 879 (6th Cir. 1988); *cf. In re Century Brass Products, Inc.*, 795 F.2d 265 (2d Cir. 1986), *cert. denied*, 476 U.S. ___, 107 S. Ct. 433 (1986) (rejection procedures required by Bankruptcy Code amendment contemplate additional bargaining over retiree benefits, but union may, because of conflict-of-interest, not be the appropriate retiree representative).

[38] Among the issues yet to be sorted out under the Internal Revenue Code (IRC) is how retiree health benefits will be taken into account under IRC section 89. To avoid being considered a "discriminatory employee benefit plan" thereunder, with resultant adverse tax consequences for any "highly compensated employees," the plan must meet either three eligibility tests and a benefits test or a coverage test and nondiscriminatory eligibility test. These tests are designed to prevent discrimination in favor of "highly compensated employees." Although the tests are stated in terms of "employees," and retirees are no longer employees, the statute does not appear meant to exclude retirees from these tests. Section 89(j)(3) provides as follows: "Except to the extent provided in regulations, this section shall be applied separately to former employees under requirements similar to the requirements that apply to employees." What exceptions the regulations might provide, and what "similar to" means in this context, is yet to be elucidated.

The legislative history, however, directs the Treasury to provide in such regulations as follows:

Employers may generally restrict the class of former employees to be tested to those who have retired on or after a reasonable retirement age, or to those who have separated from law. Moreover, the demographics of our society suggest that the issue will not go away and is only likely to grow in importance over the coming years.

Theoretically, the courts alone could fully resolve the conflicting legal principles. Indeed, they have already been forced to provide a general framework (contract law) for resolving retiree entitlement questions. The more important social questions, however, will have to be resolved by the legislative branch. Hopefully, this will not continue in a "stopgap" or narrowly focused fashion but will be part of a comprehensive examination of all relevant policies.

---

service due to disability. In addition, employers may generally limit the class further to employees who have, for example, retired within a certain number of years. Finally, in testing whatever class of employees is chosen, employers may make reasonable assumptions regarding mortality, so that they do not have to determine those former employees who are still alive.

U.S. Congress, House, *Report of the Committee on Ways and Means, House of Representatives, on the Tax Reform Act of 1986*, H.R. Rept. 426, 99th Cong, 1st sess., 1985; *Conference Report on Tax Reform Act of 1986*, H.R. Rept. 841, 99th Cong., 2nd sess., 1986; U.S. Congress, Senate, *Report of the Committee on Finance U.S. Senate, on the Tax Reform Act of 1986*, S. Rept. 313, 99th Cong., 2nd sess., 1986; see also U.S. Congress, Staff of Joint Committee on Taxation, *General Explanation of the Tax Reform Act of 1986*, Committee Print (Washington, DC: U.S. Government Printing Office, 1987).

This ability to test retirees separately from other employees is important. It will allow employers to maintain, on a tax-favored basis, retiree-only plans that meet the nondiscrimination requirements when only retirees are considered but fail those requirements when *all* former employees, including those who left the company at a relatively early age, are considered.

In addition, the ability to further limit the class tested to employees who have retired within a certain number of years will apparently make it easier for an employer to meet the nondiscrimination tests with respect to a health plan under which an employer begins to offer retiree benefits but does not reach back to cover all prior retirees. This language may also be interpreted to make it easier to meet these tests with respect to a health plan under which an employer that has explicitly stopped promising retiree benefits to new employees continues to provide for the current or future payment of benefits to employees who have already retired or to whom such benefits have already been promised.

These and other retiree health benefit issues which, as of this writing, have not been clarified, will likely be addressed in regulations under IRC section 89. Provisions included in both the House and Senate versions of the pending technical corrections would require the Treasury to issue, by October 1, 1988, rules on which employers may rely. This initial guidance is to focus primarily on issues not addressed by the statute or legislative history and needed immediately for compliance. Both versions also provide that, if the required regulations are not issued by October 1, an employer's compliance with its good faith interpretation of section 89, based on the statute and its legislative history, will constitute compliance with the statute. [Editor's note: The Internal Revenue Service issued proposed regulations on March 2, 1989.]

V. Retiree Health Benefits: The FASB Decision Process

REMARKS OF DAVID MOSSO

Introduction

Professor Alain Enthoven of Stanford University has said that fussing with the accounting and legal issues surrounding retiree health benefits is akin to rearranging the deck chairs on the Titanic. I would use that analogy a little differently: If you want to avoid hitting an iceberg, it is good to know that there is an iceberg in the vicinity, and one might describe the Financial Accounting Standards Board (FASB) retiree health accounting project as an attempt to put a telescope on every deck chair.

Let me give you a brief history of the project and then some tentative conclusions on the major issues.

History

FASB put retiree health care and other benefits on the agenda in 1979. At that time we had an active pension accounting project; retiree health benefits seemed to be similar, so we incorporated them into the pension project.

In 1982 we came out with a preliminary document that said retiree health care benefits should be accrued over the working lives of employees. We found that we could not readily follow up on that conclusion, however, because pension issues tended to dominate the board's thinking at that point. So in 1984 we separated health care benefits from pensions and basically set them aside for a couple of years. But we did issue Statement No. 81, which required disclosure of a description of the retiree health plan and the cost recognized in the income statement.

In 1986 we went back to work on the retiree health care project and have been working on it since then. An exposure draft should be issued in February 1989.* Following that, there will be six months

---

*Editor's note: On February 14, 1989, FASB released an exposure draft of a proposed accounting standard that would require companies to recognize postretirement health care and insurance benefits as a form of deferred compensation and to report these obligations on their balance sheets. Sections of the exposure draft, *Proposed Statement of Financial Accounting Standards: Employers' Accounting for Postretirement Benefits Other Than Pensions*, are included in Appendix B.

for comments on the exposure draft. Then in October 1989 we will hold public hearings at which anybody will be free to offer testimony. Sometime in 1990, probably in the first half of the year, we will issue a final statement.

The Liability Issue

The key conclusion that the board has reached is on the basic issue of whether employers have a liability, in the accounting sense, for retiree health benefits. Of course, we really reached that conclusion in 1982 and said, yes, there is a liability and it should be accrued. But we reexamined that question in great depth when we resumed work on the project in 1986. Again we concluded that, yes, it is a liability, and that postretirement health care benefits are a part of the employee compensation package.

Compensation for some current work is paid in cash, some is paid in kind; some is paid now, some is paid later during retirement. We did not see health care benefits as being any different from any other kind of compensation in that regard.

Whether or not the promise to provide retiree health benefits is legally binding is not our bailiwick, and is not really the key issue for us. If the promise is legally binding, there is no question whatsoever that an accounting liability exists. We basically operate on the presumption that a promise made in a plan document is a promise that is intended to be kept, and the obligation for that promise should be accounted for until there is some indication that the promise will not be kept.

Benefit Accrual

On the issue of how to accrue the benefits, the board has concluded that, basically, they should be accrued like pensions—that is, by estimating the future benefits that are earned during the current accounting period and then calculating the present value of those future benefits. The result is the current period cost and the increment to the liability.

A major issue in our deliberations was whether the benefits should be accrued over the entire working life of an employee or over the working life to the point at which the employee becomes fully eligible for the benefits—in other words, when the employee could retire and get the benefits, whether or not the employee chooses to retire then. The board decided to require accrual to the eligibility date rather than to the retirement date. Any funding would be offset against the liability and any income on fund assets would be offset against expense.

Transition Liability

Another major issue is what to do about the liability that has already accrued at the time a company first adopts an accounting change such as the one proposed. There has been much discussion of the magnitude of the liability and its impact on corporate equity. The board decided that the amount had to be spread over some period, and the decision was to amortize it—to [require employers to] disclose the liability immediately on adoption of the statement but not to book it on the balance sheet. Rather, it would be amortized into income and onto the balance sheet over the average remaining service life of active employees or, if that service life was relatively short, over a 15-year period.

Despite its conclusion that the transition liability should be amortized onto the balance sheet gradually, the board debated whether or not it wanted to have at least a minimum liability booked at some time prior to the time the transition obligation was fully accrued. The board decided to require that a minimum liability be booked, and that it would be the amount of the benefits that had been earned by existing retirees and those active employees who were then eligible to receive benefits.

This requirement was mitigated somewhat by the effective date provision. Basically, the accrual of current expense and current liability increments would begin for calendar year 1992. For small business and for foreign plans of U.S. companies, the accrual would be effective for calendar year 1994. The minimum liability, however, would not have to be recorded until 1997, so there would be, in effect, eight years before the minimum liability would have to be recorded on the balance sheet.

VI. FASB Accounting and Funding Issues

PAPER BY THOMAS G. NELSON

Introduction

By now most of us are aware that a large majority, approximately 80 percent, of large and medium-sized employers continue to pay for retiree life and/or health benefits for former employees. Many of us know first-hand that the cost of providing these benefits can be overwhelming. Compounding the financial difficulty is the fact that the accounting and legal requirements for retiree plans continue to change.

Many employers who pay the current retiree costs as they occur have not yet experienced the full force of the financial consequences of these plans. The relative proportion of the hidden retiree costs varies by employer, but in general these plans have two common characteristics: they are deceptive and promise to become very expensive. Take the case of one very large employer that had a long-standing plan and a mature work force. Actuarial estimations indicated that the cost of its existing plan could more than quadruple in the next 15 years, with a present value obligation totaling several billion dollars.

Another company, recently considering the adoption of a retiree health plan, benefited from our collective progress in advancing along the retiree medical learning curve. The company was aware of the rumblings regarding retiree medical plans, and wisely decided to develop financial estimates before acting. This particular employer's work force was relatively young, with very few current retirees.

The company's benefits manager had made an estimate of the next year's (modest) costs. However, an actuarial analysis that projected retirements and costs much further into the future provided quite a different picture. The estimated hidden costs—those for future years when the bulk of the retirements would be anticipated—were enormous compared with the initial costs expected by the employer. In fact, while both analyses agreed that the costs would begin modestly, the actuarial analysis projected a tenfold increase by the year 2000. The present value of all anticipated benefits was more than 100 times the initial year's expected outlay.

Long-term projections such as these demonstrate that, regardless of the group, the plan design, or any reasonable assumptions about the future, we are headed for some very expensive times that were previously unforeseen. As is usually the case, learning about the extent of the problem is a painful but essential first step in forming strategies that will enable employers to gain added control of their future benefit programs and business expenses.

Overview of the Issues

In 1974, the Employee Retirement Income Security Act (ERISA) set funding, participation, and vesting standards for retirement income plans. However, even before 1974, pension accounting and actuarial values were determined on an accrual basis.

For nonpension coverages, accounting standards are not as advanced. They are being studied by the Financial Accounting Standards Board (FASB), as are possible funding, participation, and vesting standards by the federal government. Additionally, retiree coverage has been the focal point of a number of judicial disputes that tilt toward requiring a more certain employer responsibility for retiree benefits.

Any discussion of retiree health benefits should include the following considerations.

- Our legal system has been trying to determine the extent to which retirees are entitled to benefits that are construed to have been earned during their active working lives. Despite what appears to be a legal trend toward entitlement for retirees, Congress chose, in the Deficit Reduction Act of 1984 (DEFRA), to emasculate available funding mechanisms through severe taxation of retiree plan reserves and contributions. In addition, federal budget constraints have affected governmental health programs such as Medicare, putting increasing pressure on the private sector to finance benefits for the elderly.

- The accounting standards-setters went beyond merely recognizing an important contingency-accounting omission—i.e., exclusions regarding group insurance obligations—that has existed in FASB Statement No. 5. They examined the materiality and measurability of the value of retiree health benefits as well as the apparent extent of employers' obligations to former employees. Their findings indicated a need to account for the value of such benefits over employees' working lifetimes instead of using today's nearly universal norm, cash (or pay-as-you-go) accounting. Definitive proposals by FASB on accounting standards were issued in February.*

---

*Editor's note: On February 14, 1989, FASB released an exposure draft of a proposed accounting standard that would require companies to recognize postretirement health

69

- Not only are accounting and legal issues pressuring retiree benefits, but the aging of the work force and ongoing medical inflation are causing the surprising cost increases that are being estimated for many postretirement medical benefits programs. No one knows the true aggregate cost of these plans, but the U.S. House of Representatives' Select Committee on Aging has been given estimates indicating that the liability for future retiree health benefits for the Fortune 500 companies is approximately 150 percent of total assets. This may or may not be true, but it is clear that the pay-as-you-go accounting and funding approaches generally used—along with the unavailability of more accurate data—have masked the exponential increases in retiree costs and hampered our ability to plan intelligently for our businesses' futures.

- Where the legal status of benefits is such that funding, reserving, and accrual accounting for plans are deemed appropriate, actuarial estimations of future costs are needed, using mathematical models that combine economic, demographic, and probabilistic assumptions over the next several decades.

Accounting Influences

The accounting profession, through its standards-setting process, has been instrumental in pointing out the existence and extent of the "problem." In early 1984, FASB split its long-running study of the accounting for pension and nonpension postemployment benefits into separate projects.

The pension study resulted in FASB Statement No. 87, *Employers' Accounting for Pensions*, and FASB Statement No. 88, *Employers' Accounting for Settlements and Curtailments of Defined Benefit Pension Plans and for Termination Benefits*. FASB then turned to nonpension benefits (primarily group life, health, and disability coverages).

FASB's Emerging Issues Task Force studied a number of issues related to retiree medical benefits, including materiality, measurability, the extent of employers' obligation to former employees, and accounting for these benefits in circumstances involving mergers and acquisitions. FASB staff and representatives of the American Academy of Actuaries worked closely to combine the pertinent accounting and actuarial principles to ensure that the accounting standards would be based on an appropriate conceptual foundation.

Based on FASB's study to-date, the following can be noted.

---

care and insurance benefits as a form of deferred compensation and to report these obligations on their balance sheets. Selections from the exposure draft, *Proposed Statement of Financial Accounting Standards: Employers' Accounting for Postretirement Benefits Other Than Pensions*, are included in Appendix B.

- From an accounting perspective, retiree health care benefits are considered deferred compensation earned during service.

- In the next few years, accrual methods will supersede pay-as-you-go as the acceptable accounting method.

- Actuarial projections of unfunded benefits will be used to measure costs and liabilities. Assumptions used in the projections will not be pegged; rather, explicit "best-estimate" assumptions should be employed.

- For most typical plans, expected benefits will be allocated ratably over the employee's working period from date of hire to date of eligibility for benefits.

- Minimum liabilities, to be reflected on the balance sheet, will be required for values associated with current retirees and those eligible to retire and receive benefits.

- Transition obligations will be required on the unfunded present values of benefits to be paid to current retirees, with a proportionate amount also required for active workers. The transition amount would start as a footnote to the balance sheet and be recognized over the average remaining service periods of active workers, or 15 years if longer.

- Gains and losses could be recognized either immediately or on a delayed basis.

- Accounting disclosures would be similar to those for pensions (FASB Statement No. 87), supplemented by a statement of the assumed health care trend rate and the effect of a one percentage point change in that rate on the obligation and periodic cost.

- Final standards would generally be effective for fiscal years beginning after December 15, 1991, with up to five years longer to recognize a minimum liability.

Funding

Highly publicized court cases have brought to public and congressional attention the almost total lack of prefunding for today's retiree health plans. A second general area of legal activity involving retiree benefits deals with the taxation of funded retiree plans. The passage of ERISA affected health plans in a number of ways but did not establish pension-like standards for their funding, vesting, or participation—nor has any other federal law done so since that time. DEFRA crippled available employer funding mechanisms and mandated further governmental study of funding. The inclusion of funding limitations in this legislation was a philosophically puzzling move, coming at a time when the federal government had consistently asked the private sector to shoulder a greater share of employee welfare costs. Under DEFRA, actuarial funding over employees' working lifetimes is technically allowed for in health plans but specifically may not provide for medical inflation, a critical component. Moreover, tax advantages were stripped from the holding of advance-funded retiree reserves. These provisions severely restrict employers who might wish to prefund retiree benefits as they are earned.

It may be possible for retiree health plans to regain legislatively the kind of favorable tax treatment that is accorded to pension plans. However, if this does occur, the *quid pro quo* would likely be a requirement for the sponsor to operate within specific funding, vesting, and participation rules. Thus, employers who wished to continue their plans in order to assist former employees with the financial risks associated with their health would be required to fund on a more accelerated basis than pay-as-you-go. The direction of such a potential funding/taxing change would then coincide with, rather than contradict (as do the provisions of DEFRA), the direction of expected future accounting changes.

Conclusion

In past years, plan sponsors have unknowingly granted health benefits to retirees and disabled persons worth literally billions of dollars. To a certain extent, employers were blind-sided on this retiree issue because sufficient information was generally not available to help them formulate these plans. As it turns out, the reported pay-as-you-go costs are a small portion of the total cost. Most employers did not ask for, and no one offered, better data. Even with better data and projections, however, it would have been difficult to predict the advent of the tough legal restrictions that have been established. Thus, employees have found themselves in a reactive position facing a number of tough issues.

Employers' increased interest in the financial risks associated with their retiree health plans is understandable because they may soon be faced with requirements to begin accrual accounting; to guarantee coverage for former employees in certain instances; and to establish formal vesting, funding, and participation provisions for their plans. Employers' future strategies will vary greatly, and the development of these strategies will depend on the availability of sound management, legal, and financial advice.

Employers who have not yet studied their plans' costs, or who are involved in mergers or acquisitions with companies that have not examined retiree costs, are certain to benefit greatly by studying cost projections for their plans. This information will enable them to begin an informed planning process to manage the risk involved with these benefits. The knowledge derived from a long-term projection of its retiree benefits will assist the employer in determining the amount of risk to be accepted. The employer's stance on risk will then lead either to changes in, or to an affirmation of, existing policy. Once the employer's philosophy and plan for retiree benefits are in place, periodic updates of legal, accounting, and actuarial developments will help to keep the entire retiree medical program on course.

VII. Part Two Discussion

Legal Issues

Ms. IGNAGNI: I am with AFL-CIO. I would like to begin by stating that I am still confused about some of the issues that Mr. Schmidt discussed. The documents of most of the plans that we have negotiated do not mention the issues of cost management or cost sharing. I have read some conflicting things by legal theoreticians and others who would make one argument or another, so I would like to ask you your views on the rights of a retiree versus those of a current employee in situations where the plan documents do not explicitly cover the issues of cost management and cost sharing. Are they treated differently in your mind? Should they be? What are the rights here? I am not familiar with these principles, and I do not believe anybody else is.

MR. SCHMIDT: I do not think anyone is, including the courts. I think the basic mode of analysis that I described is what would be adopted in that circumstance, which is to say, courts would try to fathom the underlying intent of the parties with respect to cost sharing, etc. You might say we did not think about it. That may be the reality of the situation and the court may believe that itself, but I think it will, nonetheless, go through that kind of an analysis. Relevant factors would be, for example: If cost sharing has been in the program for some time, has it increased? Did people claim that it was a violation of the contract when that happened? If there was no cost sharing for a while and then it was instituted, is that what started the complaint? If not, the court may say that it is not a violation of the contract. The parties did not seem to think it was a problem.

The court may be able to find other factors that shed light on this phantom intent of the parties. It is a facts-and-circumstances analysis, and parties disagree about the facts and the inferences properly drawn from the facts. I do not think you can predict, even with a stipulated set of facts sometimes, how one court or another will decide.

Ms. IGNAGNI: There is a question of utilization and management, recertification—even triple options type arrangements. We have made very little progress in obtaining information on these initiatives in the area of retiree health. We think that the initiatives should go forward, but what would your opinion be on the rights of the two parties in that situation in relation to cost sharing?

MR. SCHMIDT: Part of the problem is that you do not always have only two parties. Sometimes it is thought of as three parties, and in that case, does the collective bargaining representative represent retirees? If you pass that one for a minute and assume that they do, then it is a basic contract principle that, between themselves, two parties to a contract can do whatever they want. They can amend, modify, change it, so that if there is agreement between the union and the employer about how to implement the contract, you should not have a problem. But this raises a sticky point: Are you representing, and in effect standing in the shoes of, the retiree, and is that proper?

Modifying Contracts

MR. NELSON: A followup to that. You talked about collective bargaining. In my experience in dealing with employers, there has been a dearth of written information about the retiree portion of the contract: whether it is an insured case or a self-insured arrangement. How far are you seeing these kinds of contractual arrangements taken, for instance, in terms of cost sharing or even administration? The way the program is administered—whether it is based on coordination of benefits or a carve-out program—can mean a big difference to the retiree and to the employer in terms of how much each is responsible for. How far are you seeing that go in new contracts? Are these types of references being included in restructured plans?

MR. SCHMIDT: You are talking about people agreeing to modifications, so it is not a question of law or—

MR. NELSON: How about where an employer determines that this is going to be the program from here on, trying unilaterally to implement changes?

MR. SCHMIDT: I think when an employer is trying to implement changes and he faces a complaint from people covered by the program—and not much of anything is written—that past conduct will be an extremely important factor. In the Second Circuit decision, I believe the plan was initially not contributory. Then a contribution was made on the order of a couple hundred dollars a year, and later it went to $400 and subsequently to approximately $800. At that point the people covered first started a lawsuit. That is a little late to take a position, because there is this inference about the prior changes.

MR. NELSON: As employers attempt to modify the retiree contracts that are in effect, what level of detail is being implemented in the promises that are being made to future retirees? Are the details of cost sharing and administration being included? Have you seen any trend?

MR. SCHMIDT: I do not do labor bargaining and I cannot say what is happening at the bargaining table.

MR. RAPS: Mr. Schmidt, do you think it would carry any weight with the federal courts if an employer wanted to modify a postretirement benefit program that was found to be discriminatory by reducing the benefits to make it nondiscriminatory?

MR. SCHMIDT: I have not seen a case like that. I think one obvious response is to raise benefits to make it nondiscriminatory. The problem with that starts with the premise that there is a fixed pool and the reduction is only to make it nondiscriminatory with the limited assets available.

I work with multiemployer plans a lot and the fixed-pool issue is a reality in that context. Yet we still sometimes have a hard time selling it. My guess is that a court would not be moved very far by that notion.

MR. MARINACCI: To the extent that courts have held employers' feet to the fire on the benefits promise, has it always been on behalf of a current retiree group? Have there ever been cases where the plaintiffs were present employees, i.e., future retirees, who want to hold the employer's feet to the fire on the implied promise?

MR. SCHMIDT: Where you draw the line is certainly an issue: what the promise is, what it takes to have it sealed into a contract. For example, if the idea is that it is an offer from the employer, once an employee has worked the required time and become entitled, then it is a contract.

If it is a question of the contract providing that if you have 10 years of coverage under the plan with the employer you are entitled to lifetime benefits at normal retirement age—and the benefit has been provided to people who leave the company after 10 years and then return—I think that would be a good case for people that have not reached normal retirement age. But I cannot cite any specific case law on that.

76

New Financial Accounting Standards Board Rule

Ms. CHOLLET: I want to make sure that I understand what Mr. Mosso said. Am I right in saying that amortization of liability for retiree health benefits would involve estimating the present value of current benefits provided to current retirees, and estimating the present value, again, if it is promised, to active workers?

Amortizing for the first group would be over the 15-year period, as you do with Financial Accounting Standards Board Statement No. 87. For the second, rather than the working life, when workers become eligible, that year-to-year amortization payment goes in current liabilities. Am I right about that?

Mr. MOSSO: The liability that exists at the transition date has already been earned, and any unrecognized amount would be amortized over the longer of the remaining service life of active employees or 15 years. The accrual for a current employee's service would begin with the date of hire and would be accrued up to the date that the employee becomes eligible for benefits.*

Ms. CHOLLET: Whatever that number is in both categories, some goes in the current liability section of the balance sheet and would increase expenses, essentially, to the employer.

Mr. MOSSO: That is correct. To the extent that the prior service obligation is amortized, it would go into liabilities.

Ms. CHOLLET: Would you explain the minimum liability again?

Mr. MOSSO: The transition obligation, which is the total amount that is owed as of the date the standard is adopted, breaks down into three pieces: the piece that has been earned by existing retirees, the piece that has been earned by active employees who are eligible [for retirement], and the piece that has been earned by active employees who are not yet eligible. All of these pieces would be part of the transition obligation that would be disclosed but not immediately recognized in the financial statements. Beginning in 1997, however, the unfunded obligation for retirees and eligible active workers would be required to be reported on the balance sheet.**

---

*Editor's note: This represents a reversal of an earlier FASB decision that would have measured the obligation to provide retiree health benefits based on the portion of expected total service rendered, that is, service to the expected retirement date.

**Editor's note: This represents a reversal of earlier FASB decisions that would have defined the minimum liability as the unfunded liability for current retirees only and would have set the effective date for recognizing the minimum liability at 1994.

Ms. CHOLLET: When you say that by 1997 it would have to go on the balance sheet, am I to assume that it would go in a footnote until then?

MR. MOSSO: Yes.

Funding Vehicles

MR. LAURENT: I would like Mr. Nelson to comment on one of the key points of this discussion: What are employers going to do? I agree that the first reaction will be to try to reduce liability. The big question in my mind is, what is going to happen on the asset side? In your opinion, will there be any nontrivial level of funding before there are tax advantages greater than we have now? And if there is—if you believe people will start to fund—which of the available funding vehicles do you think are most likely to be used?

MR. NELSON: I have not seen any meaningful trend in the way employers fund retiree health care liabilities. I would be interested to know if other forum participants have a comment on that.

If not too many people are funding, I am not sure which of the vehicles are preferable. Certainly there are advantages to 401(h) in the sense that there are some standards associated with it, but it is limited. Essentially, 401(h) cannot do all that you would like to do. The voluntary employee beneficiary association approach is so emasculated that I do not see any activity in that direction. If there were reversions from pension plans, that might create some assets that would be helpful.

MR. LAURENT: Mr. Mosso, one of the FASB handouts defined plan assets that could be used to reduce liability as assets that are segregated and legally restricted. What level of restriction is required? Many people may start to fund with trust funds that may not be irrevocable. Would this kind of asset accumulation be available to offset the liability?

MR. MOSSO: I do not know for sure what you were given. It may, in fact, be the language that is likely to go into the exposure draft. We have not addressed revocability. I am not sure what the term "legally restricted" means. I do not think it goes so far as to mean that the assets have to be in an irrevocable trust, but it probably would go far enough to mean that you could not tap into them willy nilly for other corporate purposes.

MR. LAURENT: If it is not irrevocable, then it could be attacked willy nilly.

MR. MOSSO: Without being totally irrevocable, there might be conditions that would have to be met—a requirement that would protect the beneficiaries to some extent.

MR. LAURENT: So you feel that there probably would have to be some restriction on availability of the funds for them to qualify as plan assets?

MR. MOSSO: Yes.

MR. NELSON: Some of the informal discussions that I have had on this have focused on the fact that 501(c)(9) trusts typically are not segregated and dedicated to the use of the retiree program. However, my understanding is that FASB would require some kind of definite segregation in order for assets to be recognized as funding for those liabilities.

MR. LAURENT: But again, even if you set up a 501(c)(9) trust, it is my understanding that that is probably nonreversionary once the money goes in.

MR. NELSON: The 501(c)(9) trusts that I am familiar with are not specifically for the retiree segment of the population. I think that, in their initial discussions, FASB was indicating that they would need that type of trust in order to have assets recognized for the retiree evaluation.

FASB Guidance

MR. EASLEY: When FASB Statement No. 87 was issued, there was guidance on interest rates used. We have discussed the importance of the rate of medical care inflation in relation to general inflation. What type of guidance does FASB have in mind?

MR. MOSSO: It will be very general. It will not be as specific as that given for pensions, because the pension rates lean heavily on the availability of purchased annuities and use those rates as a guide. There do not seem to be similar kinds of arrangements available now, and so the guidance at this point leans more to an asset rate. If there is funding, the guidance would be related to the kinds of assets in the fund. Other than that, it would probably be related to the kinds of assets you would use otherwise. In other words, it will be very broad guidance, at least in the exposure draft.

The interest rate and the extent to which a trust would be restricted will be addressed during the public comment and public hearing process. It is very likely that they will be refined a good bit before the final statement comes out.

MR. EASLEY: I was not referring so much to the interest rate as I was to the inflation rate.

MR. MOSSO: We will give very broad guidance on that. I think about the only thing we are saying is that it should be the employer's best estimate, based on specific assumptions and the best estimate of all of the factors that go into that rate.

MR. NELSON: The discussion that I have heard to date on this point has indicated that, in terms of the explicit best-estimate assumption for medical trends, there is no prescribed relationship between the discount rate, which Mr. Mosso talked about, and the medical trend rate, which you are asking about. There is no prescription as to the levels of these rates. And in these calculations the key is the relationship between these two numbers. In addition, it was indicated that footnotes would contain information about the effect of varying the trend rate by one percentage point from whatever was assumed. Will there be some financial information for the reader in the statement also?

MR. MOSSO: That will be a proposed disclosure. I would observe, however, that we proposed that in the pension exposure draft and later dropped it. However, the board still opted to require it here, principally, I think, because the health care estimate is bound to be even softer than a pension estimate, and so the sensitivity type of disclosure would be helpful to users.

The Accrual Period

MR. EASLEY: I would like to ask a question about the early retirement provision. Why is it that many of these plans are focused heavily on early retirement? When you said that accrual would be made to the earliest eligibility date, does that also mean that the benefit available at that eligibility date would be the one used in the calculation?

What weight would be given to the fact that benefits could continue to accrue beyond that date?

MR. MOSSO: The accrual would be of the liability that exists at the retirement date, but that accrual would be made to the eligibility date. In other words, what is being accrued to the eligibility date is the final liability as it would exist on the retirement date, so that the lag between eligibility and retirement would be a factor in the calculations.

MR. EASLEY: You still use an assumed retirement that might deviate from the eligibility date?

MR. MOSSO: Yes.

MR. NELSON: The benefits are really expected benefits. If they are increased beyond the eligibility date, the present value of those additional benefits would have to be spread over an attribution period as well.

MR. FERRUGGIA: Along with many of the employers that I have been working with, I have gradually come to accept that some form of accrual-based accounting is proper recognition of these costs, albeit a pretty painful recognition. But I think most of the violent opposition that I have heard is [regarding the issue of] accruals up to the date of first eligibility.

I would like to know more about the task force's thinking. In practice, if you have liberal early retirement provisions, accrual can cease as early as age 55. Now, through the lifting of mandatory retirement, we can have employees working more than 15 years beyond first eligibility, rendering an economic benefit to the employer, yet attributing no cost to that period, and front loading the entire cost.

MR. MOSSO: FASB's basic rationale is that accounting is for contracts. Looking at the plan as a contract, if an employee is eligible as of a given date for full benefits, then the accounting would follow the contract and accrue benefits to that date. That is really the same as pension accounting, except that pension accounting does not usually run into the problem of service rendered beyond the date of full eligibility.

MR. FERRUGGIA: Nonservice related benefits?

MR. MOSSO: Right.

MR. FERRUGGIA: I am not an accountant, but I thought that one of the fundamental principles was proper income matching. These older employees generate income for the corporation, yet there is no charge to income for their benefits because they have already been charged off previously. Are you saying that they have earned everything early in their careers and are not earning anything more beyond first eligibility?

MR. MOSSO: That is correct. Matching does not override the need to accrue the cost of the benefits over the contract period in which the benefits are earned. Incidentally, the figures that we have seen—and the figures from a number of corporations—indicate that accruing to the eligibility date does not make a great deal of difference in the amount of liability or in the current period cost. What makes a greater difference, however, is in the amortization of the transition obligation. I suspect that at least some of the board members felt that they should do the accruing according to the contract terms, and, if there was going to be any amelioration of the transition impact, it would be through a slower amortization of the transition obligation.

MR. NELSON: Your point was well taken about the dates on the attribution period. I think if there is a probability that people are going to retire beyond that eligibility date, why not recognize that? But that is apparently not the way the board has decided.

MR. MOSSO: It was a very controversial issue for the board, too.

Is the Retiree Medical Benefit Vested?

MR. MCMAHON: There is a difference between a liability and a vested liability. Every employer here has worked very diligently to vest those benefits [as of] the day people retire. And in the stroke of a pen, you have vested them at early retirement.

I guarantee you that we will fight you on that. It is not a vested benefit. In America, 99 percent of the plans do not give employees a retiree medical benefit until the day they retire. The consequence, if this goes through, is that you can retire early and get your pension, but you have not earned a retiree medical benefit until the day you retire [at normal retirement age]. And therefore, from age 55 to age 65 these people are going to be on their own. That is going to be the bottom line. There is a difference between a vested pension benefit and a vested retiree medical benefit. And you will hear it louder and louder. They do not earn it until the day they retire.

MR. MOSSO: That is the question. The board is not defining or even suggesting that this benefit is legally vested. However, for accounting purposes the board has defined the eligibility date as the date the employee has earned the benefit and does not have to work any longer to get it.

MR. MCMAHON: We will wind up with the Securities and Exchange Commission telling us what accounting is. Because if you vest those benefits, we will take a qualified statement before we will put that into effect. Because you will not vest our medical benefits.

MR. MOSSO: We are not vesting anything. But the contract defines when an employee attains eligibility for benefits. It is the contract that governs, and we are accounting for the contract.

MR. MCMAHON: What contract? I told our employees that the day they retire they get a benefit. If they worked for 35 years and they die, their spouse, by law, gets one-half of their pension benefit, zero medical coverage, zero retiree medical coverage. That is the contract. There is no vesting, and that represents 99 percent of the contracts.

MR. MOSSO: Then there should be no problem. Accrual to the eligibility date would be only for expected cash payments and, in the case you described, nothing would be accrued for an employee expected to die before receiving the benefits. Such factors are considered in the actuarial measurement.

MR. FLATLEY: You have indicated that there will be some difference in the effective dates for certain types of plans, specifically foreign plans. Some of the more meddlesome issues are associated with accounting in the foreign plans. Was there much discussion in the task force or at the board level about certain unique features that are typically found in foreign plans, and are there any special provisions, other than the lag in the effective dates, for these plans?

MR. MOSSO: There was not a lot of discussion, and we do not have a large body of information about foreign plans. There are no other provisions other than the lag in application, which was modeled after FASB Statement No. 87. I do not know about the unique features.

MR. FLATLEY: Did I hear you say that you had just issued pronouncements over what you do not know much about? Is that, in fact, the case?

MR. MOSSO: It was not done without discussion with the task force and others. I do not mean to say that we did it blindly. But if there is a problem, it will come out in the comment period and it will be resolved.

MR. FLATLEY: You can count on it.

Estimating Health Cost Inflation

MR. KILLEEN: I would like to return to medical care inflation. We have all agreed that this is the most difficult item to estimate. FASB shows an awareness of this difficulty by wanting to build the sensitivity test into the footnote. But you are allowing a lot of latitude for employer judgment. It seems that there is a lot of room for the employer to arbitrarily determine the bottom line. Is the actuarial profession going to step in and develop more explicit guidelines so that employers have more specific rules under which to operate?

MR. MOSSO: I think, from the accounting point of view, it will be more a matter for the actuarial profession. They are the experts in that kind of estimation. We would expect that, as time goes on, the estimates will get better and the range will probably decrease. But even with pension estimates, the range is fairly wide.

MR. NELSON: The Actuarial Standards Board is preparing a draft of evaluation standards for these items.* It will not be prescriptive in the sense of saying "use 7 percent or 19 percent" but will be more concerned with considerations that should be taken into account in making reasonable or acceptable assumptions.

---

*Editor's note: This standard, *Recommendations for Measuring and Allocating Actuarial Present Values of Retiree Health Care and Death Benefits*, was released in October 1988.

PART THREE
THE RESPONSE OF EMPLOYERS AND
UNIONS

Employers and unions have for some time been concerned with the escalating costs of active-worker and retiree health care benefits. The proposed new accounting standard of the Financial Accounting Standards Board (FASB) has added a new dimension to the issue. FASB's rule would require employers to carry the cost of these benefits as a liability on their balance sheets. Part Three reviews how employers are responding to these challenges.

In chapter VIII, Joseph W. Duva describes Allied-Signal, Inc.'s growing awareness of the need to stabilize its active worker and retiree health plan costs and liabilities. In 1987 it became evident that the cost management strategies that had proven successful in the early 1980s had ceased to be effective. It was decided that the company could no longer afford to continue as a passive payer of medical costs, and that a new initiative was needed. Duva describes Allied-Signal's plan of action: a managed health care program for active employees and better management of current and future retiree health care arrangements.

The approach taken by a company with a predominantly young work force will necessarily differ from that taken by a company with a large proportion of older workers, says Kevin B. Flatley of American Express in Chapter IX. With an average employee age of 33 and few retirees, it is relatively easy for American Express to deal with retiree medical benefit costs. Notwithstanding these current advantages, American Express is preparing for the time when it will need to attract more middle-aged workers. It began offering a long-term care plan to employees, retirees, and their families in 1988, and has become active in the area of elder care. To combat escalating health care costs, American Express is considering instituting service-related contributions, reducing spousal coverage, and advancing the retirement age.

Flatley believes that the provision of postemployment health care benefits is an important management tool, and cautions employers against cutting back too far in response to increasing costs or to FASB's accounting requirement. If the discrepancy between health care coverage for active workers and that for retired workers is too great, people will delay retirement, he concludes.

In Chapter X, Patrick F. Killeen of the United Automobile Workers pictures employers and unions being as caught in a triple squeeze: economic restructuring, the FASB requirement, and limitations on tax-free prefunding due to the present tax code and federal budget deficits.

Killeen perceives a number of problems with the FASB rule. Many businesses do not have the cash to prefund, or desperately need this money for other purposes, he maintains. Furthermore, he contends that it is much more difficult to develop cost estimates of the liability for future health care benefits than it is to make comparable estimates for pensions.

Labor union members have been forewarned that "a crisis is coming," Killeen says, adding that union representatives have specific options and strategies under internal review.

In the discussion that follows the Part Three chapters, forum participants ask questions about specific aspects of Allied-Signal's new health care benefit plans. They debate the pros and cons of early retirement policies in terms of particular industries, question how much flexibility retirement plans should have, and discuss the use of "excess" pension assets to fund retiree health benefits. Exploring the nature of the benefit promise, they exchange opinions on whether it is the appropriate role of Congress or the courts to define employers' obligations.

VIII. Allied-Signal's Response to Rising Health Care Costs

REMARKS OF JOSEPH W. DUVA

Introduction

In 1987, we became aware that, because of the implications of the forthcoming Financial Accounting Standards Board (FASB) rule, we would have a problem with retiree medical costs and liabilities. After studying all the facts, we concluded that the major problem was health care costs; that the controls put in plans primarily for active employees in the early 1980s were no longer working; and that the retiree medical plans were not properly designed and needed to be changed in response to current business conditions and the implications of the proposed FASB rule.

Until the last few years, most companies paid little attention to the cost of continuing medical benefits after retirement. Companies began by offering postretirement medical coverage as a supplement to Medicare, then started to provide coverage to employees who retired before age 65 in order to make early retirement options more attractive. In addition, the early retiree rolls have grown substantially as a result of corporate restructuring and early retirement incentive plans.

I will review a case study of how Allied-Signal has planned to attack both problems. We decided we could not wait any longer to stabilize our active and retiree health plan costs and liabilities—we had to act immediately. As background for the discussion, table VIII.1 provides information about the structure of Allied Signal, Inc.

Inflation Projections

A comparison of Allied-Signal's overall health care cost with the consumer price index (CPI) shows that our costs for medical care increased approximately 28 percent in 1981 and approximately 15 percent in 1982 (chart VIII.1).

Allied-Signal was one of the first companies to take action to slow the significant medical care cost increases. These changes first became evident in 1984 when, for the first time, our health care cost

TABLE VIII.1
Allied-Signal, Inc.

	1986	1987
Sales	$9.9 billion	$12 billion
Employees	137,000	114,300
Retirees		50,000
Major Businesses (Sales, in billions)		
Aerospace		$5
Automotive (auto parts)		4
Engineered materials (chemicals)		3

Source: Allied-Signal, Inc.

increase of 3 percent was less than the 6.1 percent CPI medical care increase.

Since 1984, our medical care cost increases have been either at the CPI level for medical care or below, indicating that the actions taken were successful in controlling Allied-Signal's health care costs for that period.

Allied-Signal's stabilization of health care costs ran out of steam in 1987, when an increase of 39 percent occurred. Chart VIII.1 includes an estimated trend increase of 18 percent for 1988 and 17 percent for 1989 and 1990. These trends were estimated in 1987. Currently, many carriers are using trends as high as 22 percent to 25 percent. Our projections for 1988, 1989, and 1990 assume no changes in our health care plans.

To gain a better understanding of the individual business impact, we projected health care increases by sectors (table VIII.2). This table shows the 1987 health care costs by sector and projects the costs for 1988, 1989, and 1990, using the health care cost trend factors mentioned earlier. If we made no changes in the current health care plans, health care costs in the aerospace sector would increase from $204 million in 1987 to $316 million in 1990; in the automotive sector, from $58 million in 1987 to $98 million in 1990; in the engineered materials sector, from $44 million in 1987 to $74 million in 1990; and in the corporate and technology sector from $27 million to $43 million in 1990. Our overall health care costs would increase from $355 million in 1987 to $564 million in 1990. If we used a trend factor of 20 percent for the next three years, our health care costs in 1990 would be $614 million.

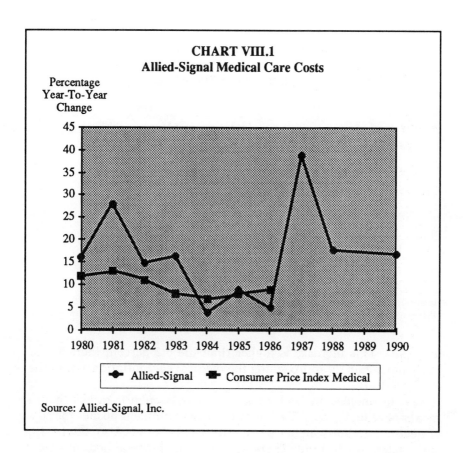

CHART VIII.1
Allied-Signal Medical Care Costs

Percentage
Year-To-Year
Change

Source: Allied-Signal, Inc.

I believe the battle to control health care costs will be even more difficult after 1990. We are now facing health care cost escalation higher than that which occurred during the early 1980s in spite of the actions taken since 1983 to control cost increases. In effect, actions taken by Allied-Signal and other companies worked for a short period. However, the providers of medical care have adjusted to the changes, and another round of significant health care escalation is upon us. We will not only have to deal with the issues of the early 1980s but with newer ones as well. Some of the problems of the early 1980s that we are familiar with are inflation, utilization, and cost shifting.

Escalating Costs—Health care costs continue to rise despite changes in the delivery system and cost-cutting measures. For more than 20 years, the rate of inflation in health care has been substantially higher than the overall CPI. The medical care component of the CPI increased at an average annual rate of between 7 percent and 8 percent in 1986

TABLE VIII.2
Actual and Projected Health Care Costs, Active and Retired Employees, by Industry[a]
(dollars in millions)

Industry	Year			
	1987	1988[b]	1989[b]	1990[b]
Aerospace	$204	$231	$270	$316
Automotive	58	72	84	98
Engineered Materials	44	54	63	74
Corporate and Technology	27	31	36	43
Closed, Divested Unit Retirees	21	24	29	33
Total	$355	$412	$482	$564

Source: Allied-Signal, Inc.
[a]If present plans were continued.
[b]Projected.

and 1987. This increase is higher than the 6.2 percent increase for 1985 and, again, is approaching the medical care inflation rate of the early 1980s.

New technology in health care is a cost escalator rather than a means of reducing cost. Each new piece of equipment pushes the cost of health care units higher as "quality" gets better. Also, the health care system is overbuilt. There are too many hospital beds, doctors, nurses, etc.

We are currently operating at a collective capacity rate of about 60 percent. The cost of that overcapacity is higher unit costs. Lastly, and unfortunately, the cost of malpractice insurance, which is passed along to the consumer, seems to have no ceiling.

Utilization—One way to control health care costs is to control the number of units used. Health care is used for many reasons. Unfortunately, many are inappropriate. The demand is driven by the industry. A hospital with low occupancy has an incentive to stimulate revenue. A physician worried about malpractice will overtreat. A hospital worried about the millions spent on a new CAT scanner will use the machine on as many patients as possible. Finally, and unavoidably, we are an aging population, and we will use more services as we grow old.

Cost Shifting—Cost shifting has been a problem for years. The government shifts costs to employers by mandating a prescribed level of benefits, by requiring employers to offer programs, and by reducing Medicare payments. In some states, employers pay a substantial amount for care used by those who have no insurance. Cost shifting will continue in the years ahead as both federal and state governments try to pass on to employers increasing responsibility for health care costs.

These three areas have been, and continue to be, very important in controlling overall health care costs.

New Challenges

There are new, and even more difficult, issues impacting on health care costs that provide a formidable challenge to U.S. employers. Companies that meet the challenge to better control these health costs for the future will have a competitive advantage. The challenges that face Allied-Signal include the following:

- The company has 50,000 retirees.
- The 1987 cost for retiree health benefits was approximately $66 million and, although one-third of the company's retirees are under age 65, they incur two-thirds of the cost.
- The plans were poorly designed (they were not based on service).
- Health care costs for retirees under age 65 are four times higher than those for active workers.
- The implications of the forthcoming FASB standard need to be addressed.

HMO Financing—Another factor that affects a corporation's health care costs is the use of health maintenance organizations (HMOs).

The existence of HMOs and the way they are financially managed within a company can no longer be ignored. Because of their number and size and the type of risk they involve, they are an important factor in our overall health care costs, and we need to know their impact on our purchasing power and leverage. Our studies indicated that the methods we were following (based on our interpretation of the federal HMO law) resulted in Allied-Signal overpaying HMOs for the risk they were assuming. Basically, they were attracting younger and healthier employees, and our indemnity plans were left with older employees who incurred more and larger claims.

Special Medical Conditions—Conditions such as mental and nervous disorders, substance abuse, and acquired immune deficiency syndrome (AIDS) are another source of significant cost. In addition, employers are seeking ways to control the staggering costs of psychiatric care. Their approaches range from severely restricting benefits to adopting managed care programs. Our information indicates that major companies pay as much as 15 percent to 20 percent of their overall claims for these special medical conditions. Included in this group are claims for alcoholism, substance abuse, and other claims that should be in this category but are not because—to protect the employee—the physician's diagnosis does not properly reflect his or her condition. Until lately, companies have not been aggressive in attempting to control these costs because of the sensitive nature of the claims and the lack of good data. However, many companies have determined that they cannot wait any longer.

There is agreement between both public- and private-sector experts that drug abuse may be the most common health hazard in the American workplace today.

Another frightening and costly area is the AIDS epidemic. An AIDS patient is expected to incur an average of between $100,000 and $120,000 in medical bills between the time he or she is diagnosed with the illness and his or her death, which usually comes within two years of diagnosis. When disability and group life insurance benefits are added, corporate costs for employees with AIDS soar even higher. As a result of the cost of caring for employees with AIDS, alternative forms of health care must be considered to hold down the treatment costs.

Allied-Signal's Action Plan for Health Care

In summary, Allied-Signal decided to change health care programs and the manner in which they are provided for the following reasons.

- As a company, we cannot afford the kinds of health care cost increases that we would be facing over the next three years.
- Prior cost containment efforts worked for the short term, but are not the answer to longer-term problems and issues.
- Cost shifting to traditional indemnity plans is increasing.
- Health care plans with managed care features are experiencing lower increases—in many cases, one-half of the increase of indemnity plans.
- Attractive opportunities currently exist to stabilize costs over the short term.

- Companies that take decisive action on health care costs will be ahead of their competition.

- Health care must be managed like a business because of its significant expense and the impact on the bottom line.

We decided that we could no longer continue to provide medical benefits, as we had in the past, as a passive payer of the cost. This decision was based on the conclusion that the approaches of the early 1980s—such as increasing deductibles and employee contributions, requiring a second opinion for surgery, and precertification programs—work for a short period of time but are not the long-term solution. Therefore, we developed a health care strategy that would: emphasize changes for active employees, on the assumption that what is done today for these employees will produce savings tomorrow for retirees; try to reduce cost of retiree medical coverage immediately; limit costs by encouraging use of alternative delivery systems; share costs with employees and retirees through deductibles, coinsurance, and premium sharing; and include the design and implementation of a retiree medical plan for workers retiring after January 1, 1989.

Managed Care Program for Current Employees—For current employees we introduced a managed care program. The new Health Care Connection program uses the existing CIGNA health plan networks throughout the United States. At present, there are 30 health care networks available to Allied-Signal. They do not cover all our locations. Accordingly, we have developed a phased-in approach for implementing the program. As of March 1, 1988, 37,000 Allied-Signal employees became eligible for the plan, or 67 percent of those ultimately eligible. Initially, the CIGNA network covers employees in southern California; Arizona; northern New Jersey; the Baltimore-Washington, DC, area; Kansas City, Mo.; Ft. Lauderdale, Fla.; Chicago; and Baton Rouge, La. As of January 1, 1989, 16,000 additional employees will become eligible, resulting in a total of 53,000 employees covered under the managed care program, out of 60,000 employees who ultimately will become eligible.

With the addition of dependents as of January 1, 1989, we will be covering 120,000 people. It is our objective to have a health care network available to all eligible employees over the next three to four years.

Under the Health Care Connection, an employee has the option at the point of medical service to opt out of the managed care program by selecting a non-network provider. He or she would then be covered for benefits under the revised indemnity plan, which has a higher

93

TABLE VIII.3
Allied-Signal's Health Care Connection

	Network Benefits	Indemnity Benefits
Deductible	None	1 percent of salary (family, 3 percent)
Coinsurance	None	80 percent
Out-of-Pocket Maximum	None	4 percent of salary (family, 12 percent)
Hospitalization	In full	80 percent after deductible
Surgery	In full	80 percent after deductible
Lab, X-Ray	In full	80 percent after deductible
Nursing Care	In full	80 percent after deductible
Prescription Drugs	$5 copayment	80 percent after deductible
Office Visits	$10 copayment	80 percent after deductible
Preventive Well-baby care	In full	Not covered
Emergency Room (appropriate use)	n/a	$25 Copayment
Restrictions	Must access via primary care physician	Preadmission certification/ concurrent stay review, mandatory second opinion

Source: Allied-Signal, Inc.

deductible and is more expensive than the managed care program. The program has been designed to encourage employees to use the managed care network.

In addition, our businesses revised the indemnity plan benefit levels in areas where networks were not presently available until they become available.

Table VIII.3 shows how the Health Care Connection is structured. When the network is available at a location, all eligible employees select a network primary care physician. At the point of medical service, the employee or dependent can elect to go outside the network and be covered under the indemnity plan. The plan is designed so that when an employee goes out of the network, it costs him or her

TABLE VIII.4
Allied-Signal's Action Plan for Retiree Health Care Benefits

Retiree Changes 1/1/89 (deferred from 7/1/88)
  Increase contributions—retiree 10 percent and dependent 15 percent
  Preadmission certification
  Increase prescription drug deductible from $3 to $5

Deferred to Later Date (1/1/90 or 7/1/90)
  Medicare carve-out
  Extend Health Care Connection plan to existing retirees under age 65

Future Retirees (1/1/90 or 7/1/90)
  Defined dollar plan
  • limit buildup of retiree medical liabilities
  • reduce charge to earnings
  Plan to be developed by 7/1/89

Source: Allied-Signal, Inc.

more. The Health Care Connection has one overall financial arrangement with CIGNA for three years.

Retiree Medical Plan—Table VIII.4 shows our action plan to better manage the retiree medical plans now and in the future. As I mentioned earlier, in 1987 and 1988 employers for the first time looked seriously at retiree medical program design and financing and determined exactly what they should be doing in the future. We believe the actions that Allied-Signal is taking will permit us to provide this important protection to our retirees on a better-managed and cost-effective basis.

Conclusion

Allied-Signal is seeking an innovative solution with the adoption of its Health Care Connection program, which has a managed health care option added to a revised indemnity plan for its active employees. This new program provides us with an opportunity to stabilize our health costs for the short term (three years) and a better long-term opportunity than if we had not taken this aggressive action. We concluded that aggressive action is required in an attempt to find a more cost-effective approach to provide employees and dependents with quality care at a more affordable cost to the company and its employees.

With regard to retiree medical benefits, we believe the program we have adopted will manage these benefits more effectively for the future and provide Allied-Signal with plans that are affordable for both the company and retirees, while preserving valuable protection.

IX. Health Care Benefits for a Changing Work Force

Remarks of Kevin P. Flatley

Introduction

I think that American Express is unique in some ways and this uniqueness makes me somewhat of a contrarian with regard to some of the things that I have heard at this forum.

During the last few years, American Express has been committed to a decentralized philosophy of management. We have four main operating subsidiaries: our travel-related services business, which is our card, check, and travel division; Shearson, Lehman, Hutton, our brokerage and investment banking operation; IDS, which deals with financial planning and investments; and American Express Bank, which is principally located outside the United States and is involved in international banking.

As a result of these separate operating subsidiaries and decentralized philosophy, we have different benefit plans in each of these operations. They are in different industries, even though they are under a general umbrella of financial and travel services, and they have different work forces. We have found over time that to develop an American Express position in benefit matters is a challenge because each of these industries needs a different approach.

We are a young company, notwithstanding the fact that we are over 100 years old. The average age of our employees is about 33. That varies a little, but in no event is it over age 40. The average length of service is less than five years. We have 95,000 employees around the world, the majority of whom are in the United States, and we have less than 3,000 retirees. This small number of retirees makes dealing with retiree medical benefits easier for us than it is for companies like Bethlehem Steel.

Our turnover tends to be a bit higher than average. In some of our operations, particularly back office operations, nonexempt turnover can be as high as 40 percent to 50 percent per year. One of the things that differentiates American Express from our competition is that we deliver a quality level of services. We are fanatics about delivering that quality, so we are very concerned with the effect that benefit changes, and particularly benefit cutbacks, might have on our ability to attract and keep the kind of workers we need.

What we do now in regard to retiree funding is probably not different from what everyone else does. Generally, we cover retirees as active employees until they reach age 65. We have a mix of Medicare supplement and carve-out coordination.

Currently, given the Financial Accounting Standards Board's (FASB) initiative on retiree medical benefits, we do fully accrue the benefit to age 55, which is our early retirement date. Employees earn the right to the benefit at that age, with varying levels of service. We fund the benefit on a pay-as-you-go basis, although last year we established a voluntary employee beneficiary association to handle run-off claims for the prior year. So we have some form of prefunding infrastructure in place, although we are not now taking advantage of it.

We have been concerned about the impact of the new FASB standard. According to our most recent statistics, which are based on 1988 data, our annual expense for the retiree medical portion of our benefits will be about $40 million. This compares with about $6 million for the portion paid on a pay-as-you-go basis and about $100 million for the portion covering active employees.

Our projected liability for our current work force is just over $300 million. Our accrued liability—the obligation we expect FASB will require us to report—amounts to $152 million. We have never believed that they would allow accrual all the way to the expected retirement date; that is why we retained our earliest possible retirement date.

One thing that makes us a bit contrarian is that the projected $306 million liability represents about one-quarter of American Express' net earnings, and the annual expense represents about seven working days' worth of net income for the company.

We told this to management and they said, "And then what?" The point is that when you have the luxury of having the kind of work force that we have, retiree medical benefits are not the problem that they might be in other kinds of industries. A much bigger concern to our management is the overall cost of health care.

We are more concerned with getting the right kind of people to work for us. One major strategic issue that we keep facing is the so-called "middle aging" of the work force. We have counted on an ever-increasing, ever-available source of youthful labor to operate our business. This has been possible because one-half of the work force is

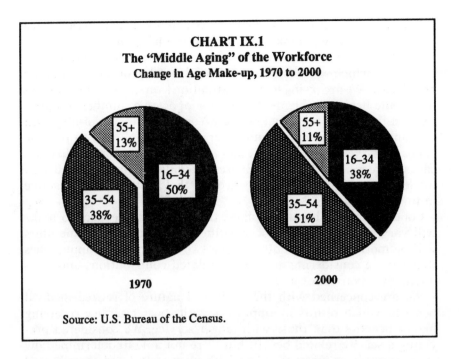

CHART IX.1
The "Middle Aging" of the Workforce
Change in Age Make-up, 1970 to 2000

55+
13%

16–34
50%

35–54
38%

55+
11%

16–34
38%

35–54
51%

1970

2000

Source: U.S. Bureau of the Census.

under age 34. As we look to the future, that is going to flip, and one-half of the work force will be middle aged (chart IX.I).

Nontraditional Policies: Long-Term Care and Elder Care

We will need to attract and keep middle-aged people in the years ahead. We are trying to direct the focus of our benefits into somewhat nontraditional areas. For example, in addition to our typical benefit plans, we have become active in the field of long-term care. In 1988, we became one of the first companies to provide a long-term care plan for employees, retirees, and their families. The plan is currently fully paid by the employees, and we have had a phenomenal enroll-ment. The people in the travel-related service business became the prime movers behind the project when they learned that an enormous number of employees were caught between caring for young children and caring for aging parents.

It is interesting that, with a work force as young as ours, almost 8 percent of our employees signed up for long-term care for themselves.

We clearly struck a chord. And if this particular kind of coverage were not so expensive, we think even more would have signed up.

Another somewhat nontraditional area that we are involved in is elder care, which we consider an essential element of retiree or aging health care. We are trying to direct attention from catastrophic illness to chronic health problems. We have supported a number of initiatives in the New York City and New York state area, working with city and state government and other private employers to provide education, referral, and other resources to acquaint people with elder care providers. The American Express Foundation has provided seed money to various organizations around the country that are active in this area.

Concerning health benefit plans, the changes we expect to make will vary by unit. Because of our different work forces, some units will be more active than others. The two most popular approaches that we are considering are service-related contributions and a reduction in spousal coverage.

We are concerned with the backward nature of retiree medical benefits, which results in employees with shorter service receiving higher benefits than those with longer service. We considered providing a service-related benefit but were not able to determine how to structure it, so we may end up with a service-related contribution instead. We think that over the long term there will be a way to address this problem.

We are considering a defined contribution approach, which has the advantage of helping to redefine some costs; service-related benefits; and an increase in retirement age.

The New Accounting Standard

In talking to American Express management and others, I have become aware that there is a danger that the benefits industry will respond in a knee-jerk way to the FASB requirement for increased current provision for retiree medical benefits. Such a response could lead to the question, "Why do we have this kind of program at all?" There is a danger that we will go a bit too far in this direction. This leads me to the somewhat heretical notion that postemployment medical benefits are good for you.

The cost of the retiree health benefits program that was promised to employees will not change because FASB requires it to be recognized on the balance sheet. If an employer considered it affordable when the commitment was made, I do not know why it would be unaffordable now. The costs themselves have not changed. Some people have argued that the FASB rule would actually reduce the cost, because it would require some advance funding. I guess that it is a question of whether you think you can make more money investing inside or outside your business. We happen to think we can probably do pretty well if we keep it inhouse.

As employers consider the effect of the FASB rule, I think they must ask themselves why they are providing postemployment medical benefits. If they think it is a good thing to do, then I think they have to be careful not to cut back too far. It is helpful to me to imagine what would happen if it was not provided: no one would retire because they could not afford to. Presumably employers will continue to provide health care benefits to active employees. If there is a great discrepancy between the coverage for active and retired workers, people will not retire.

Attracting Older Workers

I think that there will be no older worker mobility. At American Express we will need to hire people in the older age group and to recycle retirees back into our work force. However, people are not going to work for you if it means that they forfeit postemployment coverage from another employer and you do not provide adequate coverage.

The point is that there is a place for postemployment health benefits. They are an important management tool. I think we need to guard against short-term thinking with regard to current expense.

Having said that and admitting to being a contrarian, I freely admit that the nature of our work force at American Express gives us the ability to think in these terms. I am not sure that, were I representing some other employer, I would have similar thoughts on this issue.

I would like to sound a note of caution for employers: As you cut back more and more, you may be raising a political issue that will exacerbate the problem of the 37 million Americans who are uncovered. And as business abrogates what is being seen as its responsibility to provide health care coverage to active workers and retirees, there is a risk that these benefits will become less voluntary and flexible.

X. The Retiree Health Benefits Quandary

PAPER BY PATRICK F. KILLEEN

Introduction

Labor unions began bargaining for retiree health care benefits in the late 1950s and early 1960s, when health care costs were relatively low by today's standards. Furthermore, it was quite clear at that time that the anticipated advent of Medicare would largely solve the problem of retiree health care protection.

What Has Happened?

What has happened? There are several factors. Medical care costs have soared as a result of price increases, marketplace failure, inappropriate utilization, proliferation of advanced technology, and for a number of other reasons. Moreover, for over 20 years we experienced a steady erosion of Medicare protection that is only now somewhat offset by the enactment of Medicare catastrophic coverage. In addition, there has been a notable increase in the ratio of retired employees to active employees as a result of the trend toward early retirement; the overall maturing of the population; and the restructuring of certain industries, particularly in the manufacturing sector. With the drastic decline of jobs in industries such as steel, auto manufacturing, and agricultural implements—caused to a considerable extent by Reagan-Bush trade policies—we have had to look for places to put people, and one place was into retirement.

All United Automobile Workers (UAW) benefits and other compensation are costed on a cents-per-hour worked basis. Greater retiree health insurance costs are spread over fewer workers and fewer hours worked, thereby resulting in increased labor costs.

More recently, the Financial Accounting Standards Board (FASB) intends to require businesses to show as a liability on the balance sheet the present value of the future cost of lifetime retiree health coverage.

Finally, the courts, pursuant to litigation brought by UAW and others, have tended to determine that health care benefits for retirees represent a lifetime promise by employers, unless there is substantial, specific evidence to the contrary. The lifetime promise, and the present value of its projected costs, have been a major factor in a growing number of bankruptcy settlements.

The question of the lifetime promise also has arisen as a result of some corporate takeovers and plant sales. The new owners often do not feel a sense of loyalty to newly acquired employees. Also, new owners may not have been aware of the promise and the liability at the time of purchase.

Where Are We Now?

The costs of retiree health care protection in collective bargaining have risen exponentially as a result of the foregoing factors. These costs are not faced by foreign competitors in many industries such as steel, auto, and farm implements. Employers cannot terminate or materially reduce the coverage due to legal, moral, and/or collective bargaining constraints.

FASB is going to require that the present value of the lifetime cost of such benefits be carried as a liability on the balance sheet. To offset the balance sheet liability, some are proposing prefunding to create a corresponding asset. There are at least four problems with this.

- Many businesses simply do not have the cash to prefund or desperately need it for other business purposes.

- Employers who consider prefunding may want to count the cost against current collective bargaining settlements, this despite the fact that the promise and obligation were made under earlier collective bargaining settlements and workers traded off other economic objectives at that time.

- Inadequate mechanisms exist under current tax law to allow for adequate funding with pretax dollars. Prefunding is not recognized by the tax code as a legitimate business expense.

- It is far more difficult to develop cost estimates of the liability for future health care benefits than it is for pensions. Projecting medical care inflation and the extent of Medicare coverage 50 or 70 years into the future is tricky business. The UAW Social Security department actuaries have been developing such estimates since the White Motor bankruptcy in 1982, and we are all too aware of the uncertainties involved. Therefore, how do you know how much to prefund?

Legislation has been proposed to require prefunding and to make appropriate tax code vehicles available. There are two main problems with this.

104

- Congress will be very reluctant to make changes that will result in a reduction in federal revenues. This is another legacy of the Reagan-Bush tax cut of 1981.

- Those who propose mandatory prefunding typically talk about phasing it in over time in order to mitigate the financial consequences of compliance for employers with large liabilities. They point out, quite appropriately, that in the long run, the costs of pay-as-you-go and prefunding are exactly the same, which is mathematically correct. They say the problem is merely one of transition. The trouble is that many of the companies and industries with the greatest liabilities are also struggling with several other transitions at the same time: restructuring and downsizing of the work force; growing retiree-to-active-worker ratios; loss of market share to foreign competitors that do not have a retiree health cost problem; new pension funding standards under the Employee Retirement Income Security Act of 1974; increased Pension Benefit Guaranty Corporation premiums; and new pension accounting rules.

How many such transitions can these businesses and their employees survive at one time?

In short, employers and unions are caught in a triple squeeze: economic restructuring, the FASB requirement, and limitations on prefunding due to present tax code and federal budget deficits.

I recently participated in the production of an AFL-CIO educational video on these issues. Dramatizations, formal presentations, and panel discussions presented the problems clearly but offered no specific solutions. Frankly, neither the AFL-CIO nor any of its major affiliate unions have officially adopted a formal policy on these issues. We wanted to avoid making policy by video, but we had to alert labor union people around the country that a crisis is brewing. The name of the program is "Danger Ahead."

Where Do We Go?

Where do we go? I have written two endings to this paper. The first is to say that anyone who is familiar with UAW knows that we must have several specific options and strategies under internal review and under quiet discussion with other unions and that we are just awaiting the right moment to announce our definitive and comprehensive response.

The other ending is to suggest that an acceptable solution can only be found in some social insurance type of approach: expansion of Medicare, national health insurance, and/or socialization of the risk for lifetime health insurance, so that this liability effectively is recognized on a pay-as-you-go basis only. Is that sufficiently vague?

105

Possible approaches currently are being discussed in some business and labor circles in a very tentative way.

It would be ironic if the next major step toward universal health insurance protection were to owe much of its impetus to the staid Financial Accounting Standards Board.

XI. Part Three Discussion

Allied Signal's Innovations

MR. GARRETT: Mr. Duva, you spoke of bringing the retiree contributions up to 10 percent, and commented that that obviously was an increase for some. I wonder if that would be the first time some people had to contribute. Either way, were your plan documents ambiguous or unambiguous on that point, or are you waiting for the first lawsuit?

MR. DUVA: Our attorneys reviewed all the language in the documents that employees were given—both the plan and booklets—and they told us to proceed.

MR. GARRETT: Did you make some contributions for the first time on retirees?

MR. DUVA: I think in almost all cases the payments were already in. There may have been an isolated case where it was not.

MR. MARINACCI: You mentioned that several companies have already done major surgery on their retiree health care plans. I was aware of the Pillsbury Company. What other companies have gone beyond the study stage and are actually doing it?

MR. DUVA: I have problems with "major surgery." I think when you manage a business, you have to take changing times and situations into consideration. I do not think what has been done in terms of defined dollars is major surgery. Some companies are setting their contribution at the current level of health care costs, so that anyone retiring in the near future has monies for health care coverage. Companies are projecting the future cost of these programs and are concluding that retirees should share more of the cost. To me this is a good business approach in handling a needed benefit whose costs will be considerable in the future. TRW is one company now using the defined dollar approach for retiree medical.

MR. PAUL: CMD Corporation put in a dollar-per-year-of-service medical savings account allowance for future retirees, effective about 15 months ago. It was described in *Investor* magazine recently.

MR. DUVA: We are trying to preserve health care coverage for our retirees. I think we have to find a way to do it. I do not think anyone is considering eliminating it. We are merely trying to provide these benefits on a more affordable basis.

MR. FERRUGGIA: The defined dollar concept that Mr. Duva mentioned obviously gives an employer a lot more control, in terms of being able to predict costs accurately, by removing the inflation component. And obviously, by removing the inflation component, we are talking about taking a major ax to the liability. I do not think anyone is naive enough to believe that there will not be regular ad hoc increases needed in these dollar amounts. How do you feel that these increases might be reflected in terms of accounting practices?

MR. DUVA: I have a problem with that. I share the view that the problem we have is one of health care costs. Unless we attempt to control that, it all becomes academic. My feeling is that we have to provide cost-effective plans for retirees. We have to change the way we provide benefit programs to a more cost-effective way.

Concerning ad hoc increases, when you start a plan you would like to know what your liability is, so that it does not escalate before you even start the program. Then it is up to you to make a determination of whether you want to make an increase or not.

MR. FERRUGGIA: But if you do not make regular ad hoc increases, you effectively eliminate the program, unless you control inflation.

MR. DUVA: We face the same problem in our plan for active employees. They said, "Why don't you just increase our contributions and not make a change to managed care?" We replied, "If we constantly passed on to you the 39 percent or 40 percent increases, you will be very unhappy. . . ." So we went to what we believe is a more cost-effective program. I think the jury is still out on whether managed care is cost effective in the long term.

MR. FLATLEY: If the question is whether the accountant is going to force you to recognize ad hoc increases in advance, so that you end up in the same place or nearly the same place, I suggest that you look at the pension model, which has a longer track record. Observe the difference between career average and final average pay plans. The pension model works fairly well, and I have not heard anyone suggest in a career average plan any absence of actual approved updates in the past service base requiring advance recognition of the fact that you might have them. So I think it is highly unlikely, at least in the short run, that the accounting field would require advance recognition of future possible ad hoc increases.

MR. MIKKELSEN: Mr. Duva, I think most of us regard you as a very creative pioneer. Unfortunately, pioneers have a tendency to wind up with arrows in their backs. Has there been any employee relations fallout?

MR. DUVA: I think that any time you are an innovator or you start something on a nationwide basis, especially in health care, there is fallout. In our situation, the program has operated for seven months, and the problems we have center on claims and administration. It took us a couple of months to overcome an initial employee perception that if you go to a network you are not going to get quality care.

We have many problems in the United States that result from the belief that the more you pay, the better the quality is. We are finding that as you move through the program, in five, six, or seven months you learn that no one can judge quality. Employees who are using the network are finding that their medical services are just as good as they were before in terms of quality.

I would say that companies can learn a lot from our experience, but none of the things that we have encountered to date have been unmanageable.

We felt when we designed the indemnity plan that we would give participants an incentive to use the managed care networks because of the 1 percent of pay and 3 percent of pay deductibles. But many companies are now making these kinds of changes to their indemnity plans without a network because of the significant rate increases in health care costs. With our indemnity plan, the only people that the deductible increases affects are the higher paid people, because we had in our prior plans a 1 percent deductible for up to $50,000 and we removed the cap so now the 1 percent deductible is on all base compensation.

I think the results are very interesting: after seven months, over 74 percent of our employees are using the network 95 percent to 100 percent. In some locations, we have network usage of over 90 percent.

I think that is very interesting considering the importance that Americans assign to their relationship with their physicians. The most fortunate people in the program were those whose doctors were also in the network.

MR. ENTHOVEN: Mr. Duva, I either read or heard that CIGNA was not planning to undertake any other arrangements similar to the one you described. Do you have any comment on that?

MR. DUVA: We met with the CIGNA people recently and I think they have had trouble digesting 120,000 people in a very short time—March 1988 through January 1989. There are a lot of administrative requirements. CIGNA has assured us that they are interested in offering products similar to ours in each of the areas in which we have our employees in their networks.

I can say this, every one of CIGNA's networks is better today than it was before we became a part of it.

Universal Health Insurance

MR. ENTHOVEN: Mr. Killeen, you ended by saying that perhaps FASB will provide the impetus for universal publicly financed health insurance. I think this is a two-edged sword. In our democracy, incrementalism is one of the first laws of behavior, and it is a means that public policies use to avoid creating large windfalls, gains, or losses for any parties as they go into effect. I think that one of the problems related to universal health insurance is that it would require the taxpayers to relieve the automobile companies of tens of millions of dollars of liabilities unless there were some transition rule.

MR. KILLEEN: The social insurance approach that I talked about does not necessarily have to be the type of program that we considered 20 years ago—a completely tax-supported, government-administered program. There are different concepts now, such as the Massachusetts initiative.* There might be some type of mechanism that would enable the retirees of a bankrupt company to move automatically into some kind of pool. And perhaps FASB would not require that liability to be shown on the books. I cannot tell FASB what to require and what not to require. They make the rules, but that is the type of mechanism that some people are considering.

MR. MOSER: How do companies that are considering a defined dollar contribution plan present the issue? Their retirement planning was supposed to provide employees a level of income that would sustain a standard of living comparable to what they had before retiring. If employers cap the dollar spent under the medical plan, won't retirees ask for an increase in their pension benefit to offset what they are losing in medical benefits? How is that going to turn out? It seems to me that you are trading one kind of dollar for another, or you are lowering the standards for what people will have in retirement.

---

*Editor's note: On April 21, 1988 Gov. Michael Dukakis signed a universal health care bill for the state of Massachusetts that would expand health coverage to the uninsured population, primarily by requiring employers to cover their employees.

MR. DUVA: What I have seen so far in companies that are either changing to defined dollar contribution plans or considering them is that they are grandfathering certain groups of employees. In other words, they are redefining their promise for the future, but for certain groups of people to whom they feel they have made a commitment, they are grandfathering the benefits.

MR. MOSER: In effect, are you saying that the percentage of final income that you are going to provide to future retirees is going to be less?

MR. DUVA: No, however, the coverage will be provided in a different way or method for a portion of new retirees.

MR. MOSER: Through a medical plan adjustment you have altered your pension plan considerably, too.

MR. DUVA: You could broaden this and say that every time we paid for an increase in health care, we should recognize that as part of the total retirement income, too. It is a total employee benefit package. You can make the case that you are making, but I think a broader case could be made.

MR. FLATLEY: We are doing some modeling to study potential future changes requiring a percentage of postretirement net income to be contributed toward medical care as a way of a cost sharing. We are looking at various levels, from 13 percent to 15 percent of postretirement income, as a retiree contribution. This would allow for various income-related levels but would preserve a constant standard of living that could be predefined. It does not totally answer the problem, because the amount would still be frozen at retirement.

MR. DUVA: Obviously, you must work on making the health care plans more cost effective.

MR. MOSER: My point is that I hope that that kind of response or solution does not diminish industry's attention to what the real problem is.

MR. DUVA: I agree, and I think that the first responses that I have seen do not address that problem. They merely provide one program, an indemnity program, which in effect will increase the amount of money a retiree needs to buy insurance, because the actual health care costs have not been contained. I think we must come up with more cost-effective options for retirees to solve the problem.

Ms. YOUNG: I am curious about how the Allied-Signal program works for your active workers, not just your retirees. What happens to workers who have an ongoing illness, such as cancer, that requires treatment for a long time? Do they have to change their doctors in midstream, or do you have special provisions for them?

MR. DUVA: We have special transition situations. Each one is handled individually, so that would not happen. Fortunately for us, the carrier that was selected was also the incumbent carrier for most of our employees, so the transition was a lot easier. In some cases where employees and/or dependents had serious illnesses they were permitted to continue with their physicians until they adequately recovered. We had hardly any transition problems.

MR. WELLER: Mr. Duva, could you define more specifically what you mean by "managed care network," for example, at one of your sites? What percentage of the hospital do you include? What percentage of the physicians?

MR. DUVA: We need to define managed care. It is operated by doctors or hospitals? Is it an individual practice association or a staff model? Is the financial model a discount fee-for-service or capitation? The variations are unbelievable. After working through this for two years, you get a feeling of what the best financial arrangement is in the long-term.

What we bought was CIGNA's health plan network, and they had the doctors and hospitals under contract or other arrangements. Every network that we had in the first wave was one that already existed with CIGNA, except in northern New Jersey, where a new network was set up for our corporate office.

MR. WELLER: How big is the panel?

MR. DUVA: It is quite large now. It includes over 350 primary care physicians and more than 500 specialties.

MR. WELLER: What percentage of the hospitals and doctors in northern New Jersey were included in the managed care plan?

MR. DUVA: I do not have those numbers, but we started off not having the right number of doctors and the right hospitals in the right geographical locations, in the opinion of our employees. That is no longer the case. We have heard from a number of doctors who would not join the network in the beginning but have indicated that when it hurts them enough financially not to be in the network, they will reconsider. More and more doctors are now writing and calling us, wanting to be network physicians. Others have indicated that as more companies follow our example, they will have to reevaluate their position. So it is really a question of money, leverage, and time.

We have found that when a primary care physician makes enough money on a capitated basis, he or she is very anxious to work in the program. When only a few people have selected him or her, and there is not enough money coming in, there will be less interest.

MR. PETERTIL: I was glad to hear a number of people say that the defined dollar plan will work only in conjunction with strong managed care. The modeling we have done showed that even a defined dollar plan would have some ad hoc increases in the future which would result in cost shifting to employees and mean that a substantial number of retirees would devote all of their pension money to contributions for health care.

Mr. Duva, you mentioned that your company was deferring the carve-out in a number of plans and you made the point that efficient short-term cost savings can be realized by moving to a carve-out from coordination of benefits. Is your deferral related to the legal questions that were mentioned earlier?

MR. DUVA: Yes. About 80 percent or 85 percent of our retirees are in plans with carve-outs now, and we saw that as not an important issue at the moment. But we agree that this is the proper plan design.

MR. PETERTIL: Then you are not too concerned about the legal question of having gotten somebody into a plan administered that way?

MR. DUVA: I think we may have some concern about that and that is why we deferred it.

Section 89

MR. MCMAHON: Mr. Killeen, a number of your members have very good salaries and medical care. When section 89 goes into effect and some of the retirees' benefits are taxed, what will the American Federation of Labor's (AFL) position be?

MR. KILLEEN: I cannot speak for the whole AFL. I only represent the United Automobile Workers. And we are still, like everyone else, trying to sort out exactly what section 89 means. I suggest that that is probably one area in which labor and management may work together for the first time to get an exemption. Perhaps, working together, we can beat this. I do not think that we want to throw the

113

baby out with the bathwater in the matter of antidiscrimination, but section 89 certainly needs to be altered. I am not sure that most of our members, or many of our members, are in such high income brackets that they are going to be affected by it. We do not have it all sorted out yet because of the complexities.

Reconsidering Early Retirement

Ms. IGNAGNI: Mr. Flatley, you said that the retiree medical obligation was less of an issue at American Express because your work force was younger than most. Given the cost of offering and providing retiree health insurance benefits for retirees under age 65, do you foresee a change in your attitude toward early retirement and of your policy to encourage it?

MR. FLATLEY: Absolutely. We now have a series of proposals that will substantially modify our position. In hindsight, we think that we applied a long-term solution to a short-term problem in managing the work force. Like most American industries, we felt that, as a way of covering up poor performance-based appraisals, we would offer humane ways of easing superannuated employees off the payroll. Unfortunately, that proved to be a bad idea because no one thought of the long-term implications in terms of changing work force demographics.

We are thinking of substantially curtailing subsidized early retirement and pension plans, increasing the normal retirement age, and requiring a longer career. Again, it is a lot easier to make these changes in a company with a large number of 35-year-old employees. I do not propose our company as a model, but we are probably going to make these changes.

MR. KILLEEN: In some industries, like automobiles, this is a critical issue. We negotiated last year with General Motors (GM) and Ford, and GM was initially talking about limiting early retirement. We took a serious look at the issue. In the end, as the negotiations progressed, we realized that we had about 350,000 people to fit into about 275,000 future jobs and we did not know where to put them. One place was early retirement. We did not put any limitations on early retirement, and we actually opened up a window for a short period for people who were even younger and had less experience to retire, knowing that this was going to raise the pension costs and therefore the labor costs.

MR. DUVA: I suppose each company has a different perspective on what the real bottom line pressures are. Different industries have different kinds of needs. The aerospace industry could be completely different from the automotive industry. The first challenge we had was to be competitive worldwide, and that meant restructuring and becoming lean and mean. Once you get there, other kinds of real-world things take place. Should you continue to do it? I think that is now where we are.

MS. IGNAGNI: I would say becoming lean and mean has a cost that is not recognized.

MR. FLATLEY: I think if people had recognized some of the retirement costs and had been aware of the fact that the regulatory environment was going to institutionalize and in some sense ossify the status quo, they might have had a different feeling about using pension plans as opposed to window programs, which I think will clearly be the direction of the future. This is unfortunate hindsight.

Flexible Retirement Plans

VOICE FROM THE AUDIENCE: I have heard it said that we need to maintain the ability to adjust retirement plans and make them flexible. Indeed, the trend in plan documents is to incorporate provisions that allow them to be changed at any time. There is talk about using this kind of thing to encourage early retirement. I am puzzled by this need for employers to maintain maximum flexibility. Workers will retire thinking they have something, when, in fact, what they have can be changed at will by the employers.

As a retiree, I would want some certainty about what I was going to receive. If the plan document said that the benefit could be adjusted at the employers' discretion, it would not give me much comfort.

MR. KILLEEN: You used the term "maximum flexibility." I do not think you can have maximum flexibility. If an employee retires with an expectation of receiving a certain level of health care benefits, the employer should maintain, in general terms, that level of benefit protection. But this does eliminate all flexibility. That would be irrational; I hope we do not have court decisions that take away all flexibility.

We have never had a major collective bargaining agreement in which we did not make adjustments in retiree health coverage, and I am not merely talking about improvements such as adding dental care or vision care. We have raised the prescription drug copayment. That could be considered a benefit reduction, but we have done it in a package of other adjustments.

115

We think that you can provide a certain basic level of health care protection through managed care alternatives without breaking the promise to people. You can put in cost containment programs, managed care, predetermined hospital stays, and other administrative provisions. What I oppose would be sudden substantial increases in deductibles or in the retiree contribution to premiums.

MR. DUVA: Our approach is to try to provide a variety of cost-effective programs that retirees can join. These programs would have to be evaluated from time to time and possibly revised, but the idea is to make health care more cost effective, rather than continue to pay the 25-percent- or 30-percent-a-year increases associated with indemnity plan increases. The cost of a typical managed care program that provides full benefits and includes some copayments is now increasing at a slower rate than that for indemnity plans. The managed care trends are not as low as we would like them to be, but still they are lower than the indemnity plans. We need the flexibility to adopt arrangements that are more cost effective.

Funding Health Benefits with Pension Assets

MS. COLLAZO: Could the speakers comment on the use of excess pension assets to fund these benefits?

MR. FLATLEY: American Express used excess pension assets. We terminated a defined benefit pension plan, reestablished it in accordance with agency guidelines, and used the money for several different corporate purposes, not specifically for the pension program.

You have to answer a fundamental question concerning whose money it is before you ask what you will do with it. People who claim ownership of pension assets might want input into that decision. My opinion, which I suspect represents the American Express philosophy, is that it is the company's and the shareholders' money because they assumed the risk involved in providing a defined benefit.

To the extent that a corporation wants to deploy assets in a different manner, to secure different liabilities as they promised, I think it ought to have the ability to do that. If you are talking about taking the money out on a tax-efficient basis, rather than paying a tax collector, that is a political question. That depends on what party is in power.

Ultimately, I think the corporation should have the ability to redeploy its assets, and to the extent that the government wants to impose a toll on the privilege of doing that, that is a political decision.

116

The Nature of the Benefit Promise

MR. JACKSON: I would like to challenge Mr. Killeen's statement that the promise and obligation made by employers was made under earlier collective bargaining settlements, and workers traded off other economic objectives at that time.

Group insurance has operated on a one-year term insurance basis. In the past, retirees were handled on a year-to-year basis. The bargaining agreements operated on a three-year-and-out basis. At the end of three years there was a new agreement. No one promised anything to retirees beyond a current continuation of a benefit. It is very easy to criticize employers for promising too much. It is easy to blame unions for demanding too much, but the problem is Congress and the courts, which have repromised everything that was originally promised, with a tremendous emphasis on security.

I submit that the situation with regard to Congress and the courts is totally uncontrolled. There is nothing to prevent a judge from simply saying, "This meant something else and some more benefits ought to be paid."

Thirty-five years ago, when I was with the Aetna Life Insurance Company, the cost of continuing coverage medical and life insurance was known, and there was no promise to continue these benefits for life. Reading that into the promise has caused the problem we are discussing today. The problem was not caused by employers or by unions. It was caused by Congress and the courts.

MR. KILLEEN: I tend to disagree with that. I think that the expectation of most workers who retired 20 years ago was that retirement benefits would continue for life. They were told, "Here are the terms under which you get a pension," and that health care came with it.

At that time, I do not think the question of the duration of these benefits was even raised. Not only was the economy expanding, but the major sectors of the economy were expanding. The period during the late 1950s and early 1960s was very optimistic, economically. I think the retirees who retired at that time, or those who negotiated benefits, clearly thought they were negotiating something for life. Retirement benefits only became an issue later when plant closings and industrial contractions occurred. Then employers ended up in court trying to reinterpret the contract language, the language of the brochures given to employees, and what they were told in exit interviews as they retired. I do not particularly blame the courts, but I think they have had a difficult time sorting out what was agreed upon and not agreed upon.

MR. JACKSON: I sat in on bargaining sessions and I am aware that union demands for pension benefits were defined in terms of the price and the cents-per-hour cost. The determinations were based on a projected, funded pension cost.

The cost for medical and similar benefits was based on the cost in the next two or three contract years. In bargaining, the unions never gave up enough in earnings to cover a lifetime of medical coverage or life insurance coverage for the retirees. They did give up enough to cover a lifetime pension. There was no promise to continue medical benefits for life.

MR. KILLEEN: The costs in those days were so small compared with what we are faced with today, that, again, I think no one thought about it. If we had known then what we know now about what these costs would be, I think we would have funded them.

Long before the Employee Retirement Income Security Act (ERISA) was in existence, UAW went on strike to get funded pension plans. We struck Chrysler in the early 1950s. They wanted to give us a pay-as-you-go pension plan. We educated our membership about that kind of funding and said, "There is no security there."

We worked to get the standards in ERISA. Before ERISA was created, we got standards into our own negotiated agreements. I think that if we had known that the medical care costs were going to be so high, we would have tried to fund them, too, for retirees. But that is with the vision of hindsight. Logically, I would want to do it that way. Today we are asking ourselves to unscramble the omelet.

MR. KAHN: Congress has not required anything in this area. If anything, it went the other way a few years ago when it backed off on voluntary employee beneficiary associations. The courts have acted, but I think that the FASB rule changes clearly show that FASB is trying to recognize what they think is reality and that reality is a promise.

You can say that companies ought to be able to pull out any time they want, and they surely can, but the courts are saying that they want to stop them from doing that. But I do not think that the government, whether in the form of the courts or in the form of Congress, is pointing the finger.

FASB is a private-sector entity. It says to the private sector, "This [promise to provide retiree health benefits] is an obligation. It is something you have been living with all these years and ignoring." FASB's proposed change in the status of retiree medical benefits is quite different from a move by Congress and courts to impose something on employers.

PART FOUR
PUBLIC POLICY CONCERNS

With the security of some retiree health benefits now in question, Congress is faced with deciding whether and to what extent the federal government should become more involved.

In Chapter XII, Gary Hendricks places the issue of retiree health benefits in the larger context of health policy. He describes five approaches to funding health care benefits and explains why none of them will be effective as long as medical costs are not brought under control.

A lack of consensus on how public policy should approach this issue makes congressional action uncertain, he says.

In Chapter XIII, Charles N. Kahn reviews possible congressional responses to this issue, the most likely of which, he believes, may be an initiative resembling the Employee Retirement Income Security Act of 1974. Such an approach would be voluntary and would include vesting, portability, and caps on the amount that could be contributed tax free.

Kahn believes that the 101st Congress may consider the retiree health care benefit issue within a larger framework that would include long-term care and the uninsured. Ultimately, he says, the issue must be seen in terms of the long-term implications of health care inflation.

In Chapter XIV, Burma H. Klein reviews the results of a study undertaken by the U.S. General Accounting Office (GAO) to help Congress address the issue of retiree health care benefits. The study estimated companies' liabilities for current and future retirees' health care benefits, assuming that they continue to provide current benefits; estimated the annual amounts needed to advance fund these liabilities and compared them with companies' pay-as-you-go expenses; obtained companies' views on their flexibility to change their health plans to accommodate rising costs; and described how companies are using this flexibility to make changes.

According to Klein, GAO believes that Congress should consider the desirability of legislation to preserve retiree health care benefits, especially for retirees under age 65, who are not covered by Medicare. She discusses possible policy approaches and points out their advantages and drawbacks.

In the Part Four discussion, questions are raised about the assumptions GAO made concerning the real growth rate in per capita spending for health benefits and the real interest rates that produced the $227 billion that GAO estimates to be the present value of future retiree health benefits. The chapter concludes with a five-point summary of the forum's presentations and discussions.

XII. Public Policy and Retiree Health Benefits

Remarks of Gary Hendricks

Introduction

I think that it is fair to say that the issue of employer-sponsored retiree health benefits is clearly on the back-burner as far as the Executive Branch and Congress are concerned. There are several reasons for this.

First, the issue has been overtaken by other, much larger, health concerns that were not on the table when these benefits were first discussed in 1985 and 1986. There are 37 million uninsured persons in the United States, and Sen. Edward Kennedy (D-MA) introduced a proposal* in the 100th Congress to have the private sector insure at least 24 million of them. That is a much larger issue. It is difficult to argue, when there are so many uncovered workers, that we should spend tax dollars and our time and energy on retiree health benefits. That does not mean that there will not be congressional activity on the issue, but I do not think any significant action will be taken.

Congressional Priorities

I think the 101st Congress will pay more attention to long-term care, because it has a higher priority in the minds of many senators and congressmen. Retiree health benefits is an example of an issue that has received little or no coverage.

One thing that makes moving this particular issue of retiree health benefits on the Hill very difficult is that there is no agreement on how public policy should address it. It is much easier to act once there is a consensus, but there seems to be very little agreement on this issue except with regard to prefunding. If special tax preferences are to be instituted for this type of benefit, it is generally agreed that there must be standards. That would involve the Employee Retirement Income Security Act (ERISA) in any initiative that involves prefunding. However, those in the business community who might most strongly support prefunding do not like ERISA.

---

*Editor's note: The Minimum Health Benefits for All Workers Act (S.1265) was approved by the Senate Labor and Human Resources Committee but was not brought to a vote in the Senate during the last Congress.

Tax Considerations

Any tax-favored prefunding must be considered in the context of the budget. Where do we get the money? We could tax other benefits, but I think the deficit problem is so great that Congress will consider taxing other benefits and giving nothing in return to the community. Taxing benefits itself is highly controversial, and there is little consensus there. If we do tax employee benefits or find some money elsewhere, I think Congress will decide to spend that money on some other area of health.

Managing Health Care Costs

One thing that bothers me most about the issue of retiree health benefits is that it is part of a more fundamental problem, which is the problem of health care costs in general. These costs are rising so quickly that it is difficult to get a handle on them. Management utilization seemed to work for Allied-Signal for about two or three years, and then it ceased to work. This seems to happen again and again. You think you are managing costs, and then you lose control.

It seems to me that any solution we might arrive at would be unworkable if we have no handle on health care costs. I think that Congress and the Executive Branch would be loath to work on the problems associated with "ERISA-fication," establishing standards, finding tax dollars, and justifying and selling a solution when it is not clear that employers could afford the solution eight or ten years from now, and the employers that you would want to prefund probably cannot afford to do so.

We have to do something about Bethlehem Steel, about the automobile companies. What do you do when more than 50 percent of the people covered by their health plans are retirees? How do you start them out with prefunding? Would it happen fast enough when, for instance, General Motors has 350,000 workers to fill 270,000 jobs in the next few years?

As public policymakers, we are concerned about who is at risk and who is likely to lose retiree health benefits.

There are five fundamental approaches to funding retiree health care benefits, and I say nothing will work if you cannot manage health care costs. You can establish an individual health account approach, but that will not work because you do not know how much money to put in it. You do not know what amount would be sufficient to allow retirees to continue to pay their premiums.

122

The defined contribution approach, on the employer's side, involves the same problem, as does the defined dollar approach. If an employer contributes a certain amount of money to each retiree each year, a retiree who lives to be 90 or 95 could end up using his or her entire pension income to cover the remaining portion of health costs.

The defined benefit approach we have now offers a set of benefits; it has been mentioned repeatedly that employers must have flexibility in these benefits. Why do they need this flexibility? Why will they not lock in? Because of costs.

Is National Health Insurance the Answer?

We could take a public approach and adopt national health insurance. I think the problem there would be exactly the same. We cannot manage health care costs. No matter what strategy we take, we may end up in a situation similar to that of the United Kingdom, where they charge little or nothing for medical care but patients over age 55 cannot get kidney dialysis. The national health system will not pay for it. That is the way the British control costs and keep them from consuming 35 percent their Gross National Product.

I also think that the pressure from the Financial Accounting Standards Board (FASB) will dissipate. The new FASB rule will take effect slowly. It will be 1997 before employers are required to report the first large liability on the balance sheet. By then labor markets are projected to be much tighter. If older workers are going to become more valuable and employers are going to want to keep them around, policies will change and there will be less pressure for public policy solutions that specifically address retiree health benefits as opposed to including this group in the broader context of health policy.

Is Government Action Necessary?

A question I have to ask is, what is the public good? Alain Enthoven has suggested that we do not like to have people die in the streets. The people whose retiree health benefits we are discussing are largely middle-class, blue-collar workers. I do not think they are necessarily the class of people we are going to see dying in the streets.

If the employers cut off the benefits, workers will not retire, so that would mitigate the problem somewhat. I do not know why I, as a public policymaker, should worry. We all value income security in retirement, and that is one of the reasons I think this issue reached the Hill in the first place. We do not like insecure contracts. We want things to be more secure.

These are high-risk contracts. And our society does not favor the kind of contract that would allow both parties to agree that benefits can be stopped. Perhaps these contracts should not be permitted. There should be prefunding.

I have difficulty finding the public good here. I would like to hear arguments that would persuade me to put this issue high on my priority list and take it to an assistant secretary for pensions and welfare benefits at the Department of Labor and say, "We have to worry about this one."

XIII. A Congressional Perspective

REMARKS OF CHARLES N. KAHN*

Introduction

Retiree health benefits are clearly not at the top of the U.S. congressional agenda now, but the House Ways and Means Committee has started considering the issue. In the next couple of years, I believe heightened attention will be paid to retiree health benefits, as the implications of the Financial Accounting Standards Board's (FASB's) new accounting standards become clearer, and as companies reevaluate their retiree benefit "promise."

There are two factors to keep in mind when considering how Congress views retiree benefits. One, because we are dealing with the federal budget, this is a zero sum game. If Congress provides a tax incentive to prefund retiree health benefits, money must be found to make up the difference. Companies must ask themselves, then, what are they willing to trade off? Second, I expect that in return for tax breaks to prefund retiree health benefits, there would be some kind of policy *quid pro quo* to ensure the security of the benefit. Mandating the benefit is unlikely, but some type of "ERISA-fication"—that is, vesting, portability, and benefit caps—may be required.

Defined contribution arrangements may be a good way to deal with the benefits. However, there will be a tremendous amount of cost shifting likely in the out years because health care costs—if they continue as in the past—will increase. Retirees will be unhappy about this, and probably quite vocal about it.

Regardless of what Congress does or does not do, many companies must contend with FASB's new accounting requirements, higher health care costs, and a growing retiree-to-active-worker ratio. Someone has to pay and no one wants to. Pressures are building. Spiraling health care costs are driving all health care issues today, and we must deal with this factor sooner or later.

---

*The views expressed in these remarks are the author's own and do not represent the views of the House Committee on Ways and Means, its health subcommittee, or its members.

Health Care Priorities of the 101st Congress

If there is any action in the retiree health area, it may be within the broader context of health care issues, such as long-term care, the uninsured, and Medicare.

Long-Term Care—It is unlikely that Congress will take action on long-term care in 1989 because of the large expense associated with it. The more modest entitlement plans being discussed cost between $18 billion and $20 billion, with the high price-tag, full coverage plans costing $50 billion to $60 billion. It can be argued that a comprehensive long-term care program for nursing home and home health care might reduce the federal contribution to Medicaid, but with a $140 billion to $150 billion deficit that must be reduced by at least $40 billion to $50 billion, it will be difficult to justify a tax increase to pay for the program. Raising the money, whether through estate or payroll taxes, would not be popular.

The Uninsured—The 101st Congress *is* likely to examine the issue of the 37 million Americans uninsured for health care. Proposals to mandate employer-sponsored coverage will be back, as will risk pool proposals. While the costs for covering the uninsured may be high, proposals thus far try to push that cost on to employers and avoid new federal expenditures. And, while the issue does not have the kind of vocal constituency that long-term care has from the elderly and elderly groups, Congress may find it hard to ignore a problem that so many find socially unacceptable.

Medicare Catastrophic—We have probably not heard the last of the Medicare Catastrophic Coverage Act of 1988. Cards and letters sent to senators and congressmen indicate that many elderly people are not happy with Medicare catastrophic coverage—at least the 40 percent who are going to pay for 66 percent of it.

The Congressional Budget Office has determined that if the new benefits and premiums were in place in 1988 and some assumptions are made about how much is spent on Medigap policies, about 30 percent of the elderly are, on average, approximately $278 a year worse off than they were before the Medicare legislation was passed. And the premium will increase every year.

One could argue that this makes sense. The logic behind the legislation was that the premiums would be income related, on the assumption that those who could pay more should pay more. However, I do not think that the elderly realize that they made that deal.

Conclusion

Health care costs have been an intractable issue that Congress has only focused on directly once during the last eight years—when it wanted to reduce the government's cost for Medicare. It will be difficult for Congress to continue to avoid the issue of rising health care costs in the economy as a whole and merely look at what is paid through the entitlement programs.

It is not clear to me whether we will return to the types of cost containment proposals that were made during the late 1970s, but in the next decade Congress will have to focus on the long-term implications of health care inflation for our society. The issue cannot be avoided much longer, because it has broad and inescapable economic ramifications. The American people may want to have it all, but sooner or later they may not be satisfied with the implications of spending 15 or 20 percent of Gross National Product on health care, with that portion growing yearly.

XIV. Future Security of Retiree Health Benefits in Question*

PAPER BY BURMA H. KLEIN

Introduction

The private sector plays an important role in providing retirees access to affordable health care coverage. Not only is the cost of medical care under group plans generally less expensive than that purchased by retirees individually but companies often pay some or all of the costs. The benefits provided through company plans are especially important to retirees under the age of 65 because most are not covered by Medicare. In 1988, retirees under age 65 comprised one-third of all retirees covered by company health plans, but they received about two-thirds of the benefits.

Faced with significantly increasing costs, some companies are taking action to control their current costs and limit their obligations for retiree health care benefits. Retirees now receiving these benefits and active workers who expect to receive retiree benefits have limited protection from benefit modification or termination. For example, when the LTV Corporation, one of the largest companies in the United States, filed for bankruptcy in July 1986, it attempted to terminate the health benefits of more than 78,000 retirees. Only congressional action maintained these benefits.

Because the security of some retiree health benefits is in question, Congress is faced with deciding whether and to what extent the federal government should become more involved.

To help them address this issue, the U.S. General Accounting Office (GAO) was asked to: (1) estimate companies' liabilities for current and future retirees' health benefits, assuming that companies continue to provide health care as they currently do; (2) estimate the annual amounts needed to advance fund these liabilities and compare them with companies' pay-as-you-go expenses; (3) obtain companies' views on their flexibility to change their health plans to accommodate

---

*Editor's note: This paper was presented as testimony before the Subcommittee on Oversight, House Committee on Ways and Means, by the Assistant Comptroller General, Lawrence H. Thompson, on September 15, 1988.

rising costs; and (4) describe how companies are using this flexibility to make changes.

Liabilities and Annual Contributions to Advance Funding

About seven million retirees are receiving health benefits through company plans, and about $10 billion will be paid by companies in 1988 for these benefits, according to our estimates. Assuming coverage and benefit provisions do not change, in the year 2008 these companies will pay $25 billion in today's dollars for nine million retirees.

GAO estimates that the present value of future retiree health benefits accrued to date is $227 billion. This amount is about one-twelfth of the value of the stocks of American corporations ($2.6 trillion) in 1986. This estimate includes accrued liabilities of $100 billion for retirees and $127 billion attributable to the past service of active workers (chart XIV.1). The remaining $175 billion is for benefits that workers will earn from now until they retire. The amount the nation's private employers would need for investment today to pay future health benefits for retirees and for all covered workers during their retirement is $402 billion.

We did not consider employers' savings resulting from the passage of the Medicare Catastrophic Coverage Act of 1988 in our estimates. Sufficient information was not available to us to determine how overall employer costs might be affected.

It has been the practice of the Financial Accounting Standards Board (FASB) to require material costs to be disclosed on a company's accounting statements to help ensure that the statements accurately represent the company's financial condition. Since 1979 disclosure of postemployment benefit costs, such as those for company health care, has been on FASB's agenda. As an interim step, FASB required current retiree health costs to be reported on companies' financial statements beginning with accounting periods after 1984. FASB has announced its intention to issue an exposure draft that will detail its rules for recognizing and disclosing retiree health liabilities.

Most companies do not advance fund their retiree health benefits but rather pay them on a pay-as-you-go basis. Companies and others have expressed concern that the disclosure of unfunded retiree health liabilities could adversely affect their operations, including their ability to obtain capital financing. This could prompt some companies to reduce or terminate their health benefits, require retirees to pay more of the plans' cost, or start advance funding the benefits.

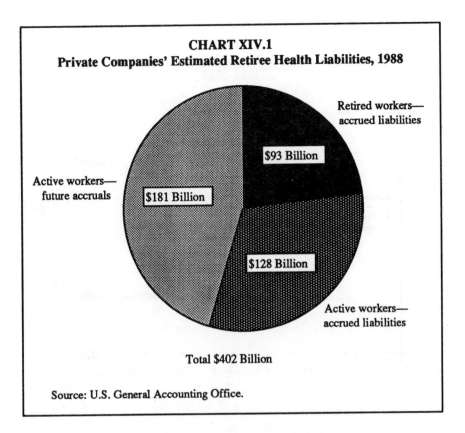

CHART XIV.1
Private Companies' Estimated Retiree Health Liabilities, 1988

Retired workers—
accrued liabilities

$93 Billion

Active workers—
future accruals

$181 Billion

$128 Billion

Active workers—
accrued liabilities

Total $402 Billion

Source: U.S. General Accounting Office.

Advance funding of retiree health liabilities would stabilize companies' annual expenditures. Moreover, the accumulation of assets would result in added security for retired workers. However, this would be very costly.

If employers were to start advance funding their retiree health liabilities the way they fund pensions, they would contribute $32 billion in 1988 under current coverage and benefit provisions and under our methods and assumptions.[1] This is about three and one-half times their current pay-as-you-go costs of $9 billion and one-eighth of the estimated 1988 pretax profits of American corporations.

---

[1]GAO used different values for selected variables in the model to determine low and high estimates of first-year contributions and accrued liabilities. First-year contributions could range from $26 billion to $47 billion to fund accrued liabilities as low as $174 billion or as high as $295 billion, respectively.

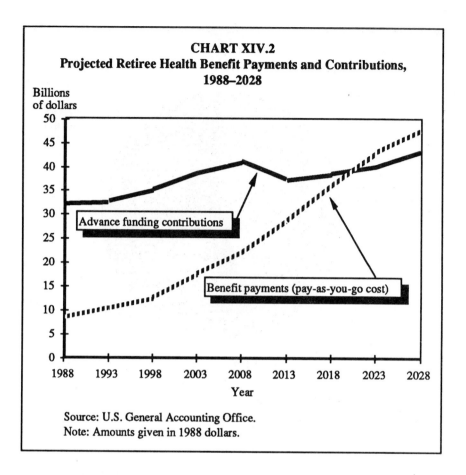

CHART XIV.2
Projected Retiree Health Benefit Payments and Contributions, 1988–2028

Billions of dollars

Advance funding contributions

Benefit payments (pay-as-you-go cost)

Year

Source: U.S. General Accounting Office.
Note: Amounts given in 1988 dollars.

GAO projected contributions and benefit payments assuming current retiree health coverage and benefit provisions to not change. As shown in chart XIV.2, annual contributions would continue to be higher than pay-as-you-go costs (in today's dollars) until the year 2018. Thereafter, pay-as-you-go costs would exceed annual contributions. If companies wait to begin advance funding, first-year contributions will be even greater relative to pay-as-you-go costs.

Companies' Changes to Manage Their Health Costs

Recognizing that companies may change or terminate their retiree health plans, GAO asked company officials about their flexibility to

132

change health plans to cope with rising costs and how they are using this flexibility to make changes. We looked at the retiree health plans of 29 companies in the Chicago area. We selected a sample of companies that had plans in 1984 to determine whether they had reduced or terminated benefits since then. We also interviewed company officials to obtain their views and concerns about the security of these benefits.

Short of terminating benefits, companies can control their costs by changing health plan provisions and cost-sharing arrangements to: (1) limit the services covered; (2) restrict eligibility for coverage and the period of coverage; and (3) require plan participants to share more of the costs. A comparison of two of the companies GAO surveyed shows the range of possibilities. One company allowed access to group plan coverage but did not share the costs. In 1987, this company charged retirees and their families enough in monthly contributions to fully cover plan costs. In contrast, another company, which did not require contributions, paid almost $4,000 per retiree.

Company actions to modify or terminate retiree health coverage have been challenged in court. In some cases, the courts have ruled that companies may not terminate the benefits being provided persons who are already retired. In other cases, the courts have upheld the companies' right to modify or terminate the benefits if the companies have previously taken explicit actions to reserve this right.

Officials at all 29 of the companies we surveyed told us they believe their companies have the right to modify or terminate health benefits for active workers and retirees; 27 of the 29 include explicit language to that effect in their health plans. This is not a new development: 25 companies already had plans with this language at least four years ago. Since then, one company has clarified the wording, and two others have added new language to this effect.

According to company officials, concerns about rising medical costs have led 24 of the companies in our survey to modify their health benefits since 1984. The modifications consisted of (1) implementing cost containment measures to help ensure that the health services are medically necessary and economical, (2) increasing deductibles and coinsurance payments, and (3) raising monthly contributions. These changes were directed at both active workers and retirees.

Officials at 26 of the 29 companies told us that they are committed to providing health benefits to their retirees but are uncertain about their companies' continued ability to pay for these benefits. Officials at 16 companies specifically said they were concerned about the effects of the proposed FASB disclosure requirement on their companies' reported financial condition.

Officials at 21 companies said they were considering additional changes to their retiree health plan structures. The current and future costs of providing retiree health insurance may be more than they can afford, and future court rulings could reduce their ability to modify plans. Some provisions being considered are much different from those already in place and would result in new benefit structures. These include offering: (1) health benefits that vary with length of employment, (2) defined dollar benefits that would cap annual medical payments based on years of employment, or (3) flexible compensation packages that would allow workers to choose from among a variety of pension and welfare benefits.

Company officials said they were planning to wait for FASB to publish its proposed guidelines and for other possible legislative and regulatory actions before deciding what additional changes are needed. They indicated that an expanded tax preference would provide a major incentive for advance funding their benefit payments.

Issues for Consideration by Congress

The private sector has played an important role in providing retirees with access to company-sponsored health benefits and helping to pay for their costs. However, this role may be changing. Current and future retirees have limited protection against company actions to reduce or stop providing health benefits. In fact, to control their current and future costs, some companies are already taking action to require retirees to pay more for their medical care. Projected future costs and requirements to disclose unfunded liabilities on financial statements may increase such actions and erode retiree benefits.

GAO believes that Congress should consider the desirability of legislation to preserve retiree health benefits, especially for retirees under age 65, who are not covered by Medicare. In considering the type of action it might take, the Congress should be aware of some likely consequences. For example, any broadening of tax preferences will obviously create tax losses for the federal treasury at a time when reducing the budget deficit is both extremely difficult and very important. Even with tax advantages, employers' higher annual contributions under advance funding could affect companies' willingness to offer retiree health benefits.

If Congress decides it should take steps to increase benefit security, it can consider actions ranging from applying pension policies to

134

retiree health benefits to requiring companies with health plans to allow their pre-age-65 retirees to purchase coverage at group rates similar to the coverage now provided terminated employees.

To apply pension-type policies to retiree health benefits, Congress, among other things, will need to define vested benefits, expand tax preferences for advance funding, develop funding standards, and consider establishing an insurance program similar to the one administered by the Pension Benefit Guaranty Corporation. This approach would provide more secure health benefits for some retirees but may cause some companies to discontinue retiree benefits for others. In addition, the federal government may have to establish additional organizational structures to administer the system.

Another option would be to give companies the choice of maintaining their retiree health plans on a pay-as-you-go basis or advance funding their liabilities within a pension-type framework. Companies that wished to advance fund could take advantage of expanded tax preferences but would become subject to regulations and restrictions similar to those covering pension plans. Companies that did not want to be subject to pension-type regulations could maintain their pay-as-you-go plans if they desired. Under this option, the benefits of some current and future retirees would be more secure than others.

A less comprehensive approach would be for Congress to provide more incentives for companies to advance fund their retiree health liabilities on a voluntary basis but not to impose the full pension regulations. Standards for advance funding and for the distribution of plan assets in events such as plan termination would need to be established. This approach lessens burdens on companies, but it also does less to promote the security of these benefits. Under this approach, more companies may be willing to increase benefit security through advance funding, but the absence of vesting rules and other protections lowers the level of security provided to individual retirees.

Under any of the above approaches, Congress could also consider adopting current legislative proposals to let companies use excess pension assets to help advance fund retiree health plans.

To avoid some of the adverse effects of requiring advance funding, Congress might take a less ambitious tack. For example, one approach not requiring advance funding would be to require all health plans to extend coverage to retirees at group rates. Under this approach, retirees would bear all of the cost of their health benefits, although payments would be at group rates which are usually lower than individual rates. An advantage is that this approach might well expand the availability of retiree health coverage.

Objectives, Scope, and Methodology

To prepare our estimates of companies' total and accrued liabilities, we updated and expanded an economic model used by the Department of Labor in a 1986 report on employer-sponsored retiree health insurance. Total liabilities—the present value of future benefits—represent the amount of money one would need to have available for investment to provide currently covered workers and retirees with retiree health benefits. If these benefits were advance funded and assumed to be earned over workers' careers, the accrued liabilities would be the portion of total liabilities assigned to workers' and retirees' past years of employment.

To make our calculations, we made several simplifying assumptions. For example, we based our model on our own and others' estimates of average national retiree health costs and of the number of current and future workers covered by employer-provided retiree health plans. We assumed current levels of coverage and benefit provisions would continue, even though companies can modify or cancel their plans. We treated the 1988 accrued liabilities as unfunded, even though we know a few firms are currently funding these liabilities in advance. Finally, we used a projected unit credit funding method with accruals for service after age 40 and no terminations other than death.

For specific model parameters, we analyzed data on numbers of active workers and retirees with retiree health benefit coverage, health care costs, rates of retirement, life expectancy and interest rates, and we reviewed available studies of retiree health costs. Because precise, up-to-date information does not exist for many of the factors affecting companies' total liabilities and annual contributions, we performed sensitivity analyses of our liability estimates by varying our coverage, retirement, mortality, and inflation assumptions.

To estimate the contributions companies would have to make to start advance funding their liabilities in 1988, we used a closed group of workers and retirees. Our estimates of benefit payout and advance funding contributions in the year 2008 were based on an open group valuation allowing for new entrants through the year 2032. Annual contributions include an amount to cover accruals for active workers as well as a 25-year amortization payment on initial (unfunded) accrued liabilities.

To assess companies' flexibility to modify retiree health plans and examine recent changes that companies have made in these plans,

136

we surveyed 29 medium-sized and large companies with retiree health plans in the Chicago area. These companies had from 186 to more than 50,000 active workers; the number of retirees ranged from 12 to 39,000. We also met with company officials and other experts and reviewed recent public- and private-sector studies and court decisions to better understand the kinds of changes that companies were making. Our findings on specific changes cannot be generalized beyond the 29 plans we surveyed.

XV. Part Four Discussion

State Pools

MR. WELLER: Mr. Kahn, what do you think about requiring states to set up risk pools?

MR. KAHN: I do not see any meaningful risk pool legislation passing in isolation, but it could be attached to a larger piece of legislation.

MR. WELLER: Such as the tax bills, where Congress originally had it in 1987?

MR. KAHN: No. I mean it could pass as a component of a big mandated benefits bill, but not in isolation. The Senate has objected consistently to the way the idea has been proposed, and I do not know why, because it would not affect that many people. The amount of money that would have to be raised to pay for it would not be large. I am still confused about why business is so up in arms about it. I understand it would set precedent. But I think it is much ado about nothing; it would be a marginal program to help the dramatically uninsured. If it is not mandated either through a tax penalty or a clear mandate from the federal government, I do not know what there is to be upset about.

The Cost of Prefunding

MR. ENTHOVEN: Ms. Klein, would you please tell us the assumptions that were made, and a little about the alternative assumptions, with respect to the real growth rate in spending per capita for health benefits and the real interest rates that produced the $227 billion that you say the General Accounting Office (GAO) estimates to be the present value of future retiree health benefits? And does the $32 billion needed to begin advance funding include the current $9 billion pay-as-you-go costs? Are you saying that if a company switched over to full prefunding and continued payment of its obligations for current retirees, its total cost would be $32 billion a year? Or is that $32 billion, plus $9 billion?

MS. KLEIN: I will answer the second question first. The $9 billion is to be subtracted from the $32 billion. Obviously, we are not talking about all companies advance funding this year, but if they all did, it would be $32 billion to start advance funding.

MR. ENTHOVEN: That would be their contributions to the unfunded obligations and the currently accrued obligations, and it would also cover the out-of-pocket payment for the current retiree expenses?

Ms. KLEIN: Yes.

MR. ENTHOVEN: It is not $32 billion-plus, then?

Ms. KLEIN: That is correct. It is the past liability and the amortization. Concerning the assumptions, Donald Snyder, the economist who did the estimates, will give us a quick rundown.

GAO's Methodology

MR. SNYDER: When I started out, I built on the work that the U.S. Department of Labor had done in its estimates of 1983 liabilities. Many of our assumptions are the same as theirs, because we can change the discount rate, with the same medical inflation assumption, and change the size of the liabilities. We used a discount rate of 7 percent. It is not the exact interest rate and discount rate that matter so much; it is the differential between the consumer price index (CPI) and medical care cost increases that is really the issue.

You can start with a 7 percent discount rate. If you have 10 percent inflation of medical care, you have a 3 percent differential. In that regard, our medical inflation differential is 1.5 percent for 14 years, three-fourths of 1 percent for 14 years, and then it caps out at 14.7 percent of Gross National Product (GNP). We have a very *de minimus* assumption about the future of health care inflation. We should all get on our knees and pray that GAO is correct in that. Were there other assumptions you were concerned about?

MR. ENTHOVEN: Yes. What is the real interest rate you used to get the present values?

MR. SNYDER: Two percent.

MR. ENTHOVEN: Two percent for how many years?

MR. SNYDER: The real interest rate? It is 2 percent for all time.

MR. ENTHOVEN: What about for the automobile industry?

MR. SNYDER: We assume a 5 percent inflation rate and a 2 percent real rate of interest for a 7 percent discount rate. Two percent is an historically derived figure with which reasonable people could disagree. Maybe 1½ percent or 2½ percent would be appropriate.

MR. ENTHOVEN: Then you use the excess of the medical CPI over the CPI of 2 percent? In other words, are you saying that the medical inflation is equal to the real interest rate, or the real growth in medical spending is below the real interest rate?

MR. SYNDER: It comes down to that in 30 years. The medical rate starts at 3.5 percent over the CPI, falls to 2.75 percent over it, and is always 2 percent higher than the CPI thereafter. However, we do not maintain that medical inflation is equivalent to the CPI-Medical Component.

MR. MAHONEY: What was the percentage of GNP?

MR. SNYDER: It would grow to 14.7 percent in 30 years. We should be clear about the share of GNP. The best data we have, and the easiest data to use, are from the *Economic Report of the President* and the consumer price index for medical care. That is what I used and what most people use because we do not have better information. A particular company with a very generous plan might have much higher price experience. This is an aggregate estimate. If you apply this differential between the CPI and medical care components and the real growth of the economy, and take the share of GNP that goes to health care expenditures, then you get 14.7 percent in our model with our assumptions.

MR. MAHONEY: Is GAO low, medium, or high on that assumption?

MR. SNYDER: I consider it to be low; "conservative" is probably an understatement.

MR. LAURENT: Is this a public document? If so, what is the document number?

MS. KLEIN: If you are interested in the testimony that we gave September 15, 1988, before the Oversight Subcommittee of the Ways and Means Committee, it is GAO T-HRD88-30. There will be a technical appendix that will describe the assumptions and all the details. This document does not go into that kind of detail.

MR. LAURENT: Would the reinvestment rate you used assume that the proceeds were taxable or not taxable?

MS. KLEIN: We assumed they were not taxable.

MR. LAURENT: Chart XIV.2 shows your premium curves. Usually under premium scenarios, the area above the curve in the early part equals the area under the curve in the later part. If you add the areas under these curves, obviously prefunding is a lot higher than cumulative costs. Is that because you did not just carry it out far enough? Presumably after 2028 the pay-as-you-go method keeps going up.

Ms. KLEIN: That is correct.

Wrap-Up

MR. GARBER: I have summarized five points from our discussion that I think start in one place and end back at the same place. First, I think there is general agreement that the FASB action is correct in principle, if not necessarily in all of its details. Recognizing retiree health care costs on a current basis rather than on a pay-as-you-go basis is an appropriate accounting action and an appropriate way for companies to measure their financial situation.

The second point would be that this is a difficult problem, principally because the cost of health care is out of control, creating a risk that employers cannot accept. Therefore, the fundamental problem is to come to terms with health care costs, which must be done in any event, regardless of what is done about retiree health.

The third point is that action at the federal level to permit funding is probably not likely for the reasons you have heard. These reasons are basically on the revenue side; we would end in a zero sum game in which there would be questionable tradeoffs. Moreover, if there were advance funding, ERISA-type provisions would be required, and I think ultimately this probably would not be helpful to industry because what they would gain by receiving the ability to fund might not be worth what they would lose.

Fourth, there are the legal limitations on what employers can do with respect to the retired and near-retired employees, because of the obligations that are already in place. They can change policies at the margin but not in a fundamental way. For active workers, however, employers can take actions to offset long-term costs, although these actions will not offset current costs.

Which leads me back to FASB, my fifth point. FASB has started a process and employers have until 1992 to complete the first installment. It seems to me that companies will begin by fine tuning their numbers. They will begin to adjust and adopt plans to affect their longer-term liabilities, which are related to active employees. Thus the process of bringing these long-term costs up to date and into current income statements or balance sheets will, in the long term, ensure the elimination of a large part of these costs.

Appendix A. Retiree Health Benefits: Given the Tax Incentives, Corporations Can Solve the Problem

PAPER BY A. HERBERT NEHRLING

A. Herbert Nehrling, assistant treasurer of E.I. du Pont de Nemours & Company, delivered the following address at the Sixth National Conference of Americans for Generational Equity, July 29, 1988.

Let me briefly summarize the retiree health care dilemma faced by U.S. companies.

U.S. industry's aggregate unfunded future cost for retiree health care is estimated at between $100 billion and $2 trillion. In the 1992 to 1994 time frame, the Financial Accounting Standards Board (FASB) will require accrual accounting for retiree health care, which will have severely adverse consequences for corporations' balance sheets and income statements. Mainly as a result of revenue considerations, Congress will not permit tax-favored funding for retiree health care, which would offset some of these consequences. At the same time, Congress worries that companies cannot keep their promises to retirees. The dilemma for industry is: How can we reduce future FASB income statement charges and balance sheet liabilities and at the same time make our health care promises to retirees more secure?

I have been asked to say a few words on the premise that "given the tax incentives, corporations can solve the retiree health benefits problem." Let me say, to begin, that I cannot honestly say that this premise is true. However, I can say with certainty that, absent such tax incentives, there is no way that corporations can solve the problem, and that with such incentives, there is a chance that we can indeed solve the problem—a good chance, I believe.

What incentives do we need? I would like to suggest a three-step legislative program. The first step would be to permit companies to pay their current retiree health benefits directly from excess pension assets. The second step would be to permit companies to transfer a portion of their excess pension assets to a separate fund that would pay retiree health benefits for current and future retirees. The third step would be to establish the same type of ongoing tax-favored funding for retiree health care as we already have for pensions.

143

Before briefly discussing each of these steps, I would point out that the key question is: Would business use the vehicles provided by such legislation?

I recognize that individual companies would make decisions in terms of their own situations with regard to cash flow, earnings, and alternative investments. However, there is a new, powerful motivator which will affect every company. The FASB rules, which will be effective between 1992 and 1994, will have such a severely adverse impact on corporate earnings and liabilities that companies will be faced with a choice of either finding a way to fully or partially offset the liability or reducing or eliminating their retiree health care benefits. The only way I know to offset the liability is to set assets aside to cover it—either the assets we have already set aside for pensions that are in excess of the need for that purpose or new assets purchased through an advance tax-favored funding vehicle.

This leads us back to our proposed three-step legislative program. First, let us permit companies to pay their current retiree health benefits directly from excess pension assets in their pension funds rather than from general corporate funds.

This provision could be in effect for a limited period of time—for example, from two to five years—and it would move us in the direction of permitting transfers of excess pension assets into a separate retiree health care fund and eventually permitting full advance funding of retiree health benefits. Meanwhile, the proposal would increase tax revenues by $500 million to $1 billion annually. This would occur because payments of retiree health benefits from excess pension assets would not be tax deductible, whereas current payments on a pay-as-you-go basis from general corporate funds are tax deductible. Moreover, the proposal would make retiree health care promises more secure for retirees without jeopardizing the security of their pension promises. Excess pension assets are now estimated at more than $200 billion, while the annual corporate payout for retiree health care is only $5 billion. Thus, a cushion could easily be retained in pension plans to provide further protection for pension promises.

Our second proposed legislative step would be to allow employers whose pension plans are overfunded to transfer a portion of the excess assets to a separate fund that would pay retiree health benefits for current and future retirees. This would be another move in the direction of eventually permitting full advance funding of retiree health benefits. This second step would also increase tax revenues. Payments from a retiree health care fund would not be tax deductible, while current payments on a pay-as-you-go basis from general corporate funds are tax deductible. Finally, this step would also make retiree health care promises more secure for retirees without jeopardizing the security of their pension promises, because the rules should leave a cushion in the pension fund.

As stated earlier, excess pension assets are now estimated at more than $200 billion. An aggregate of funds in this amount should go a long way toward solving the problem, thus minimizing corporate actions to reduce or eliminate retiree health care benefits. In return, employers should be willing to accept a prohibition on reversions of pension assets for any other purpose.

While we firmly believe that pension plan benefits, not pension assets, represent the substance of the employer's pension promise to employees, we should be willing to agree to a restriction on reversions but only if the *quid pro quo* is the permitted transfer of excess pension fund assets just described and the ongoing ability to prefund postretirement medical benefits on a tax-favored basis.

This brings us to our third and final proposed legislative step, which would be the establishment of the same type of ongoing funding vehicle for retiree health care as we already have for pensions. That is, the ability to prefund postretirement medical benefits on a tax-favored basis. In return, employers should be prepared to accept a "retiree health care ERISA." That is, if a company elects to provide retiree health care, it would have to advance fund for the benefit and, further, it would have to meet vesting and participation standards in return for a tax deduction for the contributions and for tax-free accumulation of earnings on the funds contributed.

However, even with ERISA-type rules, the country's budget deficit situation would seem to preclude tax-favored funding in the foreseeable future, because such funding would reduce tax revenues. Therefore, if we are to have a funding vehicle—and we must ultimately have one if we are to solve the problem—business must be willing to put some revenue raisers on the table. Such items could be in or outside of the benefits area. I am not speaking here either for my company or for the business community. Furthermore, I am not going to advocate specific give-ups. I am merely pointing out, as one knowledgeable professional in the field, that the retiree health care problem is symptomatic of the fact that business, labor, and government have not sorted out their priorities in the employee benefits area, in particular, regarding health care. We all need to decide how much our society can afford and who should pay for what. If employer-sponsored retiree health care is deemed by all parties to have a high priority, a tax-favored funding vehicle will give business a good chance to solve the problem, and the terms and conditions of such a solution must result from statesmanlike compromises by all parties.

Perhaps the debate on retiree health care will focus attention on the urgent need for developing a comprehensive national retirement income and retiree health care policy. We, in the benefits community, at one time believed that this policy should be developed independently of revenue considerations. However, in today's world, this is not realistic. Revenue issues must be considered for the foreseeable future.

In this connection, I would especially like to commend the legislation proposed by Rep. Rod Chandler (R-WA)* as a statesmanlike effort to begin crafting a comprehensive national retirement income and retiree health care policy, taking into account the practical revenue realities. I urge your serious consideration of Rep. Chandler's major proposals.

To summarize, the FASB rules will have such an adverse impact on corporate earnings and liabilities that companies will be faced with a choice of either finding a way to fully or partially offset their retiree health benefits liability or reducing or eliminating the retiree health care benefit. The only way I know to offset the liability is to set aside assets to cover it, either assets already set aside for pensions that are in excess of what is needed for that purpose or new assets purchased through an advance-funding vehicle. As Rep. Chandler has said, "It's time we recognized that the need for adequate retirement income *and* financing retiree health care are part of the same fabric." Accordingly, if assets set aside for pensions are excessive for that purpose, they should be used to satisfy retiree health needs. And, if retirement *income* warrants tax-favored funding, then retiree *health care* should receive the same treatment.

---

*Editor's note: The Retiree Health Benefits and Pension Preservation Act (H.R. 5309) was introduced in the 100th Congress on September 18, 1988. It would have permitted defined benefit plan sponsors to prefund a retiree's medical or long-term care premiums in amounts of up to $2,500 per year. Funds from defined contribution plans would also have been allowed to be used to pay for the premiums.

Appendix B
Proposed Statement of Financial Accounting Standards: Employers' Accounting for Postretirement Benefits Other Than Pensions*

FEBRUARY 14, 1989

Summary

This proposed Statement would establish accounting standards for employers' accounting for postretirement benefits other than pensions (hereinafter referred to as postretirement benefits). Although it would apply to all forms of postretirement benefits, this proposed Statement focuses principally on postretirement health care benefits. It would significantly change the prevalent current practice of accounting for postretirement benefits on a pay-as-you-go (cash) basis by requiring accrual, during the years that the employee renders the necessary service, of the expected cost of providing those benefits to an employee and the employee's beneficiaries and covered dependents.

The Board's conclusions in this proposed Statement result from the view that a defined postretirement benefit plan sets forth the terms of an exchange between the employer and the employee. In exchange for services provided by the employee, the employer promises to provide, in addition to current wages and other benefits, health and other welfare benefits during the employee's retirement period. It follows from that view that postretirement benefits are not gratuities but are part of an employee's compensation for services rendered. Since payment is deferred, the benefits are a type of deferred compensation. The employer's obligation for that compensation is incurred as employees render the services necessary to earn their postretirement benefits.

The ability to measure the obligation for postretirement health care benefits and the recognition of that obligation have been the subject of controversy. The Board believes that measurement of the obliga-

---

*Editor's note: Included in this appendix are selected sections of the Financial Accounting Standards Board exposure draft document. For more detail, refer to the actual document.

tion and accrual of the cost based on best estimates are superior to implying, by a failure to accrue, that no obligation exists prior to the payment of benefits. The Board believes that failure to recognize any obligation prior to its payment impairs the usefulness and integrity of the employer's financial statements.

The Board's objectives in issuing this proposed Statement are to improve employers' financial reporting for postretirement benefits in the following manner:

a. To enhance the relevance and representational faithfulness of the employer's reported results of operations by recognizing net periodic postretirement benefit cost as employees render the services necessary to earn their postretirement benefits, pursuant to the terms of the plan
b. To enhance the relevance and representational faithfulness of the employer's statement of financial position by including a measure of the obligation to provide postretirement benefits based on the terms of the underlying plan
c. To enhance the ability of users of the employer's financial statements to understand the extent and effects of the employer's undertaking to provide postretirement benefits to its employees
d. To improve the understandability and comparability of amounts reported by requiring employers with similar plans to use the same method to measure their accumulated postretirement benefit obligation and the related cost of the postretirement benefits.

Similarity to Pension Accounting

The provisions of this proposed Statement are similar, in many respects, to those in FASB Statements No. 87, *Employers' Accounting for Pensions*, and No. 88, *Employers' Accounting for Settlements and Curtailments of Defined Benefit Pension Plans and for Termination Benefits*. To the extent the promise to provide pension benefits and the promise to provide postretirement benefits are similar, the provisions of this proposed Statement would be the same as or similar to those prescribed by Statements 87 and 88; different accounting treatment would be prescribed only when the Board has concluded that there is a compelling reason for different treatment. Appendix B [of full FASB document] identifies the major similarities and differences between this proposed Statement and employers' accounting for pensions.

Basic Tenets

This proposed Statement relies on a basic premise of generally accepted accounting principles that accrual accounting provides more relevant and useful information than does cash basis accounting. The importance of information about cash flows or the funding of the postretirement benefit plan is not ignored. Amounts funded or paid are given accounting recognition as uses of cash, but the Board believes that information about cash flows alone is insufficient. Accrual accounting goes beyond cash transactions and attempts to recognize the financial effects of noncash transactions and events as they occur. Recognition and measurement of the accrued obligation to provide postretirement benefits will provide users of financial statements with the opportunity to assess the financial consequences of employers' compensation decisions.

Accrual accounting is concerned with expected future cash receipts and disbursements as a result of transactions and events that have already occurred and recognizes assets, liabilities, and earnings on that basis. The Board believes that for postretirement benefits, as in other areas, the resulting accounting information is more representationally faithful and more relevant to financial statement users than accounting information prepared solely on the basis of cash transactions.

In applying accrual accounting to postretirement benefits, this proposed Statement would adopt three fundamental aspects of pension accounting: delayed recognition of certain events, reporting net cost, and offsetting liabilities and related assets.

Delayed recognition means that certain changes in the obligation for postretirement benefits, including those changes arising as a result of a plan initiation or amendment, and certain changes in the value of plan assets set aside to meet that obligation would not be recognized as they occur. Rather, those changes would be recognized systematically over future periods. All changes in the obligation and plan assets would ultimately be recognized unless they are first reduced by other changes. The changes that have been identified and quantified but not yet recognized in the employer's financial statements as components of net periodic postretirement benefit cost and as a liability or asset would be disclosed.

Net cost means that the recognized consequences of events and transactions affecting a postretirement benefit plan would be reported as a single amount in the employer's financial statements. That single amount would include at least three types of events or

149

transactions that might otherwise be reported separately. Those events or transactions—exchanging a promise of deferred compensation in the form of postretirement benefits for employee service, the interest cost arising from the passage of time until those benefits are paid, and the returns from the investment of plan assets—would be disclosed separately as components of net periodic postretirement benefit cost.

Offsetting means that plan assets restricted for the payment of postretirement benefits would offset the accumulated postretirement benefit obligation in determining amounts recognized in the employer's statement of financial position and that the return on those plan assets would offset postretirement benefit cost in the employer's statement of income. That offsetting would be reflected even though the obligation has not been settled, the investment of the plan assets may be largely controlled by the employer, and substantial risks and rewards associated with both the obligation and the plan assets are borne by the employer.

Recognition and Measurement

The Board is sensitive to concerns about the reliability of measurements of the postretirement health care benefit obligation. The Board recognizes that limited historical data about per capita claims cost are available and that actuarial practice in this area is still developing. The Board has taken those factors into consideration in its decisions to delay the effective date for the proposed standard and to emphasize disclosure while phasing in recognition of the transition obligation in an employer's statement of financial position. However, the Board believes that those factors are insufficient reason not to utilize accrual accounting for postretirement benefits in financial reporting. With increased experience, the reliability of measures of the obligation and cost should improve.

This proposed Statement would require that an employer's obligation for postretirement benefits expected to be provided to or for an employee be fully accrued by the date that employee attains full eligibility for the benefits expected to be received by that employee, any beneficiaries, and covered dependents (the full eligibility date), even if the employee is expected to render additional service beyond that date. That accounting reflects the fact that at the full eligibility date the employee has provided all service necessary to retire and receive all of the benefits that employee is expected to earn under the plan.

The beginning of the attribution (accrual) period is the employee's date of hire unless the plan only grants credit for service from a later date, in which case benefits are generally attributed from the beginning of that credited service period. An equal amount of the expected postretirement benefit obligation is attributed to each year of service in the attribution period unless the plan otherwise specifies the benefits earned for specific periods of service. The Board concluded that, like accounting for other deferred compensation agreements, accounting for postretirement benefits should reflect the explicit or implicit contract between the employer and its employees.

Single Method

The Board believes that understandability, comparability, and usefulness of financial information are improved by narrowing the use of alternative accounting methods that do not reflect different facts and circumstances. The Board has been unable to identify circumstances that would make it appropriate for different employers to use fundamentally different accounting methods or measurement techniques for similar postretirement benefit plans or for a single employer to use fundamentally different methods or measurement techniques for different plans. As a result, a single method would be prescribed for measuring and recognizing an employer's accumulated postretirement benefit obligation.

Minimum Liability

Certain aspects of the delayed recognition features of this proposed Statement cause the liability that is recognized in the employer's statement of financial position to differ from the best available current measurement of the unfunded accumulated postretirement benefit obligation. This proposed Statement would require recognition of a minimum liability to limit the extent to which delayed recognition of the transition obligation, changes in the plan, and loss recognition would otherwise understate the employer's recognized obligation. That minimum liability would be measured as the unfunded accumulated postretirement benefit obligation for retirees and other fully eligible plan participants.

Transition

Unlike the effects of most other accounting changes, a transition obligation for postretirement benefits generally reflects, to a considerable extent, the failure to accrue the accumulated postretirement benefit obligation in earlier periods as it arose rather than the effects of a change from one acceptable accrual method of accounting to another. The Board believes that accounting for transition from one method to another is a practical matter and that a major objective of that accounting is to minimize the cost and mitigate the disruption to the extent possible without unduly compromising the ability of financial statements to provide useful information.

This proposed Statement measures the transition obligation as the unfunded and unrecognized accumulated postretirement benefit obligation for all plan participants. The initial emphasis of this proposed Statement is on disclosure of that transition obligation, with recognition of the effect of that obligation in the statement of financial position and in the statement of income being phased in over future periods. However, that delayed recognition would not be permitted to result in less rapid recognition than accounting for the transition obligation on a pay-as-you-go basis.

Effective Date

This proposed Statement generally would be effective for fiscal years beginning after December 15, 1991, except that the application of this proposed Statement to non-U.S. plans and certain small, non-public employers would be delayed to fiscal years beginning after December 15, 1993. The provisions requiring recognition of a minimum liability would be delayed for all employers to fiscal years beginning after December 15, 1996.

152

Contents

Introduction

1. This Statement establishes standards of financial accounting and reporting for an employer that offers **postretirement benefits other than pensions**[1] (hereinafter referred to as **postretirement benefits**) to its employees.[2] The Board added a project on postemployment **benefits** other than pensions to its agenda in 1979 as part of its project on accounting for pensions and other postemployment benefits. In 1984, the subject of accounting for postemployment benefits other than pensions was identified as a separate project. As interim measures, in November 1984, the Board issued FASB Statement No. 81, *Disclosure of Postretirement Health Care and Life Insurance Benefits*, and in April 1987, issued FASB Technical Bulletin No. 87-1, *Accounting for a Change in Method of Accounting for Certain Postretirement Benefits*.

2. Most employers have accounted for postretirement benefits on a pay-as-you-go (cash) basis. As the prevalence and magnitude of employers' promises to provide those benefits have increased, there has been increased concern about the failure of financial reporting to identify the financial effects of those promises.

3. The Board views a **postretirement benefit plan** as a deferred compensation arrangement whereby an employer promises to exchange future benefits for employees' current services. Since the obligation to provide benefits arises as employees render the services necessary to earn the benefits pursuant to the terms of the **plan**, the Board believes that the cost of providing the benefits should be recognized over those employee service periods.

4. This Statement addresses, for the first time, the fundamental accounting issues related to measuring and recognizing the exchange that takes place between an employer that promises to provide postretirement benefits and the employees who render services in exchange for those benefits. The Board believes the accounting recognition required by this Statement should result in more useful and repre-

---

[1] Words that appear in the glossary are set in **boldface type** the first time they appear.

[2] The Board will consider the accounting for benefits paid after employment but before retirement (for example, layoff benefits) in a separate phase of its project on accounting for postemployment benefits other than pensions. The fact that this Statement does not apply to those benefits should not be construed as discouraging the use of accrual accounting for those benefits.

sentationally faithful financial statements. However, this Statement is not likely to be the final step in the evolution of more useful accounting for postretirement benefit arrangements.

5. The Board's objectives in issuing this Statement are to improve employers' financial reporting for postretirement benefits in the following manner:

a. To enhance the relevance and representational faithfulness of the employer's reported results of operations by recognizing **net periodic postretirement benefit cost**[3] as employees render the services necessary to earn their postretirement benefits, pursuant to the terms of the plan
b. To enhance the relevance and representational faithfulness of the employer's statement of financial position by including a measure of the obligation to provide postretirement benefits based on the terms of the underlying plan
c. To enhance the ability of users of the employer's financial statements to understand the extent and effects of the employer's undertaking to provide postretirement benefits to its employees
d. To improve the understandability and comparability of amounts reported by requiring employers with similar plans to use the same method to measure their **accumulated postretirement benefit obligation** and the related cost of the postretirement benefits.

Standards of Financial Accounting and Reporting

Scope

6. This Statement is applicable to all postretirement benefits expected to be provided by an employer to current and future **retirees** (including those employees deemed to be on a disability retirement), their beneficiaries, and covered dependents, pursuant to the terms of an employer's undertaking to provide those benefits. Postretirement benefits include, but are not limited to, postretirement health care, which is thought to be the most significant in terms of cost and prevalence; life insurance provided to retirees outside a pension plan; and other welfare benefits such as tuition assistance, day care, legal

---

[3]This Statement uses the term *net periodic postretirement benefit cost* rather than *net postretirement benefit expense* because part of the cost recognized in a period may be capitalized along with other costs as part of an asset such as inventory.

156

services, and housing subsidies provided after retirement. Often those benefits are in the form of a reimbursement or direct payment to providers for the cost of specified services as the need for those services arises, but they may also include benefits payable as a lump sum, such as death benefits.

7. This Statement also applies to **settlement** of all or part of an employer's accumulated postretirement benefit obligation or **curtailment** of a postretirement benefit plan and to an employer that provides postretirement benefits as part of a special termination benefits offer.

8. An employer's promise to provide postretirement benefits may take a variety of forms and may or may not be funded. This Statement applies to any arrangement that is in substance a postretirement benefit plan, regardless of its form, or the means or timing of its funding. This Statement applies both to written plans and to plans whose existence may be implied from a well-defined, although perhaps unwritten, practice of paying postretirement benefits. For the purposes of this Statement, a postretirement benefit plan is an arrangement whereby an employer undertakes to provide its employees with benefits during their retirement in exchange for their services over a specified period of time, upon attaining a specified age while in service, or both. Benefits may commence immediately upon termination of service or may be deferred for payment upon attaining a specified age.

9. An employer's practice of providing postretirement benefits to selected employees under individual contracts with specific terms determined on an individual-by-individual basis does not constitute a postretirement benefit plan under this Statement. Those contracts shall be accrued individually, following the terms of the contract. If the contract does not define the specific years of service to be rendered in exchange for the benefits, the contract should be accrued in accordance with paragraphs 34–36. This Statement does apply to deferred compensation contracts with individual employees if those contracts, taken together, are equivalent to a postretirement benefit plan.

10. A postretirement benefit plan may be part of a larger plan or arrangement that provides benefits currently to active employees as well as to retirees. In those circumstances, the promise to provide benefits to present and future retirees under the plan shall be seg-

regated from benefits provided currently to active employees and shall be accounted for in accordance with the provisions of this Statement.

11. This Statement does not apply to pension or life insurance benefits provided through a pension plan. The accounting for those benefits is set forth in FASB Statements No. 87, *Employers' Accounting for Pensions*, and No. 88, *Employers' Accounting for Settlements and Curtailments of Defined Benefit Pension Plans and for Termination Benefits*.[4] This Statement also does not apply to temporary benefits that are provided only to certain employees after their employment and are not provided to employees who retire.

12. This Statement supersedes FASB Statement No. 81, *Disclosure of Postretirement Health Care and Life Insurance Benefits*. Paragraphs 13 and 84 of this Statement amend APB Opinions No. 12, *Omnibus Opinion—1967*, and No. 16, *Business Combinations*, respectively. Paragraph 108 rescinds FASB Technical Bulletin No. 87-1, *Accounting for a Change in Method of Accounting for Certain Postretirement Benefits*.

Amendment to Opinion 12

13. The following sentences replace the first four sentences of paragraph 6 of Opinion 12:

> FASB Statements No. 87, *Employers' Accounting for Pensions*, and No. XXX, *Employers' Accounting for Postretirement Benefits Other Than Pensions* (this Statement), apply to deferred compensation contracts with individual employees if those contracts, taken together, are equivalent to a postretirement income or health or welfare benefit plan. Other deferred compensation contracts with specific terms determined on an individual-by-individual basis should be accounted for individually on an accrual basis in accordance with the terms of the underlying

---

[4]Two Special Reports prepared by the FASB staff, *A Guide to Implementation of Statement 87 on Employers' Accounting for Pensions* and *A Guide to Implementation of Statement 88 on Employers' Accounting for Settlements and Curtailments of Defined Benefit Pension Plans and for Termination Benefits*, provide accounting guidance on implementation questions raised in connection with Statements 87 and 88. Many of the provisions in this Statement are the same as or are similar to the provisions of Statements 87 and 88. Consequently, the guidance provided in those Special Reports should be useful in understanding and implementing many of the provisions of this Statement.

contract. If the contract does not define the specific years of service to be rendered in exchange for the future payments, the amounts expected to be paid should be accrued in a systematic and rational manner over the period of active employment from the date the contract is entered into to the date the employee attains full eligibility (as defined in Statement XXX) for the benefits expected to be received by that employee, any beneficiaries, and covered dependents.

Use of Reasonable Approximations

14. This Statement is intended to specify accounting objectives and results rather than specific computational means of obtaining those results. If estimates, averages, or computational shortcuts can reduce the cost of applying this Statement, their use is appropriate, provided the results are reasonably expected not to be materially different from the results of a detailed application.

Single-Employer Defined Benefit Postretirement Plans

15. This Statement primarily focuses on an employer's accounting for a **single-employer plan** that defines the postretirement benefits to be provided to retirees. For purposes of this Statement, a **defined benefit postretirement plan** is one that defines the postretirement benefits in terms of (a) monetary amounts (for example, $100,000 of life insurance) or (b) benefit coverage (for example, up to $200 per day for hospitalization, 80 percent of the cost of specified surgical procedures, and so forth) to be provided. (Specified monetary amounts and benefit coverage are hereinafter collectively referred to as benefits.) **Full eligibility** for postretirement benefits may be defined in terms of compensation levels, years of service, attained age while in service, or a combination of those factors and may or may not coincide with full eligibility for pension benefits.

16. A postretirement benefit is part of the compensation paid to an employee for services rendered. In a defined benefit plan, the employer promises to provide, in addition to current wages and benefits, future benefits during retirement. Generally, the amount of those benefits depends on the **benefit formula** (which includes factors such as the number of years of service rendered or the employee's compensation before retirement or termination) and how long the retiree and any beneficiaries and covered dependents live and the incidence

of events requiring benefit payments (for example, illnesses affecting the amount of health care required). In most cases, services are rendered over a number of years before an employee retires and begins to receive benefits or is entitled to receive benefits as a need arises. Even though the services rendered by the employee are complete and the employee has retired, the total amount of benefits the employer has promised and the cost to the employer of the services rendered are not precisely determinable but can be estimated using the plan's benefit formula and estimates of the effects of relevant future events.

Basic Elements of Accounting for Postretirement Benefits

17. Any method of accounting that recognizes the cost of postretirement benefits over employee service periods (before the payment of benefits to retirees) must deal with two factors that stem from the nature of the arrangement. First, estimates or **assumptions** must be made concerning the future events that will determine the amount and timing of the benefit payments. Second, an **attribution** approach that assigns benefits and the cost of those benefits to individual years of service must be selected. The basic elements of accounting for postretirement benefits are described in paragraphs 18–20.

18. The **expected postretirement benefit obligation** for an employee is the **actuarial present value** as of a date of the postretirement benefits expected to be paid to or for the employee, the employee's beneficiaries, and any covered dependents pursuant to the terms of the plan. Measurement of the expected postretirement benefit obligation is based on the expected amount and timing of future benefits, taking into consideration future costs and the extent to which the benefit promise encompasses cost increases. An employee's future compensation is considered in that measurement if the benefit formula is based on compensation. Plans that base benefits on compensation may be referred to as **pay-related plans**. Plans that do not base benefits on compensation may be referred to as **non-pay related plans**.

19. Net periodic postretirement benefit cost comprises several components that reflect different aspects of the employer's financial arrangements. The **service cost** component of net periodic postretirement benefit cost is the actuarial present value of benefits attributed to services rendered by employees during the period (the proportion of the expected postretirement benefit obligation attributed to service in the period). The service cost component is the same for an unfunded

160

plan, a plan with minimal funding, and a well-funded plan. The other components of net periodic postretirement benefit cost are **interest cost**[5] (interest on the accumulated postretirement benefit obligation, which is a discounted amount), **actual return on plan assets, amortization** of **unrecognized prior service cost,** amortization of the **transition obligation or asset,** and the **gain or loss component.**

20. The accumulated postretirement benefit obligation as of a particular date is the actuarial present value of all future benefits attributed to employees' service rendered to that date pursuant to paragraphs 34–37, assuming the plan continues in effect and that all assumptions about future events are fulfilled. Prior to the date on which an employee attains full eligibility for the benefits that employee is expected to earn under the terms of the postretirement benefit plan (the **full eligibility date**),[6] the accumulated postretirement benefit obligation for an employee is a portion of the expected postretirement benefit obligation. On and after the full eligibility date, the accumulated postretirement benefit obligation and the expected postretirement benefit obligation for an employee are the same. Determination of the full eligibility date is not affected by measurement assumptions such as when the benefit payments will commence, **dependency status,** salary progression, and so forth.

Measurement of Cost and Obligations

21. The Board believes that measuring the net periodic postretirement benefit cost and accumulated postretirement benefit obligation based on best estimates is superior to implying, by a failure to accrue, that no cost or obligation exists prior to the payment of benefits. This Statement requires the use of **explicit assumptions,** each of which individually represents the best estimate of a particular future event, to measure the expected postretirement benefit obligation. A portion of that expected postretirement benefit obligation is attributed to

---

[5]The interest cost component of postretirement benefit cost shall not be considered interest for purposes of applying FASB Statement No. 34, *Capitalization of Interest Cost.*

[6]For example, for a plan that provides 100 percent benefit coverage to employees who render at least 10 years of service and attain age 55 while in service, the full eligibility date is the date at which an employee first meets both of those conditions. For a plan that provides 50 percent benefit coverage to employees who render 20 years of service and 3 percent benefit coverage for each year of service thereafter, up to a maximum of 80 percent benefit coverage, the full eligibility date is the earlier of the date at which an employee has rendered 30 years of service or retires (terminates) with at least 20 years of service.

each period of an employee's service associated with earning the postretirement benefits, and that amount is accrued as service cost for that period. The accumulated postretirement benefit obligation is the aggregation of the expected postretirement benefit obligation attributed to **plan participants'** prior service periods associated with earning the postretirement benefits together with interest thereon less benefits paid.

22. The **vested postretirement benefit obligation** provides information about the amount of benefits expected to be paid to or for retirees, former employees, and active employees assuming they terminated immediately, including benefits expected to be paid to or for beneficiaries and any covered dependents. The vested postretirement benefit obligation for active employees measures the obligation for postretirement benefits for which employees' rights to receive those benefits are not contingent on remaining in the service of the employer; it may exceed the employer's accumulated postretirement benefit obligation for those employees.[7] The vested postretirement benefit ogligation for former employees, including retirees, is the same as the accumulated postretirement benefit obligation for those employees.

Assumptions

23. The service cost component of postretirement benefit cost, any **prior service cost**, and the accumulated postretirement benefit obligation are measured using actuarial assumptions and present value techniques to calculate the actuarial present value of the expected future benefits attributed to periods of employee service. Each assumption used shall reflect the best estimate solely with respect to that individual assumption. All assumptions shall presume that the plan will continue in effect in the absence of evidence that it will not continue. Principal actuarial assumptions include the time value of money (**discount rates**); the amount and timing of future benefit pay-

---

[7]For example, for a plan that provides 100 percent benefit coverage commencing upon retirement (termination of service) to employees who render at least 10 years of service and attain age 55 while in service, the accumulated postretirement benefit obligation for a 55-year-old employee who has rendered at least 10 years of service and is expected to retire at age 62 would be measured as the actuarial present value of the benefits expected to be paid to or for that employee commencing upon retirement at age 62. The vested postretirement benefit obligation would be measured as the actuarial present value of the benefits that would be paid to or for that employee assuming benefits commenced immediately (as though the employee retired immediately).

ments, which for **postretirement health care benefits** consider past and present **per capita claims cost by age, health care cost trend rates, Medicare reimbursement rates**, and so forth; salary progression (for pay-related plans);[8] and the probability of payment (turnover, retirement age, dependency status, mortality, and so forth).

24. Assumed discount rates shall reflect the interest rates inherent in the amount at which the postretirement benefit obligation could be effectively settled (that is, the interest rates that determine the single amount that, together with returns on that amount equal to the discount rates, would provide the cash flows necessary to provide the benefits, assuming no future experience **gains or losses**). In making that assumption, employers may also look to rates of return on high-quality fixed-income investments currently available and expected to be available during the period until the benefits are expected to be paid. Assumed discount rates are used in measurements of the expected, accumulated, and vested postretirement benefit obligations and the service cost and interest cost components of net periodic postretirement benefit cost.

25. The **expected long-term rate of return on plan assets** shall reflect the average rate of earnings expected on the existing assets that qualify as **plan assets** and contributions to the plan expected to be made during the period. In estimating that rate, appropriate consideration should be given to the returns being earned by the plan assets currently invested and the rates of return expected to be available for reinvestment. If the return on plan assets is taxable to the plan, the expected long-term rate of return shall be reduced to reflect the expected income tax accrual rate under existing law determined in accordance with FASB Statement No. 96, *Accounting for Income Taxes*. If the return on plan assets is taxable to the employer, the expected long-term rate of return shall not reflect the effect of taxes. The expected long-term rate of return on plan assets is used (with the **market-related value of plan assets**) to compute the **expected return on**

---

[8]Unlike Statement 87, this Statement includes salary progression in the measurement of the accumulated postretirement benefit obligation of a pay-related plan. Statement 87 refers to the measurement that excludes salary progression as the accumulated benefit obligation and the measurement that includes salary progression as the projected benefit obligation. In both this Statement and Statement 87, the accumulated benefit obligation is disclosed in and, as discussed in footnote 30, either all (Statement 87) or a portion (this Statement) of the unfunded accumulated benefit obligation is used to measure the **minimum liability**.

plan assets. (Refer to paragraph 50.) There is no assumption of an expected long-term rate of return on plan assets for plans that are unfunded or that have no assets that qualify as plan assets pursuant to this Statement.

26. The service cost components of net periodic postretirement benefit cost and the expected and accumulated postretirement benefit obligations shall reflect future compensation levels to the extent the postretirement benefit formula defines the benefits wholly or partially as a function of future compensation levels.[9] Future increases in benefits for which a present commitment exists as described in paragraph 37 shall be similarly reflected. Assumed compensation levels shall reflect the employer's best estimate of the actual future compensation levels of the individual employees involved, including future changes attributed to general price levels, productivity, seniority, promotion, and other factors. All assumptions shall be consistent to the extent that each reflects expectations of the same future economic conditions, such as future rates of inflation. Measuring service cost and the expected and accumulated postretirement benefit obligations based on estimated future compensation levels entails considering any indirect effects, such as benefit limitations, that would affect benefits provided by the plan.[10]

27. Automatic benefit increases[11] specified by the plan that are expected to occur shall be included in measurements of the expected,

---

[9]For pay-related plans, salary progression is included in measuring the expected postretirement benefit obligation. For example, a postretirement health care plan may define the deductible amount or copayment, or a postretirement life insurance plan may define the amount of death benefit, based on the employee's average or final level of annual compensation. Refer to the discussion in footnote 8 regarding inclusion of the salary progression assumption in measurement of the accumulated postretirement benefit obligation.

[10]For example, a plan may define the maximum benefit to be provided under the plan (an unadjustable cap). In measuring the expected postretirement benefit obligation under that plan, the projected benefit payments would be limited to that cap. For a plan that adjusts the maximum benefit to be provided under the plan for the effects of inflation (an adjustable cap), the expected postretirement benefit obligation would be measured based on adjustments to that cap consistent with the assumed inflation rate reflected in other inflation-related assumptions.

[11]For purposes of this Statement, a plan that promises to provide retirees a benefit in kind, such as health care benefits, rather than a defined dollar amount of benefit, is considered to be a plan that specifies automatic benefit increases. (The assumed increase in the future cost of providing health care benefits, the assumed health care cost trend rate, is discussed in paragraph 31.) A benefit in kind includes the direct rendering of services, the payment directly to others who provide the services, or the reimbursement of the retiree's payment for those services.

164

accumulated, and vested postretirement benefit obligations and the service cost component of net periodic postretirement benefit cost. Also, retroactive **plan amendments** shall be included in the computation of the expected and accumulated postretirement benefit obligations once they have been contractually agreed to, even if some provisions take effect only in future periods. For example, if a plan amendment grants a different benefit level for employees retiring after a future date, that increased or reduced benefit level shall be included in current-period measurements for employees expected to retire after that date.

Assumptions Unique to Postretirement Health Care Benefit Measurements

28. Measurements of the expected, accumulated, and vested postretirement benefit obligations, the service cost component of net periodic postretirement benefit cost, and determination of prior service cost for postretirement health care benefits require the use of several assumptions in addition to those addressed in paragraphs 23–27. Most significantly, they include assumptions about the amount and timing of future benefits, which require consideration of historical per capita claims cost by age, health care cost trend rates (for plans that provide a benefit in kind), and medical coverage by governmental authorities and other providers of health care benefits.

29. The **assumed per capita claims cost by age** is the future per capita cost, after the **measurement date**, of providing the postretirement health care benefits at each age from the earliest ages at which plan participants could begin to receive benefits under the plan through their remaining life expectancy or the covered period, if shorter. To determine the assumed per capita claims cost by age, the per capita claims cost by age based on historical claims costs is adjusted for assumed health care cost trend rates and the effects of coverage by Medicare and other providers of health care benefits. The resulting assumed per capita claims cost by age reflects expected future costs and is applied with the plan **demographics** to determine the amount and timing of expected future benefits.

30. Past and present claims data shall be used in developing an employer's assumed per capita claims cost by age to the extent that those data are considered to be representative of the employer's expected future experience. That assumption also may be based on or

may consider a historical pattern of claims by age (claims curve) and claims experience of other employers with similar participant demographics. The latter information may be developed by insurance companies, actuarial firms, or employee benefit consulting firms from information in data banks. The per capita claims cost by age developed on those bases shall be adjusted to best reflect the employer's circumstances. For example, the information should be adjusted, as necessary, for differing demographics, such as health care utilization patterns by men and women at various ages, the expected geographical location of retirees and their dependents, the age and sex of plan participants, and the plan's terms to the extent that different benefits are provided.

31. The health care cost trend rates assumption represents the expected annual changes in the incurred claims cost of health care benefits currently provided by the postretirement benefit plan due to factors other than changes in the demographics of the plan participants. That assumption shall consider estimates of health care inflation, changes in health care utilization or delivery patterns, technological advances, and changes in the health status of plan participants.[12] Differing services, such as hospital care and dental care, may require the use of different health care cost trend rates. It is appropriate to reflect in that assumption the fact that health care cost trend rates change over time.

32. Assumed discount rates include an inflationary element that reflects the expected general rate of inflation. Assumed compensation levels include consideration of future changes attributable to general price levels. Similarly, assumed health care cost trend rates include an element that reflects expected general rates of inflation for the economy overall and for health care costs in particular. To the extent that those assumptions consider similar inflationary effects, the assumptions about those effects shall be consistent.

33. Certain medical claims may be covered by governmental programs under existing law[13] or by other providers of health care ben-

---

[12]An assumption about changes in the health status of plan participants considers, for example, the probability that certain claims costs will be incurred based on expectations of future events, such as the likelihood that some retirees will incur claims requiring technology currently being developed or that historical claims experience for certain medical needs may be reduced as a result of participation in a wellness program.

[13]For example, under existing U.S. law, certain health care benefits are provided by the Health Care Financing Administration through Medicare.

efits.[14] Benefit coverage by those providers shall be assumed to continue at the level provided by the present law or plan, absent evidence to the contrary. Enacted changes in the law or amendments of plans of other health care providers that will affect the future level of their benefit coverage shall be considered in current-period measurements for benefits expected to be provided in future periods. Future changes in the law or future amendments of benefits provided by others shall not be anticipated.

Attribution

34. For purposes of this Statement, except as described in paragraphs 35–37, the expected postretirement benefit obligation for a plan participant ordinarily shall be attributed to periods of employee service to the full eligibility date based on the plan's benefit formula to the extent that the formula states or implies how that obligation should be attributed. An equal amount of benefits will not necessarily be attributed to each period of employee service to the full eligibility date.

a. The beginning of the **attribution period** shall be the date of hire[15] unless the plan's benefit formula grants credit only for service from a later date, in which case benefits shall be attributed from the beginning of that **credited service period**.[16]
b. An equal amount of the expected postretirement benefit obligation shall be attributed to each year of service in the attribution pe-

---

[14]For example, a retiree's spouse also may be covered by the spouse's present (or former) employer's health care plan. In that case, the spouse's employer (or former employer) may provide primary or secondary postretirement health care benefits to the retiree's spouse or dependents.

[15]For example, for a plan that provides benefit coverage to employees who render 30 or more years of service or who render at least 10 years of service and attain age 55 while in service, without specifying when the credited service period begins, the expected postretirement benefit obligation is attributed to service from the date of hire to the earlier of the date at which a plan participant has rendered 30 years of service or has rendered 10 years of service and attained age 55 while in service.

[16]For example, for a plan that provides benefit coverage to employees who render at least 20 years of service after age 35, the expected postretirement benefit obligation is attributed to a plan participant's first 20 years of service after attaining age 35 or after the date of hire, if later than age 35.

riod[17] (a benefit/years-of-service approach)[18] *unless the plan's benefit formula specifies the benefits earned for specific periods of service,*[19] in which case benefits shall be attributed in accordance with the plan's benefit formula.[20]

35. Some plans may have benefit formulas that define benefits in terms of specific periods of service to be rendered in exchange for those benefits but attribute all or a disproportionate share of the expected postretirement benefit obligation to employees' later years of service.[21] For those plans, the expected postretirement benefit obligation shall be attributed to employee service as described in paragraph 36. A plan benefit formula is considered to attribute all or a

---

[17]For example, for a plan that provides health care benefits of up to $800 per year in incurred claims for life to employees whose attained age plus years of service equals at least 80 when they retire, an equal amount of the expected postretirement benefit obligation is attributed to each year of service from the date of hire to the date at which a plan participant's age plus years of service equals 80. For an active plan participant who is expected to have rendered 20 years of service upon attaining age 60, the amount of the benefit attributed to each of the first 20 years of that plan participant's service is $40 multiplied by the number of years of life expectancy after retirement (assuming that the plan participant is expected to receive the maximum benefit of $800 in each of those years); the service cost attributable to each of those years of service is the actuarial present value of that benefit. Stated another way, because this plan does not specify different benefits for different years of service, each year prior to the plan participant's full eligibility date, one twentieth of the expected postretirement benefit obligation for that plan participant is recognized as service cost.

[18]Except as noted in footnote 19, that method is the same as the projected unit credit or unit credit with service prorate actuarial cost method for pay-related plans. For non-pay related plans, it is the same as the unit credit actuarial cost method.

[19]Some plans have benefit formulas that define different benefits for different years of service. For example, a step-rate plan might provide a benefit of 1 percent of final pay for each year of service up to 20 years and 1.5 percent of final pay for years of service in excess of 20. Another plan benefit formula might define the benefit as 1 percent of final pay for each year of service but limit the total annual benefit to no more than 20 percent of final pay. For plans that define different benefits for different years of service, the attribution called for by this Statement will not assign the same amount of benefits to each year of service and is not the same as the actuarial cost methods identified in footnote 18.

[20]For example, for a plan that provides 50 percent benefit coverage to employees who render 20 years of service and 3 percent benefit coverage for each year of service thereafter, the actuarial present value of the cost of providing 2.5 percent benefit coverage is attributed to service in years 1–20, and the actuarial present value of the cost of providing 3 percent benefit coverage is attributed to each year of service thereafter.

[21]For example, a plan with a benefit formula that defines no benefits for the first 19 years of service after age 35 and benefits of $10,000 for the 20th year of service after age 35 is substantively the same as a plan with a benefit formula that defines benefits of $500 for each of the first 20 years of service after age 35, with employees only eligible for the benefits upon completion of the 20th year of service after age 35.

disproportionate share of the expected postretirement benefit obligation to later years of service if (a) a disproportionate share of the expected postretirement benefit obligation is attributed to later years of service in the credited service period or (b) an employee is fully eligible for benefits upon completion of the credited service period and the years of service in the credited service period are nominal relative to the total years of service prior to the full eligibility date.

36. For plans with a benefit formula that attributes all or a disproportionate share of benefits to employees' later years of service, the expected postretirement benefit obligation shall be attributed as follows:

a. For plans with a benefit formula that attributes all or a disproportionate share of the benefits to employees' later years of service in the credited service period, an equal amount of a plan participant's expected postretirement benefit obligation shall be attributed to each year of that plan participant's service in the credited service period.[22]
b. For plans with a benefit formula that attributes the benefits to a credited service period that is nominal in relation to employees' total years of service prior to their full eligibility date, an equal amount of a plan participant's expected postretirement benefit obligation shall be attributed to each year of that plan participant's service prior to full eligibility for benefits.[23]
c. For plans with a benefit formula (1) that attributes all or a disproportionate share of the benefits to later years of service in the credited service period and (2) that defines a credited service period that is nominal in relation to employees' total years of service prior to their full eligibility date, an equal amount of a plan par-

---

[22]For example, a plan that attributes 1 percent benefit coverage to each of the first 19 years of service after age 35 and 61 percent benefit coverage to service in the 20th year of service after age 35 attributes a disproportionate share of the benefit to later years of service in the credited service period (service after age 35). For plan participants expected to render at least 20 years of service after age 35 under that plan, the service cost recognized each year during their credited service period is an equal portion (1/20) of the expected postretirement benefit obligation.

[23]For example, a plan with a benefit formula that defines 100 percent benefit coverage for service in the year employees attain age 60 has a 1-year credited service period. If plan participants are expected to have rendered an average of 20 years of service at age 60, the credited service period is nominal in relation to their total years of service prior to their full eligibility date. In that case, the service cost recognized each year of a plan participant's service to age 60 is an equal portion of the expected postretirement benefit obligation.

ticipant's expected postretirement benefit obligation shall be attributed to each year of that plan participant's service prior to full eligibility for benefits.[24]

37. In some situations a history of regular increases in benefits and other evidence may indicate that an employer has a present commitment to make future improvements to the plan and that the plan will provide benefits attributable to prior service that are greater than the benefits defined by the written terms of the plan. In those situations the commitment shall be the basis for the accounting, and the existence and nature of the commitment to make future amendments shall be disclosed.

Recognition of Net Periodic Postretirement Benefit Cost

38. As with other forms of deferred compensation, the cost of providing postretirement benefits shall be attributed to the periods of employee service rendered in exchange for those future benefits pursuant to the terms of the plan. That cost notionally represents the change in the **unfunded accumulated postretirement benefit obligation** for the period, ignoring employer contributions to the plan, plan settlements, and payments made by the employer directly to retirees. However, changes in that unfunded obligation arising from experience gains and losses and the effects of changes in assumptions may be recognized on a delayed basis. In addition, the effects of a plan initiation or amendment are generally recognized on a delayed basis.

39. The following components shall be included in the net postretirement benefit cost recognized for a period by an employer sponsoring a defined benefit postretirement plan:

a. Service cost
b. Interest cost

---

[24]For example, a plan with a benefit formula that defines 5 percent benefit coverage for service in years 20–24 and 80 percent coverage for service in year 25 attributes a disproportionate share of benefits to later years of service in the credited service period (service in years 20–25), and the credited service period is nominal in relation to employees' total years of service prior to their full eligibility date. For a plan participant expected to render 25 or more years of service, the service cost recognized in each of that plan participant's first 25 years of service is an equal portion (1/25) of the expected postretirement benefit obligation.

c. Actual return on plan assets, if any

d. Amortization of unrecognized prior service cost, if any

e. Gain or loss (including the effects of change in assumptions) to the extent recognized (paragraphs 52–54)

f. Amortization of the unrecognized obligation or asset existing at the date of initial application of this Statement (hereinafter referred to as the **unamortized transition obligation**[25] or **unamortized transition asset**). (Refer to paragraphs 105 and 106.)

Service Cost

40. The service cost component recognized in a period shall be determined as the actuarial present value of the expected postretirement benefit obligation attributed to employee service during that period. The measurement of the service cost component requires use of assumptions and an attribution method, which are discussed in paragraphs 21–37 of this Statement.

Interest Cost

41. The interest cost component recognized in a period shall be determined as the increase in the accumulated postretirement benefit obligation to recognize the effects of the passage of time. Measuring the accumulated postretirement benefit obligation as a present value requires accrual of an interest cost at rates equal to the assumed discount rates.

Actual Return on Plan Assets

42. For a funded plan, the actual return on plan assets shall be determined based on the **fair value** of plan assets (refer to paragraphs

---

[25]The term *unamortized* is used rather than *unrecognized* because in recognizing an additional liability pursuant to paragraph 56, the amount recognized as an intangible asset may at least partially represent a previously unrecognized transition obligation. However, for purposes of (a) recognition of the effects of a negative plan amendment pursuant to paragraph 48; (b) the constraint on immediate recognition of a net gain or loss pursuant to paragraph 53; (c) settlement accounting pursuant to paragraphs 87 and 88; (d) **plan curtailment** accounting pursuant to paragraphs 92–94; and (e) the constraint on delayed recognition of the unrecognized transition obligation pursuant to paragraph 106, the amount of the transition obligation or asset referred to is the amount that has not been recognized in the income statement (as opposed to the amount that has not been recognized in the statement of financial position). The term *unamortized* has been used to distinguish that unrecognized amount.

61 and 62) at the beginning and end of the period, adjusted for contributions and benefit payments. If the plan is a taxable entity, the actual return on plan assets shall reflect the tax expense or benefit for the period determined in accordance with Statement 96. If the return on plan assets is taxable to the employer, no provision for taxes shall be included in the actual return on plan assets.

Prior Service Cost

43. Plan amendments (including initiation of a plan) may include provisions that attribute the increase or reduction in benefits to employee service rendered in prior periods (**retroactive benefits**).[26] Similarly, plan amendments may include provisions that attribute the increase or reduction in benefits only to employee service to be rendered in future periods (**prospective benefits**).[27] In other cases, plan amendments may not specify how the increase or reduction in benefits is attributed to employee service periods. In the absence of plan provisions defining the specific period of service to which the plan amendment applies, the plan amendment shall be viewed as retroactive.[28] That is, for purposes of measuring the accumulated postretirement benefit obligation, the effect of the plan amendment on a plan participant's expected postretirement benefit obligation shall be attributed to each year of service in that plan participant's attribution period, including years of service already rendered by that plan participant, in accordance with the attribution discussed in paragraphs 34–36.

44. Plan amendments are granted with the exception that the employer will realize economic benefits in future periods. Consequently, this Statement does not require the cost of providing retroactive benefits (that is, prior service cost) to be included in net periodic postretirement benefit cost entirely in the year of the amendment. Rather, paragraph 45 of this Statement provides for recognition of prior service cost arising from benefit increases during the remaining years

---

[26]For example, if a plan amendment increases the benefits of **fully eligible plan participants**, the additional benefits are implicitly retroactive (attributable to employee service rendered in prior periods).

[27]For example, if a plan amendment increases benefits by $25 annually for each year of service rendered after the date the plan is amended, any additional benefits are earned prospectively (attributable only to employee service rendered in future periods).

[28]For example, if a plan amendment increases benefit coverage provided to all plan participants who render at least 20 years of service, the plan amendment is viewed as retroactive.

172

of service prior to full eligibility for benefits of those plan participants active at the date of the plan amendment. (Refer to paragraph 48 for plan amendments that reduce benefits.)

45. The cost of retroactive benefit improvements (including improved benefits that are granted to fully eligible plan participants) is the increase in the accumulated postretirement benefit obligation as a result of the plan amendment, measured at the date of the amendment. Except as specified in the next sentence and in paragraphs 46 and 47, that prior service cost shall be amortized by assigning an equal amount to each remaining year of service to full eligibility for benefits of each plan participant active at the date of the amendment (who was not yet fully eligible for benefits at that date). If all or almost all of a plan's participants are fully eligible for benefits, the cost of retroactive plan amendments shall be amortized based on the remaining life expectancy of those plan participants rather than on the remaining years of service prior to full eligibility of the **active plan participants**.

46. To reduce the complexity and detail of the computations required, consistent use of an alternative amortization approach that more rapidly reduces the unrecognized cost of retroactive amendments is permitted. For example, a straight-line amortization of the cost over the average remaining years of service to full eligibility for benefits of the active plan participants is acceptable.

47. In some situations, a history of regular plan amendments and other evidence may indicate that the period during which the employer expects to realize economic benefits from an amendment granting increased benefits retroactively is shorter than the remaining years of service to full eligibility for benefits of the active plan participants. Identification of those situations requires an assessment of the individual circumstances and the substance of the particular plan situation. In those circumstances, the amortization of prior service cost shall be accelerated to reflect the more rapid expiration of the employer's economic benefits and to recognize the cost in the periods benefited.

48. A plan amendment can reduce, rather than increase, the accumulated postretirement benefit obligation. A reduction in that obligation shall be used first to reduce any existing unrecognized prior service cost, then any remaining unamortized transition obligation.

The excess, if any, shall be amortized on the same basis as specified in paragraph 45 for prior service cost. Immediate recognition of the excess is not permitted.

Gains and Losses

49. Gains and losses are changes in the amount of either the accumulated postretirement benefit obligation or plan assets resulting from experience different from that assumed or from changes in assumptions. This Statement does not distinguish between those sources of gains and losses. Gains and losses include amounts that have been realized, for example, by the sale of a security, as well as amounts that are unrealized. Because gains and losses may reflect refinements in estimates as well as real changes in economic values and because some gains in one period may be offset by losses in another or vice versa, this Statement does not require recognition of gains and losses as components of net postretirement benefit cost in the period in which they arise. (Gain and loss recognition in accounting for settlements and curtailments is addressed in paragraphs 85–94).

50. The expected return on plan assets shall be determined based on the expected long-term rate of return on plan assets (refer to paragraph 25) and the market-related value of plan assets. The market-related value of plan assets shall be either fair value or a calculated value that recognizes changes in fair value in a systematic and rational manner over not more than five years. Different methods of calculating market-related value may be used for different classes of assets (for example, an employer might use fair value for bonds and a five-year-moving-average value for equities), but the manner of determining market-related value shall be applied consistently from year to year for each class of plan assets.

51. Plan asset gains and losses are differences between the actual return on plan assets during a period and the expected return on plan assets for that period. Plan asset gains and losses include both (a) changes reflected in the market-related value of plan assets and (b) changes not yet reflected in the market-related value of plan assets (that is, the difference between the fair value and the market-related value of plan assets). Plan asset gains and losses not yet reflected in market-related value are not required to be amortized under paragraphs 52 and 53.

52. As a minimum, amortization of an **unrecognized net gain or loss** (excluding plan asset gains and losses not yet reflected in market-related value) shall be included as a component of net postretirement benefit cost for a year if, as of the beginning of the year, that unrecognized net gain or loss exceeds 10 percent of the greater of the accumulated postretirement benefit obligation or the market-related value of plan assets. If amortization is required, the minimum amortization[29] shall be that excess divided by the average remaining service period of active plan participants. If all or almost all of a plan's participants are inactive, the average remaining life expectancy of the inactive participants shall be used instead of the average remaining service period.

53. Any systematic method of amortization of unrecognized gains and losses may be used in place of the minimum amortization specified in paragraph 52 provided that (a) the minimum is used in any period in which the minimum amortization is greater (reduces the unrecognized amount by more), (b) the method is applied consistently, (c) the method is applied similarly to both gains and losses, and (d) the method used is disclosed. If an enterprise uses a method of consistently recognizing gains and losses immediately, any gain that does not offset a loss previously recognized in income pursuant to this paragraph shall first offset any unamortized transition obligation; any loss that does not offset a gain previously recognized in income pursuant to this paragraph shall first offset any unamortized transition asset.

54. The gain or loss component of net periodic postretirement benefit cost shall consist of (a) the difference between the actual return on plan assets and the expected return on plan assets and (b) the amortization of the unrecognized net gain or loss from previous periods.

Recognition of Liabilities and Assets

55. This Statement requires that an employer's statement of financial position report a liability for postretirement benefits that is the greater of (a) the **accrued postretirement benefit cost** or (b) the accumulated postretirement benefit obligation for fully eligible plan participants

---

[29]The amortization must always reduce the beginning-of-the-year balance. Amortization of an unrecognized net gain results in a decrease in net periodic postretirement benefit cost; amortization of an unrecognized net loss results in an increase in net periodic postretirement benefit cost.

in excess of the fair value of the plan assets (minimum liability).[30] That requirement is intended to limit the extent to which the delayed recognition of any transition obligation, prior service cost, and losses can result in omission of a liability for those participants' benefits from an employer's statement of financial position.

56. If an employer's measure of the accumulated postretirement benefit obligation for plan participants fully eligible for benefits exceeds the fair value of the plan assets, an additional liability may be required to be recognized. The amount of that additional liability is determined as follows:

a. If an employer has recognized net periodic postretirement benefit cost in excess of amounts the employer has contributed to the plan[31] (accrued postretirement benefit cost), an additional liability shall be recognized equal to the amount, if any, by which the employer's minimum liability *exceeds* that accrued postretirement benefit cost.

b. If an employer has recognized an asset for amounts contributed to the plan in excess of net periodic postretirement benefit cost (**prepaid postretirement benefit cost**),[32] an additional liability shall be recognized equal to the employer's minimum liability for that plan *plus* the amount of prepaid postretirement benefit cost.

c. If an employer has not recognized either accrued or prepaid postretirement benefit cost, an additional liability shall be recognized equal to the employer's minimum liability for that plan.

57. The offset to any additional liability recognized pursuant to paragraph 56 shall be recognized as an intangible asset, provided that the asset recognized shall not exceed the amount of any unrecognized prior service cost.[33] If the additional liability required to be recog-

---

[30]Measurement of the minimum liability to be recognized pursuant to this Statement differs from that required to be recognized by Statement 87 because the unfunded accumulated benefit obligation is defined differently (refer to footnote 8) and because the Statement 87 minimum liability includes the unfunded accumulated benefit obligation for all active plan participants, not just those plan participants who have attained full eligibility for benefits.

[31]Benefit payments made directly by the employer to or on behalf of participants in an unfunded plan are considered to be amounts contributed to the plan.

[32]Refer to paragraph 106 regarding limitations on recognition of prepaid postretirement benefit cost.

[33]For purposes of this paragraph, any unamortized transition obligation (paragraph 105) shall be treated as unrecognized prior service cost.

nized exceeds unrecognized prior service cost, the excess (which would represent a net loss not yet recognized as net periodic postretirement benefit cost) shall be reported as a separate component (that is, a reduction) of equity, with that component of equity reported net of any tax benefits that result from considering such a loss as a temporary difference for purposes of applying the provisions of Statement 96. The additonal liability is unaffected by those tax considerations.

58. Each year-end (refer to paragraph 63) an employer shall determine the amount of additional liability to be recognized pursuant to paragraph 56. Any previously recognized additonal liability and offsetting intangible asset and component of equity shall be adjusted as necessary to recognize the amount of any additional liability currently required to be recognized pursuant to paragraphs 56 and 57.

Measurement of Plan Assets

59. Plan assets are assets—usually stocks, bonds, and other investments (except certain insurance contracts as noted in paragraph 75)—that have been segregated and restricted (usually in a trust) to be used for postretirement benefits. The amount of plan assets includes amounts contributed by the employer (and by plan participants for a **contributory plan**) and amounts earned from investing the contributions, less benefits, taxes, and other expenses incurred. Plan assets ordinarily cannot be withdrawn by the employer except under certain circumstances when a plan has assets in excess of obligations and the employer has taken certain steps to satisfy existing obligations. Securities of the employer held by the plan are includable in plan assets provided they are transferable.

60. Assets not segregated in a trust, or otherwise effectively restricted, so that they cannot be used by the employer for other purposes are not plan assets for purposes of this Statement, even though the employer may intend that those assets be used to provide postretirement benefits. Those assets shall be accounted for in the same manner as other employer assets of a similar nature and with similar restrictions. Amounts accrued by the employer but not yet paid to the plan are not plan assets for purposes of this Statement.

61. For purposes of measuring the minimum liability required by paragraph 56 and for purposes of the disclosures required by paragraph 66, plan investments, whether equity or debt securities, real

estate, or other, shall be measured at their fair value as of the measurement date. The fair value of an investment is the amount that the plan could reasonably expect to receive for it in a current sale between a willing buyer and a willing seller, that is, other than in a forced or liquidation sale. Fair value shall be measured by the market price if an active market exists for the investment. If no active market exists for an investment but an active market exists for similar investments, selling prices in that market may be helpful in estimating fair value. If a market price is not available, a forecast of expected cash flows may aid in estimating fair value, provided the expected cash flows are discounted at a current rate commensurate with the risk involved.[34] (Refer to paragraph 75.)

62. Plan assets used in plan operations (for example, buildings, equipment, furniture and fixtures, and leasehold improvements) shall be measured at cost less accumulated depreciation or amortization for all purposes.

Measurement Date

63. The measurements of plan assets and obligations required by this Statement shall be as of the date of the financial statements or, if used consistently from year to year, as of a date not more than three months prior to that date. Even though the postretirement benefit measurements are required as of a particular date, all procedures are not required to be performed after that date. As with other financial statement items requiring estimates, much of the information can be prepared as of an earlier date and projected forward to account for subsequent events (for example, employee service).

64. The additional liability reported in interim financial statements ordinarily will be based on the additional liability (paragraph 56) recognized in the previous year-end statement of financial position to reflect the minimum liability, adjusted for subsequent accruals and contributions.[35] However, if measures of both the obligation and

---

[34]For an indication of factors to be considered in determining the discount rate, refer to paragraphs 13 and 14 of APB Opinion No. 21, *Interest on Receivables and Payables*. If significant, the fair value of an investment shall reflect the brokerage commissions and other costs normally incurred in a sale.

[35]This determination of the reported additional liability applies to the first interim period of the first fiscal year for which paragraph 56 is effective even though no such liability was "recognized" in the previous year-end financial statements.

the plan assets are available as of a more current date or a significant event occurs, such as a plan amendment, settlement, or curtailment, that ordinarily would result in new measurements, those more recent measurements shall be used.

65. Measurements of net periodic postretirement benefit cost for both interim and annual financial statements shall be based on the assumptions at the beginning of the year (assumptions used for the previous year-end measurements) unless more recent measurements of both plan assets and the accumulated postretirement benefit obligation are available or a significant event occurs, such as those noted in paragraph 64, that ordinarily would call for remeasurement of net periodic postretirement benefit cost from the date of the event to the year-end measurement date.

Disclosures

66. This Statement requires disclosures about an employer's obligation to provide postretirement benefits and the cost of providing those benefits that are intended to enhance the usefulness of the financial statements to investors, creditors, and other users of financial information. An employer sponsoring one or more defined benefit postretirement plans (refer to paragraph 70) shall disclose separately, if applicable, the following for those plans that provide primarily postretirement health care benefits and those plans that provide primarily other postretirement welfare benefits:

a. A description of the plan(s) including employee groups covered, types of benefits provided, benefit formula, **funding policy**, types of assets held and significant nonbenefit liabilities, and the nature and effect of significant matters affecting the comparability of information for all periods presented
b. The amount of net periodic postretirement benefit cost for the period showing separately the service cost component, the interest cost component, the actual return on plan assets for the period, amortization of the unamortized transition obligation or transition asset, and the net total of other components[36]

---

[36]The net total of other components is the net effect during the period of certain delayed recognition provisions of this Statement. That net total includes:

a. The net asset gain or loss during the period deferred for later recognition (in effect, an offset or a supplement to the actual return on plan assets)
b. Amortization of the net gain or loss from earlier periods
c. Amortization of unrecognized prior service cost.

c. A schedule reconciling the funded status of the plan(s) with amounts reported in the employer's statement of financial position, showing separately:

(1) The fair value of plan assets
(2) The accumulated postretirement benefit obligation
(3) The amount of unrecognized prior service cost
(4) The amount of unrecognized net gain or loss (including plan asset gains and losses not yet reflected in market-related value)
(5) The amount of any remaining unamortized transition obligation or transition asset
(6) The amount of any additional liability recognized pursuant to paragraph 56
(7) The amount of net postretirement benefit asset or liability recognized in the statement of financial position, which is the net result of combining the preceding six items

d. The vested postretirement benefit obligation
e. The weighted-average assumed discount rate, rate of compensation increase, and health care cost trend rate used to measure the accumulated postretirement benefit obligation and the weighted-average expected long-term rate of return on plan assets and, for taxable plans, the estimated income tax rate included in that rate of return
f. The effect of a one-percentage-point increase (or decrease) in the weighted-average assumed health care cost trend rate on the net periodic postretirement health care benefit cost and the accumulated postretirement benefit obligation for postretirement health care benefits
g. The amounts and types of securities of the employer and related parties included in plan assets, and the approximate amount of future annual benefits of plan participants covered by **insurance contracts** issued by the employer and related parties
h. Any alternative amortization method used pursuant to paragraphs 46 and 53 and the existence and nature of any commitment as discussed in paragraph 37
i. The amount of gain or loss recognized during the period for a settlement or curtailment and a description of the nature of the event(s) (Refer to paragraphs 85–94.)
j. The cost of providing special or contractual **termination benefits** recognized during the period and a description of the nature of the event(s). (Refer to paragraphs 96 and 97.)

Employers with Two or More Plans

67. Postretirement benefits offered by an employer may vary in nature and may be provided to different groups of employees. As discussed in paragraph 68, in some cases an employer may aggregate data from unfunded plans for measurement purposes in lieu of performing separate measurements for each unfunded plan (including plans whose designated assets are not appropriately segregated and restricted and thus have no plan assets as that term is used in this Statement).

68. The data from all unfunded postretirement health care plans may be aggregated for measurement purposes if (a) those plans provide different benefits to the same group of employees or (b) those plans provide the same benefits to different groups of employees. Data from other unfunded postretirement welfare benefit plans may be aggregated for measurement purposes in similar circumstances. However, a plan that has plan assets (as defined herein) shall not be aggregated with other plans but shall be measured separately.

69. Net periodic postretirement benefit cost, liabilities, and assets shall be determined for each separately measured plan or aggregation of plans by applying the provisions of this Statement to each such plan or aggregation of plans. In particular, unless an employer clearly has a right to use the assets of one plan to pay benefits of another, a liability required to be recognized pursuant to paragraph 56 for one plan shall not be reduced or eliminated because another plan has assets in excess of its accumulated postretirement benefit obligation or because the employer has prepaid postretirement benefit cost related to another plan.

70. Except as noted in paragraph 66 and below, disclosures required by this Statement may be aggregated for all of an employer's single-employer defined benefit plans, or plans may be disaggregated in groups to provide more useful information. For purposes of the disclosures required by paragraph 66(c), plans with plan assets in excess of the accumulated postretirement benefit obligation shall not be aggregated with plans that have accumulated postretirement benefit obligations that exceed plan assets. Disclosures for plans outside the United States shall not be combined with those for plans in the United States unless those plans use similar economic assumptions.

181

Insurance Contracts

71. For purposes of this Statement, an insurance contract is defined as a contract in which an insurance company unconditionally undertakes a legal obligation to provide specified benefits to specific individuals in return for a fixed consideration or premium. The insurance contract must be irrevocable and must transfer significant risk from the employer to the insurance company.

72. Some insurance contracts (**participating insurance contracts**) provide that the purchaser (either the plan or the employer) may participate in the experience of the insurance company. Under those contracts, the insurance company ordinarily pays dividends to the purchaser, the effect of which is to reduce the cost of the plan. If the participating insurance contract[37] causes the employer to remain subject to all or most of the risks and rewards associated with the benefit obligation covered or the assets transferred to the insurance company, that contract is not an insurance contract for purposes of this statement, and the purchase of that contract does not constitute a settlement pursuant to paragraphs 85–90.

73. The purchase price of a participating insurance contract ordinarily is higher than the price of an equivalent contract without a **participation right**. The difference is the cost of the participation right. The cost of the participation right shall be recognized at the date of purchase as an asset. In subsequent periods, the participation right shall be measured at its fair value if the contract is such that fair value is reasonably estimable. Otherwise the participation right shall be measured at its amortized cost (not in excess of its net realizable value), and the cost shall be amortized systematically over the expected dividend period under the contract.

74. To the extent that **nonparticipating insurance contracts**[38] are purchased during the period to cover postretirement benefits attributed

---

[37]If the insurance company is controlled by the employer or if there is any reasonable doubt that the insurance company will meet its obligations under the contract, the purchase of the contract does not constitute a settlement for purposes of paragraphs 85–90 of this Statement.

[38]If the insurance company providing the contract does business primarily with the employer and related parties (a **captive insurer**) or if there is any reasonable doubt that the insurance company will meet its obligations under the contract, the contract is not an insurance contract for purposes of paragraphs 74 and 75 of this Statement.

to service in the current period (such as life insurance benefits), the cost of those benefits shall be the cost of purchasing the coverage under the contracts. If all the postretirement benefits attributed to service in the current period are covered by nonparticipating insurance contracts purchased during that period, the cost of the contracts determines the service cost component of net postretirement benefit cost for that period. Benefits attributed to current service in excess of benefits provided by nonparticipating insurance contracts purchased during the current period shall be accounted for according to the provisions of this Statement applicable to plans not involving insurance contracts.

75. Benefits covered by insurance contracts shall be excluded from the accumulated postretirement benefit obligation. Insurance contracts shall be excluded from plan assets. Other contracts with insurance companies shall be accounted for as investments and measured at fair value. For some contracts, the best available evidence of fair value may be contract value. If a contract has a determinable cash surrender value or conversion value, that is presumed to be its fair value.

Multiemployer Plans

76. For purposes of this Statement, a **multiemployer plan** is a post-retirement benefit plan to which two or more unrelated employers contribute, usually pursuant to one or more collective-bargaining agreements. A characteristic of multiemployer plans is that assets contributed by one participating employer may be used to provide benefits to employees of other participating employers since assets contributed by an employer are not segregated in a separate account or restricted to provide benefits only to employees of that employer. A multiemployer plan usually is administered by a board of trustees composed of management and labor representatives and may also be referred to as a "joint trust" or "union plan." Generally, many employers participate in a multiemployer plan, and an employer may participate in more than one plan. The employers participating in multiemployer plans usually have a common industry bond, but for some plans the employers are in different industries, and the labor union may be their only common bond. Some multiemployer plans do not involve a union. For example, local chapters of a not-for-profit organization may participate in a plan established by the related national organization.

77. An employer participating in a multiemployer plan shall recognize as net postretirement benefit cost the required contribution for the period and shall recognize as a liability any contributions due and unpaid.

78. An employer that participates in one or more multiemployer plans shall disclose the following separately from disclosures for a single-employer plan:

a. A description of the multiemployer plan(s) including the employee groups covered, the type of benefits provided (defined benefit or defined contribution), and the nature and effects of significant matters affecting comparability of information for all periods presented
b. The amount of cost recognized during the period.

79. In some situations, withdrawal from a multiemployer plan may result in an employer's having an obligation to the plan for a portion of its unfunded accumulated postretirement benefit obligation. If withdrawal under circumstances that would give rise to an obligation is either probable or reasonably possible, the provisions of FASB Statement No. 5, *Accounting for Contingencies*, shall apply.

Multiple-Employer Plans

80. Some postretirement benefit plans to which two or more unrelated employers contribute are not multiemployer plans. Rather, those **multiple-employer plans** are in substance aggregations of single-employer plans, combined to allow participating employers to pool plan assets for investment purposes and to reduce the costs of plan administration. Those plans ordinarily do not involve collective-bargaining agreements. They also may have features that allow participating employers to have different benefit formulas, with the employer's contributions to the plan based on the benefit formula selected by the employer. Those plans shall be considered single-employer plans rather than multiemployer plans for purposes of this Statement, and each employer's accounting shall be based on its respective interest in the plan.

Non-U.S. Postretirement Benefit Plans

81. Except for its effective date (paragraph 103), this Statement includes no special provisions applicable to postretirement benefit ar-

rangements outside the United States. To the extent those arrangements are in substance similar to postretirement benefit plans in the United States, they are subject to the provisions of this Statement for purposes of preparing financial statements in accordance with accounting principles generally accepted in the United States. The substance of an arrangement is determined by the nature of the obligation and by the terms or conditions that define the amount of benefits to be paid, not by whether (or how) a plan is funded, whether benefits are payable at intervals or as a single amount, or whether the benefits are required by law or custom or are provided under a plan the employer has elected to sponsor.

Business Combinations

82. When an employer is acquired in a business combination that is accounted for by the purchase method under Opinion 16 and that employer sponsors a single-employer defined benefit postretirement plan, the assignment of the purchase price to individual assets acquired and liabilities assumed shall include a liability for the accumulated postretirement benefit obligation in excess of the fair value of the plan assets or an asset for the fair value of the plan assets in excess of the accumulated postretirement benefit obligation. The accumulated postretirement benefit obligation assumed shall be measured based on the benefits attributed by the acquired entity to employee service prior to the date the business combination is consummated, adjusted to reflect any changes in assumptions based on the purchaser's assessment of relevant future events (as discussed in paragraphs 23–33). If it is expected that the plan will be terminated or curtailed, the effects of those actions shall be considered in measuring the accumulated postretirement benefit obligation. Otherwise, no future changes to the plan shall be anticipated.

83. As a result of applying the provisions of paragraph 82, any previously existing unrecognized net gain or loss, unrecognized prior service cost, or unamortized transition obligation or transition asset is eliminated for the acquired employer's plan. Subsequently, to the extent that the net obligation assumed or net assets acquired are considered in determining the amounts of contributions to the plan, differences between the purchaser's net postretirement benefit cost and amounts it contributes will reduce the liability or asset recognized at the date of the combination.

Amendment to Opinion 16

84. The following footnote is added to the end of the last sentence of paragraph 88 of Opinion 16:

> *Paragraphs 82 and 83 of FASB Statement No. XXX, *Employers' Accounting for Postretirement Benefits Other Than Pensions* (this Statement), specify how the general guidelines of this paragraph shall be applied to assets and liabilities related to postretirement benefit plans.

Accounting for Settlement of a Postretirement Benefit Obligation

85. For purpose of this Statement, a settlement is defined as a transaction that (a) is an irrevocable action, (b) relieves the employer (or the plan) of primary responsibility for a postretirement benefit obligation, and (c) eliminates significant risk related to the obligation and the assets used to effect the settlement. Examples of transactions that constitute a settlement include making lump-sum cash payments to plan participants in exchange for their rights to receive specified postretirement benefits and purchasing long-term nonparticipating insurance contracts for the accumulated postretirement benefit obligation for some or all of the plan participants.

86. A transaction that does not meet the three criteria of paragraph 85 does not constitute a settlement for purposes of this Statement. For example, investing in a portfolio of high-quality fixed-income securities with principal and interest payment dates similar to the estimated payment dates of benefits may avoid or minimize certain risks. However, that investment decision does not constitute a settlement because that decision can be reversed and investing in that portfolio does not relieve the employer (or the plan) of primary responsibility for a postretirement benefit obligation nor does it eliminate significant risks related to that obligation.

87. For purposes of this Statement, the maximum gain or loss subject to recognition in earnings when a postretirement benefit obligation is settled is the unrecognized net gain or loss defined in paragraphs 49-53 plus any remaining unamortized transition asset.[39] That max-

---

[39]As discussed in paragraph 106, in measuring the gain or loss subject to recognition in earnings when a postretirement benefit obligation is settled, it shall first be determined whether recognition of an additional amount of any unamortized transition obligation is required.

imum gain or loss includes any gain or loss resulting from remeasurements of plan assets and the accumulated postretirement benefit obligation at the time of settlement.

88. If the entire accumulated postretirement benefit obligation is settled and the maximum amount subject to recognition is a gain, the settlement gain shall first reduce any remaining unamortized transition obligation; any excess gain shall be recognized in earnings. If the entire accumulated postretirement benefit obligation is settled and the maximum amount subject to recognition is a loss, the maximum settlement loss shall be recognized in earnings. If only part of the accumulated postretirement benefit obligation is settled, the employer shall recognize, in a similar manner, a pro rata portion of the maximum settlement gain or loss equal to the percentage reduction in the accumulated postretirement benefit obligation.

89. If the purchase of a participating insurance contract constitutes a settlement (refer to paragraph 72), the maximum gain (but not the maximum loss) shall be reduced by the cost of the participation right before determining the amount to be recognized in earnings.

90. If the cost of all settlements[40] in a year is less than or equal to the sum of the service cost and interest cost components of net periodic postretirement benefit cost for the plan for the year, gain or loss recognition is permitted but not required for those settlements. However, the accounting policy adopted shall be applied consistently from year to year.

Accounting for a Plan Curtailment

91. For purposes of this Statement, a curtailment is an event that significantly reduces the expected years of future service of active plan participants or eliminates the accrual of defined benefits for some or all of the future services of a significant number of active plan participants. Curtailments include:

---

[40]For the following types of settlements, the cost of the settlement is:

a. For a cash settlement, the amount of cash paid to plan participants
b. For a settlement using nonparticipating insurance contracts, the cost of the contracts
c. For a settlement using participating insurance contracts, the cost of the contracts less the amount attributed to participation rights. (Refer to paragraph 72.)

a. Termination of employees' services earlier than expected, which may or may not involve closing a facility or discontinuing a segment of a business
b. Termination or suspension of a plan so that employees do not earn additional benefits for future service. In the latter situation, future service may be counted toward eligibility for benefits accumulated based on past service.

92. The unrecognized prior service cost associated with the future years of service that are no longer expected to be rendered as the result of a curtailment is a loss. For purposes of measuring the effect of a curtailment, unrecognized prior service cost includes the cost of retroactive plan amendments and any remaining unamortized transition obligation. For example, a curtailment may result from the termination of a significant number of employees who were plan participants at the date of a prior plan amendment.[41] The loss associated with that curtailment is (a) the portion of the remaining unrecognized prior service cost related to that (and any prior) plan amendment that is attributable to the remaining years of service in the attribution period that had been expected to be rendered by those employees who were terminated and (b) the portion of the remaining unamortized transition obligation that is attributable to the remaining expected future years of service of the terminated employees who were plan participants at the date of transition.

93. The accumulated postretirement benefit obligation may be decreased (a gain) or increased (a loss) by a curtailment.[42]

a. To the extent that gain exceeds any unrecognized net loss (or the entire gain, if an unrecognized net gain exists), it is a curtailment gain.
b. To the extent that loss exceeds any unrecognized net gain (or the entire loss, if an unrecognized net loss exists), it is a curtailment loss.

---

[41]A curtailment also may result from terminating the accrual of additional benefits for the future services of a significant number of employees. The loss in that situation is (a) the portion of the remaining unrecognized prior service cost attributable to the remaining years of service in the attribution period of those employees who were plan participants at the date of the plan amendment and whose future accrual of benefits has been terminated and (b) the portion of the remaining unamortized transition obligation that is attributable to those same employees.

[42]Increases in the accumulated postretirement benefit obligation that reflect termination benefits are excluded from the scope of this paragraph. (Refer to paragraphs 96 and 97.)

For purposes of applying the provisions of this paragraph, any remaining unamortized transition asset shall be treated as an unrecognized net gain and shall be combined with unrecognized net gain or loss arising subsequent to transition to this Statement.

94. If the sum of the effects identified in paragraphs 92 and 93 is a net loss, it shall be recognized in earnings when it is probable that a curtailment will occur and the net effect is reasonably estimable. If the sum of those effects is a net gain, it shall be recognized in earnings when the related employees terminate or the plan suspension or amendment is adopted.

Relationship of Settlements and Curtailments to Other Events

95. A settlement and a curtailment may occur separately or together. If benefits expected to be paid in future periods are eliminated for some plan participants (for example, because a significant portion of the work force is dismissed or a plant is closed) but the plan remains in existence and continues to pay benefits, to invest assets, and to receive contributions, a curtailment has occurred but not a settlement. If an employer purchases nonparticipating insurance contracts for the accumulated postretirement benefit obligation and continues to provide defined benefits for future service, either in the same plan or in a successor plan, a settlement has occurred but not a curtailment. If a **plan termination** occurs (that is, the obligation is settled and the plan ceases to exist) and the plan is not replaced by a successor defined benefit plan, both a settlement and a curtailment have occurred (whether or not the employees continue to work for the employer).

Measurement of the Effects of Termination Benefits

96. Postretirement benefits offered as special or contractual termination benefits shall be recognized in accordance with paragraph 15 of Statement 88. That is, an employer that offers special termination benefits to employees shall recognize a liability and a loss when the employees accept the offer and the amount can be reasonably estimated. An employer that provides contractual termination benefits shall recognize a liability and a loss when it is probable that employees will be entitled to benefits and the amount can be reasonably estimated. A situation involving special or contractual termination benefits may also result in a curtailment to be accounted for under paragraphs 91–94 of this Statement.

97. The liability and loss recognized for employees who accept an offer of special termination benefits to be provided by a postretirement benefit plan shall be the difference between (a) the accumulated postretirement benefit obligation for those employees assuming that those employees (active plan participants) not yet fully eligible for benefits would terminate at their full eligibility date and that fully eligible plan participants would retire immediately, without considering any special termination benefits, and (b) the accumulated postretirement benefit obligation as measured in (a) adjusted to reflect the special termination benefits.

Disposal of a Segment

98. If the gain or loss measured in accordance with paragraphs 87–89, 92–94, or 96 and 97 is directly related to disposal of a segment of a business or a portion of a line of business, it shall be included in determining the gain or loss associated with that event. The net gain or loss attributable to the disposal shall be recognized pursuant to the requirements of APB Opinion No. 30, *Reporting the Results of Operations—Reporting the Effects of Disposal of a Segment of a Business, and Extraordinary, Unusual and Infrequently Occurring Events and Transactions.*

Defined Contribution Plans

99. For purposes of this Statement, a **defined contribution postretirement plan** is a plan that provides postretirement benefits in return for services rendered, provides an individual account for each plan participant, and has terms that specify how contributions to the individual's account are to be determined rather than the amount of postretirement benefits the individual is to receive. Under a defined contribution plan, the postretirement benefits a plan participant will receive are limited to the amount contributed to the plan participant's account, the returns earned on investments of those contributions, and forfeitures of other plan participants' benefits that may be allocated to the plan participant's account.

100. To the extent a plan's defined contributions to an individual's account are to be made for periods in which that individual renders services, the net postretirement benefit cost for a period shall be the contribution called for in that period. If a plan calls for contributions for periods after an individual retires or terminates, the estimated cost shall be accrued during the employee's service period.

101. An employer that sponsors one or more defined contribution plans shall disclose the following separately from its defined benefit plan disclosures:

a. A description of the plan(s) including employee groups covered, the basis for determining contributions, and the nature and effect of significant matters affecting comparability of information for all periods presented
b. The amount of cost recognized during the period.

102. A postretirement benefit plan having characteristics of both a defined benefit plan and a defined contribution plan requires careful analysis. If the *substance* of the plan is to provide a defined benefit, as may be the case with some "target benefit" plans, the accounting and disclosure requirements shall be determined in accordance with the provisions of this Statement applicable to a defined benefit plan.

Effective Dates and Transition

103. Except as noted in the following sentences of this paragraph and in paragraph 108, this Statement shall be effective for fiscal years beginning after December 15, 1991. For plans outside the United States and for defined benefit plans of employers that (a) are **nonpublic enterprises** *and* (b) sponsor no defined benefit postretirement plan with more than 100 plan participants, this Statement shall be effective for fiscal years beginning after December 15, 1993. For all plans, the provisions of paragraphs 56 and 57 shall be effective for fiscal years beginning after December 15, 1996. In all cases, earlier application is encouraged. Restatement of previously issued annual financial statements is not permitted. If a decision is made in other than the first interim period of an employer's fiscal year to apply this Statement early, previous interim periods of that year shall be restated.

104. If at the transition date an employer has excluded assets in a **postretirement benefit fund** from its statement of financial position and some or all of the assets in that fund do not qualify as plan assets as defined herein, the employer shall recognize in the statement of financial position the fair value of those nonqualifying assets as the employer's assets (not prepaid postretirement benefit cost) and an equal amount as an accrued postretirement benefit obligation pursuant to the transition to this Statement and before applying para-

graph 105. Thereafter, those assets shall be accounted for in accordance with generally accepted accounting principles applicable to those types of assets, including their presentation in the employer's statement of financial position based on any restrictions on their use. The fair value of those assets at the transition date shall be used as their cost.

105. For a defined benefit plan, an employer shall determine as of the measurement date (paragraph 63) for the beginning of the fiscal year in which this Statement is first applied (the transition date), the amounts of (a) the accumulated postretirement benefit obligation and (b) the fair value of plan assets plus any recognized accrued postretirement benefit cost or less any recognized prepaid postretirement benefit cost. Except as required by paragraph 106, the difference between those two amounts, whether it represents an unrecognized transition obligation or an unrecognized transition asset, shall be amortized on a straight-line basis over the average remaining service period of active plan participants, except that (1) if the average remaining service period is less than 15 years, the employer may elect to use a 15-year period, and (2) if all or almost all of the plan participants are inactive, the employer shall use the average remaining life expectancy period of those plan participants. Any unrecognized transition obligation related to a defined contribution plan shall be amortized in the same manner.

106. Amortization of the transition obligation shall be more rapid than otherwise required by paragraph 105 in the following situations:

a. Cumulative benefit payments subsequent to the transition date to fully eligible plan participants at the transition date exceed the sum of (1) the cumulative amortization of the entire transition obligation and (2) the cumulative interest on the **unpaid transition obligation**.
b. Cumulative benefit payments subsequent to the transition date to all plan participants exceed the cumulative accrued postretirement benefit cost recognized subsequent to the transition date (including amounts required to be recognized pursuant to subparagraph (a) above).

An additional amount of the unamortized transition obligation shall be recognized equal to the excess cumulative benefit payments in one or both of those situations. For purposes of applying this paragraph,

192

cumulative benefit payments shall be reduced by any plan assets or any recognized accrued postretirement benefit obligation at the transition date. Payments made pursuant to a settlement, as discussed in paragraphs 85–89, shall be included in the determination of cumulative benefit payments made subsequent to the transition date.

107. If at the measurement date for the beginning of an employer's fiscal year it is expected that additional recognition of any remaining unamortized transition obligation will be required pursuant to paragraph 106, amortization of the transition obligation for interim reporting purposes shall be based on the amount expected to be amortized for the year, except for the effects of applying paragraph 106 for any settlement required to be accounted for pursuant to paragraphs 85–89. Those effects shall be recognized when the related settlement is recognized. The effects of changes during the year in the initial assessment of whether additional recognition of the unamoritized transition obligation will be required for the year shall be recognized over the remainder of the year. The amount of the unamortized transition obligation to be recognized for a year shall be finally determined at the measurement date for the end of the year based on the constraints on delayed recognition discussed in paragraph 106; any difference between the amortization of the transition obligation recognized during interim periods and the amount required to be recognized for the year shall be recognized immediately.

Rescission of Technical Bulletin 87-1

108. Effective with the issuance of this Statement, FASB Technical Bulletin No. 87-1, *Accounting for a Change in Method of Accounting for Certain Postretirement Benefits,* is rescinded. If a change in method of accounting for postretirement benefits is adopted subsequent to the issuance of this Statement, the new method shall comply with the provisions of this Statement.

**The provisions of this Statement need
not be applied to immaterial items.**

Glossary

476. This appendix contains definitions of certain terms used in accounting for postretirement benefits.

Accrued postretirement benefit cost

Cumulative net postretirement benefit cost accrued in excess of the employer's cumulative contribution or, in the case of an unfunded plan, of cumulative benefits paid by the employer.

Accumulated postretirement benefit obligation

The actuarial present value of benefits attributed to employee service rendered to a specific date. Prior to an employee's full eligibility date, the accumulated postretirement benefit obligation as of a specified date for an employee is the portion of the expected postretirement benefit obligation attributed to that employee's service rendered to that date; on and after the full eligibility date, the accumulated and expected postretirement benefit obligations for an employee are the same.

Active plan participant

Any active employee who has rendered service during the credited service period and is expected to receive benefits, including benefits to or for any beneficiaries and covered dependents, under the postretirement benefit plan. Also refer to **Plan participant**.

Actual return on plan assets (component of net periodic postretirement benefit cost)

The change in the fair value of the plan's assets for a period including the decrease due to expenses incurred during the period (such as income tax expense incurred by the plan, if applicable), adjusted for contributions and benefit payments during the period.

Actuarial present value

The value, as of a specified date, of an amount or series of amounts payable or receivable thereafter, with each amount adjusted to reflect (a) the time value of money (through discounts for interest) and (b) the probability of payment (for example, by means of decrements for events such as death, disability, withdrawal, or retirement) between the specified date and the expected date of payment.

Amortization

Usually refers to the process of reducing a recognized liability systematically by recognizing revenues or of reducing a recognized asset systematically by recognizing expenses or costs. In accounting for postretirement benefits, amortization is also used to refer to the systematic recognition in net periodic postretirement benefit cost over several periods of previously *unrecognized* amounts, including unrecognized prior service cost, unrecognized net gain or loss, and any unamortized transition obligation or asset.

Assumed per capita claims cost by age

The future per capita cost of providing postretirement health care benefits, after the measurement date, at each age from the earliest ages at which plan participants could begin to receive benefits under the plan through their remaining life expectancy or the covered period, if shorter. To determine the assumed per capita claims cost by age, the per capita claims cost by age based on historical claims costs is adjusted for assumed health care cost trend rates and the effects of coverage by Medicare and other providers of health care benefits. The resulting assumed per capita claims cost by age reflects expected future costs and is applied with the plan demographics to determine the amount and timing of future benefits. Also refer to **Per capita claims cost by age**.

Assumptions

Estimates of the occurrence of future events affecting postretirement benefit cost, such as turnover, retirement age, mortality, dependency status, per capita claims costs by age, health care cost trend rates, levels of Medicare and other health care providers' reimbursements, and discount rates to reflect the time value of money.

Attribution

The process of assigning postretirement benefits or cost to periods of employee service.

Attribution period

The period of an employee's service to which the expected postretirement benefit obligation for that employee is assigned. The beginning of the attribution period is the employee's date of hire unless the plan's benefit formula grants credit only for service from a later date, in which case the beginning of the attribution period is generally the beginning of that credited service period.

195

The end of the attribution period is the full eligibility date. Within the attribution period, an equal amount of the expected postretirement benefit obligation is attributed to each year of service unless the plan's benefit formula specifies the benefits earned for specific periods of service. In that case, benefits are attributed in accordance with the plan's benefit formula.

Benefit formula

The basis for determining benefits to which participants may be entitled under a postretirement benefit plan. A plan's benefit formula specifies the years of service to be rendered, age to be attained while in service, or a combination of both that must be met for an employee to be eligible to receive benefits under the plan. A plan's benefit formula may also define the beginning of the credited service period and the benefits earned for specific periods of service.

Benefits

The benefits or benefit coverage to which participants may be entitled under a postretirement benefit plan, including health care benefits, life insurance not provided through a pension plan, and legal, educational, and advisory services.

Captive insurer

An insurance company that does business primarily with related entities.

Contributory plan

A plan under which employees contribute part of the cost. In some contributory plans, employees wishing to be covered must contribute; in other contributory plans, employee contributions result in increased benefits.

Credited service period

Employee service period for which benefits are earned pursuant to the terms of the plan. The beginning of the credited service period may be the date of hire or a later date. For example, a plan may provide benefits only for service rendered after a specified age. Service beyond the end of the credited service period does not earn any additional benefits under the plan. Also refer to **Attribution period**.

196

Curtailment
Refer to **Plan curtailment**.

Defined benefit postretirement plan
A plan that defines postretirement benefits in terms of monetary amounts (for example, $100,000 of life insurance) or benefit coverage (for example, up to $200 per day for hospitalization, 80 percent of the cost of specified surgical procedures, and so forth) to be provided. Any postretirement benefit plan that is not a defined contribution postretirement plan is, for purposes of this Statement, a defined benefit postretirement plan.

Defined contribution postretirement plan
A plan that provides postretirement benefits in return for services rendered, provides an individual account for each plan participant, and specifies how contributions to the individual's account are to be determined rather than specifies the amount of benefits the individual is to receive. Under a defined contribution postretirement plan, the benefits a plan participant will receive depend solely on the amount contributed to the plan participant's account, the returns earned on investments of those contributions, and the forfeitures of other plan participants' benefits that may be allocated to that plan participant's account.

Demographics
The characteristics of the plan population including geographical distribution, age, sex, and marital status.

Dependency status
The status of a current or former employee having dependents (for example, a spouse or other relatives) who are expected to receive benefits under a postretirement benefit plan that provides dependent coverage.

Discount rates
The interest rates inherent in the amount at which the postretirement benefit obligation could be effectively settled (that is, the interest rates that determine the single amount that, together with returns on that amount equal to the discount rates, would provide the cash flow necessary to provide the benefits, assuming no future experience gains or losses). Discount rates are used to reflect the time value of money. Also refer to **Actuarial present value**.

197

Expected long-term rate of return on plan assets

An assumption about the rate of return on plan assets reflecting the average rate of earnings expected on existing plan assets and contributions to the plan expected to be made during the period.

Expected postretirement benefit obligation

The actuarial present value as of a date of the benefits expected to be paid to or for an employee, the employee's beneficiaries, and any covered dependents pursuant to the terms of the postretirement benefit plan. The expected postretirement benefit obligation for an employee is measured using assumptions about the employee's expected retirement date and the employee's future compensation (if the benefit formula is based on future compensation levels).

Expected return on plan assets

An amount calculated as a basis for determining the extent of delayed recognition of the effects of changes in the fair value of plan assets. The expected return on plan assets is determined based on the expected long-term rate of return on plan assets and the market-related value of plan assets.

Explicit (approach to) assumptions

An approach under which each significant assumption used reflects the best estimate of the plan's future experience solely with respect to that assumption.

Fair value

The amount that a plan could reasonably expect to receive for an investment in a current sale between a willing buyer and a willing seller, that is, other than in a forced or liquidation sale.

Full eligibility (for benefits)

The status of an employee having rendered all the service necessary to have earned the right to receive all of the benefits that are expected to be received by that employee (including any beneficiaries and covered dependents) under a postretirement benefit plan upon the occurrence of a specified event or as the need for those benefits arises during the retirement period. Full eligibility for benefits is earned by meeting specified age, service, or age and service requirements of the postretirement benefit plan.

Full eligibility date

The date at which an employee attains full eligibility for the benefits that employee is expected to earn under the terms of a postretirement benefit plan. Determination of the full eligibility date is not affected by measurement assumptions such as when benefit payments commence, dependency status, salary progression, and so forth.

Fully eligible plan participants

Collectively, that group of former employees (including retirees) and active employees who have rendered service to or beyond their full eligibility date and who are expected to receive benefits under the plan, including benefits to their beneficiaries and covered dependents.

Funding policy

The program regarding the amounts and timing of contributions by the employer(s), plan participants, and any other sources to provide the benefits a postretirement benefit plan specifies.

Gain or loss

A change in the value of either the accumulated postretirement benefit obligation or the plan assets resulting from experience different from that assumed or from a change in an actuarial assumption. Also refer to **Unrecognized net gain or loss.**

Gain or loss component (of net periodic postretirement benefit cost)

The sum of (a) the difference between the actual return on plan assets and the expected return on plan assets and (b) the amortization of the unrecognized net gain or loss from previous periods. The gain or loss component is the net effect of delayed recognition of gains and losses (the net change in the unrecognized net gain or loss) except that it does not include changes in the accumulated postretirement benefit obligation occurring during the period and deferred for later recognition.

Health care cost trend rates

An assumption about the rates of annual changes in the per capita claims cost of benefits currently provided by the postretirement benefit plan due to factors other than changes in the composition of the plan population by age and dependency status. The health care cost trend rates consider estimates of health care inflation, changes in health care utilization or delivery patterns, technological advances, and changes in the health status of the plan participants. Differing types of services, such as hospital care and dental care, may have different trend rates.

Insurance contract

A contract in which an insurance company unconditionally undertakes a legal obligation to provide specified benefits to specific individuals in return for a fixed consideration or premium. An insurance contract is irrevocable and involves the transfer of significant risk from the employer (or the plan) to the insurance company.

Interest cost (component of net periodic postretirement benefit cost)

The accrual of interest on the accumulated postretirement benefit obligation due to the passage of time.

Market-related value of plan assets

A balance used to calculate the expected return on plan assets. Market-related value can be either fair value or a calculated value that recognizes changes in fair value in a systematic and rational manner over not more than five years. Different methods of calculating market-related value may be used for different classes of plan assets, but the manner of determining market-related value shall be applied consistently from year to year for each class of plan asset.

Measurement date

The date of the financial statements or, if used consistently from year to year, a date not more than three months prior to that date, as of which plan assets and obligations are measured.

Medicare reimbursement rates

The health care cost reimbursements expected to be received by retirees through Medicare as mandated by enacted legislation. Medicare reimbursement rates vary by the type of benefits provided.

Minimum liability

The accumulated postretirement benefit obligation for retirees and other fully eligible plan participants in excess of the fair value of plan assets.

Multiemployer plan

A postretirement benefit plan to which two or more unrelated employers contribute, usually pursuant to one or more collective-bargaining agreements. A characteristic of multiemployer plans is that assets contributed by one participating employer may be used to provide benefits to employees of other participating employers since assets contributed by an employer are not segregated in a separate account or restricted to provide benefits only to employees of that employer. A multiemployer plan is usually administered by a board of trustees composed of management and labor representatives and may also be referred to as a "joint trust" or "union plan." Generally, many employers participate in a multiemployer plan and an employer may participate in more than one plan. The employers participating in multiemployer plans usually have a common industry bond, but for some plans the employers are in different industries and the labor union may be their only common bond.

Multiple-employer plan

A postretirement benefit plan maintained by more than one employer but not treated as a multiemployer plan. Multiple-employer plans are generally not collectively bargained and are intended to allow participating employers, commonly in the same industry, to pool their plan assets for investment purposes and to reduce the cost of plan administration. A multiple-employer plan maintains separate accounts for each employer so that contributions provide benefits only for employees of the contributing employer. Multiple-employer plans may have features that allow participating employers to have different benefit formulas, with the employer's contributions to the plan based on the benefit formula selected by the employer.

Net periodic postretirement benefit cost

The amount recognized in an employer's financial statements as the cost of a postretirement benefit plan for a period. Components of net periodic postretirement benefit cost include service cost, interest cost, actual return on plan assets, gain or loss, amortization of unrecognized prior service cost, and amortization of the unrecognized transition obligation or asset.

Nonparticipating insurance contract
An insurance contract that does not provide for the purchaser to participate in the investment performance or in other experience of the insurance company.

Non-pay-related plan
A plan that has a benefit formula that does not base benefits or benefit coverage on compensation.

Nonpublic enterprise
An enterprise other than one (a) whose debt or equity securities are traded in a public market, either on a stock exchange or in the over-the-counter market (including securities quoted only locally or regionally), or (b) whose financial statements are filed with a regulatory agency in preparation for the sale of any class of securities.

Participating insurance contract
An insurance contract that provides for the purchaser to participate in the investment performance and possibly other experience (for example, morbidity experience) of the insurance company.

Participation right
A purchaser's right under a participating contract to receive future dividends or retroactive rate credits from the insurance company.

Pay-related plan
A plan that has a benefit formula that bases benefits or benefit coverage on compensation, such as a final-pay or career-average-pay plan.

Per capita claims cost by age
The amount required to be paid to provide postretirement health care benefits for one year at each age from the youngest age to the oldest age at which plan participants are expected to receive benefits under the plan.

Plan
An arrangement whereby an employer undertakes to provide its employees with benefits during their retirement period in ex-

change for their services over a specified period of time, upon attaining a specified age while in service, or a combination of both. A plan may be written or it may be implied from a well-defined, although perhaps unwritten, practice of paying postretirement benefits.

Plan amendment

A change in the terms of an existing plan. A plan amendment may increase or decrease benefits, including those attributed to years of service already rendered. Also refer to **Retroactive benefits.**

Plan assets

Assets—usually stocks, bonds, and other investments—that have been segregated and restricted (usually in a trust) to provide for postretirement benefits. The amount of plan assets includes amounts contributed by the employer (and by employees for a contributory plan) and amounts earned from investing the contributions, less benefits, income taxes, and other expenses incurred. Plan assets ordinarily cannot be withdrawn by the employer except under certain circumstances when a plan has assets in excess of obligations and the employer has taken certain steps to satisfy existing obligations. Assets not segregated in a trust or otherwise effectively restricted so that they cannot be used by the employer for other purposes are not plan assets even though it may be intended that those assets be used to provide postretirement benefits. Amounts accrued by the employer as net periodic postretirement benefit cost but not yet paid to the plan are not plan assets. Securities of the employer held by the plan are includable in plan assets provided they are transferable. If a plan has liabilities other than for benefits, those nonbenefit obligations are considered as reductions of plan assets.

Plan curtailment

An event that significantly reduces the expected years of future service of active plan participants or eliminates the accrual of defined benefits for some or all of the future services of a significant number of active plan participants.

Plan participant

Any employee or former employee who has rendered service in the credited service period and is expected to receive benefits under the postretirement benefit plan, including benefits to or for any beneficiaries and covered dependents. Also refer to **Active plan participant.**

Plan termination
An event in which the postretirement benefit plan ceases to exist and all benefits are settled by the purchase of insurance contracts or by other means. The plan may or may not be replaced by another plan. A plan termination with a replacement plan may or may not be in substance a plan termination for accounting purposes.

Postretirement benefit fund
Assets accumulated in the hands of a funding agency for the sole purpose of paying postretirement benefits when the claims are incurred or benefits are due. Those assets may or may not qualify as plan assets. Also refer to **Plan assets.**

Postretirement benefit plan
Refer to **Plan.**

Postretirement benefits
All forms of benefits, other than retirement income, provided by an employer to retirees. Those benefits may be defined in terms of specified benefits, such as health care, tuition assistance, or legal services, that are provided to retirees as the need for those benefits arises, such as certain health care benefits, or they may be defined in terms of monetary amounts that become payable on the occurrence of a specified event, such as life insurance benefits.

Postretirement benefits other than pensions
Refer to **Postretirement benefits.**

Postretirement health care benefits
A form of postretirement benefit provided by an employer to retirees for defined health care services or coverage of defined health care costs, such as hospital and medical coverage, dental benefits, and eye care.

Prepaid postretirement benefit cost
Cumulative employer contributions in excess of cumulative accrued net periodic postretirement benefit cost.

Prior service cost

The cost of retroactive benefits granted in a plan amendment (or initiation). Also refer to **Unrecognized prior service cost.**

Prospective benefits

Benefits granted in a plan amendment (or initiation) specifically in exchange for employees' future service only. That is, only future service of the employee counts towards eligibility for the benefits. The cost of those benefits is included in the service cost component of net periodic postretirement benefit cost during the periods that that future service is rendered.

Retirees

Collectively, that group of plan participants that includes retired employees, their beneficiaries, and covered dependents.

Retroactive benefits

Benefits granted in a plan amendment (or initiation) that are attributed to prior years of service by the plan benefit formula. In the absence of a benefit formula that defines the specific years of service to be rendered in exchange for the benefits, they are the benefits that are allocated based on the provisions of this Statement to employee services rendered in periods prior to the plan amendment (or initiation). The cost of the retroactive benefits is referred to as prior service cost. Also refer to **Plan amendment.**

Service cost (component of net periodic postretirement benefit cost)

The portion of the expected postretirement benefit obligation attributed to employee service during a period.

Settlement

An irrevocable action that relieves the employer (or the plan) of primary responsibility for a postretirement benefit obligation and eliminates significant risks related to the obligation and the assets used to effect the settlement. Examples of transactions that constitute a settlement include (a) making lump-sum cash payments to plan participants in exchange for their rights to receive specified postretirement benefits and (b) purchasing nonparticipating insurance contracts for the accumulated postretirement benefit obligation for some or all of the plan participants.

Single-employer plan
A postretirement benefit plan that is maintained by one employer. The term also may be used to describe a plan that is maintained by related parties such as a parent and its subsidiaries.

Termination benefits
Benefits provided by an employer to employees in connection with their termination of employment. They may be either special termination benefits offered only for a short period of time or contractual benefits required by the terms of a plan only if a specified event, such as a plant closing, occurs.

Transition asset
The unrecognized amount, as of the date this Statement is initially applied, of (a) the fair value of plan assets plus any recognized accrued postretirement benefit cost or less any recognized prepaid postretirement benefit cost in excess of (b) the accumulated postretirement benefit obligation.

Transition obligation
The unrecognized amount, as of the date this Statement is initially applied, of (a) the accumulated postretirement benefit obligation in excess of (b) the fair value of plan assets plus any recognized accrued postretirement benefit cost or less any recognized prepaid postretirement benefit cost.

Unamortized transition asset
The portion of the transition asset that has not been recognized as a part of net periodic postretirement benefit cost, as an offset to certain losses, or as a part of accounting for the effects of a settlement or a curtailment.

Unamortized transition obligation
The portion of the transition obligation that has not been recognized as a part of net periodic postretirement benefit cost, as an offset to certain gains, or as a part of accounting for the effects of a settlement or a curtailment.

Unfunded accumulated postretirement benefit obligation
The accumulated postretirement benefit obligation in excess of the fair value of plan assets.

Unpaid transition obligation

The transition obligation (a) reduced for subsequent benefit payments to plan participants who were fully eligible for benefits at the date of transition and (b) increased for subsequent interest at the discount rates used at the date of transition. The unpaid transition obligation is used in determining the constraint on delayed recognition of the transition obligation pursuant to paragraph 106(a)

Unrecognized net gain or loss

The cumulative net gain or loss that has not been recognized as a part of net periodic postretirement benefit cost or as a part of the accounting for the effects of a settlement or a curtailment. Also refer to **Gain or loss.**

Unrecognized prior service cost

The portion of prior service cost that has not been recognized as a part of net periodic postretirement benefit cost, as a reduction of the effects of a negative plan amendment, or as a part of the accounting for the effects of a curtailment.

Vested postretirement benefit obligation

The actuarial present value as of a date of the benefits expected to be paid to or for retirees, former employees, and active employees assuming they terminated immediately, including benefits expected to be paid to or for beneficiaries and any covered dependents of those plan participants.

Appendix C. Forum Participants

Moderator

Robert D. Paul
Vice Chairman
Martin E. Segal Company

Authors and Speakers

Deborah J. Chollet
Senior Research Associate
Employee Benefit Research
  Institute

Joseph Duva
Corporate Director, Employee
  Benefits
Allied-Signal, Inc.

Alain C. Enthoven
Professor of Public and Private
  Management and Health Care
  Economics
Stanford University

Kevin P. Flatley
Vice President, Employee Benefits
American Express Company

Gary Hendricks
Chief Economist, Director of
  Office of Research and
  Economic Analysis
Pension and Welfare Benefits
  Administration
U.S. Department of Labor

Charles Kahn
Minority Health Counsel
Committee on Ways and Means
U.S. House of Representatives

Patrick Killeen
Assistant Director, Social Security
  Department
United Auto Workers Union

Burma Klein
Assistant Director, Pension Equity
  Group
U.S. General Accounting Office

Carl Marinacci
General Manager, Compensation
  and Benefits
AMOCO Corporation

David Mosso
Assistant Director of Research and
  Technical Activities
Financial Accounting Standards
  Board

Thomas Nelson
Associate Member
Milliman & Robertson, Inc.

K. Peter Schmidt
Partner
Arnold & Porter

Participants

Keith P. Ambachtsheer
President
Keith P. Ambachtsheer &
  Associates, Inc.

Wally Anderson
Group Insurance Manager
Southland Corporation

Gerald Anderson
Director of the Center for Hospital
  Finance and Management
Johns Hopkins University

Robert Ball
Consultant on Social Security,
  Health, and Welfare Policy

Nancy Barrand
Program Officer
Robert Wood Johnson Foundation

John Bauer
Actuary
Metropolitan Life Insurance
  Company

Nancy Bern
Second Vice President
John Hancock Mutual Life
  Insurance Company

Fred Betts
Vice President
Capital Guardian Trust

Tom Bierley
Associate Director
The Principal Financial Group

John Blodger
Vice President-Human Resources
American Newspaper Publishers
  Association

Diane Braunstein
Legislative Affairs Director
U.S. Social Security
  Administration

Craig Campbell
Associate Director, Benefit
  Planning
Southwestern Bell Corporation

Lou Ann Cash
Manager, Benefit Planning and
  Administration
American Express Travel Related
  Services Company, Inc.

Sharon Canner
Assistant Vice President
National Association of
  Manufacturers

William Cartwright
Chief of Demography and
  Economics
National Institute on Aging

David Certner
Legislative Representative
American Association of Retired
  Persons

Denice Collazo
Vice President
Citibank, N.A.

Joyce Cowan
Associate
Epstein, Becker & Green

Albert B. Crenshaw
Reporter
Washington Post

Royal Dellinger
Principal Deputy and Chief
  Negotiator
Pension Benefit Guaranty
  Corporation

James Dorsch
Washington Counsel
Health Insurance Association of
  America

Joanne Duarte
Vice President
American International Group

Lloyd Duxbury
Professional Staff Member
Special Committee on Aging
U.S. Senate

Matthew S. Easley
Associate Vice President
Department of Annuity and
  Pension Actuarial
Nationwide Insurance

Marion Ein-Lewin
Director of Health Policy
  Fellowship Programs
Institute of Medicine
National Academy of Sciences

Thomas Feeney
Project Manager, Employee
  Benefits
Quantum Chemical Corporation

Jason Feer
Assistant Editor
Thompson Publishing Group

Bob Feldman
Associate
Goldman, Sachs & Company

Steven Ferruggia
Consulting Actuary
Buck Consultants, Inc.

Mary Jane Fisher
Correspondent
National Underwriter

John Fleming
Administrative Director
Bakery and Confectionery Union
   and Industry International
   Health Benefits and Pension
   Funds

Joyce Frieden
Associate Editor
Health Business

Beth Fuchs
Analyst in Social Legislation
Congressional Research Service
Library of Congress

Harry Garber
Vice Chairman
The Equitable Life Assurance
   Society of the United States

Harper Garrett
Vice President, Director of
   Professional Services
The Alexander Consulting Group,
   Inc.

Ed Gilroy
Associate Director, Employee
   Benefits and Compensation
National Association of
   Manufacturers

Marian Gornick
Director, Division of Beneficiary
   Studies
Health Care Financing
   Administration
U.S. Department of Health and
   Human Services

Joseph Grant
Assistant Counsel
Subcommittee on Oversight
Committee on Ways and Means
U.S. House of Representatives

Jim Henderson
Executive Director, Human
   Resources Policy and Planning
Pacific Telesis Group

Jack Hoadley
Senior Research Associate
National Health Policy Forum

Kathleen Holness
District Manager
AT&T

Neil J. Horgan
Director, Compensation and
   Benefits
Sun Company, Inc.

Mac Howland
Manager, Benefit Accounting
Harvard University

Renee Hubbard
Consultant
A. Foster Higgins & Company, Inc.

Karen Ignagni
Associate Director, Department of
   Occupational Safety, Health,
   and Social Security
AFL-CIO

Lynn Jacobs
Assistant Vice President, Legal
   and Public Affairs
CIGNA

Paul Jackson
Vice President and Director
The Wyatt Company

Judy Miller Jones
Director of National Health
National Health Policy Forum

Michael Kahn
Retirement and Benefits Specialist
National Education Association

Jeanne Kardos
Director, Employee Benefits
Southern New England Telephone

Mark Laurent
Director, Product Development
Lincoln National Pension
   Insurance Company

211

C. William Lee
Director, Compensation and
  Benefits Division
E.I. du Pont de Nemours &
  Company, Inc.

Robert F. Leonard, Jr.
District Staff Manager, Benefits
  Planning
NYNEX Corporation

Arthur Lifson
Vice President
Equicor, Inc.

Brendan Lynch
Vice President
The Travelers Companies

Cynthia Maher
Evaluator
U.S. General Accounting Office

Michael J. Mahoney
Actuary and Principal
Milliman & Robertson, Inc.

Patricia Mansfield
Staff Assistant
Subcommittee on Labor-
  Management Relations,
Committee on Education and
  Labor
U.S. House of Representatives

Leslie Mardenborough
Director of Corporate Personnel
The New York Times Company

Frank B. McArdle
Consultant
Hewitt Associates

Thomas M. McMahon
Vice President, Administration
  and Finance
Pacific Maritime Association

R.G. Merrill
Executive Vice President
The Prudential Insurance
  Company of America

Gene Michael
Manager, Health Care Benefits
Mobil Oil Corporation

Curtis Mikkelsen
Vice President
Morgan Guaranty Trust Company
  of New York

Jim Moberge
Executive Vice President Human
  Resources
Pacific Telesis Group

Marilyn Moon
Director, Public Policy Institute
American Association of Retired
  Persons

Gina Mitchell
Senior Technical Associate
Financial Executives Institute

John Morgan
Assistant Vice President
Union Labor Life Insurance
  Company

Warren Moser
Vice President, Planning and
  Development
United Health Care, Inc.

John M. Naughton
Executive Vice President
Massachusetts Mutual Life
  Insurance Company

Ralph Nelson
Director of Compensation and
  Benefits
General Foods Corporation

Jeffrey Petertil
Principal
William M. Mercer-Meidinger-
  Hansen, Inc.

William Poole
Research and Development
  Analyst
National Rural Electric
  Cooperative Association

Pam Power
Senior Consultant
Peat Marwick Main & Co.

Eric Raps
Manager
Arthur Andersen & Co.

Michael J. Reynolds
President
Godwins, Inc.

Melvyn J. Rodrigues
Manager, Benefit Plans Research
  and Compliance
Atlantic Richfield Company

Richard Schultz
Vice President
Chemical Bank

Wendy Schick
Legislative Analyst
Association of Private Pension and
  Welfare Plans

Ray Schmitt
Specialist in Social Legislation
Congressional Research Service
Library of Congress

Nancy Simmons
Editor
BNA/Benefits Today
Bureau of National Affairs

Donald Snyder
Economist
U.S. General Accounting Office

Steve Snyder
Vice President, National Accounts
Vision Service Plan

Denise Spence
Senior Research Analyst
Brookings Institution

John E. Stettler
Director, Employee Benefits
  Investments
Georgia-Pacific Corporation

Charles Stunkard
Trust Officer
Mellon Bank, N.A.

Ed Tasca
Assignment Manager
U.S. General Accounting Office

Richard G. Tomlinson
Vice President
Upjohn Company

Al Turco
Legal Director
Aetna Life & Casualty

Kathleen Utgoff
Executive Director
Pension Benefit Guaranty
  Corporation

Susan Vucurevich
Manager, Health & Wellness
  Program
IBM Corporation

Craig Wainscott
Assistant Vice President and
  Senior Research Analyst
Frank Russell Company

Daniel Wartonick
Special Assistant for Policy
  Development
U.S. Social Security
  Administration

Craig Webb
Correspondent
McGraw Hill News

Chuck Weller
Attorney
Jones, Day, Reavis & Pogue

James White
Reporter
Wall Street Journal

Patricia Willis
Employee Benefit Plan Specialist
U.S. Department of Labor

Thomas Woodruff
Vice President
Mutual of America Life Insurance
  Company

Richard Wyman
Vice President
Howard Johnson & Company

Leah Young
Reporter
Journal of Commerce

214

Index

215

L.A. TIMES

Also by Stuart Woods
in Thorndike Large Print ®

Santa Fe Rules
Under the Lake

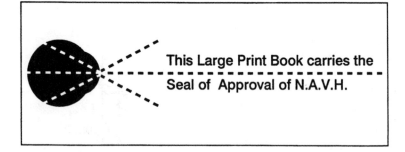

This Large Print Book carries the
Seal of Approval of N.A.V.H.

L.A. TIMES

STUART WOODS

Thorndike Press • Thorndike, Maine

Thorndike Large Print ® Cloak & Dagger Series edition published in 1993 by arrangement with HarperCollins Publishers.

The tree indicium is a trademark of Thorndike Press.

Set in 16 pt. News Plantin by Penny L. Picard.

This book is printed on acid-free, high opacity paper. ∞

Library of Congress Cataloging in Publication Data

Woods, Stuart.
   L.A. times / Stuart Woods.
     p. cm.
   ISBN 0-7862-0006-5 (alk. paper : lg. print)
   ISBN 0-7862-0007-3 (alk. paper : lg. print : pbk)
   1. Large type books. I. Title.
  [PS3573.O642L18 1993b]
  813′.54—dc20

93-5160
CIP

This book is for Steven and Barbara Bochco.

ACKNOWLEDGMENTS

I am grateful to my former editor, Ed Breslin, who is now writing his own novel, for his fine work in editing this book; to Gladys Justin Carr, my new editor, for working so hard for the book's success; to all the other people at HarperCollins for their help; to my agent, Mort Janklow, his principal associate, Anne Sibbald, and their colleagues at Janklow & Nesbit, who have been so important to my career over the past dozen years; and to Chris Connor, for helping me to understand Hollywood.

PROLOGUE

1975

Vincente Michaele Callabrese blinked in the midafternoon sunlight as he emerged from the darkness of the York Theater on the Upper West Side after the noon performance of *The Strange One*, a revival starring Ben Gazzara and George Peppard. He sprinted for the subway, and as he rode downtown toward his next movie he was still gripped by the performances of the two young actors who had been among the most promising of their generation.

Woody Allen's movie *Bananas* was next, at the Bleecker Street Cinema, and he would make a seven o'clock double feature of Orson Welles's *The Magnificent Ambersons* and *Othello*. He was short of his record of seven movies in sixteen hours, but that had been made possible by two three-screen houses next

7

door to each other on Third Avenue, so he'd only had to take one subway.

It was after midnight when Vinnie left the Eighth Street Playhouse and started home; each step he took toward Little Italy was taken with more foreboding. He had cut school again, and he was already a grade behind; his mother would be waiting up for him, and his father, if he were home . . . well, he didn't want to think about that.

Vinnie was fourteen and big for his age. He was already shaving every day, and girls three and four years older were taking him seriously. He didn't have a lot of time for girls, though — when he wasn't in school or at the movies, he was running errands for a loan shark in the neighborhood, which paid for his movie tickets. Since the age of six, when he had belatedly seen his first film, Vinnie Callabrese had been to the movies nearly two thousand times. His friend and benefactor, an older boy named Tommy Provensano, who was very smart, was always telling Vinnie that he should keep his moviegoing a secret, because nobody would take him seriously.

He had seen some favorite films four or five times, but *Othello* had been a new experience for Vinnie. He hadn't understood much of the dialogue, but he had been able to follow the story, and the dark drama had riveted him to his seat. He knew guys like Iago on his own block. He admired them; he learned from them.

Vinnie walked up the five flights, his heart pounding from more than the exertion. What if the old man were home? He inserted his key into the lock and turned it as silently as possible, then slipped into the four-room railroad flat. All was quiet; he sagged with relief as he stood still in the kitchen, letting his breathing return to normal. It would be easier if his mother didn't see him until morning, when her anger would have abated a little.

"Bastard!" a voice behind him said.

Vinnie spun around to find his father, Onofrio, sitting in a kitchen chair, leaning against the wall, a pint bottle of cheap whiskey in his hand. Onofrio didn't bother using a glass anymore.

"Bastard from hell!" his father said. "You were never mine; your mother laid down with the mailman, the butcher — somebody."

"Don't you talk about my mother that way," Vinnie said, his voice trembling.

Onofrio stood up and took a long swig from the bottle, then set it on the sink beside him. "You talk back to me?" He unbuckled his wide belt and slipped it from his trousers. "You want this, huh?"

9

"Don't you talk about my mother that way," Vinnie repeated.

"Your mother is a whore," Onofrio said, almost conversationally. "That's why you are the bastard." He flicked the belt out to its full length.

This time the buckle was not in his hand, but at the swinging end of the belt. This time would be bad, Vinnie thought.

Onofrio swung the buckle at his son. It made a whirring sound as it moved through the air.

Instinctively, Vinnie ducked, and the heavy buckle passed over his head.

"Stand still and take your beating, bastard!" Onofrio shouted.

There was a hammering on a door down the hall, and Vinnie heard his mother's voice faintly pleading with his father. "You beat her again, didn't you?" Vinnie asked.

"She gave me a bastard, didn't she? I beat her good this time."

Without thinking, Vinnie swung a fist at his father's head. The blow caught Onofrio solidly on the jaw, and he staggered back against the wall, dropping the belt.

Vinnie's father stared at him, his eyes wide with anger. "You would raise a hand to your father?"

Vinnie swallowed hard. "I would beat the shit out of my father," he said. Onofrio reached down for the belt, but Vinnie kicked it out of his reach, then straightened him up with an uppercut that would have laid out most men. His father was tough, though; he had been the neighborhood bully in his youth — Vinnie had heard this from his mother, when she had warned him never to resist a beating from his father.

"Now I kill you with my hands," Onofrio said, pushing off the wall and rushing at his son.

Vinnie was as tall as his father, but fifty pounds lighter. On his side he had quickness and, tonight, the fact that his father was drunk. He stepped aside and let Onofrio hit the opposite wall of the tiny kitchen, then stepped in and threw a hard left to the bigger man's right kidney. Onofrio sagged to his knees, groaning, and then Vinnie went to work, choosing his punches and his targets, feeling cartilage and bone break under his fists, hammering his father until the man could only lie on the floor defenseless while his son kicked him into unconsciousness.

Vinnie stopped only because he was tired. He wet a dishcloth and wiped the sweat from his face and neck, and when his breathing had slowed, he went down the hall to his parents' bedroom and unlocked the door. His mother fell into his arms, weeping.

11

★ ★ ★

Much later, after he had helped his mother get his bleeding father onto the living room couch, after she had bathed Onofrio's battered face, after sleep had finally come to his parents, Vinnie lay awake and relived the pleasure of what he had done to his father. It was fuller and more complete than any pleasure he would know until he was much more experienced sexually. He felt not the slightest guilt, because Vinnie never felt guilt about anything. He had learned in his short life that other people felt guilt; he understood the emotion, but he did not know it. Now he devoted himself to thinking about the worst possible thing he could do to his father, worse than the beating he had just given him. It did not take long for Vinnie's bright mind to alight on the brown bag.

Onofrio collected numbers money each evening from two dozen locations in Little Italy, then remitted it to Benedetto, a rising soldier in the Carlucci family, the following morning. Onofrio's life was his bond. If he did not take the money to Benedetto, he would die for his greed. Benedetto had a foul temper and a reputation for swift vengeance at any hint of disrespect.

Vinnie got slowly out of bed and tiptoed next door to his parents' bedroom. Silently, he opened the door and crossed the room to the bed, then dropped to his knees beside his sleeping mother. He felt under the bed for the bag, and its handle met his hand. As quietly as he could, he extracted the little satchel, then returned to his own room and switched on the light.

There was nearly three thousand dollars in the bag. Vinnie moved his bed out from the wall and removed the floorboard that covered his secret hiding place. He moved aside the *Playboy* magazines and the condoms and the hundred dollars he had saved and placed the money in the hole; then he replaced the floorboard and the nail that made it look permanently fixed.

He took the brown bag into the kitchen and dropped it out the window into the air shaft, where he knew it would be found; then he returned to his room and stretched out on the bed.

By this time tomorrow, he thought as he drifted off, Onofrio Callabrese would be at the bottom of Sheepshead Bay. Vinnie's sleep was not disturbed by the prospect.

CHAPTER

1

1989

Vinnie Callabrese stood on the southeast corner of Second Avenue and St. Mark's Place in New York City and watched the candy store across the street. The fat man was due any minute.

Vinnie felt neither guilt nor anxiety about what he was going to do. In fact, the only emotion he felt at that moment was impatience, because he could see the marquee of the St. Mark's Theater 80 in the next block, and he knew that *Touch of Evil* started in eight minutes. Vinnie didn't like to be late for a movie.

Vinnie's nose was Roman, his hair and beard thick and black, his eyes dark. He knew how to concentrate those eyes on another man and induce fear. Vinnie wasn't the heaviest muscle who worked for Benedetto, but he stood six-two and weighed a tightly packed one hundred and ninety pounds.

The fat man weighed more than three hundred pounds, but he was soft to the bone. Vinnie wasn't worried, except about the time.

With six minutes left before the movie, the fat man double-parked his Cadillac Sedan De Ville at the opposite corner, struggled out of the big car, and waddled into the candy store. Vinnie gave him long enough to reach his office, then crossed the street. The place was empty, except for the old man who made the egg creams and sold the cigarettes. Vinnie closed the door, worked the latch, and flipped the OPEN sign around. He looked at the old man and gave him a little smile. "You're closed," he said, "for five minutes."

The old man nodded resignedly and picked up the *Daily News*.

Vinnie strode past the magazine racks, his leather heels echoing off the cracked marble floor, and put his hand on the doorknob of the back room. He opened it very gently and peeked into the little office. The fat man sat, his gut resting on the battered desk. With one hand he was flipping quickly through a stack of small bills, and the fingers of his other hand flew over a calculator in a blur. Vinnie was momentarily transfixed. He had never seen anything quite like it; the fat man was

15

a virtuoso on the calculator.

The man looked up and stopped calculating. "Who the fuck are you?" he asked.

Vinnie stepped into the office and closed the door behind him. "I'm a friend of the guy who loaned you five thousand dollars nine weeks ago," he said. His accent was heavy — New York and Little Italy.

The fat man managed a sour grin. "And you've just come to make a polite call, huh?"

Vinnie shook his head slowly. "No. The polite guy was here last week, and the week before that, and the month before that."

"So you're the muscle, huh?" the fat man said, grinning more widely and leaning back in his chair. His right hand remained on the edge of the desk. It was a long reach over his gut, and it didn't look natural. "You ever heard of the law, guinea? You ever heard that what your friend does is against the law? That he has no legal claim on me, not even a piece of paper?"

"You gave my friend your word," Vinnie said slowly. "That was good enough for him. Now you've disappointed him." The fat man's fingers curled over the top of the desk drawer and yanked it open, but Vinnie moved faster. He caught the fat man by the wrist, then turned and drove an elbow into his face. The fat man grunted and made a gurgling sound but didn't let go of the desk drawer. Without a pause, Vinnie lifted a foot and kicked the drawer shut. A cracking sound was heard in the room.

The fat man screamed. He snatched his hand from Vinnie's grasp and held it close to his bleeding face. "You broke my fingers!" he whimpered. He wouldn't be doing any calculating for a while.

Vinnie bent over, grabbed a leg of the chair in which the fat man sat, and yanked. The fat man fell backwards into a quivering heap. Vinnie opened the desk drawer and found a short-barrelled .32 revolver. He lifted his shirttail and tucked it into his belt. "This is a dangerous weapon," he said. "You shouldn't have it; you'll end up hurting yourself." Vinnie reached for the stack of bills on the desk and started counting. The fat man watched with an expression of pain that had nothing to do with his bleeding face or his broken fingers. Vinnie stopped counting. "Five hundred," he said, sticking the wad into his pocket and returning a few ones to the desktop. "My friend will apply this to the interest on your loan. On Friday, he'll want all the back interest. A week from Friday, he'll want the five grand."

"I can't raise five thousand by then," the fat man whined.

"Sell the Cadillac," Vinnie suggested.

"I can't; it's got a loan on it."

"Maybe my friend will take the Cadillac in payment," Vinnie said. "I'll ask him. You could go on making the payments."

"Are you nuts? That car is new — it cost me thirty-five thousand."

"Just a suggestion," Vinnie said. "It would be cheaper just to come up with the five grand."

"I can't," the fat man whimpered. "I just can't do it."

"I'll tell my friend you promised," Vinnie said. He left the office and closed the door behind him.

Vinnie was in his seat, eating buttered popcorn, in time to raptly watch Orson Welles's incredibly long, one-take opening shot of Charlton Heston and Janet Leigh crossing the border into Mexico. He'd seen it at least a dozen times, and it never failed to amaze him. So much happening all at once, and yet the shot worked. He loved Welles; he loved the deep rumbling voice. Vinnie could do a very good impression of the Welles voice. He was a talented mimic.

CHAPTER

2

Vinnie's beeper went off as he left the movie
house. "Shit," he muttered under his breath.
"The sonofabitch couldn't wait until tomorrow." He glanced at his watch; he could still
make it if he hurried.

He grabbed a cab to Carmine Street in Little
Italy. "Wait for me," he said to the cabbie
as they pulled up in front of the La Boheme
Coffee House.

"C'mon, mister," the cabbie moaned, "it's
six bucks. I ain't got time to wait."

Vinnie fixed him with the gaze he used on
delinquent debtors. "Stay here," he said, then
got out of the cab without waiting for a reply.
He hurried into the coffeehouse, past old men
at tiny tables, and stopped at a table outside
the door of the back room. An enormous man
wearing a hat jammed on his head sat there,

his gross fingers gripping a tiny espresso cup.

"Hey, Cheech," Vinnie said.

"You din' ansa da beep," Cheech said.

"It was quicker just to come."

Cheech made a motion with his head. "He's in dere."

Vinnie waited for Cheech to press the button, then opened the door. Benedetto sat at a small desk, a calculator before him. Vinnie was reminded of the fat man. Both counted their money every day. Vinnie's old friend Thomas Provensano, now Benedetto's bagman and bookkeeper, sat at a table in a corner, working at a calculator. Tommy Pro winked at Vinnie.

"Vinnie," Benedetto said, not looking up from the tally sheet on the desk. Benedetto was in his late thirties, prematurely graying, a dapper dresser.

"Mr. B.," Vinnie said, "I talked to the fat man."

"Was he nice?"

Vinnie produced the five hundred in cash and placed it on the desk. "He was nice for five hundred after I broke his fingers."

Benedetto held up a hand. "Vinnie, you know it's not good for me to know those things."

Vinnie knew, but he also knew Benedetto loved hearing them. "Just between you and me, Mr. B., I told the fat man all the vig by Friday and the whole five grand in another week."

"Will he do it?"

"He's got a new Cadillac. I told him you'd take that, and he could keep making the payments."

Benedetto laughed. "I like that. You're a smart boy, Vinnie; you could go places, if you could ever stop going to the movies."

This was high praise as well as scorn from Benedetto, and Vinnie nodded gratefully. Benedetto was a capo in the Carlucci family, and rumor was he'd be the new don when the present don's appeals on a triple murder conviction were exhausted. Keeping Benedetto happy was Vinnie's constant worry. The man had the disposition of an unhappy rattlesnake, and there were corpses planted far and wide, men who had once displeased Mr. B., not the least of them Vinnie's father, Onofrio Callabrese.

Benedetto handed the money to Tommy Pro, who quickly counted it, entered the sum into the calculator, then put the money into the safe. Tommy extracted another envelope from the safe and handed it to Benedetto.

"Payday, kid," Benedetto said, handing the envelope to Vinnie.

Vinnie pocketed the envelope quickly.

"Thanks, Mr. B.," he said.

"Make sure the fat man keeps his new schedule," Benedetto said. "Come see me after you collect the vig. How's the rest of your list doing?"

Vinnie knew that Benedetto knew the status of every account; he just wanted to hear it aloud.

"Everybody's on schedule this week," Vinnie replied.

"That's what I like to hear," Benedetto replied. "Keep it up."

"Right, Mr. B." Vinnie turned to go.

"And Vinnie . . ."

"Yes, Mr. B.?"

"Next time, bring me the money right away; don't take in a movie first."

"Yes, Mr. B."

"What is it with you and the movies, huh? I never seen anything like it."

"It's kind of a hobby, you know?"

Benedetto nodded. "You're getting too old for hobbies. How old are you now, Vinnie?"

"Twenty-eight, Mr. B."

"Time you was making your bones."

Vinnie didn't speak. Sweat broke out in the small of his back.

"Maybe the fat man don't come through, you can make your bones on him."

"Whatever you say, Mr. B.," Vinnie said. "Getoutahere."

Vinnie got out. The taxi was waiting, and he gave the cabbie an address in Chelsea, then sat back in the seat, drained. He opened the envelope and counted: three thousand bucks — his best week ever. Working for Benedetto had its advantages, but this thing about making his bones was beginning to weigh on Vinnie. Once he did that, he'd be a "made man," a full member of the family. And once he did that, Benedetto would own him forever. Vinnie didn't like the idea of being owned.

CHAPTER

3

Vinnie paid the cabbie, tipped him five, then ran up the steps of the Chelsea brownstone. As far as Benedetto and the rest of the family knew, Vinnie lived in his dead mother's place on Bleecker Street, but he spent fewer and fewer nights there; his real home was three rooms in Chelsea.

He unlocked the mailbox labeled "Michael Vincent." Three years before, he had picked a lawyer out of the phone book, legally changed his name, gotten a Social Security number, a driver's license, a voter registration card and a passport, and opened a bank account. After two years of filing tax returns, listing his occupation as freelance writer, he had obtained credit cards and charge accounts in his new name, signed a lease on the Chelsea apartment, and had even taken out and repaid a bank loan. He made his bank deposits in cash at a different branch each time, he never bounced a check, and he had twelve thousand dollars in a savings account, plus a stash of fifties and hundreds. Michael Vincent was the most respectable of citizens.

"How do you do?" Vinnie said aloud to himself as he climbed the stairs to his second-floor apartment. "I'm very pleased to meet you." After a lot of experimenting, he had settled on the Tyrone Power voice. "One, two, three, four, five, six, seven, eight, nine, ten." Power was the star whose vocal sounds most closely matched Vinnie's own, and the actor's accentless California speech and silken delivery was what Vinnie strived for. He had seen *The Razor's Edge* only the day before, and Vinnie tried to project the serenity of Larry as played by Power into his speech. "I'm extremely pleased to meet you," he said as he unlocked the three locks on the front door of the apartment.

The interior was classic New York Yuppie. Vinnie had exposed the brick on the wall with the fireplace; the furniture was soft and white, with a sprinkling of glass and leather; the art was a few good prints and a lot of original movie posters — *Casablanca*, *For Whom the Bell Tolls*, and *His Girl Friday* among them. Nearly everything in the place had fallen off the back of a truck, including the posters, which Vinnie had stripped from a broken-down revival movie house before a wiseguy acquaintance of his had torched the place for the strapped owner. There were nearly a thousand videotapes of movies neatly catalogued by title on bookshelves.

He checked his answering machine; there was one message. "Michael, darling," a woman's low voice said. "Dinner's at nine. Don't be late. In fact, try and be early."

Vinnie got out of the black clothes he habitually wore on his collection rounds — his mob outfit, as he thought of it. He took a shower, shampooed his hair, and carefully blow-dried it. He dumped the two gold chains and the flashy wristwatch into a basket on the dresser top and slipped on a steel-and-gold Rolex and a small gold signet ring engraved with a family crest. He had selected a Vincent crest from the files of the genealogical department of the New York Public Library and had taken it to Tiffany's, where he had chosen a ring and had it engraved. The ring was very nearly the only thing Vinnie had ever paid retail for.

He had a small wardrobe of Ralph Lauren suits and jackets that a shoplifter of his acquaintance had systematically acquired for him on order from half a dozen Polo shops, and he selected a plaid tweed jacket and a pair of flannel trousers. Vinnie slipped into a Sea Island cotton shirt and Italian loafers, and he was ready for class. He glanced at the Rolex; he had twenty minutes.

Vinnie arrived at Broadway and Waverly Place with five minutes to spare. He was seated in a classroom of the New York University Film School by the time the professor walked in. The class was on production budgets.

Waring, the professor, held up a sheaf of papers. "Mr. Vincent?" he said.

Vinnie raised his hand.

"Do you really think you can shoot this film for two million six?"

The class of thirty turned as one and looked at Vinnie.

"I believe I can," Vinnie replied in his silky Tyrone Power voice.

"Tell us why, Mr. Vincent," Waring said.

Vinnie sat up. "Well, just because the piece is set in New York doesn't mean it has to be shot in New York. My budget is for an Atlanta shoot with some stock street footage of New York. That's in the budget, by the way."

Across the room a young man with curly red hair slapped his forehead.

"And in what areas did you achieve savings by shooting in Atlanta?" Waring asked.

"In almost every area," Vinnie said. "Cost of housing, transportation, sets. And no Teamsters or craft unions to worry about. I knocked off half a million because of that."

"Can you give me a single example of a film set in New York that was successfully shot in Atlanta?" Waring asked.

"I saw a TV movie, 'The Mayflower Madam,' last week. That was a New York story shot in Atlanta, and it looked good to me."

"Didn't my instructions specify a New York shoot?" Waring asked.

Vinnie pulled out a piece of paper and glanced at it. "Where?" he asked. "You may have implied a New York shoot, but you didn't specify it."

"You're right, Mr. Vincent," Waring said, "and you were the only one in the class who figured that out. That's why you came in eight hundred thousand dollars under anybody else's budget. Congratulations, it was a good, workable budget, and you saved your investors a lot of money."

"Thank you," Vinnie said, feeling very proud of himself.

After class the redheaded young man approached Vinnie. He was wearing jeans, an

28

army field jacket with an outline where sergeant's stripes had been, and wire-rimmed glasses. He needed a haircut. "I'm Chuck Parish," he said, sticking out his hand.

"How do you do?" Vinnie replied. "I'm very pleased to meet you."

"You're Michael Vincent, right?"

"That's right."

"Can I buy you a cup of coffee? There's something I'd like to talk to you about."

Vinnie glanced at the Rolex. "I've got twenty minutes," he said, "before I'm due somewhere."

The waitress put the coffee on the table. Chuck Parish paid her, and when she had gone he pulled a script from a canvas briefcase. "I'd like you to read this and cost it for me. I'm going to shoot it in New York, and I need a production manager."

Vinnie flipped through the pages, one hundred and nineteen of them.

"It's a caper movie, about some Mafia guys who steal two million dollars of their godfather's money and nearly get away with it."

"Who's financing?" Vinnie asked.

"I can raise three hundred thousand," Parish said. "Family connections."

"You think that's enough?"

"That's what I want you to tell me. My

girlfriend's doing the female lead, and there are enough people in her acting classes to cast from. There's one guy I think looks good for the male lead."

"Do you have a distributor?"

"No."

Vinnie nodded. "I'll read it and call you."

"My number's on the back of the script."

They shook hands and parted.

Fifteen minutes later a cab dropped Vinnie at a prewar apartment building on Fifth Avenue near the Metropolitan Museum of Art.

"Good evening, Mr. Vincent," the doorman said, opening the door for him.

"Good evening, John," Vinnie said smoothly. He took the elevator to the top floor, emerged into a marbled vestibule, and opened a door with his key.

"In here, darling," she called.

Vinnie walked down the long hall past twenty million dollars' worth of art and turned into the huge master bedroom. She was in bed; a rosy-tipped breast peeked out from under the sheet. She had wonderful breasts for a woman of forty-one, Vinnie thought.

"We have half an hour before our guests arrive," she said, smiling. "Don't muss my makeup."

CHAPTER

4

Vinnie had met Barbara Mannering at a benefit for the NYU Film School eight months before. He had been waiting in line for a drink when she appeared at his elbow.

"Shit," she said.

He turned and looked at her. A blonde of five-seven or -eight, expensively coiffed and dressed, discreet but very real diamonds. "I beg your pardon?" he said.

"I am unaccustomed to standing in lines," she replied. "Would you be a prince and get me a double scotch on the rocks?"

"Of course," Vinnie had replied.

"Are you a budding movie director?"

"A budding producer," he said.

"You look a little old for NYU."

Vinnie knew he looked thirty-five. "I'm not a full-time student."

31

"What do you do full-time?"

"I'm a writer."

"Of what?"

"Books, magazine pieces, speeches sometimes."

"Anything I would have read?"

"Of course."

"Such as?"

"I have a rather peculiar specialty; I'm a ghostwriter."

"And whom do you ghost for?"

"If I told you, I'd no longer be a ghost. Business people, the odd politician."

"How do you find your clients?"

"They seem to find me — a sort of grapevine, I guess."

"You must do very well."

"Not all that well. I didn't write the Trump book or the Chuck Yeager book. My clients are more modest."

"So that's why you want to be a film producer, to do better?"

"I want to produce because I love film. I think I love it enough to do very well at it."

"I'm inclined to believe you will," she said. "Do you know, you sound just like Tyrone Power?"

Vinnie smiled more broadly than he had intended. "Do I?"

He took her home, and they began making

love while still in the elevator. They had been making love ever since, once or twice a week. She gave a dinner party regularly, twice a month; Vinnie was invited about every other time. He had met a couple of ex-mayors, some writers, and a great many other interesting people.

Vinnie kissed a breast, unstuck his body from hers and headed for the shower. When he came out of the bathroom she was leafing through Chuck Parish's script.

"What's this?"

"A guy in my budgeting class asked me to cost it for him. He's scraped up some money and wants to shoot it."

"Is it any good?"

"I haven't had a chance to read it yet, but he has a reputation at NYU as a kind of genius. I've seen a couple of short films he's done, and they were extremely good. My impression is that he doesn't have much business sense." He went to the closet that held the wardrobe Barbara had chosen for him and selected a dinner jacket and a silk shirt. Both had been made by a London tailor who visited New York quarterly, and Barbara had picked up the bill. The clothes were the only thing he'd ever taken from her, although the first time he had seen the twelve-room Fifth Avenue

33

apartment and its art and furnishings, his first impulse had been to tell Benedetto about it and get the place cleaned out some weekend when she was out of town. He'd liked her, though, and he'd thought she might be more useful to him as a friend. He'd been right. "Who's coming to dinner?" he asked.

"Senator Harvey and his wife; Dick and Shirley Clurman — Dick's retired from Time & Life — he was chief of correspondents — and he's got a wonderful new book out about the Time-Warner merger; Shirley's a producer at ABC; Leo and Amanda Goldman. We're just eight tonight."

"Leo Goldman of Centurion Pictures?"

"I thought you'd like that. Quite apart from running the studio of the moment, he's an interesting man. Very bright."

Vinnie pulled his bow tie into a perfect knot, exactly the way Cary Grant had in *Indiscreet*. "I'll be interested to meet him," he said.

Everybody arrived almost at once. Vinnie shook Goldman's hand but made a point of not talking to him before dinner. Instead, he listened quietly to a conversation between the senator and Dick Clurman that was practically an interview. Clurman was quick and asked very direct questions, and he got very direct answers from the senator. Vinnie learned a lot.

At dinner he was seated between Shirley Clurman and Amanda Goldman; Leo Goldman was one place away, but still Vinnie did not press conversation with him. He was charming to Mrs. Clurman and devoted a lot of attention to Amanda Goldman, a beautiful blonde in her early forties, but not so much attention as to irritate her husband.

It was not until after dinner, when they were having brandy in the library that Vinnie said more than two words to Goldman, and luckily, Goldman initiated the exchange.

"I hear you're at NYU Film School," he said. He was a balding, superbly built man in his mid-forties, obviously the product of a strenuous daily workout.

"Part-time," Vinnie replied.

"What's your interest in film?"

"Production."

"Not the glamour stuff — writing or directing?"

"No."

"What draws you to production?"

Vinnie took a deep breath. "It's where the control is."

Goldman laughed. "Most people would say the director has control."

"Producers hire and fire directors."

Goldman nodded. "You're a smart guy, Michael," he said. "You think you have any sense of what makes a good movie?"

"Yes."

Goldman fished a card from his pocket. "When you've got something you think is good, call me. That's the private number."

Vinnie accepted the card. He smiled. "I'll call you when you least expect it."

Vinnie spent an hour in bed with Barbara, and when he had finally exhausted her, he slipped into the shower again, got into a robe, and took the Parish script into the library. He read it in an hour, then got a legal pad from the desk and started breaking it down into scenes and locations. By daylight he had a rough production schedule and budget. He didn't need a calculator to add up the figures. Vinnie had always had a facility for numbers and an outstanding memory.

He got an hour's sleep before Barbara woke him for breakfast.

"What were you doing all night?" she asked over eggs and bacon.

"Reading Chuck Parish's script and working up a production budget."

"Was it any good?"

He turned and looked at her. "Barbara, it is very, very good. It's a caper film, but it's funny. It moves like a freight train, and if it's properly produced it can make money."

"What do you need to produce it?"

"I can bring it in for six hundred and fifty thousand," Vinnie replied. "Parish has already got three hundred thousand."

"Sounds like a low budget to me," she said.

"It is. Leo Goldman wouldn't believe it."

"Are you going to take it to Goldman?"

"No. If Parish is game, I'm going to make it before anybody sees it."

"Risky."

"Not as risky as you think. You haven't read the script."

"Why don't I invest?"

"I don't want your money, Barbara." He smiled. "Just your body." He knew that she was heir to a very large construction fortune.

"The project interests me," she said. "I'll put up two hundred thousand; you come up with the rest."

"I'll think about it," Vinnie said.

He had already thought about it.

As he was leaving she said, "You know what Leo Goldman said about you last night?"

Vinnie looked at her questioningly; he didn't want to ask.

"He said, 'Your friend Michael is a hustler,

but he doesn't come on like a hustler. I like that.' "

Vinnie smiled and kissed her good-bye. He was going to have to be very careful with Leo Goldman.

CHAPTER

5

Vinnie worked on the production budget for two days, between collecting debts for Benedetto. He sat at his computer in the Chelsea apartment and constructed beautiful schedules and documents. He was impressed with his own work.

When he was ready, he went to see Tommy Pro. Vinnie had known Thomas O. Provensano since childhood. Tommy was two years older, but they had formed a friendship early. Vinnie thought Tommy was, in some ways, the smartest guy he had ever known. He had gotten an accounting degree from CUNY, passed the CPA exam, then gone to NYU Law School. Tommy knew as much about Benedetto's business as Benedetto did — maybe more.

The office was behind an unmarked door

upstairs over the coffeehouse that was Benedetto's headquarters. Tommy had two rooms — one for an assistant, a fiftyish Italian widow — and one for himself and his computers. Tommy had three computers, and it seemed to Vinnie that all three of them were going full blast all the time. The furniture was spartan — a steel desk and filing cabinets that had come from a restaurant Benedetto had bankrupted some years back, and a very large safe. Tommy had told him once how all the real records were kept on computer disks, and how the safe was wired to destroy them — from a remote location, if necessary. Tommy left work each evening with a duplicate set of disks in a substantial briefcase, and *nobody* knew where he kept that.

Tommy wheeled his considerable bulk from computer to computer in a large executive chair, his only concession to comfort or luxury. "What's happening, kid?" he asked when Vinnie had been admitted to the inner sanctum.

"I'm going to make a movie, Tommy," Vinnie said, sitting down and opening his briefcase.

Tommy Pro spread his hands and grinned. "It was only a matter of time," he said. "Can I help?"

"I want to show you what I got here, and

see what you think." Vinnie spread out his schedules and budgets and explained the whole thing to Tommy, who was the only person Vinnie trusted even a little. When he had finished, he sat back. "So, how'm I doing?"

Tommy smiled broadly. "It works for me," he said. "Except you gotta come up with a hundred and fifty grand, clean. How you gonna do that?"

"Between you and me, I've got nearly seventy," Vinnie replied. He had never told anybody about his stash.

"If I know you, you'll find the other eighty."

"Believe it," Vinnie said.

"This stuff amounts to a real good business plan," Tommy said, leafing through the budget. "What do you need from us?"

"From you," Vinnie said. "Not Benedetto. I've got this thing trimmed to the bone to make it work, and if Mr. B. gets wind of it he'll want a rake-off." He allowed himself a small smile. "You," he said, "I can owe."

Tommy Pro laughed. "Okay, so what are you going to owe me for?"

"Logistical help, mostly. I want to shoot in the neighborhood, and I don't want any flak from anybody."

"I can do that."

41

"I'm shooting this strictly nonunion, and I don't want any pickets."

"A phone call," Tommy said.

"And I want you to draw all the contracts," Vinnie said.

"Well, I haven't done a lot of entertainment work, but I've got a lot of boilerplate in the computer. You'll want to incorporate, of course."

"Of course," Vinnie said. He hadn't thought of that.

The two young men spent three hours listing contracts to be drawn and looking for holes in Vinnie's business plan. There weren't many.

When Vinnie was about to leave, Tommy Pro said, "I know a pretty good actress who's available."

"Sure; I'll find something for her. Who is she?"

"Remember Carol Geraldi?"

"Sure, *Widow's Walk*, four or five years ago. I haven't seen anything of her for a while."

"Neither has anybody else; she's on the skids — a junkie."

"Too bad."

"I think she could still work, and she's still got a name."

"How do you know about this?"

"I've got a couple pushers on the street; one of 'em's supplying her. She owes me eight grand. If you want her, pick up her tab, and I'll make you a gift of her."

"I'll think about that, Tommy, and thanks."

Vinnie was as nervous as he ever got. Chuck Parish was on his way over to the Chelsea apartment, and Vinnie made sure everything was neat and that his papers were laid out. He jumped when the doorbell rang.

Chuck was accompanied by one of the most beautiful girls Vinnie had ever seen.

"This is Vanessa Parks," Chuck said. "She's my girl and my leading lady."

"Great," Vinnie said, shaking the girl's hand. She was tall and willowy, with lovely light brown hair. Her skin was without blemish, her breasts were full and high, and her mouth was wide and lush, with excellent teeth. Vinnie wanted her immediately.

He put them on the sofa, got them a drink, then sat opposite them.

"Nice place," Vanessa said, looking around.

"Thank you, Vanessa," Vinnie said. He had found it effective to address women by their names often early in a relationship.

"So," Chuck said, "what've you got for me?"

Vinnie placed the screenplay on the coffee

43

table. "First of all," he said, "I want to tell you that I think your screenplay is extremely good. You're a very fine writer."

Chuck glowed a little. "Thanks," he said, "but let's get down to it. What's it going to cost to produce?"

"There are three ways you can make this picture," Vinnie said. "Actually, there are dozens of ways, but only three make sense."

Chuck leaned forward. "What are they?"

Vinnie held up a finger. "One," he said, "you can make this film as a project. You can take your three hundred thousand dollars, hire some students as cast and crew, and make a nice little movie that will probably win you the NYU Film School award for best picture and best screenplay. It will be unreleasable in that form, but you can take it to the studios and use it to get a shot at writing and directing a feature, or you might get a contract to do a TV movie."

"Sounds good to me," Chuck said.

"But — and you should think seriously about this — it will be the most expensive master's thesis in history, and you'll no longer have your three hundred thousand."

"I could live with that if it helped me launch a career," Chuck said.

"It's your own money, then."

Chuck nodded. "An inheritance."

44

"Chuck, it's my view that a man ought to be paid for his work. If you do this, you won't be paid, and you'll squander your inheritance as well."

"I see your point," Chuck replied. "What are the other two ways?"

"You can get an agent — I've got some contacts — and sell your screenplay to a studio. It's good enough that you might get two, three hundred thousand for it."

"I like the sound of that," Chuck said, grinning.

"But they'll never let you direct it."

"Oh."

"You'll have to rewrite it half a dozen times for the studio, then, when they're happy, you'll have to rewrite it for the director, and when he's happy, you'll have to rewrite it for the star. That's the way it's done, and I don't think what you'd end up with would much resemble what you started out with."

"I see your point," Chuck said. He was looking discouraged. "What's the third option?"

"The third option," Vinnie said, "is to make a releasable film and then take it to the studios. Hire professionals for all but the menial work; cast good people who will work for scale."

"Can I do it for three hundred grand?"

"No. You'll need six hundred and fifty grand."

"I can't raise the rest," Chuck said.

"I can," Vinnie replied.

"You'd invest in my movie?" Chuck asked, astonished.

"If I produce it," Vinnie replied.

Chuck sat back on the sofa and sipped his drink. "I want to write, produce and direct my own stuff."

Vinnie sat back too. "If that's what you want, then that's what you should do."

Chuck looked at him cautiously. "But you won't bring your investors in if I do."

Vinnie shook his head. "I couldn't do that, and I'll tell you why. You're an intelligent man, a good writer, and, from what I've seen at the film school, a good director. You ought to concentrate on what you're good at, and my guess is you're not a very good businessman. I am. I can organize this project, run the business side, and leave you free to do what you do best. That's what you need, Chuck, whether it's me or somebody else. You need a producer."

"What have you produced?"

"Nothing," Vinnie said. "But let me take you through the business plan I've worked out and show you how I'd do it." He went to his desk, picked up copies, and handed them to Chuck and Vanessa. "Page one," he said, "are overall costs, broken down by category."

When he had finished, Vinnie got up and fixed himself a drink, his first. Chuck and Vanessa whispered back and forth while he was gone. When he returned, Vanessa smiled at him, and he knew he was home free.

"I like this," Chuck said.

"It's not going to be a piece of cake," Vinnie replied. "You and I are going to have to defer compensation. It's a twenty-three-day schedule, and you're going to have to be very well prepared to bring that off. You're going to have to shoot with Mitchell cameras instead of Panavision; you'll have to edit on a Movieola, not a Steenbeck — in fact, it would be best if you could edit at school, use their stuff — even if you have to do it in the middle of the night."

"I don't need much sleep," Chuck said. He flipped through the pages quickly. "I don't see a Steadicam in here," he said. "I specified a Steadicam for three scenes."

"You can't have a Steadicam," Vinnie said. "You can have a rented wheelchair, if we can't steal one, and all the sheets of ply-

47

wood you can borrow, for track."

"How much time for preproduction and casting?" Chuck asked.

"A month. That's ample, I think. I've already found all the locations."

"All of them?" Chuck asked incredulously.

"I've put the addresses by each scene."

"What about interiors?"

"We'll borrow them. You can use this place for the girl's apartment. We won't be renting any soundstages."

"That's gotta mean a lot of looping, then."

"It's in the budget," Vinnie replied.

"Holy shit," Chuck said, wiping his brow. "This is really possible, isn't it?"

"It is."

"How do you know we can sell it to a studio when it's finished?"

"I have contacts. I believe it's doable, or I wouldn't bring my investors into it. You're going to have to depend on my business judgment, though, when we do the deal."

Vanessa put a hand on Chuck's. "I think you should do it Michael's way," she said.

Chuck looked at her, then turned back to Vinnie and stuck out a hand. "You've got a deal," he said. "When do we start?"

Vinnie took the hand in both of his. "We start tomorrow at a meeting with our lawyer. You can bring your own lawyer, of course.

You should do that."

"I don't have a lawyer," Chuck said.

Vinnie smiled reassuringly. "Don't worry about it," he said.

CHAPTER

6

Vinnie loved the work. He tried to get his collection business done in the mornings, then devoted his afternoons and evenings to mounting the production. He wheeled and dealed, offered cash for discounts, rounded up equipment, hired crew, attended casting sessions. He was a *producer*.

There was one thorn in his flesh: the fat man. He had come up with the vigorish on schedule and had made two payments. Then, when Vinnie stopped by the candy store to collect the next payment, he walked in and saw a cop. The man was loitering near the office door, reading a magazine from the rack; he was in plainclothes, but Vinnie made him in a second. The old man behind the counter raised an eyebrow and glanced at the cop. Vinnie left before he was made.

The sonofabitch, he thought as he walked on to his next customer. Benedetto would definitely lose patience now. The fat man had called the cops! Was he insane?

Benedetto was pissed off. "Why should this man treat me this way?" he asked Vinnie plaintively.

"You're right, Mr. B.," Vinnie said. "He needs a real shock to the system."

"He needs getting dead," Benedetto said flatly.

"Give me one more shot at him," Vinnie said. "After all, he won't pay you if he's dead. I'll have him on schedule by next collection day."

"All right, Vinnie, I'll leave it in your hands."

"Right, Mr. B. I'll take care of it right away." He turned to go.

"And Vinnie?"

Vinnie stopped. "Yeah, Mr. B.?"

"I'm holding you responsible."

Vinnie didn't like the sound of that. He got out fast.

Later in the day Vinnie sat in on a casting session in a basement room at NYU and watched actors read for the three principal male roles. Vanessa Parks was reading with

51

them, and Vinnie didn't like what he heard. He thought she had the makings of an actress, but she was too young for the part, too inexperienced for the role. A week of rehearsals started in a few days. Time was short.

He got up and went to a pay phone.

"Yeah?" Tommy Pro said.

"Tommy, it's Vinnie. I need some personnel," Vinnie said.

"What kind?"

"Somebody with some medical training and a knowledge of drugs. A little muscle wouldn't hurt."

"I think I know what's in your mind, Vinnie," Tommy said. Vinnie could hear him grinning. "When?"

"Over the weekend." Vinnie could hear pages turning.

"Roxanne," Tommy said. "She's an R.N. Them that knows her well calls her Roxy Graziano."

"Perfect," Vinnie said.

At 3:00 A.M. Vinnie turned into an upper-middle-class street in Queens and cruised slowly down the block, checking each window in each house. Not a light was on. He spotted the Cadillac, parked in a driveway; the house number was right. Vinnie drove to the end of the block, made a U-turn, and came slowly back, his headlights off. He parked and got out.

The device was a quart bottle of gasoline and a detonator with a two-minute fuse. Looking carefully up and down the street, he approached the Cadillac, set the device on the ground under the gas tank, and activated it. He walked quickly back to his car and drove away, not hurrying.

At the end of the block, he turned the corner, then stopped. He could still see the Cadillac. There was a "whomp" sound as the detonator lit the gasoline, then, after a short delay, a big fireball of an explosion. Vinnie smiled to himself and drove back toward Manhattan. The sonofabitch would pay on time now.

The following afternoon Vinnie dressed in his blue pinstriped suit and met Roxanne in a delicatessen on West Eighth Street. "It's a short walk," he said.

"Suits me."

Roxanne was a good six feet tall and weighed about a hundred and sixty, Vinnie guessed. She listened to him as they walked, nodding occasionally.

"I can handle that," she said.

"Did you bring the stuff?"

She patted her large handbag.

They came to a handsome brownstone on West 10th Street, on the elegant block between Fifth and Sixth Avenues. Michael rang the bell and waited.

She looked like hell when she came to the door. She was dressed in clean jeans and a work shirt, but her hair was dirty, and she looked older than her thirty-four years. "Yes?" she said.

"Miss Geraldi," Vinnie said, "my name is Michael Vincent. I'm a film producer. There's a script I hope you'll read — a wonderful part — and I wanted to deliver it myself." He handed her a brown envelope.

"Oh," she said, surprised and pleased. "Thank you. I'll read it over the weekend."

"This is one of my production assistants, Roxanne," he said, gesturing toward the large woman. "I wonder if we could come in for just a moment? I'd like to tell you about the project."

"Well, the place is a mess," she said, "But . . ."

"Thank you," Vinnie said, brushing past her. She had been right; the place was a mess. Vinnie moved a pizza box from a sofa and sat down.

Carol Geraldi sat opposite him, and Roxanne stood quietly in the doorway.

Vinnie told Geraldi about the film, about

her part. "There are only four scenes," he said, "but it's the only female part of any consequence, and the quality of the writing, I think you'll agree when you read it, is extraordinary. I don't want to oversell it, but I think there's an opportunity for an Academy Award nomination in this part."

"Well," Geraldi said, taking the script from the envelope. "*Downtown Nights.* It's an interesting title."

"Why don't you read the scenes now?" Vinnie suggested. "The pages are flagged."

She glanced at her watch. "I'm sorry, but I don't have time right now; I'm expecting someone."

"Take the time," Vinnie said. "You certainly won't be sorry."

"Mr. . . . Vincent, is it?" she said, an edge in her voice. "I really am expecting someone, and I'm in no mood to read this at the moment."

"I'm afraid the man you're expecting isn't coming, Miss Geraldi."

She looked alarmed. "I beg your pardon?"

"The man with the drugs is not coming."

She was trembling now. "I don't know what you're talking about. Who are you, anyway?"

"I'm a film producer, as I told you a moment ago. I assure you, this is a genuine offer."

"Offer? You haven't made an offer. You'll have to call my agent," she said, rising.

"I'm afraid you don't have an agent anymore, Miss Geraldi. You haven't had one for some time."

She sat down again. "What is this, exactly?"

"I won't waste your time," he said. "I'll be direct with you."

"I'd appreciate that." She was twitching now.

"I have bought your debt from your pusher. Eight thousand dollars — that's a lot of drugs, Miss Geraldi. You're up to two grams of cocaine a week now, plus whatever else you can get your hands on."

"I'm going into rehab next week," she said.

"Not just yet," Vinnie replied. "You have a part to do first."

"Look, I don't know if this film is real or not, but I'm in no shape to deliver any kind of performance right now. And I really am expecting someone."

"He was about to cut you off anyway. Look at me as a rescuing angel."

"You're going to supply me with drugs?" she asked incredulously.

"That's right, Miss Geraldi, and Roxanne here is going to administer them. Roxanne is going to see that you feel just fine right through a week's rehearsals and ten days of shooting. I'm arranging to shoot your scenes almost back to back, so that we won't take any more of your time than absolutely necessary. And as soon as you've finished shooting, we'll get you into rehab, I promise."

Geraldi looked at Roxanne. "Can you give me something now?" she asked.

"Of course she can," Vinnie said, rising. "I'm just about finished. But I want to be sure you understand me clearly. Roxanne is moving in with you from this moment. She's going to maintain you through the weekend, the rehearsals, and the shoot, and I don't want you to give her the slightest difficulty. Is that clear?"

Geraldi nodded dumbly.

"You must understand that I'm giving you a great opportunity, and I expect your full cooperation. If you don't cooperate with me, the director, and Roxanne at all times, I'm going to drop you right back into the frying pan; I'm going to sell your debt to a man who's not nearly as nice as I am and who deals in a different kind of movie than I do — then you'll have to work your debt off, and it will take a long, long time. Do you understand me, Carol?"

"I understand," Geraldi said weakly. She turned to Roxanne. "Now, please?" she whimpered.

"Help her, Roxanne," Vinnie said. "Carol, your first reading will be at one o'clock on Monday afternoon. Be sure you know your lines." He smiled. "Roxanne will read with you."

CHAPTER

7

Vinnie sat in the rehearsal hall at Central Plaza on Second Avenue and watched Chuck Parish rehearse his cast. They spent the morning running through the four scenes between Vanessa Parks and the three male leads. Chuck moved quickly, only occasionally stopping to make a suggestion. Vinnie was impressed with the way he handled the actors, never criticizing, always encouraging.

At noon, lunch was delivered from a delicatessen, and Vinnie took the opportunity to call Chuck aside. When they were alone in the stairwell Vinnie spoke quietly. "Chuck, at the risk of insulting you, I'm going to tell you something you already know."

"What's that?" Chuck asked warily.

"Vanessa is wrong for the part. Wrong for the movie, in fact."

"What the hell are you talking about?" Chuck demanded defensively. "I've cast her, and that's it."

"Come here," Vinnie said, leading him over to the door to the rehearsal hall. They looked in at the group of actors eating lunch. "Look at that group and tell me this: who's out of place?"

Chuck looked at his cast — most of them Italian, all of them ethnic-looking in some way.

"Look at them," Vinnie repeated. "We've got Italians, Jews, Puerto Ricans, a couple of blacks. It's a gritty group." He paused. "And then there's Vanessa."

Chuck said nothing, but continued to stare at the group.

"She's a promising actress, I'll give you that, but she's too WASPy, she's too delicate, she's too young, she's too green. We need an older, more experienced actress, someone who can bring some personal weight to the part."

"If I tell her that she'll walk right out on me," Chuck said.

"If she loves you she won't," Vinnie said smoothly. "She'll understand you're doing it for the production."

"I just can't do it," Chuck said. "Will you tell her?"

"If she hears it from me she'll never forgive you."

Chuck turned away from the door. "But we're too far along now. How can we recast the part in the time we've got? You're always bitching at me about schedule."

"I understand that Carol Geraldi is available," Vinnie said.

Chuck looked at him. "You think we could get her?"

"I do."

"Can we afford her?"

"Yes."

"Where has she been the past couple of years? I haven't seen her in anything since she won the Oscar for *Widow's Walk*."

"She took some time off."

Chuck walked back to the door and looked at Vanessa. "She's so goddamned beautiful," he said. "I always wanted somebody as beautiful as that."

"Your career is at stake here, Chuck. She can't carry the part, and nobody will blame her; they'll blame you for casting her."

Chuck leaned against the wall and wiped his brow with his sleeve. "I guess I just have to be ruthless, huh?"

"It won't be the last time, Chuck; it's a tough business. I think maybe Vanessa understands that better than you. When she's

61

had time to think about it, she'll see that you're doing it as much for her career as yours. Everybody who'd see the film would know she was out of her depth."

"You're right," Chuck said. "I can't let her do that to herself."

Vinnie put a hand on Chuck's shoulder. "You're a good man. Best to tell her now."

Chuck nodded. "Just give me a minute, okay?"

"Sure," Vinnie said. "I'll have Carol Geraldi here at one o'clock."

Chuck nodded and looked at his feet.

Vinnie walked downstairs and out onto the street, breathing more easily. He looked up to see Carol Geraldi and Roxanne getting out of a taxi. He walked over to them. "You look terrific," he said to Geraldi, taking her hand.

"I had a good weekend," she said.

"Good, good. Now, you're a few minutes early, so you and Roxanne go across the street and get a cup of coffee. At one, go up to Studio A and introduce yourself to the director, Chuck Parish."

"Won't you be there?" she asked nervously.

"I have to do something else for a couple of hours, but Chuck is expecting you, and he's very excited about working with an actress of your caliber."

She smiled. "That's nice."

"Now go get your coffee." He watched the two women cross the street, then went and stood inside the door to the building, waiting. Five minutes later he heard a door slam, then the ring of high heels on the steel stairs, then Vanessa Parks nearly fell into his arms. She was weeping and nearly hysterical.

"Vanessa, honey, take it easy," he said, holding her at arm's length and looking at her closely.

"The bastard!" she said. "The bastard fired me!"

"Are you all right?" he asked.

"Of course I'm not all right! My boyfriend just fired me off his picture! Don't you understand?"

"Come on," Vinnie said, putting an arm around her. "Let's get out of here." Outside, he hailed a cab and bundled her into it. He gave the driver the address of the Chelsea apartment, then turned to Vanessa, who was trembling with fury, tears streaming down her face. "Take it easy now. We'll talk this whole thing out and see what we can do about it." He pulled her head to his shoulder and let her do her sobbing there.

In the Chelsea apartment he mixed her a strong Scotch. She wolfed down half of it.

"The bastard," she kept saying.

Vinnie pulled her onto the sofa and stroked her hair. "Listen, it's just a job," he said. "You're going to have better parts than that, I promise you."

"You think so?" she asked, wiping her nose with a tissue.

"Vanessa, look at me," he said, cupping her face in his hands.

She looked up at him, doe-eyed, snuffling.

"You have something very special, something the camera can see, something an audience can identify with."

"I do?" she whimpered.

"More than being very beautiful, you have a rare talent that, properly developed, is going to propel you to a high place in the film business."

"Do you really think so?" she asked. She had stopped crying.

"Absolutely. Chuck is going to do okay, I'm going to do okay, but you are going to be a very great star. I promise you that."

"Oh, Michael," she said, placing a hand on his cheek. "You always believed in me from the start, didn't you? I knew you did, I could tell. Chuck just wanted to fuck me."

"Listen, Chuck thinks you're great, but let me tell you, as good as you would have been in that part, the part wouldn't have been good for you."

"Why?"

"Because the character isn't anywhere near as young and beautiful as you are. I'm going to find you parts, create parts for you that will send you to the top of this business."

"You'd do that for me?" she asked.

"I'll do it for you, I'll do it for myself. I want to see you on top, and I want to be the one who puts you there."

She kissed him.

He kissed her back, but he held himself away. Her mouth was incredible and he wanted more of it, but he wanted her to be the aggressor.

She did not disappoint him. She pushed him back on the sofa, got his zipper undone, and in a moment she had him in her mouth.

If he thought her mouth had been incredible on his lips, then where it was now was right next to heaven, he thought. He looked at the top of her head, ran his hand through her thick hair, played his fingers at the corner of her mouth, felt himself swelling, swelling, then exploding. She kept sucking until he pulled her head away, got an arm around her waist and swept her into the bedroom, both of them shedding clothes along the way.

***

Vinnie made it back to the rehearsal hall before the reading broke for the day. "How did it go?" he asked Chuck.

"Geraldi is absolutely wonderful," Chuck replied. "She walked in here, and in five minutes, she *was* the part, and everybody in the cast knew it. She was inspired casting, Michael."

"I'm glad you're happy."

"I'm delirious. Did you see Vanessa when she left?"

"No, I had to go uptown and fix a hassle with the lighting. It's okay now."

"I dread seeing her when I get home," Chuck said. "I feel just terrible about this."

"You'll get over it, and so will she," Vinnie replied. "She'll probably throw herself into your arms the moment you walk in."

An hour later, the phone rang in the Chelsea apartment.

"Hello," Vinnie said.

"Michael," Chuck Parish sobbed, "she's gone!"

"Take it easy now," Vinnie replied soothingly.

"All her stuff is gone; she's vanished. None of her friends knows where she is."

"It's how it had to be, Chuck," Vinnie said. "Let her go. Get your head back into the film.

Don't think about anything else."

Chuck heaved a deep sigh. "You're right," he said. "The film is the important thing. I don't know why I let the cunt upset me so much."

"Get a good night's sleep. I'll see you in the morning."

"Sure, Michael. Thanks." He hung up.

Vinnie hung up and looked toward the kitchen, where Vanessa, dressed only in a shirt, was making pasta.

"You like a lot of garlic?" she asked, smiling at him.

CHAPTER

8

Vinnie sat straight up in bed. Something had awakened him, some noise, but it was gone. Vanessa was stretched out beside him, sleeping quietly. He looked at the bedside clock: just after 3:00 A.M. The noise came again, and this time he knew what it was: his beeper, sending muffled signals from his trousers pocket.

He got out of bed, switched off the beeper, and went to the living room phone. He didn't like this; Benedetto had never once called him in the middle of the night. The fat man's collection day was tomorrow — that must be what it was about. He dialed the number.

"Yeah?" the voice of Cheech, the bodyguard, said.

"It's me. What the fuck?"

"Now," Cheech said.

"Right now?" He tried to keep his voice down so as not to wake Vanessa. "Does he have any idea what the fuck time it is?"

"Gee, I dunno," Cheech said. "You want I should ask him?"

"I'll be there in twenty minutes," Vinnie said, exasperated.

"Make it ten," Cheech said.

"Tell him I'm not at home, and I have to find a cab."

"Yeah," Cheech said, then hung up.

Vinnie got into the clothes he had taken off at bedtime. He hated wearing clothes twice, but he couldn't afford to waste time. He didn't like being on the streets of New York at this time of night, either; he opened a drawer and found the fat man's gun, then left the building. A miracle; it took him only five minutes to find a cab going south on Seventh Avenue.

They were two thirds through shooting the film, and Vinnie had already shaved a day off the schedule. He was proud of himself, but he was nervous, too. He was right on budget, but most of Chuck's and Barbara's investment was gone, and soon he was going to have to come up with his hundred and fifty thousand. He had seventy, which he hated to think of using, but he needed another eighty at least.

The cab driver was on his way home to

Brooklyn and refused to go any farther south than Houston Street. Vinnie jogged the rest of the way.

The streets of Little Italy were deserted, and his soft Italian loafers made little sound as he ran along. He was swept back to his childhood, when running had meant that somebody was chasing him, usually for stealing. As he approached the La Boheme Coffee House, he slowed to a walk, willing his heart to slow down. He stood outside the door and panted for a moment. Suddenly the glass behind him rattled. Vinnie spun around, his heart racing again, to find Cheech standing there, his bulk filling the doorway.

"Christ, Cheech, you scared the shit out of me," he panted.

"You better get in there," Cheech said, indicating the back room with a thumb. "He's pissed off."

Vinnie walked quickly through the dark coffeehouse, aiming at the light under the door of the back room. His shirt was sticking to him, and he didn't have his breathing under control yet. He hated not being perfectly in control of himself, hated it that Benedetto was going to see him this way. He knocked, then opened the door.

Benedetto was sitting in his usual place, and there were stacks of money on the table. The door to the big safe was ajar. Cheech went and sat at the desk where Tommy Pro often worked.

"Evening, Mr. B.," Vinnie said, trying to calm his breathing.

"Evening, my ass," Benedetto said, becoming red in the face.

"What's up? How can I help?" Vinnie asked.

"This is your problem, not mine," Benedetto replied. "You can fucking fix it."

"What's the problem, Mr. B.?" He had a sickening feeling that he knew what the problem was.

"You see the late news tonight?"

"No."

"The fat man was the star of it. Oh, they had a goddamned coat over his head, but it was him getting into the car."

"The fat man's been busted?" Vinnie asked, mystified.

"Not exactly," Benedetto replied snidely. "The fat man is trying to get *me* busted. He's been to the DA, who has a hair up his ass about loan-sharking, and who now has a warrant out for me. I couldn't even get into my office until an hour ago. There's been cops all over."

Vinnie was stunned. The fat man didn't know his name, but he could certainly give

71

the cops a good description. "I don't believe it," he said. "The man can't be that crazy."

"Well, he is that crazy," Benedetto said, "and it was your job on his car that pushed him over the edge."

"He'd never testify against you, Mr. B.," Vinnie said. "He'd know what that'd mean. He's not *that* crazy."

"They got him sequestered," Benedetto said.

"Oh, shit."

"Exactly, except I found out where. Cost me ten big ones."

"You know where they got him?"

"Fortunately, yeah. Otherwise Cheech would right now be breaking your head like a walnut."

Vinnie looked at Cheech, who seemed disappointed that he was not breaking Vinnie's head. "Mr. B.," he said, "just tell me what you want me to do."

Benedetto took a slip of paper from his pocket and pushed it across the table. "That's where he is," the capo said. "It's a place in Oyster Bay, on the North Shore. You go do it."

"Do what, Mr. B.?"

"Make him dead. Cheech'll give you a gun." He turned and looked at his bodyguard. "Give Vinnie something heavy to make his bones with. I don't want no surprise recovery."

Vinnie's mind went into a kind of crazy fast-forward. He would try to get to the fat man, and the cops would kill him. He would never see his film released, never make love to Vanessa again, never go to another dinner party at Barbara Mannering's to meet the rich and powerful.

But then again, maybe not. Maybe he would pull it off and get the credit for saving Benedetto's ass. He would make his bones and be one of the boys. And Benedetto would have him by the balls for the rest of his life, tell him what and what not to do, rule his life, *own* him.

Benedetto was turning back toward him; Cheech had a .45 automatic by the barrel, wiping it with an oily cloth.

Decide! Decide! He decided. His hand went to the waist of his trousers and grasped the fat man's revolver. He was moving too slowly, he knew; Cheech was big, but he was quick as a cat. Vinnie started up with the gun, saw the surprise in Benedetto's face. Vinnie shot him in his surprise.

The bullet went in under the left eye, and Benedetto spilled backward from his chair. Vinnie knew he might not be dead, but Cheech was doing something with his hands. Vinnie

73

turned, crouched, and fired twice. The first one got Cheech in the left shoulder, the second hit him in the neck. He still had the .45 in his hand, clasped in the oily cloth. He was having trouble getting a finger on the trigger through the cloth.

Vinnie quickly walked toward him, stopped three feet away. He put one into Cheech's head, saw some skull come away and blood splash the desk. He fired one more into the forehead.

There was a noise behind him. Benedetto was on his hands and knees struggling toward him. His face was contorted with pain and rage. He reached up and got hold of Vinnie's trouser leg. Vinnie backhanded him with the pistol; he didn't want blood all over him. Benedetto reeled, but recovered and started toward him again, blood pouring from his face. Vinnie shot him twice more in the top of the head, and the pistol was empty.

Vinnie turned back to Cheech, terrified that the giant might still be able to fire the heavy pistol at him, but Cheech was on his back, bleeding into the floorboards. He wheeled back to Benedetto, but Mr. B. was very dead too.

Vinnie stood, frozen, in the middle of the room, the gun in his hand, taking deep breaths, trying to stop his heart from flying from his chest. Then a deep voice behind him shook him to his roots.

"Well, Vinnie," Tommy Pro said, "you've really made a mess, haven't you?"

Vinnie whipped around, the pistol out in front of him, to find Tommy standing in the doorway, a sawed-off shotgun in his hands.

"Your piece looks empty," Tommy said.

"Empty," Vinnie said, recovering. "Yeah, it's empty."

"Is it yours?"

"No, I got it from a guy."

"It's clean, then?"

"Yeah, I guess so."

Tommy reached out and took the pistol from Vinnie's hand and pocketed it. "I was upstairs working late; an all-nighter. I'm glad it was you." He looked at Vinnie closely. "Thank Christ you were empty, I think."

"Yeah," Vinnie said. "I probably would have kept shooting. You scared me bad." He was feeling numb now, tired to the bone. "You gonna give me to the Don, Tommy?" he asked weakly.

"Are you insane?" Tommy Pro asked. "Look around here, don't you see what I see?"

"I see Benedetto dead," Vinnie said.

"You don't see any money on the table, Vinnie? You don't see the safe open?" Tommy

75

chuckled. "Even *I* don't have the combination to that safe."

Vinnie began to recover; the numbness was leaving him. "You and me, Tommy? We take everything?"

"Not exactly, Vinnie," Tommy Pro said. "You take half the money. I take everything else."

"What else?" Vinnie asked, looking around the nearly empty room. Then he understood.

Tommy went to the safe and opened it wide. He took two bank bags from a shelf and began to stuff money into both of them. When he had finished, he stood up and began bagging the money on the table. Finally, he held out both bags to Vinnie. "No time for counting. I divided it up; you got dibs."

Vinnie took one of the bags.

"You remember how we used to run across the roofs?" Tommy asked.

"Yeah," Vinnie replied.

"You go out the back way, go up the fire escape, across the roofs to your mother's place. Hide the money somewhere *good*. Stay at your mother's until you hear from me. People are going to want to talk to you. I'll handle things here."

"I've got another place, in Chelsea," Vinnie said.

"Can anybody put you there tonight?"

"Yeah, there's a girl."

"Wait'll morning, when there's people on the street. Go back to Chelsea and call me around ten. Act surprised on the phone."

Vinnie nodded. Without speaking again, he left through the back door. A moment later he was flying across the roofs, a child again with Tommy Pro, running from somebody.

CHAPTER

9

Vinnie lay on his dead mother's bed and tried to think. For an airtight alibi, he needed to get back to Chelsea before Vanessa woke up. Thank God, he thought, she sleeps like a rock. But how would he do that? He'd never get a cab at this time of night, and he might be noticed at this hour on the subway. He certainly didn't want to be walking the streets in the middle of the night with a lot of money in a bag. Then he remembered something.

He got off the bed and went to the chest of drawers where his old clothes were. He got into some athletic shorts, a sweatshirt, and sneakers, then picked up the money and left the apartment. As silently as he could, he tiptoed down the stairs. There it was, at the bottom. A bicycle, with a helmet dangling from the handlebars. The kid who lived downstairs worked for a messenger service. Vinnie stuffed the money into a saddlebag, donned the helmet, and very quietly got the bike out of the building. The gears were a little crazy, but he soon got the hang of it. He peddled through the silent streets, past the groceries and coffeehouses he had known since boyhood, and soon he was headed uptown.

At Sixth Avenue and Twelfth Street a police car gave him a bad moment when it pulled up next to him. He gave them a smile and a wave and kept peddling.

He left the bicycle leaning against a bus stop shelter on Seventh Avenue and jogged the rest of the way home.

Back in the apartment, he got a knife and cut through the plastic bonding material that held four bricks in place. He stuffed the moneybag into the hole and replaced the bricks, carefully filling the cracks again. A little soot from the fireplace and the filling matched the cement holding the other bricks together. It was near dawn when he gratefully crawled into bed next to the sleeping Vanessa.

She was up first; she had a modeling job that morning. "Where were you last night?" she asked. "I got up and went to the bathroom, and you were gone."

He knew what kind of sleeper she was.

"Sweetheart, you had a dream. I never budged at all last night."

"Oh," she said, then kissed him and went on her way.

When she had gone, he resisted the temptation to count the money. Instead, he called Tommy Pro. "Just checking in," he said.

"Bad news," Tommy said. "Benedetto got hit last night. Cheech too."

Vinnie always assumed the line was tapped. "No shit," he said, sounding as astonished as he could. "Who did it?"

"We're working on it, and so are the cops, but no leads so far. They cleaned out the safe, too. Wasn't much in it, just the proceeds from the coffeehouse for a couple days."

"Anything I can do?"

"I'll let you know," Tommy replied, then hung up.

The phone rang.

"Hello?"

"It's Barbara. How about tonight?"

"Dinner party?"

"Just you and me, babe."

He didn't have to think long. "I'll look forward to it."

He stayed away from the shoot that day, since they were still in Little Italy and he didn't want to be seen there, even though

80

there was no reason for the cops to question him. They were only a couple of weeks away from a rough cut of the picture, and he had to think about the next stage.

Finally he was unable to resist the temptation; he took out the bricks and had a look at the money. It was in bills of all sizes, and it came to a little over a hundred and ninety thousand. He could finish the picture now, even if he went over budget, but he was determined not to do that. He hid the money again.

Barbara Mannering ran a long fingernail down Vinnie's chest to his pubic hair. "Again, lover?" she asked sweetly.

Vinnie still hadn't caught his breath from the first time. "Barbara, you are insatiable, you know that?"

She chuckled. "I know that. I'll give you a minute."

"Thanks."

"How's your movie coming?"

"We wrap next week."

"When can I see it?"

"I want it finished before you see it — scored, the titles and the opticals in."

"Oh, all right, I'll be patient."

"You know anybody at the New York Film Festival?"

81

"Sure. A girl I knew at Bennington is the executive director."

"Can you get her to look at the picture?"

"I expect so. The festival's next month, though. She'll need to see it very soon if she's to schedule it. In fact, it might be too late already."

"Tell her I'll have a rough cut in ten days. I'll book a screening room at the film school."

"I'll see what I can do. You all rested now?"

He turned back to her. "I'm all rested."

Since there were no titles yet, the film just stopped.

"I love it," the woman said. "I just love it. But we've booked the whole festival."

"Surely you can squeeze us in somewhere," Vinnie said. "Look, this is a homegrown New York product, with a score by a student at Juilliard and a director from the NYU film school who's going to be very hot. A couple of months from now you'll look very smart to have had this in the festival."

"Can you finish it in time?" she asked.

"We can," Vinnie replied. He hoped that was true.

"Tell you what. We've only got a single feature scheduled for the second night — a new film from England. I'll run yours first."

"Run it second," Vinnie said. "Everybody will show up for the English film. We'll be dessert."

She stuck out a hand. "You're on."

Vinnie held his breath and dialed the number. "Mr. Goldman's office," a businesslike female voice said.

"Hello, this is Michael Vincent. May I speak to Leo, please?"

"Does he know you, Mr. Vincent?"

"How else would I have this number?" Michael said, laughing.

"Just a moment."

There was a very long wait, but finally the voice was male. "Leo Goldman," he said briskly.

"This is Michael Vincent; how are you?" God, is he going to remember?

"Barbara's friend. What can I do for you?"

"Will you be in New York for the film festival?"

"I'm there for the opening, then I have to go on to London."

"I've got a film showing the second night."

"Bring it to our screening room — the Centurion Building, on Fifth Avenue. Let's see . . ."

Vinnie could hear pages turning.

"Three o'clock on opening day."

"That's good."

"See you then." Goldman hung up.

Vinnie replaced the receiver and held his breath for a moment. Then he exploded in laughter. "A screening with Leo Goldman!" he shouted to the empty room.

10

Vinnie sat in a taxicab and sweated. He had less than ten minutes before his appointment with Leo Goldman and he was still forty blocks away. The film lab had been late finishing the print, and he was nearly crazy. He had meant to have the film delivered to the Centurion offices, but now he had to hump the cans up there himself. He found a handkerchief and patted his face; he breathed deeply, settled himself into a kind of mild trance. There was nothing he could do about this; he would go with the flow.

He was ten minutes late for his appointment, and when he reached Goldman's office, his secretary said he was waiting in the screening room. He took the elevator down, handed all the film cans to a waiting projectionist, straightened his tie, and entered the screening room.

Leo Goldman sat hunched in a chair, cigar smoke rising from him. He nodded at Vinnie, then pressed a button, and said, "Let's go, Jerry."

Vinnie took a seat as the film began to run. They were thirty seconds into the titles when a phone rang.

Goldman picked it up and started to talk rapidly, alternately puffing on the cigar.

Vinnie reached over and pressed the intercom button. "Jerry, please stop the film and back it up to the beginning."

Goldman stopped talking and placed a hand over the receiver. "I was watching," he said.

"Leo," Vinnie said calmly, "all I want is ten minutes of your undivided attention. If you'd like to take calls after that, feel free."

Goldman looked at him oddly for a moment, then spoke into the phone again. "I'll get back to you." He hung up and pressed the intercom. "Let's go, Jerry."

The film started again, and Vinnie made every effort not to look at Goldman. This was easy for him, for he had not seen the finished film himself, and he was entranced.

Ten minutes into the film Goldman glanced at his watch, then picked up the telephone.

Oh, shit, Vinnie thought, *I blew this one.*

"Bernice," Goldman said into the telephone, "hold my calls."

Vinnie sank back into the big chair and started to enjoy the film again.

Goldman had gone through two more cigars during the film, but he had not shifted in his seat. He waited until the final credit had rolled before he spoke. "Who owns this movie?" he asked.

"The Downtown Nights Company, Incorporated," Vinnie replied.

"And who owns the corporation?"

"I do."

"A hundred percent of the stock?"

"That's correct."

"What about your investors?"

"They invested in the film, not the corporation."

"So you're free to deal, without encumbrance?"

"I am."

"Who else has seen this film?"

"Nobody but you; not even the director has seen this print, and it's one of only two prints. The other is for the festival."

"What do you want for the negative?"

"Make me an offer."

"I'll give you two million dollars for it, lock, stock, and barrel."

"No."

"Are you crazy?"

"Leo, tomorrow night the film is going to be shown at the New York Film Festival. The reviews will appear in the *Times* the following morning. It won't be a secret anymore."

"All right, two and a quarter million."

Vinnie shook his head slowly. He was waiting to be asked again what he wanted.

Leo stood up. "See you around, kid," he said, and strode up the aisle of the little theater.

Keep functioning, Vinnie said to himself. He pressed the button on the intercom. "Jerry, please rewind the reels."

Goldman walked through the swinging doors.

Vinnie sat and waited for the projectionist to finish rewinding. He willed himself not to run after Goldman. *Never mind,* he was thinking, *they'll all see it tomorrow night.*

Goldman came back through the swinging doors, strode down the aisle, and sat down next to Vinnie. "All right, let's see how smart you are," he said. "Tell me what you want. Be reasonable, be realistic. If you do that, I'll buy it."

"I want three million dollars cash," Vinnie said. "I want ten gross points — that's me, personally, not the corporation — a separate contract; I want a guarantee of a minimum of eight million dollars spent on advertising and promotion; I want a guarantee that it will open on not less than one thousand screens; I want a guarantee that nobody will touch one frame of it."

"I don't do gross points," Goldman said.

"Leo, you're going to have a terrific finished film in the theaters for a third of what it would cost you to produce it yourself."

"It may have to be edited for television."

"You can dub language, you can't edit."

"I want you to come to work in development for me. I'll give you six hundred grand a year and a good expense account, five-year contract."

"I don't want to develop, Leo, I want to produce. I want a production deal."

"What kind of a deal?"

"Three-quarters of a million a year, the expense account, and overhead of three hundred thousand; a million a year in development money; three-year contract."

"Three years and an option for two more; any budget over a negative cost of twenty million, you fund elsewhere."

"All right, but you get thirty days to green-light; after that, I can take it anywhere I want, but shoot at Centurion. If you pick up my option, I get a million and a half a year."

"Six weeks to green-light."

"Done," Vinnie said.

Goldman picked up a phone and punched in a number. "Murray, I want a negative buyout contract right now; the price is three million; the film is called *Downtown Nights*, we're buying from Downtown Nights Company, Incorporated. I said *now*. Further, I want a separate contract giving ten gross points personally to one Michael Vincent. Further, I want a producer's contract drawn." He dictated the terms exactly as he and Vinnie had agreed. "One more thing," he said. "Cut me a check for three million dollars to the corporation and another one for a hundred thousand to Vincent. I want everything in my office in half an hour." He hung up.

"You can generate those contracts in half an hour?" Vinnie asked incredulously.

Goldman waved a hand. "It's all boilerplate; he'll insert the numbers and spew the whole thing out of a word processor. It'll take him forty-five minutes." He got up. "Where's the negative?"

"In your screening room," Vinnie replied.

"I like the way you do business, Michael. Come on."

Vinnie followed Goldman at a near-trot to his office. It was a square room, about thirty feet on a side, and the walls were hung with a mixture of abstract paintings and impressionists.

"A beautiful collection," Vinnie said.

"You should see the stuff at my house," Goldman replied. He riffled through his calendar. "Let's see, I'm back from London on Saturday. You show up on the lot on Monday morning; come to dinner on Tuesday. Want me to arrange a girl?"

"I've got one of those."

"Married?"

"No."

"Smart."

The contracts arrived. Vinnie went through them carefully, taking his time, while Goldman caught up on his phone messages. He complained about some clauses, quibbled about others. Goldman was reasonable. By seven in the evening the contracts had been revised, and Goldman and Vinnie signed.

Goldman handed him two checks. "There's your buyout. Here's another for a hundred grand, the first payment on your contract."

Vinnie stood up and shook Goldman's hand. "Thank you, Leo."

"Let me ask you something, Michael: what did it cost you for the negative?"

"Six hundred and thirty thousand dollars," Vinnie replied.

Goldman roared with laughter. "I love it!" he shouted. "I figured a million eight! I paid you more than you wanted! Of course, you're screwing your investors, taking the ten points directly to you."

"I only have two investors, and they'll make out like bandits. You got a good deal, too; you don't make bad deals."

"It's always like this, kid; two guys make a deal, they both always know something the other doesn't. It works out in the end."

Vinnie looked at Goldman sharply. "Leo, what do you know that I don't know?"

Goldman permitted himself a small smile. "Carol Geraldi checked out this morning. An overdose. That's going to guarantee ten million dollars worth of free publicity for this movie, and I'm going to get her a posthumous Academy Award. You wait and see."

Vinnie sat back in the cab and looked at his two checks. If he had known about Geraldi's death, he could have gotten at least another million, he thought. Never mind, he reasoned, he'd make out just fine with his gross points.

CHAPTER

11

Vinnie had three meetings on the morning of the showing of *Downtown Nights* at the New York Film Festival. First, he met Chuck at the coffeeshop where they had first talked about making *Downtown Nights*.

"Where have you been?" Chuck asked. "I ran the film last night, and it looks great. You haven't even seen it."

"I saw it yesterday afternoon with Leo Goldman of Centurion Pictures."

"How did you get to Goldman?"

"I told you I had some connections."

"What did he think?"

"He loved it. He paid me three million dollars for it."

Chuck's mouth fell open; he seemed unable to speak.

"Is that all right with you, Chuck?" Vinnie asked.

"Well . . . I don't know. Is that a good deal? You never checked with me."

"It's a very good deal, Chuck, and our contract stipulates that I conduct all negotiations and have the final say."

"Well, if that's what it says. When do I see some money?"

Vinnie produced an envelope. "Here's your first payment," he said.

Chuck ripped open the envelope. "A hundred and fifty grand, all at once!"

"That's your fee for writing and directing." Vinnie produced another check.

Chuck's hands were trembling as he opened the envelope. "Five hundred ninety-seven thousand, four hundred and twenty-five dollars," he said weakly.

"That's your investment of three hundred thousand, plus the earnings."

"That's . . . that's . . . " Chuck was looking at the ceiling, concentrating.

"That's a total of seven hundred forty-seven thousand dollars and change," Vinnie said. "Let me tell you how it breaks down. We spent six hundred and fifty thousand shooting the film. We got three million for it, leaving two million, three hundred and fifty thousand. Out of that, your fee for directing and writing was a hundred and fifty thousand; my fee for producing was two hundred and fifty thousand . . ."

"How come you get more than me?" Chuck demanded. "It was my film."

"For two reasons," Vinnie said calmly. "First, I'm picking up the legal work, which is going to be expensive. Second, none of this would have happened without me; you wouldn't have three quarters of a million dollars in your hand, and your film wouldn't be showing at the New York Film Festival tonight."

"You're right, Michael," Chuck said sheepishly. "I didn't mean to be ungrateful."

"To continue: that leaves a million nine hundred and fifty thousand dollars profit. Taxes are something over six hundred and fifty thousand, leaving a net of a little under a million three to distribute to investors. Your share is forty-six percent. It's all right here," he said handing Chuck a document. "Believe me, if a studio had done the film they'd have raked off most of the profits."

Chuck was looking at the checks and nodding. "*Yes!*" he shouted.

Vinnie's second meeting took place later that morning. He and Tommy Pro sat in the little office at the back of La Boheme and drank espresso.

"Is this place clean?" Vinnie asked, looking around the room. There was a constant fear of electronic bugs in the place.

"It was swept this morning," Tommy replied. "You hear from the cops?"

"Not a word."

"I know you didn't hear from our people; I kept you out of it."

"Thanks, Tommy."

"So, how's your movie coming along?"

"It's finished. It's being shown at the New York Film Festival tonight."

"Fantastic! So maybe a studio will pick it up?"

"A studio picked it up yesterday."

"Wonderful, Vinnie; how'd you do?"

"I did okay." Vinnie shoved a briefcase across the table. "Your legal fees," he said.

Tommy Pro lifted the lid of the case and peeked inside, then closed the case and shoved it back across the table. "Completely unnecessary," he said.

"Tommy, you did the legal work, and you . . . made it possible for me to make the movie."

"I did all right too, remember?"

"I remember, but it's not enough."

"I got a lot more than you did out of all this."

"How do you mean?"

96

Tommy shrugged. "Look around you. Where are we sitting?"

"You're the new . . . ?"

"I am. And if I say so myself, the family couldn't have done better."

"You're right, they couldn't do better."

"So what's next for you, Vinnie? Another movie?"

"A lot of movies," Vinnie replied. "I got a production deal at Centurion Pictures. I leave the day after tomorrow for L.A."

"So I'm going to know somebody in Hollywood? I get starlets when I come out?"

"You get whatever you want, and it'll always be on me."

"I'm looking forward," Tommy said.

"By the way, from now on I'm known as Michael Vincent. Think you can handle that?"

Tommy Pro stood up, grabbed Vinnie, and hugged him. "Michaele," he said.

"I still owe you," Vinnie replied.

Vinnie's third meeting took place at Le Cirque, at lunch. Barbara, who was a regular, had booked the table. When the champagne had arrived he handed her the check.

"Just over a hundred percent profit in less than three months," she said, tucking it into her purse.

"Here's a statement of where all the money

went," he said, handing her a sheet of paper.

She tore it up and put the pieces in the ashtray. "Honey, I've made a profit, and that's all I want. I don't care how much you skimmed off the top."

"Barbara, I assure you . . ."

She put a hand over his mouth. "I know you would never cheat me. I'm happy as a clam." She sipped her champagne. "But," she said, "I have the feeling I'm not going to be seeing as much of you."

He told her about his production deal with Centurion. "And it was all because you introduced me to Leo Goldman. I won't forget that."

She kissed a finger and placed it on his lips. "As long as you don't forget me," she said.

That afternoon, he picked up Vanessa from a modeling job and took her to the Palm Court of the Plaza for tea. When they had been served he handed her a slim book.

"What is it?" she asked, leafing through it.

"It's a little-known nineteen-twenties novel called *Pacific Afternoons*," he said. "It's a wonderful book, and it's going to be your first starring vehicle."

Vanessa jumped up and down and made little squealing noises.

Vinnie took a sheaf of papers from his briefcase and handed it to her with a pen. "You'll be under contract to me, personally, for five years, starting at five thousand dollars a week, with raises each year."

She took the pen and signed the contract.

"I think you should have your lawyer read it before you sign it," Vinnie said.

"I don't need a lawyer," she said. "I've got you."

Vinnie took a thick envelope from his briefcase. "Here's your first month's salary," he said. "Why don't you go shopping this afternoon? Save something for Rodeo Drive, though."

Her eyes widened. "Are we going to California?"

"The day after tomorrow, first class," he replied.

Vanessa got up from her chair, walked around the table, sat in his lap and began kissing him.

That night, *Downtown Nights* got a standing ovation at the film festival, and at a cocktail party afterward, Vinnie and Chuck received the congratulations of hundreds. The evening was marred only by Chuck's first sight of Vinnie with Vanessa.

The morning following the screening,

Vinnie and Vanessa boarded an MGM Grand flight to Los Angeles. They settled into the luxurious seats and ordered champagne. Vinnie had a cashier's check in his pocket for six hundred and sixty thousand dollars, representing his profits thus far from *Downtown Nights*, and in a carry-on bag in the overhead compartment was two hundred and sixty thousand dollars in cash, representing his savings and the proceeds from the murder of Benedetto. He was not quite a millionaire.

As the airplane left Kennedy Airport and turned west, Vinnie looked down at lower Manhattan and raised his glass. "Good-bye Vinnie Callabrese," he whispered, "and hello Michael Vincent!"

CHAPTER

12

Michael opened his eyes and listened hard. There was a noise, a sound he was unaccustomed to. The room was dark, and he wasn't sure where he was; then he recognized the sound.

He got out of bed and stumbled across the room, groping for the curtain pull. He swept open the drapes and blinked in the morning sunlight. A limb of a giant tree spanned the length of the windows, and on it sat two fat birds, singing loudly. Birds singing, Michael thought to himself. California!

Vanessa slept soundly, a mask over her eyes. Michael went to his luggage and dug out a small box, then went into the bathroom and regarded his image in the mirror. Vinnie Callabrese stared back at him. He opened the box and installed the batteries in the electric clippers. It took two minutes to dispose of Vinnie. He whipped up some lather and shaved off the remaining stubble. *There,* he said to himself, *finally.* Michael Vincent smiled back at him.

"Jesus," Vanessa said from behind him.

He turned and looked at her. "I thought you were sound asleep."

"The birds woke me up," she said. "You are gorgeous — you look so much better without the beard. All you need now is a haircut."

"It's Sunday; the barbershops are closed."

She dragged a stool over to the mirror and dug into her makeup kit, coming up with a shiny pair of scissors. "How do you think I made my living before I got a modeling job?"

"Are you any good?"

"Trust me," she smiled. "Now sit down and shut up. I know exactly how you should look."

Michael sat down nervously. "Not too much off," he said.

"I told you to shut up," she said, running her fingers through his thick hair, snipping away.

When she had finished, he stood up and looked closely at his reflection while she held a mirror behind his head. "It's a lot shorter," he said.

"It's a lot *better*," she replied. "Now you look like a businessman instead of a film student."

She ordered breakfast sent to the suite, and he went through the real estate section of the *Los Angeles Times*, occasionally marking something.

"What are you doing?" she asked.

"Looking for a place for us to live," he replied, marking another apartment.

"We'd better rent a car," she said, "if we're going house-hunting."

"That won't be necessary," he said. "I've arranged something."

At 10:00, Michael left the suite. "Meet me out front in fifteen minutes," he said to Vanessa, picking up his briefcase and the newspaper.

"Okay. How shall I dress?"

"Like a Californian out for a Sunday drive." He closed the door and stepped out onto a shaded walkway. He loved the Bel-Air Hotel, he thought as he walked through the densely planted gardens. He walked through the lobby and out the front entrance, then over a bridge. Below him, swans paddled up and down a little stream.

As he came to the parking lot an attendant approached. "Good morning, Mr. Vincent," the young man said. "There's a gentleman waiting for you just over there." He indicated the other side of the lot, where a man waited in the shade of a tree, leaning against a car.

Michael walked over to him, looking the car over closely.

"Mr. Vincent?" the man said, sticking out his hand. "My name's Torio. What do you think of the car?"

Michael walked slowly around the machine, a new Porsche Cabriolet, painted metallic black, with a black leather interior. "Have you got the title?" he asked.

The man opened a briefcase and handed him a sheet of paper. "It's the real thing," he said. "All registered in your name."

"How do you do this?" Michael asked, looking at the title. "This looks genuine."

"It *is* genuine," the man replied, sounding hurt. "You think I'd palm off bad paper on a friend of Tommy Pro's?"

"I suppose not," Michael said.

"We got our own man at motor vehicle registrations," the man said, looking around him to make sure no one was listening. "When we yank a car we already got the numbers from a vehicle that's already trashed. This car has got less than a hundred miles — real miles on it, but it's registered as last year's model. We turned up the speedometer to show three thousand miles. Our guy registers the car, and your title is absolutely clean, I guarantee it. You want to drive the car? It's perfect, I promise."

"That won't be necessary; I'll take your word for it." Michael opened his briefcase, took out a thick envelope, and handed it to the man. "Twenty-five thousand cash, as agreed."

He accepted the envelope. "I won't need to count it," he said, sticking out his hand again. "Give Tommy my best when you see him."

"I'll do that," Michael replied, shaking the man's hand.

"Oh," the man said, producing a business card. "If it ever comes up, you bought the car from this dealership out in the Valley, okay?"

"Okay," Michael replied and watched the man climb into a waiting car and be driven away. He got into the Porsche, started the engine, and drove up to the portico just as Vanessa appeared.

"Wow!" she said, running a hand over the car.

"Hop in, Ms. Parks," Michael replied,

grinning. "Let's go find a place to live."

Late in the afternoon, after looking at half a dozen houses and apartments, Michael and Vanessa stood in the living room of a large penthouse in Century City.

"It's available for a year," the agent was saying. "The owner is making two films in Europe and will be based in London."

"We'll take it," Michael said.

"Well," the woman said, "I'm afraid there are three more people to see the place, then we'll pick the best-qualified tenant. There will be some formalities to go through."

"I don't think we need worry about formalities," Michael said.

"I beg your pardon?"

"I'll pay the year's rent in advance," he said, opening his briefcase, "in cash. Right now."

"In *cash?*"

"That's what I said. Now I'm sure you have a standard lease form in your briefcase, and if we can wrap this up *right now* there's a two-thousand-dollar bonus in it for you. In cash. And I don't think we'll find it necessary to mention this to your broker."

The woman licked her lips. "You say you're at Centurion?"

"Starting tomorrow. Leo Goldman's office will confirm."

"Well," she said, "I don't see why we can't forget the formalities."

When she had gone and the keys were in Michael's pocket, he and Vanessa stood on the terrace and looked out over the city. "Right out there," he said, pointing.

"Where?"

"Follow my finger; see the gate and the big sign?"

"Centurion Pictures," she said.

"I like being able to see it from here," he said.

"Michael, what'll we do when the year's lease is up?"

"Don't you worry, babe," he said, giving her a hug. "We'll find something a *lot* nicer."

When they had moved their things into the new apartment, Michael drove them out to Malibu, and they found a restaurant and a table overlooking the Pacific. As the sun went down, they raised their glasses. "To Hollywood," Michael said. "It's going to be ours."

CHAPTER

13

Michael approached the gates of Centurion Pictures slowly. He had seen photographs and film of this famous entrance all his life, and he wanted to savor the moment.

He stopped at the little guardhouse, and for a moment he felt as though he were an intruder.

A uniformed guard stepped out. "May I help you?"

"My name is Michael Vincent," he said. "I . . ."

"Oh, yes, Mr. Vincent," the guard said, smiling. "Just a moment." He disappeared into the guardhouse and came back with a plastic sticker, which he affixed to the Porsche's windshield. "That'll get you in any time and without delay," he said. "The Executive Building is at the other end of the grounds. Take your first right and follow your nose. My name is Bill, if I can ever be of any service."

"Thank you, Bill," Michael said, smiling at the man. "I'll remember that." He drove slowly past a row of neatly painted bungalows; each had a sign out front with the occupant's name painted on it. He recognized the names of directors and writers. Then he turned right and found himself on a New York City street.

Downtown, he thought. Not Little Italy — the Village, maybe. Rows of neat brownstones ran down the block, with small shops interspersed. On an impulse he stopped the car and ran up the front steps of a house, peering through the glass of the front door. As he had expected, there was nothing beyond but a weeded lot and the back of another row of façades. The whole street was propped up with timbers.

He continued to the Executive Building and drove slowly around the parking lot, looking for a place. To his surprise, he found one marked by a freshly painted sign reading MR. VINCENT. He paused. Could there be another Vincent at Centurion? Then he decided the paint was so fresh, it must be his. He parked the Porsche, noting the distance from his parking place to the front entrance of the building. Not too far, he noted — at least, not as far as some.

The Executive Building was a substantial structure with a stone façade and a row of columns. There was an air of permanence about it. Michael trotted up the front steps and entered the building. A large desk straddled the broad hallway, occupied by two very busy telephone operators and a receptionist. She smiled coolly at him. "Good morning," she said. "May I help you?"

"My name is Michael Vincent," he said. "I'm . . ."

"Oh, yes, Mr. Vincent," she interrupted. "Just a moment, I'll ring Mr. Goldman's secretary for you. Won't you have a seat?"

Instead of sitting, Michael wandered up and down the entrance hall, inspecting the original posters that hung there — posters for movies that were like a history of his life, movies he'd seen at dozens of New York movie houses from his earliest years. There were many Academy Award–winners among them.

Shortly, a small, plump woman in a business suit appeared. "Mr. Vincent? I'm Helen Gordon, Mr. Goldman's secretary. Mr. Goldman isn't in yet — still recovering from jet lag, I believe. He's asked me to take care of you."

"How do you do?" Michael said, taking the woman's hand and turning on a businesslike charm. "I'm sure I'll be in good hands."

"Mr. Goldman thought one of two offices might be to your liking," she said. "Please follow me, and I'll show them to you."

Michael followed her up the broad staircase behind the reception desk, past a set of heavily varnished mahogany doors, then down a hallway that ran the length of the building. At the very end, she showed him a large office with a reception room of its own.

"It's very nice," Michael said noncommittally. He wanted to know what the second one was like before he chose.

"The other office is really a little building of its own," she said, leading him back down the hallway and out of the building. "It's only a short walk." She led him down a broad sidewalk that ran between two rows of huge, hangarlike soundstages. At the end, she turned a corner, and they approached a small adobe building, one end of which was half a story higher than the other. Producing a key, she led him inside.

"This is very interesting," Michael said, looking around the empty reception area.

She opened the doors of two good-sized offices, then led him toward a large pair of double doors. "In the old days they used to shoot screen tests in this room," she said, opening the doors and stepping back for him to enter.

The room was large, with a very high ceiling. This was the extra half-story he had noticed from outside. Sunlight poured in through high windows at one end.

"By shooting tests here, they didn't take up time on the big stages," she said. "I think it's rather nice, don't you?"

"I do," he replied, turning to her. "May I ask your advice? Which should I take?"

Helen Gordon nearly blushed. "Well," she said haltingly, "there is a body of opinion which holds that it is not wise to work too close to Mr. Goldman's office. He does rather have a tendency to look over one's shoulder."

"I see," Michael laughed. "Well, I think I'll be very happy in this building. I'm going to need some space for one or two other people anyway."

"Good," she said. "Now, let's see about getting you some furnishings. Follow me." She led him out of the building and down the street. At a small door in what he assumed was a soundstage, she pressed a bell and waited. "I'll introduce you to George Hathaway," she said.

"The art director?" Michael asked. "I'd assumed he was dead."

"He's very much alive, I assure you, though he's sort of retired. He manages props and costumes now. Mr. Goldman has kept a number of the old-timers on retainer. They seem to prefer it to a pension."

The door opened and a tall, slender, elderly man with a clipboard in his hand waved them in. "Good morning, Helen," he said.

"Good morning, Mr. Hathaway. I'd like you to meet Michael Vincent, who's going to be producing on the lot."

"I'm an admirer of your work," Michael said to the man, shaking his hand. "I've always been particularly impressed with your designs for *Fair Weather* and *Border Village*."

Hathaway beamed. "How very nice of you to say so." He seemed to have a slight English accent.

"George," Helen Gordon said, "Mr. Vincent has decided to use the old screen test building. Do you think you could put together some furnishings for him? Mr. Goldman says he's to have whatever he wants."

"Why, of course, Helen," Hathaway replied. "I'd be delighted. I'm always happy to have a new producer for a client."

"Mr. Vincent," Helen said, "I'll leave you in George's capable hands. When you've finished here, come on back to the Executive Building; Mr. Goldman should be in by that time, and he'll want to greet you himself."

"Thank you, Helen," Michael replied.

She left the building, and George Hathaway

beckoned for Michael to follow. He led the way to another door and opened it.

Michael stepped through the door and stared. What he had thought was a soundstage was a vast warehouse of furniture and other objects stacked high on steel shelving. The central aisle seemed nearly to vanish into the distance. "It's like something out of *Citizen Kane*, Mr. Hathaway," he said wonderingly.

George Hathaway laughed. "Yes, I suppose it is. And please, you must call me George."

"And I'm Michael."

"Let's have a wander around, and if you see a desk or a sofa or anything else that catches your eye, you just let me know."

Michael followed the old man slowly through the building, gazing at the collection of seventy years of movie making — furniture, paintings, objets d'art, hat racks, spittoons, bars from English pubs and Western saloons. At the end of a row, Michael spotted something familiar. Leaning against the outside wall was an eight-foot-wide stretch of oak panelling surrounding a stone fireplace. "George, isn't that the fireplace from Randolph's study in *The Great Randolph*?"

"It is," George beamed, "and how nice it is to find someone with the eye to recognize it."

"I always loved that room," Michael said.

"When I was about twelve, I had this fantasy of living in it."

"Tell me," George said, scratching his chin, "were you thinking of using the tall room for your office?"

"Yes, I was."

"Well, you know, that whole study is here in this warehouse — the desk, furniture, books — everything, and I think it might fit the tall room, with an adjustment or two. How would you like it if I reassembled it for you?"

"You could do that?"

"Of course. Mr. Goldman says you're to have whatever you want."

"That would be absolutely wonderful, George. I'll feel like Randolph himself."

"Consider it done. Will you want the other rooms furnished?"

"Yes, I'll be hiring a few people soon."

"Well, if you'll leave it to me, I'll choose some things for them."

"Thank you very much."

George picked up a phone against the wall and punched in a number. "I'll get a crew on it right away," he said. "We're not too busy at the moment, so I should be ready for you tomorrow."

"Tomorrow? As soon as that?"

"Well, Michael," George Hathaway said,

"this is Hollywood, after all."

Michael left the warehouse and started back toward the Executive Building walking on air, headed for his first meeting with Leo Goldman. He passed a small bungalow, and through the open windows came the sounds of a string quartet, playing something Michael didn't know. He thought it must be recorded, but when he stopped and looked inside, he saw three elderly men and a woman playing their instruments, lost in the music. He continued on toward the Executive Building. This was indeed Hollywood, he thought.

14

Michael entered the Executive Building again and found Helen Gordon waiting for him.

"Oh, good," she said. "Mr. Goldman has just come in. Let's go up to his office."

At the top of the stairs she opened one of the large, gleaming mahogany doors he had noticed before and led him through an elegant waiting room where two young women were typing furiously on word processors. Helen rapped on an inner door, then opened it and showed Michael into Leo Goldman's office. The room was large enough to contain a huge desk, a pair of leather sofas in front of a fireplace, a grand piano, and a conference table with seating for twelve. One wall was a floor-to-ceiling bookcase with a ladder on rails. Leo Goldman sat in a large leather chair, his feet on his desk, talking into a telephone headset that was plugged into one ear. He waved Michael to one of the sofas and continued talking rapidly.

Michael sat down and regarded the room's furnishings. Every object seemed to be the best of its kind, carefully chosen to make the enormous room comfortable and beautiful.

Leo tossed the headset onto his desk, walked the twenty feet to where Michael sat, shook his hand, and sprawled on the opposite sofa. "Well, did you have a good flight?"

"Yes, just fine, Leo."

"Your rooms at the Bel Air all right?"

"Perfect. We enjoyed it, but we've already found an apartment in Century City."

"Good; fast work. Who's *we?*"

"My lady friend, Vanessa Parks."

Goldman nodded. "Have you moved in yet?"

"Vanessa is moving us today."

"Will we meet her tomorrow night at dinner?"

"You will."

"Good; Amanda will be delighted. By the way, is there anybody special you'd like to meet?"

"At dinner?" Michael asked, a little nonplussed.

"Sure. Anybody in town you'd like me to ask?"

118

"I don't know a soul here."

Leo shook his head. "I mean, is there *any-body* you'd like to meet?"

Jesus, Michael thought, can he just summon anybody he wants? "Well, there are lots of people I'd like to meet."

"Name somebody."

Michael thought. "Yes. I'd like to meet Mark Adair." He had read in the *Times* that the novelist was in town.

"I'll see what I can do," Leo said.

"And I'd like to meet Robert Hart."

"Well, at least you want to meet movie stars, just like everybody else," Leo said, laughing. "Bob Hart is just back from a month at Betty Ford's," he said. "Booze, not drugs. He hasn't worked in over a year."

"If you don't think it's a good idea . . ."

"No, it's fine; I like Bob, and I've always loved his work. His wife can be a little hard to take." He picked up a phone on the coffee table between the sofas, pressed a button, and spoke. "Helen, invite Bob and Sue Hart to dinner tomorrow night; you've got the number. And call the Beverly Hills and see if Mark Adair is there; ask him, too. Let me know." He hung up. "If they're not in town, think of somebody else."

"This is very kind of you, Leo," Michael said, meaning it.

"Not at all." Leo leaned back on the sofa and threw a leg onto the cushions. "Now. Let me tell you about Centurion. You may already have heard some of it, but I'll tell you again."

"Fine."

"Centurion was founded in 1937 by Sol Weinman, who had run an important unit at MGM for Irving Thalberg. When Thalberg died, Sol couldn't stomach being directly under L. B. Mayer, so he got out. Sol was a rich man — inherited — and he got some other rich men together and started Centurion. They bought a broken-down Poverty Row studio that had some good real estate, built four soundstages, and started to make pictures. It was tough at first, because they had to borrow talent from the majors and that was expensive, but they had a string of hit pictures, and by the time the war was over Sol had bought out his partners and had a profitable studio. He ran his own show, the way Sam Goldwyn did, and his pictures were at least as good. When TV came along, he didn't get hurt quite as badly as MGM and the other big studios; his overhead was lower, and he kept on making good pictures until he died twenty years ago.

"The studio floundered around for a while, had some hits and some flops, but it was going downhill pretty fast. Fifteen years ago, I borrowed a lot of money and put together a deal with some investors to buy the studio from Sol's widow. I kept control. I moved in here, sold the back lot to some developers, paid off most of the debt with the proceeds, and Centurion was back in business. I expect you know our output pretty well since then."

"Yes, I do, and I admire it."

"Thanks, you ought to; we do good work here. I keep the overhead low; we rent a lot of space to people whose work I like — you've seen the signs outside the buildings."

"Yes."

"I hung onto props and costumes, mostly out of sentiment, I guess, and we rent to everybody; just about breaks even. We've still got the four soundstages Sol built, plus two more, and we keep 'em busy. We make a dozen or so pictures a year, and a lot more get made on the lot by independents." Leo leaned forward and rested his elbows on his knees.

"What I want from you is a new picture next year, while you're getting your feet on the ground, and then two pictures a year after that. I want good work on tight budgets, commercial enough to make money. We've had a blockbuster or two around here, but that's not what pays the rent. We do it with good material, intelligently made, year in and year out. Once in a while I like a beautiful little picture, something a little arty that doesn't lose too much money. It's good for the studio, and you can get expensive talent to work cheap in a project like that. You cop an occasional Oscar that way, too.

"I have broad tastes; I like cop movies, comedies, heavy drama, classy horror, medical stories, westerns, biographies, musicals — God, I *love* musicals, but you can't make 'em any more without losing your ass. I'm *very* leery of blockbuster-type material, unless there's an absolutely *superb* script before another dime is spent. I tell you the truth, if Arnold Schwarzenegger came to me today with just an *idea* for something like that, I'd say, 'Thank you very much, Arnold, but fuck off until you've got a script that puts my blood pressure dangerously up.' I swear to God. What makes a blockbuster a blockbuster changes so quickly that it scares me to death. My idea of a nightmare is a movie — any kind of movie — that goes into production without a perfected script. I know, I know, *Casablanca* started without a finished script, but that's a very wild exception. Don't ever come to me, Michael, with a script you know is half-baked and ask me to make it. Don't ever commit me to a star without a finished script. You'll end up making a hash of it, trying to get it written while the star is still available, and you'll hurt us both. If you've got a *good* script, there's *always* a star available, believe me.

"We've got a television production company on the lot that does very nicely. If you come across something you don't want to make, but that you think would make a good TV movie, mini-series, or series, send it to me. You'll make friends on the lot that way. Speaking of making friends, you're going to have a hard time doing that. Studio executives are envious of guys with production deals, and my people are no exception. They make a lot of money for what they do, but they know that you have the *potential* of making a hell of a lot more, and that drives 'em crazy, so if you want to get along with the people in this building, work at it. Do them favors, compliment their work, kiss their asses when you can stomach it, and if somebody gets in your way, go around him, not through him.

"I know you're smart, Michael, and I don't have to tell you this, but I'm going to anyway. You're a young guy, good-looking, in a glamorous business with money to throw around. Be careful. Don't get into debt — in fact, pay cash for everything you possibly can. Don't use drugs. I've seen fifty bright young guys go right down the tubes on that stuff. Don't let your dick get in the way of your business. I'm glad to hear you've got a girl, because there are ten thousand women in this town who will suck your cock for a walk-on as a hatcheck girl in a bad movie, and a thousand who can do it so well they'll make you forget your business and do the wrong thing."

Leo sat back and took a deep breath. "That's all I can think of at the moment."

"Thank you, Leo," Michael said. "It's all good advice, and I'll try to follow it."

"Now," Leo said. "About *Downtown Nights*. I'm going to open it on a total of nine screens in New York and L.A. the week before Thanksgiving."

Michael's face fell, and he started to speak.

Leo held up a hand. "Wait a minute," he said, "let me finish. I'm going to run it for two weeks, then pull it until after the New Year. Between Thanksgiving and Christmas I'm going to screen the shit out of it on the lot, and we're going to get some good word-of-mouth going. Then, in mid-January, when a lot of big Christmas releases are starting to drop out of sight, I'm going to open it on twelve hundred screens and spend eight million dollars on advertising and promotion. It's good timing for the Academy Awards, and believe me, Carol Geraldi is going to be nominated. We'll do thirty, forty million, and with what we've got invested, that'll be a solid hit for us."

"Sounds wonderful," Michael said.

"Damn right," Leo said, looking at his watch. "I've got a lunch," he said. "I wanted to take you somewhere, but this can't be postponed. You take the rest of the day off; your office won't be ready until tomorrow anyway, and you need to get moved into your new place. Come over to the house early tomorrow night — say, six o'clock — that'll give us an hour to talk before the others get there. I want to hear about what you want to do next."

"Fine, I'll look forward to it."

Leo walked to his desk, retrieved a sheet of paper, then walked Michael to the door. "Here," he said, handing him the paper. "I had Helen put this together for you, stuff you'll need. Doctor, dentist, bank, barber, maid service, florist, caterer, whatever I could think of. There's a list of good restaurants. I've had Helen call them and tell them who you are, so don't worry about getting in. My address and home phone are there, too. See you tomorrow at six."

Five minutes later, Michael stood in the parking lot and watched Leo Goldman being driven off in an enormous Mercedes. Through the back window, he could see the phone at Leo's ear.

He got into the Porsche and just sat for a moment, remembering everything Leo had said. Michael had a superb memory. He could have recited it all verbatim.

CHAPTER

15

Michael had a prearranged appointment downtown at 2:30, and there was time to stop along the way and shop for a car phone. He bought a hand-held portable, too, and left the car for the phone installation. He took a shopping bag from the trunk and walked to his meeting a few blocks away.

He checked the directory in the lobby of a gleaming skyscraper and took the elevator to the top floor, to the offices of a discreet private bank. The Kensington Trust, the lettering on the glass doors told him, was based in London and had branches in New York, Los Angeles, Bermuda, Hong Kong, and the Cayman Islands.

At the reception desk he gave his name as Vincente Callabrese and asked for Derek Winfield. He was shown immediately to a panelled office with a spectacular view of the L.A. smog.

Winfield, a tall, thin man in his fifties wearing a Savile Row suit, rose to meet him. "Good afternoon, Mr. Callabrese," he said, extending a soft and beautifully manicured hand, "I've been expecting you." He offered Michael a chair.

"How do you do, Mr. Winfield?" Michael replied. "I expect you've been told of my banking needs."

"Yes, yes, our mutual friend in New York called a week ago. We're always happy to do business with friends of his. Have you known each other long?"

"Mr. Winfield," Michael said, ignoring the question, "I would like to open an investment account with you."

"Of course," Winfield replied. "I understood from Mr. Provensano that you also had something in mind."

"That's correct," Michael said, taking an envelope from his pocket. "Here is a cashier's check on my New York bank for six hundred and sixty thousand dollars." He placed the shopping bag on Winfield's desk. "There is a further one hundred thousand dollars cash in this bag." He endorsed the cashier's check. "I want to invest the entire amount on the street."

"I see," Winfield said. "What sort of a return were you anticipating on your investment?"

"Our friend said I could expect three percent a week; that's good enough for me."

"I think we can manage that," Winfield replied. "How would you like to collect the interest?"

"I'd like to roll it into the principal each week. From time to time I may withdraw some capital, but I expect this to be an investment of at least a year, perhaps much longer." Michael knew that if he took the interest each week, the annual income on his investment would be in excess of a million dollars, but if he let the interest ride, compounding weekly, his income would be much, much more, and it would be tax-free. The loan sharks would be lending his money at ten percent a week, so everybody would make money.

"Will you require facilities for, ah, movement of funds?" Winfield asked.

"Perhaps; I'm not certain at the moment."

"There would, of course, be a charge for that service."

"Of course. In such a case, how would the money be returned to me?"

"We could arrange for you to collect fees as a consultant to one of a number of corporations," Winfield explained. "You would have to pay taxes on the proceeds, of course, since the relevant corporation would be filing Form 1099 with the Internal Revenue Service. We could also move the funds through our Cayman branch, but in order to have safe access to them in this country you would have to travel there and return with cash. One must be careful with large sums of cash these days."

"I understand."

"If you will wait a moment, I'll get you a receipt. Oh, how shall I list the name and address of the account?"

"My name, but no address; just keep my statements on file here, and I'll pick them up when it's necessary."

Winfield smiled. "Of course," he said, then left the room.

Michael wandered around the office, inspecting paintings and looking out at the view. A few minutes later, Winfield returned.

"Here is your receipt," the banker said.

Winfield saw him to the elevator. "You may call me at any time for a confirmation of your current balance," he said.

"Thank you," Michael replied. He boarded the elevator, pressed the button for the lobby, and rode down feeling very rich.

That night, Michael and Vanessa dined at Granita, Wolfgang Puck's new restaurant in

Malibu. The headwaiter had been solicitous when Michael had called at the last minute. Leo Goldman's name worked wonders.

They sipped champagne while Michael touched on the highlights of his day. "What did you do?" Michael asked.

"Oh, I moved our luggage into the apartment and got the phone working, then I did a little shopping on Rodeo Drive."

"How much did you spend?"

"Does it matter?" she asked kittenishly.

"Not at all," he laughed. "It comes out of your pay. But then, you're very well paid, aren't you?"

"I'd like a car, Michael. Do you think that would be all right?"

"Of course; what would you like?"

"One of those new Mercedes convertibles, I think. Silver."

"I think you can afford that," he said.

"When do I start to earn my keep?" she asked.

"You mean, when do you become a movie star?"

"That's exactly what I mean," she said.

"You begin tomorrow night," Michael said, touching his glass to hers. "All you have to do is relax and be your charming self."

CHAPTER

16

Michael arrived at his offices the following morning and was not surprised to find workmen in the place. A pair of men were hammering in one of the small offices off the reception room. Hollywood or not, he thought, nobody could put all this together in a day.

The doors to his office had been replaced by a heavy, dark-stained oaken set; he passed through and stopped, staring. He was standing in the study from *The Great Randolph*, complete in every detail. One entire wall, floor to ceiling, was covered with bookcases, and they were filled with leatherbound books in matched sets. The opposite wall was panelled and covered in paintings that looked English — portraits of men in uniform and women in ball gowns, landscapes and still lifes, and one or two that appeared to be old masters. In that wall was a huge fireplace, and over the mantel hung a full-length portrait of Randolph himself, replete in white tie and tails, looking sternly toward Michael.

"A very impressive fellow, isn't he?" a voice behind him said.

Michael turned to find George Hathaway standing there.

"Sir Henry Algood as Randolph," Hathaway said. "I knew him well, before the war. Mind you, the portrait adds about a head in height to the old boy, that's why he loved it so much. He tried a dozen times to buy it, but he and Sol Weinman had some sort of falling out, and it gave Mr. Weinman the greatest pleasure to deny him the picture."

"George, I'm overwhelmed by the room," Michael said.

"Let me show you a few modifications," Hathaway said. "The width was perfect, but the room was about eight inches too long for the set. We made a false wall, then made good around the windows." He opened a cupboard to reveal a gas bottle. "This runs the fireplace. Don't ask how we did the flue, and don't, for Christ's sake, ever try to burn anything but gas in it." He walked across the room and behind the massive desk facing the fireplace, then pulled out a couple of large drawers. "We managed to conceal a couple of filing cabinets in here, but if you run out of space we'll have to add some cabinets to the reception room. Incidentally, we've found some panelling for that area that matches this pretty well, and there's a good desk for out there, too. Not a single one of the books is anything but a spine," he said, hooking a fingernail over one and pulling away a whole row of them to reveal a small wet bar. He opened another spine-concealed door and showed Michael a small refrigerator with an icemaker.

"It's astonishing," Michael said, meaning it. "This really is Hollywood, isn't it?"

"As real as it gets," Hathaway said.

Michael set his briefcase on the desk and took out a copy of *Pacific Afternoons*. "George," he said, handing him the book, "have you ever read this?"

"No," Hathaway replied, "but I know a little about it."

"I'd appreciate it if you'd read it. I'd like to get your advice on how it might be designed for a film."

"Of course, Michael, glad to."

There was a knock at the door, and Helen Gordon appeared, followed by a tall, handsome woman who appeared to be in her early forties, wearing a well-designed business suit.

"I'd better get going," Hathaway said. "I'll read this tonight." He left the room and Michael was alone with the two women.

"Mr. Vincent," Helen said, "I'd like you to meet Margot Gladstone."

"How do you do?" the woman said.

Michael shook the woman's hand, admiring her poise and the low, mellifluous voice that accompanied it. "I'm very glad to meet you, Ms. Gladstone."

Helen spoke again. "Mr. Goldman has suggested that Margot serve as your secretary. She's been with the studio for quite some time, and he thought she might help you find your feet."

"That was very kind of him," Michael said. "Perhaps Ms. Gladstone and I could have a talk?"

"Of course," Helen said. "Call me if there's anything you need." She took her leave.

"Will you have a seat, Ms. Gladstone?" Michael asked, showing her to one of the leather Chesterfield sofas before the fireplace.

"Thank you," she replied, sitting down and crossing her long legs. "And please do call me Margot."

"Thank you, Margot." Michael caught her accent. "I didn't realize at first that you were British."

135

"I was, a very long time ago," she replied. "I've been in this country since I was nineteen."

"It hasn't harmed your accent a bit," he said.

She smiled broadly, revealing beautiful teeth. "Thank you. I learned early on that Hollywood loves an English accent, so I made a point of hanging onto it."

Michael sat down opposite her and regarded her quizzically. "Certainly I can use someone who is at home in the studio," he said, "but I'm puzzled about something."

"Perhaps I can clear it up for you?"

"Perhaps you can, and I hope you'll be frank with me."

"Of course."

"Why am I, the new boy on the lot, being rewarded with such an elegant and, no doubt, accomplished assistant? Surely there are top studio executives ahead of me in line who would be very pleased to have you working for them."

She regarded him coolly. "You're very direct, Mr. Vincent."

"It saves time."

"Very well," she said. "I don't see why you shouldn't know what everybody else on the lot already knows."

"And what is that?"

"Let me begin at the beginning. I was born in a village called Cowes, on the Isle of Wight, daughter of a butcher. I exhibited some talent for drama at school, and afterwards I sought a career on the London stage. I got a small part in a Noel Coward play almost immediately, and almost immediately after that, Sol Weinman saw the play and came backstage to see me. He offered me a studio contract, and within a month I was on the Centurion lot, the perfect little English starlet.

"I played small parts and an occasional second lead for a few years, and then the studio system came crashing down around me. Being of a practical bent, I went to Mr. Weinman and asked him for a secretarial job. He put me to work as one of half a dozen girls in his office, and then, a couple of years later, he died.

"When Leo Goldman took over the studio I remained in the office and, eventually, became his secretary. We had an affair; it ended when he married. It became awkward having me around, so Leo passed me on to the studio's head of production, Martin Bell, and I became his secretary. We had an affair.

"This continued until quite recently, when, in short order, his marriage ended, and he married a girl in her twenties." She spread her hands. "So, you see, I'm awkward again, and nobody else in the executive building wants me in his office. Everyone is afraid I'll report back to either Martin or Leo. I'm regarded as something of a political bombshell."

"I see," Michael said. "Apart from your personal relationships with Leo and Bell, are you very good at your work?"

"I am very good indeed," she replied evenly.

"Didn't it occur to you to seek work at another studio? Surely with your background you would be a good candidate for secretary to some top executive."

"I am fifty-one years old," she replied. "I have twenty-three years vested in the studio pension plan, not to mention profit sharing and my Screen Actors Guild pension. All that matures in two years; then I can take my pensions and my profits and my savings and do as I please."

"Well, Margot," Michael said, "I think I would be very lucky to have you spend those two years with me."

"Thank you," she replied, "I think I would like that, as well."

"I must tell you: I'm new at this, and I'm going to need all the help I can get. You might make it your most important duty to keep me from making an ass of myself."

Margot laughed. "I am so glad you are intelligent enough to know that. I think we'll get along."

"I think we will, too," he replied. And, he thought to himself, you are not only going to keep me out of trouble, you are going to tell me, in very short order, where the bodies are buried in this studio — and who buried them. "Let's get to work."

She stood up. "Fine. Why don't we start with these?" She walked over to a table against the wall and picked up a stack of half a dozen packages.

"What are those?"

"These are scripts."

"From where?"

"From all over the place. Your deal with Centurion was reported in the trade press on Friday. You'll get more scripts tomorrow; it's best if we deal with them directly. You'll get a reputation around town as somebody who doesn't waste time."

"When am I going to have time to read them?"

"You won't have time; I'll screen them first." She began looking at the return addresses on the packages. "This one's been around for years," she said, tossing it back onto the table. "This writer's an unreliable drunk; this one's from an agent who doesn't represent anybody worth reading; this one's from a New York playwright who hasn't had anything produced since the mid-eighties — still, it might be worth reading; I'll look it over for you."

"What's next?" he asked.

"I'll order you some studio stationery and some business cards and get you subscriptions to the trades; leave restaurant bookings and screening invitations to me; I'll handle your expense reports; if you need a house, a haircut, or a whore, let me know, and I'll arrange it. I'll tell you what I know about the people you'll be working with."

That, he thought, *is what I want to know.*

"There's something you could do for me right away," he said.

"Of course."

"I want you to call every used bookstore in the Yellow Pages and buy every copy you can find of a novel called *Pacific Afternoons.* Please send a messenger to pick them up; I'd like them by four o'clock."

She smiled. "Not taking any chances, are you?"

Michael smiled back. "I never do."

CHAPTER

17

Michael and Vanessa found the Bel-Air house of Leo and Amanda Goldman on Stone Canyon, up the street from the Bel-Air Hotel. Michael pulled the Porsche into the driveway at precisely 6:00, and he thought he had never seen anything so beautiful.

There was no imposing edifice, just a comfortable-looking exterior that only hinted at what must be a large place. Michael had not yet become accustomed to the profusion of plant life that could exist in a desert when it was well watered; the landscaping looked as if it had always been there.

Leo answered the door himself, clad in a plaid sport jacket over an open-neck shirt. "Come in, come in," he said, giving Vanessa a huge smile.

"Leo," Michael said, "this is Vanessa Parks."

"She certainly is," Leo said, clasping her hand in both of his. "Welcome to Los Angeles and welcome to our home."

Amanda Goldman appeared, wearing a floral-printed silk dress and a knockout hairdo. "Michael," she said, pecking his cheek rather close to the corner of his mouth, "how nice to see you again." She turned to the younger woman. "And you must be Vanessa."

"Hello," Vanessa said shyly.

"You come with me," Amanda said to her. "I know Michael and Leo have some talking to do, so I'll show you the garden."

The two women departed together, and Leo led Michael into a small study lined with books and pictures.

"Let me get you a drink," Leo said.

"Just some mineral water. I'll have some wine with dinner."

Leo went to a butler's tray that held drinks and poured Michael a Perrier and himself a large Scotch. They sat down in comfortable chairs before the fireplace and raised their glasses to each other.

"So," Leo said. "How are you settling in?"

"Very well, thanks. We're comfortable in the new apartment and amazingly, George Hathaway has managed to put my office together in little more than a single day."

"I heard about the *Randolph* set," Leo chuckled. "It's all over the lot already. Expect people to drop in to see you just to see that room."

"I hope I haven't overdone it," Michael said.

"Don't worry about it. A little flamboyance is good for business in this business. What do you think of Margot?"

"I'm very impressed with her; thank you for sending her to me."

"She's a smart girl," Leo said, nodding in agreement with himself. "We were an item a few years back. She's a few years older than I am, but it never seemed to matter." He raised a warning finger. "Never mention her name in Amanda's presence."

Michael nodded.

"Treat her well, and she'll help you more than you can believe."

"I'll remember that; she's easy to treat well."

"What's this about you cornering the market on some book?"

"You heard about that?" Michael asked, surprised.

"Of course. My girl, Helen, doesn't miss anything on the lot." He raised a hand. "I swear, I'm not getting stuff on you from Margot."

"The book is the next project I want to do," Michael said.

"What is it? Helen didn't pick up on the title."

"*Pacific Afternoons.* It was written in the twenties by a woman named Mildred Parsons; the only thing she ever wrote."

"I read it at Stanford," Leo said. He got up and walked along a bookcase for a moment, then plucked out a slim, leatherbound volume and handed it to Michael.

"You had it bound?"

"I liked it that much," Leo said. "How the hell did you ever come across it?"

"A girl I knew in New York passed it on to me. I was enchanted."

"You think a movie could make money?"

"I do," Michael replied. "If it's a quality production using the right people."

Leo sat up straight. "Wait a minute," he said. "Now I know why you wanted Mark Adair and Bob Hart here tonight."

Michael nodded.

Leo pondered this for a moment. "They're both perfect," he said, "but Hart will never do it."

"Why not? He's not in all that much demand these days, is he?"

"Nope. He made two expensive flops — I mean flops with the best people — and then he hit the bottle hard."

"Does he look like staying sober?"

"So I hear."

"So what's the problem?"

"His wife. Susan will never let him do it."

"Does he listen to her about these things?"

"He relies on her completely. She's the one you'd have to sell, and she'll never buy it. Bob is fifty-four or -five, but Susan sees him the way he was ten years ago, still making big-time thrillers, playing cops and cowboys."

"He was at the Actors Studio, wasn't he?"

"He was, and he was outstanding there. Then he came out here and went for the big bucks, and although he helped support the Studio for years with the money he made, Lee Strasberg would barely speak to him."

"Maybe he's ready for a change of pace, then."

Leo gave a short laugh. "Sure he is, but Susan isn't. She handled his money well and he's a rich man, so he doesn't *have* to make movies."

"He's an actor, isn't he? How many actors have you known who'd turn down a really good part like this one?"

"Not many. Brando; that's about it. Sure, Bob's an actor, but never underestimate an actor's vanity. If Susan tells him it's wrong for his image, that's it, he won't do it."

"I would *really* like him for the part."

"You brought some books?"

"Yes, they're in the car."

"We're going to screen *Downtown Nights* after dinner. My advice is, give both Bob and Susan the book, then get her alone and try to sell her before they leave. For Christ's sake, don't tell her what the book is about during dinner; she'll have already made up her mind before you can talk to her."

"All right, I'll do that."

"Adair's a different sell. I think you must know that he's mainly a novelist; everything he's done as a screenplay is a small, beautiful, and vaguely important film."

"Yes, that describes it well."

"Try and challenge him in some way; don't just offer him a job."

"All right."

"Who do you want for the girl? You'll need somebody hot to make the picture noticed."

"You met her a few minutes ago."

Leo's eyebrows went up. "Your girl? Vanessa?"

Michael nodded. "Vanessa Parks."

Leo gazed into his drink. "Michael, didn't you hear anything I said to you yesterday? She's gorgeous, I'll grant you that, but you're following your cock around."

"No," Michael said, "I'm not. She's going

to be startlingly good in this picture, Leo. In some ways, Vanessa *is* the girl in the book. It will come naturally to her, and she has it in her to be a very good actress. All she needs is some confidence, and this picture will give it to her."

Leo shook his head. "I don't know."

"Leo," Michael said, leaning forward, "I've got a budget together on this. I can shoot it in northern California for eight million dollars, *if* I can keep salaries in line. If I cast an established star, her money is going to put everybody else's money up. Which would you rather have, a twenty-five-million-dollar movie with a star in that role, or an eight-million-dollar movie with a girl who will be a star as soon as it's released?"

"I like your economics," Leo said. "You feel that strongly about Vanessa in the role?"

"Yes, I do."

"Well, I'm paying you for your judgment," he said. "Just be sure you give me my money's worth."

Michael stood up. "I promise you, I will."

"By the way," Leo said, "I suppose you've optioned the book."

Michael shook his head and smiled. "The copyright expires in three weeks."

"Absolutely not," Leo said.

"What?"

"Option the book *tomorrow*. You should be able to lowball the heirs, but I'm not going to have articles in the trades saying how Centurion waited for expiration, then pounced."

"All right, I'll option it tomorrow."

"Who were you thinking about for a director?"

"George Cukor, if I could raise him from the dead. I want someone like him, who's good with women."

"How about the guy who directed *Downtown Nights* for you? He did a good job."

"He's wrong for this; believe me, I know him. I'll use him again, but not for this." Michael knew he was in a position to reap good publicity for his first film, and that if Chuck Parish directed his second film, the industry would think of them as partners, and he would be sharing the glory. He wanted somebody else.

"Let me know who you want."

The doorbell rang.

"Let's go meet the others," Leo said.

The two men rose and started for the door.

"By the way," Leo said, "Bob Hart is shorter than you think; don't look surprised."

CHAPTER

18

Robert Hart was indeed shorter than Michael had thought. Even in the cowboy boots he was wearing, he came only up to Michael's chin. He had lost weight and become grayer than in his last film, too, and Michael immediately saw him as Doctor Madden in *Pacific Afternoons*.

His wife, Susan, was very small and pretty, with graying blonde hair pulled back in a bun, but in the firmness of her handshake and the directness of her gaze, Michael saw the kind of strength that her husband lacked.

Hart was cordial, but reserved; he was obviously accustomed to homage from others, and he accepted it in a charming, almost princely way. Susan was talkative and down-to-earth. They seemed a compatible pair.

"What are you doing next?" Leo asked Hart

when they had settled in the living room for drinks.

Susan Hart spoke before her husband could. "We're looking at a couple of offers," she said. "Everybody's after Bob."

The doorbell rang again, and a moment later Amanda brought Mark Adair into the room. Adair was expansive and witty from the moment he arrived, Michael thought. He was sixtyish, white-haired, and conveyed a sort of rumpled elegance — just the right image for an eminent novelist.

When they were seated, Leo again asked the mandatory question: "What are you up to, Mark? What brings you to the Coast?"

"Turning down awful ideas, mostly," he said cheerfully. "Paramount got me out here on the pretext of doing something significant, but it was junk. Half a dozen Hollywood hacks could do it better than I. Why the hell do you think they would even consider me for that sort of stuff?"

"They want the weight of your name to give some substance to their project," Leo said smoothly.

"You're so full of horseshit, Leo," Adair said, but he basked in the compliment nevertheless.

A man in a white jacket entered the room and announced dinner.

They dined in a glassed-in room with tile floors and many plants. Since Adair had come alone, the usual man-woman alternation had not worked at Amanda Goldman's table, and Michael was seated between Amanda and Mark Adair.

"I've greatly enjoyed your work over the years," Michael said to Adair when he had a chance. "I particularly enjoyed *Halls of Ice.*" It was the only book of Adair's he had read.

"Thank you," Adair said, beaming as if he had never received a compliment. "Leo tells me you've produced an outstanding film, and that we're seeing it after dinner."

"I just learned that myself," Michael said, "and when you see it, I hope you won't think that my interests are confined to that genre."

"I'll try to keep an open mind," Adair replied.

"In fact, I'm putting something together right now, and it occurs to me that you might be the only writer I know who could do it justice."

"Michael," Adair said, "you may be new out here, but you've certainly copped on to the Hollywood horseshit in a hurry."

Michael laughed. "When you know more about the project you may think I was only speaking the truth."

"Tell me about it," Adair said.

Michael looked around to be sure everyone else was absorbed in their own conversations. "Do you remember a novel called *Pacific Afternoons*?"

Adair nodded. "I read it as a teenager, did a high school book report on it, in fact, but for the life of me the only thing I can remember about it is a scene where the middle-aged doctor sings to the young girl."

"It was Mildred Parsons's only novel; she committed suicide a year or so later, before the book had achieved a wide readership."

"I remember something about that."

"I think she would have had a brilliant career," Michael said, "and I think it's a great pity that the book isn't better known than it is."

"Well, that's a nice ambition for a dead author. I hope when I'm gone somebody will think as kindly of me. Now, why do you think I'm so uniquely qualified to adapt this book?"

"Because you're the sort of novelist that Mildred Parsons was; your sensibilities are not those of a Hollywood hack, as you put it earlier, but those of a genuine writer. The novel is highly adaptable for film, but I want it preserved as Parsons wrote it, both in structure and intent. The dialogue in the book is brilliant — you may not have considered it so

152

as a teenager, but when you read it again, you'll see what I mean."

Michael took a deep breath. "Look, this is the main reason I'd like you to do it: Writers have egos like everyone else, of course, but a Hollywood screenwriter would take this book and, in adapting it, rewrite it to make himself look good. What I want is for Mildred Parsons to look good, for her book to be seen almost as it is read, and it will take a very fine novelist to do that. The success of the book rests entirely on the feeling that she put into it — it was almost certainly autobiographical — and I want someone to get inside her head and put that very real emotion and sentiment on the screen."

Adair looked thoughtful. "Sentiment is a good word for that book," he said. "I recall it as conveying sentiment without sentimentality."

"Then you already know what I want," Michael said. "All that remains is for you to read the book again."

"I'll be glad to."

"You'll have a copy before the evening is over," Michael said.

When the screening was over and Michael had accepted the praise of those present, Leo leaned close to him and said, "I'll tackle Bob

153

Hart; you take on Susan."

Michael found her in the hallway on her way back from the ladies' room. "Susan," he said, taking her arm, "Leo is in there offering Bob a part. I'd like to talk with you about it for a moment, if I may."

"All right," she said.

He steered her through some French doors into the garden and found a bench for them to occupy. The California night air was heavy with the scent of tropical blossoms. Michael looked her in the eye. "I wanted to talk with you because I think I can say some things to you that I can't say to Bob."

"That happens all the time," she said. "Shoot."

He handed her a copy of the book. "Leo is giving Bob a copy; I wanted you both to have one. Bob has had a wonderful career; he's done some very fine work here and there, but I think that the sort of roles that have been available to him in the past have shown only a small part of what he is capable of."

Susan Hart looked thoughtful. "I think I can agree with that," she said.

"There is a role in this book that will give him an opportunity to make his audience aware of a whole new dimension of his talent, which I consider to be a very large talent." He took a deep breath. "This part will take

154

courage. Bob will have to bare himself in a way that has never been asked of him. There are no bad guys to conquer in this story; there are no drug busts or shootouts on Main Street; there is no action that takes place outside of a summer house overlooking the Pacific Ocean. But this book is full of meaning and real emotion, and the part I'd like Bob to play — Doctor Madden — is the best role in the book. He'll be playing opposite a new actress — a very talented girl, but he'll have to carry her at times. He'll speak in the idiom of a cultivated set of people in the nineteen-twenties. It is a courtly language, and there is very fine dialogue for him to speak. I've asked Mark Adair to do the screenplay.

"I wanted to talk to you about this because it will be a departure for Bob, and he may need your help to make that departure. But this role is something else: *Pacific Afternoons* will open up his career and make it possible for him to play virtually anything he wants; it will release his talent from the confinement of genre films and show the industry what hidden reserves have lurked in this man for so long. And I'll tell you this — I would never say this to Bob — it would make Lee Strasberg proud of him if he were alive to see Bob in the role."

Susan Hart regarded him with a look of

surprise. "Well, Michael, I don't know whether I'll like this book or not, or whether Bob will want the part, but I'll tell you one thing: That's the greatest line I've ever heard from a producer."

Michael laughed out loud. "You have a great surprise coming, Susan," he said.

"It's been a long time since I've been surprised, Michael."

"The surprise is, when you've read the book, you'll know that everything I've said to you is understatement."

Michael and Vanessa were the last to leave. Amanda pecked them both on the cheek, and Leo walked them to their car.

"Well, how did it go?" he asked.

"I had a chance to make my pitch to both Mark and Susan. I think they'll read the book; let's hope they like it."

"If these two guys come on board," Leo said, "I won't hold you to your eight-million-dollar budget; I'll go to twenty million. I want this to be a first-class production, and Susan's not going to let Bob do it on the cheap."

"Thanks, Leo," Michael said, "but I don't think the extra budget will be necessary. I think Bob will be on board before the end of the week, and I'll be willing to bet that

156

Mark Adair will be on the phone before lunch tomorrow."

"What on earth did you say to Mark that makes you believe that?" Leo asked incredulously. "He's a tough sale, you know; tougher than Bob Hart."

"Well, for a start," Michael said, "I gave him your beautiful leatherbound copy of the book."

Leo looked at Michael blankly for a moment, then burst out laughing. "You son of a bitch!" he crowed.

"See you tomorrow, Leo," Michael said. He put the Porsche in gear and drove away down Stone Canyon.

"Well," Vanessa said, resting her head on Michael's shoulder, "am I going to be a movie star?"

"It's in the bag, sweetheart," Michael replied. "Don't worry about a thing."

CHAPTER

19

Michael arrived in his office to find his secretary standing at her desk, holding her hand over the phone receiver. "There's somebody on the phone who will only identify himself as 'Tommy,' " Margot said, exasperated.

"It's okay," Michael replied, hurrying into his office. "You can always put him through if I'm alone." He picked up the phone. "Tommy?"

"So, how's it in Hollywood, kid? How's the big-time producer?"

"You wouldn't believe how good," Michael said, laughing. "When you coming to see me?"

"How about Saturday?"

"You serious?"

"I'm serious, kid; where should I stay?"

"The Bel-Air, and I'll take care of it. How long you gonna be here?"

"Just until Monday. I got a little business to do over the weekend. We'll have dinner Saturday, though, okay?"

"Sure, okay."

"Get me a girl?"

"Sure, no problem."

"I get in about four."

"We'll meet you in the bar at the Bel-Air at seven."

"Look forward to it," Tommy said. "See ya." He hung up.

Michael stood holding the phone and staring at the ceiling. Where the hell was he going to get a girl? He didn't know anybody in L.A.

"That was very strange."

Michael looked and saw Margot standing in the doorway. "What?"

"You were speaking in a thick New York accent. I've never heard you speak that way before."

Michael managed a laugh. "It was an old friend from New York. We talk that way to each other as a kind of joke."

"Oh."

Michael remembered something. "Margot, he's coming in on Saturday. Do you think you could find him a girl for the evening?"

"Of course. Anything in particular?"

"Somebody beautiful. And it wouldn't hurt if she's in the business in some way; he'll like that. And make it somebody discreet; he's a married man."

"Consider it done. Anything else?"

"Yes, get him a suite at the Bel-Air for Saturday and Sunday nights — something nice; tell them to send the bill to me."

"Would you like some flowers and a bottle of champagne in the room?"

"Yes, please."

"By the way, you had a call from Mark Adair ten minutes ago. He's at the Beverly Hills; want me to get him for you?"

"Please." Michael sat down at his desk and waited for the call to go through. Please, God, he muttered under his breath. Adair was the key to everything. The phone buzzed; he picked it up. "Mark?"

"Yes, Michael."

"Good morning; did you sleep well?"

"Hardly at all. I stayed up most of the night reading your goddamned book and making notes."

Making notes; that sounded good. "What do you think?"

"I think it'll make a brilliant film — *if* you can get Bob Hart to play the doctor. Get him, and I'm yours."

"That sounds wonderful, Mark." He sensed he had an advantage at this moment. "Mark, I have to tell you, Leo's got me on a very tight budget for this film."

There was a brief silence. "How tight?"

"Have your agent call me."

"Come on, Michael, what're you offering?"

"Mark, I know you're used to more money, but the best I can do is a hundred thousand."

"Jesus Christ, Michael! Do you really expect me to fall for that tight budget crap?"

"Mark, I'm being honest with you. This picture comes in under eight million, or Centurion won't fund. That's it, I'm afraid."

"I want a quarter of a million. I usually get four hundred thousand."

"Mark, I'll make it a hundred and fifty, but fifty is going to have to come out of my producer's fee. That's how much I want you to do this picture."

"Oh, shit, all right. Two drafts and a polish, and not a word more."

"Done. If you can't write this in two drafts and a polish, it can't be written."

"You're the worst kind of flatterer. I'll have a first draft in six weeks; send me fifty grand and a contract — *after* you get a commitment from Bob Hart." He slammed the phone down.

Michael did a little dance around the room, while Margot watched from the door. He saw her and froze; that was twice she'd caught him out this morning.

"George Hathaway called. He'd like a meeting at three."

"A meeting? George?"

She looked secretive. "I told him you were free for half an hour."

"Oh, all right. I guess I owe him some time for putting together these offices so fast."

"Susan Hart called, too; I wouldn't keep her waiting, if I were you."

Michael's heart nearly stopped. "Get her." He sat down and took some deep breaths; he didn't want to sound anxious. The phone buzzed. He took one more breath and picked it up. "Susan? I'm sorry to be so long; I was on the phone with Mark Adair."

"Is he going to do it?"

"He certainly is; he was up all night reading it."

"So were Bob and I. It was smart of you to give us each a copy."

"What did you think?"

"I think it's interesting. Bob's doing a thriller for Fox; he'll consider it for next fall."

"Susan, we start shooting April first. We have to get the spring season on film."

"Out of the question," she said. "The Fox project is a fifty-million-dollar production with a major female star, not an art film with a nobody. You *need* Bob for this one, Michael;

162

postpone until October and set the film in autumn."

"It can't be done without screwing up the story, Susan; it's a spring story, and that can't change."

"Michael, if you want Bob, schedule for October. He'll want two million."

Michael thought fast. Leo had said he'd up the budget for Hart. "Susan, can you hold for a minute? I've got Paul Newman incoming on the other line." He punched the hold button before she could speak. Christ, he thought, staring at the flashing light. Have I pushed her too far? He glanced at his watch; he'd have to leave her on hold for at least a minute, or she'd know he was lying. After a minute and fifteen seconds he picked up the phone.

"Susan, I'm so sorry, but I had to take that call."

"How *dare* you put me on hold!" she sputtered.

"I'm truly sorry, I really am, but I want you to know I understand Bob's position on the Fox project, and if that's what he wants to do, I'll just have to live with it. It wouldn't have worked, anyway; I'm stuck with an eight-million-dollar budget, and I could only have offered Bob half a million for the part."

"You expected Bob to work for half a million?" she asked incredulously.

163

"Sweetheart, Centurion won't let me do this unless I bring it in for eight million, and anyway, the picture is going to shoot in forty-one days, and Bob would've only had to work twenty-two."

"How could the lead work only twenty-two days on a forty-one-day shoot? That's crazy."

"I juggled the schedule for Bob, but to tell you the truth, I'm relieved I don't have to do that now. I'd rather shoot in sequence, to tell you the truth. Anyway, the girl has more scenes; Bob just has the *best* scenes."

"When do you plan to start shooting?"

"April one, in Carmel, if we can nail down the locations."

"How much time in Carmel?"

"Three weeks; the rest is interiors we can do on the lot."

"God, I haven't been to Carmel in years."

"It's gorgeous up there, isn't it?" Michael had never been to Carmel, but that was where the book was set. "I'm so looking forward to it."

"What kind of accommodations?" Susan asked.

"The best available, of course. I can do that on my budget."

"We'd want a suite at the Inn."

"You mean you're considering this, Susan?"

"I'd better not find out you're lying about

Mark Adair writing it."

"Susan."

"And Bob will want a million."

"Susan, there isn't a million in the budget. At half a million, Bob would be the highest-paid cast member. I'm only taking a hundred thousand for a fee."

"I want a copy of the budget," she said, "by noon today." She hung up.

"Margot!" he shouted.

She appeared in the doorway. "Yes?"

"Print out a copy of the budget for *Pacific Afternoons*! I've got three quarters of a million in for the male lead and three hundred thousand for script; change those figures to half a million and a hundred and fifty thousand, then spread the money over the other categories. Can you do that in an hour?"

"Sure."

"Get me legal."

When the phone buzzed Michael picked it up. "Who's this?"

"This is Mervyn White, head of the legal department," a voice said, sounding annoyed.

"Mervyn, this is Michael Vincent. I need a contract drawn immediately, for a picture called *Pacific Afternoons*."

"Nothing like that on the schedule," White said.

Michael could hear him shuffling papers.

"I don't care if it's on the schedule," he said firmly. "Draw the contract for Robert Hart at half a million dollars, working from April first of next year to May first, deluxe accommodations, travel on the Centurion jet, deluxe motor home for dressing. He can have one assistant for ten thousand bucks."

"I'll have to clear this with Mr. Goldman," White said stiffly. "Especially the part about the airplane."

"Mervyn," Michael said slowly, "when Leo sees that he's getting Bob Hart for half a million, he'll fly the airplane himself. I want that contract drawn and on my desk in . . ." he glanced at his watch, ". . . ninety minutes, and if it's not here, I'll come over there and set your desk on fire, do you hear me?"

"Oh, all right," White said petulantly.

"Good." Michael hung up the phone. He had Mark Adair and Robert Hart on board for four hundred thousand less than he'd budgeted for. He was in Hollywood heaven.

Then a niggling doubt pricked at his brain. There was something else. Oh, yes, he didn't own the film rights to the book.

"Margot," he called, "when that contract arrives, send it with the budget to Susan Hart. And by the way, find out who owns the copyright to *Pacific Afternoons*."

CHAPTER

20

Michael sat in the lawyer's office and stared at the man. He was in his mid-seventies, Michael reckoned, and a little worse for the wear. A bottle of single-malt Scotch whiskey stood on his desk, a crystal glass beside it. Michael had already refused a drink.

What was it with this guy? The whole city of L.A. *existed* on the telephone, people walked around with the phone plugged into their heads, and this guy had insisted on a face-to-face meeting.

"You're sure you won't have a taste?" Daniel J. Moriarty asked.

"Quite sure," Michael replied. "Now, can we get down to business, Mr. Moriarty?"

"Of course, of course," the lawyer replied. "What can I do for you?"

"You do remember our brief phone conversation of an hour ago?" Michael asked. He was steamed.

"I do, I do. It was film rights you wanted to meet about?"

"*I* did not want to meet, Mr. Moriarty; I am here only at your insistence. I am interested in acquiring the film rights to the novel *Pacific Afternoons* by Mildred Parsons. I understand that in some way you control those rights?"

"Indeed I do, Mr. Vincent, indeed I do. You see, Mildred's younger brother, Montague — Monty, we all called him — was my closest friend. Monty and I went to law school together. Very close, we were."

"And Montague Parsons controls the rights?"

"Monty, alas, passed on last year. I am his executor."

"Were there no other relatives surviving?"

"None. The rights to all of Mildred Parsons's works passed to Monty on her death; those rights rest in his estate. The income from those rights passes as a bequest to Carlyle Junior College. And, as I mentioned before, I am the executor."

"As executor, are you empowered to act for the estate?" Michael hoped the hell he was; he didn't want to have to deal with the trustees of some college.

168

"I am so empowered."

"You don't have to have the permission of anyone at Carlyle Junior College?"

Moriarty chuckled. "I do not. Carlyle gets the income, but as long as I'm executor, I make all the decisions."

"Good. I would like to purchase the film rights to *Pacific Afternoons*. I am in a position to offer you five thousand dollars for a one-year option, renewable for an additional year at the same rate. On exercising the option, I will pay a further twenty thousand dollars."

"And just who are you, Mr. Vincent? I mean, do you represent a major studio?"

"I am an independent producer," Michael said.

"Ah, an independent," Moriarty said, sipping his Scotch. "This town is full of them. Tell me, Mr. Vincent, do you actually *have* five thousand dollars?"

Michael checked his temper. "Mr. Moriarty, I am an independent producer with a production deal at Centurion Pictures, and as such, I have the full backing of that studio. If you like, I will have Mr. Leo Goldman call you and confirm my position there."

Moriarty held up a hand. "Please don't take offense, Mr. Vincent; it's just that this town is full of people who style themselves independent producers. Centurion is a reputable studio, and I accept that you represent them."

"Thank you. Do you accept my offer?"

"What offer was that?"

Michael tried not to grind his teeth. He repeated his offer.

"Alas, no," Moriarty said. "I cannot accept such an offer."

"What sort of price did you have in mind?" Michael asked.

"Oh, I didn't have anything in particular in mind," Moriarty said, replenishing his drink.

"All right, Mr. Moriarty, I will offer you ten thousand against twenty-five, but that is the best I can do."

"Is it, Mr. Vincent; is it, indeed?" Moriarty swivelled slightly in his chair and gazed out the window.

Michael stared at the man, fuming. What was his game? What kind of negotiation is this?

"Mr. Moriarty, you are wasting my time. What do you want for the rights?"

Moriarty jumped, as if startled from a reverie. "Mmm? Oh, the rights, the rights, yes."

"Yes," Michael said.

"Yes."

Michael wanted to strangle the man. "Mr. Moriarty, you must be aware that the copyright on *Pacific Afternoons* expires in three weeks, and, if I wish, I can simply wait and have the rights for nothing. So if you expect to earn anything for your college, put down that glass and start doing business."

"Ha-ha!" Moriarty cried. "So you were operating on the premise of the life plus fifty years copyright law! Well, my fine fellow, that doesn't apply here! The copyright to Miss Parsons's novel runs on the old copyright law — the one that was in effect when she died. So if you wish to threaten me with expiration of copyright, you'll have to wait another twenty-four years! Ha-ha!"

This is some sort of nightmare, Michael thought. It's a bad dream, and I'll wake up in a moment and it will be all right.

"Is there anything else you wish to say, Mr. Vincent?"

"Frankly, Mr. Moriarty, I'm speechless. Do you wish to sell these rights?"

"As a matter of fact, I would love to sell the rights, but I can't."

"What?"

"I promised Monty Parsons when I became his executor that I would never, ever sell the film rights to Mildred's little novel. He hated the films, you see; thought they were common and vulgar. He would never allow his sister's only work to be corrupted in such a fashion." Moriarty tossed down the remaining Scotch in his glass and emitted a low chuckle. "Did you think you were the first, Mr. Vincent? I've had a regular parade of 'independent producers' in here over the years wanting to film that book. I've always thought it would make a fine little film myself, but I had to say no to all of them."

Michael was stunned. "Then why, may I ask, did you drag me down here for this ridiculous meeting?"

Moriarty spread his hands. "Well, it gets lonesome in this office, you know, the Parsons estate being my last client. It passes the time to bandy a bit with a producer. I'm afraid, Mr. Vincent, that you'll have to wait until I've passed on. Then you can go to the trustees of Carlyle Junior College and make a deal with them. *They* didn't make any promises to Monty Parsons."

Michael stood up. "Good day, Mr. Moriarty."

Moriarty waved his glass. "Good day to you, Mr. Vincent. And thank you for your visit. Come back any time!"

CHAPTER

21

Michael drove back to the studio in a fury, whipping around corners, passing other cars, twice nearly running down pedestrians. There were two cars ahead of him at the gate, and he waited, taking deep breaths and trying to regain control of his anger. By the time he was let through he was able to smile and wave back at the guard.

He parked in his reserved spot and walked the few yards to his building, his mind still racing. He didn't have the rights to *Pacific Afternoons*. How could he make the picture? He had a top star and a top writer ready to work, and he didn't have the rights to the property!

He walked through the waiting room and Margot thrust a handful of pink message slips at him.

"We've got a request from the PR department for an interview and photographs with one of the trades," she said, following him into his office. "It's a real coup, getting that kind of space. When do you want to do it?"

"Set it up for next week," he said. "A morning."

"Fine." She wrinkled her brow. "Michael? Are you all right?"

"I'm fine," he said, sitting down at Randolph's huge desk. "I'm just thinking about something."

The phone rang and she picked it up at his desk. "Mr. Vincent's office. Oh, yes, Leo, he's right here." She punched the hold button. "It's Leo on one."

"Tell him I'll get back to him."

"I can't do that," she said, alarmed. "I've already told him you're here. Leo hates being put off; you'll have to answer."

Michael picked up the phone and forced a smile into his voice. "Leo, how are you?"

"Great, kid. I just had Sue Hart on the phone; she told me the news. Congratulations!"

"Thanks, Leo."

"And you got Mark for the screenplay, too! That's a tour de force performance, Michael. I'm proud of you."

"It's going to be a good production," Michael said lamely.

"How you coming on the rights to the book?"

Michael gulped. "It's in the works; I don't anticipate any problems."

"Good, good. I'm glad everything is going so smoothly. Catch you later, kid." Leo hung up.

Michael hung up and found that he was sweating heavily.

Margot stuck her head into the office. "George Hathaway is here; he seems pretty excited."

"Sure, sure," Michael said, struggling to put the rights problem out of his mind and concentrate on the business at hand.

George Hathaway came into the room, a thick roll of heavy paper under his arm. "Michael," he beamed, placing the roll on the desk, "I read the book, and I loved it! I was up all night thinking about it and making sketches." He unrolled the papers to reveal a sketch of a cottage.

Michael stared at the sketch. It was as if George had reached into his mind and extracted his image of the northern California house of the protagonist of *Pacific Afternoons*.

"What do you think?"

"It's perfect, George; it *is* the cottage. How did you do it?"

"Well, I used to be an art director, my boy,

175

not just in charge of the props department." He flipped through his sketches: it was all there — the cottage, the music room, her bedroom, the doctor's study — every important scene in the book had been rendered.

"I'm overwhelmed," Michael said. "How did you do all this so quickly?"

"I've always been a fast study," George said. "Would you believe I drew this set . . ." he waved a hand at *The Great Randolph*'s study ". . . in half an hour?"

Michael sat back in his chair. "George, will you do this film with me?" he asked.

George turned pink and beamed. "My boy, I'd be honored." He blinked rapidly, and his voice became husky. "It's been a long time since somebody offered me something important."

"And it is important," Michael said, standing and clapping the designer on a frail shoulder. "Mark Adair is doing the screenplay, and Robert Hart has agreed to play the doctor."

"Why, that's fabulous," George said. "Who for costumes?"

"Who would you recommend?"

"Edith Head, but she's dead, like just about everyone else I know."

"Think about it."

"There is somebody," George said. "She lives in the group of apartments where I live, and she's been trying to get work. Young, but she's very talented, I think."

"Ask her to do some sketches for me, and to call Margot for an appointment. What's her name?"

"Jennifer Fox — Jenny. I'll tell her, and I'll work with her myself on the sketches." George smiled. "You know which scene I loved best in the book?"

"Which one?"

"The one where the doctor sings to the young woman. *'Dein ist mein ganzes Herz'* — 'My Whole Heart Is Yours.' "

"Yes, that is a wonderful scene. We'll have to cut it from the film, though. I doubt if Bob Hart could carry it off."

"Why not? He doesn't have to sing — you could dub it — he's actor enough to bring it off."

"I think the scene might be too much in conflict with his previous image in films."

"Too bad, I love Lehár."

"Who?"

"Lehár, Franz Lehár."

Michael searched his mind for the reference. "Opera?" he hazarded.

"Operetta," George said. "He wrote *'Dein ist mein ganzes Herz.'* "

"Ah," Michael said. He didn't have a clue. "Have you never heard it?"

"Not for a long time," Michael lied.

"Will you give me just ten minutes more of your time?"

"Of course, George." What the hell was the old man running on about?

George ran from the room, picked up Margot's phone, and made a call. Five minutes later, two workmen appeared pushing a grand piano on a dolly and set it up at one end of Randolph's study, then two elderly men walked in. One of them was carrying a sheaf of music.

"Please," George said, waving Michael to a sofa, "sit."

Michael sat down.

"Mr. Vincent," George said formally, "may I present Anton Gruber and Hermann Hecht?"

"How do you do," Michael said. Then the Gruber name struck home. The man had written scores for dozens of films in the thirties and forties. Michael had never heard of Hecht.

Anton Gruber sat at the piano and played a soft introduction, then Hermann Hecht, assuming a concert position, his hands folded before him, began to sing.

Michael had never heard the music before. It was old-fashioned, certainly, but the melody was wonderful. The old man sang it in a slightly cracked baritone, but with such feeling that when he had finished and the piano was quiet, Michael had a lump in his throat. He stood up and clapped loudly. "Gentlemen, that was wonderful. I've never heard it done better!"

"I thought you'd like it," George said. "Now you can see why it's so important in the story, the doctor finally expressing himself to the young woman in a song, in *German* yet, when before he couldn't tell her of his feelings."

"You're right, George," Michael said. "It could be the emotional high point of the film. It could be perfectly wonderful, if I can get Bob Hart to do it."

"He's an actor, isn't he?" George asked. "All actors are hams. He'd never pass up a scene like that, even if he can't sing. Hermann here could dub it for him."

"It might work," Michael said. It damned well would work, he thought; it could bring the audience close to tears, as it had him.

It was a wonderful scene that could be played by a huge star in a film that he could not make unless he owned the rights to the novel. He could hear Daniel J. Moriarty laughing at him.

CHAPTER

22

Michael drove the Porsche slowly up Sunset Boulevard toward the Bel-Air Hotel. Vanessa sat beside him, checking her makeup in the mirror on the back of the sun visor.

"Tell me who this guy is again," she said.

"His name is Tommy Provensano," Michael said. "I knew him as a kid in New York, growing up."

"Oh, right."

"Don't be surprised if he calls me Vinnie sometimes. It's kind of a nickname."

"Okay. Is he bringing anybody?"

"Her name is Mimi; that's all I know about her. It may be their first date."

"How old a guy is Tommy?"

"A couple of years older than I am."

"If he's boring, do I still have to be nice to him?"

"Vanessa, in Hollywood, you have to be nice to *everybody*. You never know who you're talking to."

"That's a good policy, I guess."

"Believe me, it is."

Tommy opened the door and grabbed Michael in a bear hug. "Hey, *paisan*," he roared. "It's the big-time Hollywood producer!" He had slimmed down some and was wearing an expensive Italian-cut suit.

"Hello, Tommy," Michael said. "I'd like you to meet Vanessa Parks."

Tommy suddenly became the gentleman. "How do you do, Vanessa," he said. "I'd like you both to meet Mimi."

A small, dark-haired girl stood up from the sofa and shook both their hands. She was demurely dressed and very beautiful. Michael thought Margot had done her job well.

Tommy popped a bottle of champagne for them. Dom Perignon, Michael noted, remembering that he was paying for it. Tommy poured, and when their glasses were full he addressed the little group.

"This guy," he said, taking Michael's shoulder and shaking him like a rag doll, "and I were greasy kids on the street together. We stole fruit from the pushcarts, we rolled drunks, we did all the terrible things young kids on the street do, and we went home every night to our mothers."

"Tommy," Michael said reprovingly, "you know very well that we never stole any fruit." He turned to the others. "Tommy has a romantic view of our youth."

"And listen to him talk," Tommy said, pinching Michael's cheek. "He used to talk like me!"

Michael bored his gaze into Tommy, and he seemed to take the hint.

"That was a long time ago, of course," he said, glancing apologetically at Michael. "Now, where are we eating?"

"I thought you might enjoy Spago," Michael said dryly. "The pizza's great."

"I get it, I get it," Tommy said. "I'll behave."

"No," said Michael, "you'll really like the pizzas. They're different from what you're used to."

Their table overlooked Sunset and the big movie billboards. Tommy couldn't get enough of the place.

"I can't believe I'm sitting in the same restaurant as Burt Reynolds," he whispered hoarsely to Michael.

"I'm sorry there aren't more stars here," Michael replied. "There usually are." It was the first time he had been to the restaurant, but the headwaiter had been ready for him.

Vanessa stood up. "I'm for the little girls' room," she said. "Join me, Mimi?" The women left Michael and Tommy alone.

Tommy was suddenly quiet and serious. "So, tell me how it's really going, Vinnie. No bullshit, now."

"Tommy, it is difficult for me to explain coherently to you just how well it is going. *Downtown Nights* opens later in the fall, and I've already got Robert Hart starring in my next picture."

"Robert Hart the movie star?" Tommy asked, amazed.

"Movie stars are who star in pictures, Tommy. And a great novelist named Mark Adair is writing the screenplay."

"I heard of him. My wife read one of his books one time."

"How is Maria?"

"She's okay. She likes being a capo's wife, I can tell you. She's getting a lot of new respect from her friends."

"And how do you like being a capo?"

"My first taste of real power," Tommy said. "It's like fine wine; you can't get enough."

"Come on, you've had a lot of juice for a long time."

Tommy shook his head. "It's not the same

as manipulating Benedetto to get what I want. Now, I want something, I say so, and I get it." He looked around the restaurant. "I really like this place. You don't think it's bugged, do you?"

Michael laughed. "Certainly not. You have nothing to worry about."

"Listen, you always have to worry about taps these days — that and guys wearing wires. Seems like the FBI is everywhere." He leaned closer across the table. "Just between you and me, looks like the Don is going to take a fall."

Michael became Vinnie for a moment. "No shit?"

"A big fall. He's going to be inside by Christmas, the way things are going. Frankie Bigboy's blabbing his head off on the stand; he's all lined up for the witness protection program, and nobody's been able to get a shot at him."

"I never thought Frankie was the type to testify — especially against the Don. He's a dead man."

"I doubt it. A minute after the jury says 'guilty,' he'll be running a bowling alley in Peoria or someplace. We won't see him again."

Michael looked at Tommy closely. "You don't seem all broken up about the Don going away."

184

Tommy smiled slyly. "It's an ill wind that don't blow somebody some good."

"Is there going to be trouble about who succeeds?"

Tommy glanced around the room. "I'm out here to be out of it," he said. "I got word that somebody's going to get whacked this weekend. I don't want to be around."

"Am I an alibi?" Michael asked anxiously.

"Don't worry, it won't come to that. A couple stewardesses could make me on the plane, and there's always the hotel."

"If you need it, say the word," Michael said, relieved that he wouldn't be involved. "Say, Tommy, thanks for the car and the help with the banker. You wouldn't believe what a sweet deal that bank is. My dough's on the street already."

Tommy put his hand on Michael's. "Anytime, you need anything, kid, anytime. I'm connected pretty good out here."

"That you are," Michael said. "By the way," he took a deep breath, "I got a little legal problem, maybe you could help me with."

"Speak to me," Tommy said.

"I'm having a little trouble getting the rights to this book that I want to make into a film."

"Who's giving you a hard time?"

Michael took a cocktail napkin and wrote

down the name of Daniel J. Moriarty and the address of his law office, then he told Tommy about his conversation with the lawyer.

"I'll look into it," Tommy said, pocketing the napkin. "Call you when I know something." He looked up to see the women returning. "Say," he said, "that's some broad you got me. Is she gonna get mad if I want to fuck her?"

"She's yours for whatever you want," Michael said.

Tommy slapped him on the shoulder. "That's it, kid, you take care of me, I take care of you."

23

Michael jerked awake to the sound of the telephone. He glanced at the bedside clock; just past 6:00 A.M. on Monday morning. He picked it up. "Hello?" he croaked. Some goddamned wrong number, he knew it.

"Rise and shine, kid," Tommy's voice said.

"Jesus, Tommy, you know what time it is? You never got up this early in your life. Where are you?"

"In New York; where else? I just want you to know I'm taking care of that little problem of yours."

"Thanks, Tommy. I owe you."

"Forget it. You know where the corner of Sunset and Camden is?"

"Sure, in Beverly Hills."

"Park your car there at eight o'clock sharp this morning, southeast corner; a guy will pick you up. He's kind of a consultant on these things."

"What's his name?"

"You don't need to know; he won't know yours, either."

"Right."

"Listen, I left kind of a mess at the hotel; I'm sorry about that."

"Don't worry about it; they're used to it."

"Yeah? Well, you got class, kid, and I thank you for the night on the town."

"Thanks for your help too, Tommy. Keep in touch."

"Don't worry about that. *Ciao.*" Tommy hung up.

Michael rolled out of bed and put his face in his hands. Jesus, what did they drink last night? He glanced at Vanessa. Sawing away, just like always; nothing could wake the girl until she was ready.

He got out of bed, showered, and fixed himself some breakfast, feeling relieved. He didn't know how Tommy was going to fix the rights thing, but he had complete faith in him. If Tommy said it was fixed, it was fixed.

He got dressed, took the elevator down to the garage, and drove to Sunset and Camden, arriving ten minutes early. He sat idly just off Sunset, listening to a drive-time disc jockey, drumming his fingers on the wheel in time with the music.

A large Cadillac pulled up next to him and the electric window on his side rolled down. A man in his early twenties, unshaven, with greasy hair, looked at him.

"You and me got a mutual friend?"

"Yeah," Michael replied.

"Get in."

Michael got out of his car and into the Cadillac. Traffic on Sunset was full-bore rush hour now. "Where we going?"

The driver had turned down Camden and was now making a left turn.

"This guy Moriarty," he said.

"Yeah?"

"I gotta know what he looks like, right?"

"Okay, but where we going?"

The driver held up a page torn from a phone book; the lawyer's name was circled. "To have a look at him."

"Oh."

The Cadillac swung into Bedford Drive and stopped.

"Now what?" Michael asked.

"Look," said the driver, exasperated, "let me handle this, okay?"

"Okay, sorry."

"That's his house right there," the driver said. "We'll wait."

Michael switched on the radio and found

some music. They sat there for better than half an hour, then he looked up and saw Daniel J. Moriarty leaving his home, a briefcase in his hand. "That's him," Michael said. "Get a good look." The way Moriarty was swinging the case, Michael could tell it was empty, except maybe for a bottle of Scotch. Why did the old guy bother going to the office, anyway?

The driver started the Cadillac and moved slowly away from the curb, checking his rear-view mirrors. Momentarily there was no traffic. Moriarty stepped off the curb and walked around an elderly Volvo station wagon, digging for his keys. As he put the key into the door lock, the driver gunned the Cadillac.

"What the hell . . ." Michael yelled, bracing a hand against the dashboard. "What are you . . ."

The Cadillac scraped the side of the Volvo, then struck Moriarty, sending him up into the air. Michael heard him hit the top of the Cadillac, then saw the door of the Volvo spinning off in another direction. The Cadillac screeched to a stop, throwing Michael against the dashboard.

"*Are you out of your fucking mind?*" Michael screamed.

The driver was looking back over his shoulder. "Shit!" he said through his teeth. "Wait here." He got out of the Cadillac and started walking back toward Moriarty, who was not only alive but was, unaccountably, trying to pull his battered body across the street with his elbows.

Michael started to hip his way across the seat to the wheel and drive away; then he saw there were no keys in the ignition — indeed, there was no ignition. He looked across the street to where a man in a Mercedes had been pulling out of his driveway. He had stopped and was looking, first at Moriarty, then at Michael. Michael looked to his right and saw a middle-aged woman in a bathrobe and curlers holding a newspaper, looking straight at him. He turned and looked out the rear window of the car.

The driver was walking the hundred yards that separated the Cadillac from Moriarty; purposefully, but not fast. A knife was in his hand. He covered the last few yards to the struggling Moriarty, kicked him over onto his back, plunged the knife into his chest, twisted it once, then walked back toward the Cadillac, leaving the knife in the now-dead body of Daniel J. Moriarty.

Michael looked again at the man in the Mercedes and the woman with the newspaper. They were watching the driver walk back to the car and following his progress to the Cadillac, where Michael still sat.

The young man got into the car, reached under the dash, did something with some wires, and the engine came to life. He put the car in gear and drove away, turning right at the next corner. "You'd think the car would do it to an old guy like that, right? I mean, Christ, a Cadillac!"

Michael was speechless with rage and fear. He scrunched down in the seat; why hadn't he done that before? A couple of minutes later, he was left standing at his car. He got in, started the engine, drove to the corner, then turned onto Sunset, blending in with the traffic, terrified of everybody around him. He could hear police cars in the distance.

They had seen him, those two people. The man in the Mercedes, he could be in the business, somebody he might have to deal with someday. The woman could be married to somebody at Centurion; how did he know? They had bored their curious eyes into him, memorized his features; he was sure of it. He put on his dark glasses and turned toward Sacramento on the freeway. He would turn back toward the studio in a few minutes; right now, he had to swallow his heart, get his pulse back under two hundred. Driving would do it.

CHAPTER

24

Driving didn't do it. When he got to the studio an hour later, Michael's heart was still pounding. He slammed the car door and walked into his office.

"Morning," Margot said, handing him his messages.

Michael said nothing, but went into his office and sat down heavily at his desk.

Margot followed him in. "There's a problem."

"Huh?" He hadn't been listening.

"At the Bel-Air."

"What are you talking about?"

"Your friend, he beat up the girl I arranged."

"*What?*"

"Put her in the hospital. I'm afraid that I am in trouble with her madam, and you are

193

in trouble with the Bel-Air."

"Tommy beat her up?"

"Michael, try and listen to me. Your friend made such a mess of that girl that she may never look the same again. Her madam is up in arms, the hotel is up in arms — I persuaded them not to call the police — and you are going to find this very expensive."

"What do you mean?"

"The girl wants twenty-five thousand dollars before noon today, or she says she'll go to the police."

"Tell her okay."

"The madam is probably raking some of that off. I can try to get it down some."

"Tell her it's okay, I'll pay the money." He flipped through his address book, found the number, and dialed. The banker came on the line. He waved Margot out of the office. "This is Callabrese."

"Yes, Mr. Callabrese; what can I do for you?"

"I want twenty-five thousand in cash left at your reception desk immediately. A woman will ask for it; don't ask for I.D., just give it to her."

"As you wish."

Michael hung up the phone and went to the door. "Margot, please go to this address and pick up an envelope; there'll be money inside; pay the madam and do what you can to see that she keeps her mouth shut." He handed her a slip of paper.

Margot grabbed her handbag and headed for the door. "You'll have to cover your own phones."

Michael picked up the phone and called home.

"What?" a sleepy Vanessa said.

"Vanessa, wake up and listen to me carefully."

"Huh?"

"Goddamnit, wake up and listen!"

"All right, Michael, I'm listening!"

"This is what you and I did this morning: we woke up early, made love, then took a shower together. I left the house about nine-thirty — later than usual — for the office. You got that?"

"If you say so."

"It's important, if anybody should ask."

"All right. Can I go back to sleep now?"

Michael slammed down the phone. Where were his fingerprints on the Cadillac — on the door handle? Yes, and on the dashboard, where he'd braced himself. Christ, if they ever found that car . . . The phone rang.

"Hello?"

"Mr. Vincent? Is that you?"

"Yes, who is this?"

"My name is Larry Keating; I sent you a screenplay? I'd like to set up a meeting."

"Call my secretary this afternoon." He hung up. The phone rang again, and he let it ring. He sat and let the phone ring until Margot got back.

"Is it all right?" he asked.

"It's all right. The madam can control the situation. She's extremely annoyed that this has happened, but she'll keep her mouth shut, and she'll keep the girl quiet, too."

"Good."

"I didn't get a chance to tell you earlier, but your appointment with the trade paper is tomorrow, for an interview and photographs."

"Fine," he said, then sat bolt upright. "No!"

"Tomorrow's bad? Your book was clear."

"I'll do it on the phone."

"Michael, they can't take pictures on the phone."

"No pictures. I haven't got time to mess with these people; tell the guy if he wants to talk to call me tomorrow morning."

"All right."

"And hold all my calls until I tell you. I've got some thinking to do."

"All right."

He tried to think but couldn't. Finally, he buzzed Margot. "Find out who's the chairman

196

of the Board of Trustees of Carlyle Junior College, then make me an appointment as soon as possible." This was dangerous, but he had to do it now, or he would go completely crazy.

The chairman's name was Wallace Merton, and his office was in a downtown law firm. Michael was made to wait a few minutes, increasing his nervousness. When he was finally announced, he drew a deep breath and tried to relax.

"Good morning, Mr. Vincent, what can I do for you?" Merton asked, waving Michael to a chair. He clearly was not accustomed to spending time with strangers.

Michael sat down and set his briefcase on the floor. "Good morning, Mr. Merton; I won't take much of your time."

"Good."

"I am a producer at Centurion Pictures, and I am interested in the film rights to a property which I understand has been left as a bequest to the college."

Merton looked at him blankly. "I don't have the slightest idea what you're talking about."

"The estate of Mildred Parsons?"

"Oh, yes; that man Moriarty."

Best to tell as much of the truth as possible. "I saw him last week, but frankly, he was a little worse for the wear, and I couldn't make much sense of what he had to say. I did understand that the Board of Trustees had it in its power to sell the rights."

"Well, we didn't last week — only Moriarty did, but some hit-and-run driver ran him down in front of his house this morning."

"I'm very sorry to hear it."

"It seems most of my day has been taken up with Mr. Moriarty and his problems."

"If I'd known about this I certainly would have waited a decent interval, but as long as I'm here, may I explain myself?"

"Go ahead."

"I read the book recently and thought it might make a nice little art film, if I can fit it into our schedule. We normally have a couple of dozen projects like that floating around the studio at any given time."

Merton looked at Michael sharply. "I've done some business with you movie people in my time, and it sounds to me like you're trying to buy a valuable property cheap."

Michael stood up and put his card on the man's desk. "I'm sorry to have taken up your time, Mr. Merton; you're obviously very busy today. If you have any interest in selling the rights, call me." He turned to go.

"Oh, sit down, Vincent," Merton said. "At least tell me what you've got in mind."

198

Michael sat down. "What I have in mind, sir, is offering you ten thousand dollars for a year's option against a twenty-five-thousand-dollar purchase price."

"Let's get this done, Mr. Vincent: twenty-five thousand against fifty. I have a fiduciary responsibility to the college to get a decent price."

"Twenty against forty. That's as far as I can go without the board's permission."

Merton stood up and stuck out his hand. "Done. Send me a contract and a check."

Michael shook the man's hand. "I'm sorry about Mr. Moriarty."

"Drunken oaf," Merton said. "He had a liver the size of a watermelon. He told me his doctor gave him six months, and that was nearly a year ago; I shouldn't think he'd have lived another month."

When Michael got back to his office there were two men in his waiting room.

"Mr. Vincent, these two gentlemen are police officers," Margot said. "They'd like a word with you."

CHAPTER

25

Michael sat and looked at the two police officers. This was a new experience for him. In the past he had always avoided talking with policemen.

"I'm Sergeant Rivera," said the larger of the two men. "This is Detective Hall."

"What can I do for you, gentlemen?" Michael asked, more calmly than he felt.

"Are you acquainted with a lawyer named Daniel J. Moriarty?" Rivera asked.

"Yes, I am, if you can call it acquainted."

"What do you mean?"

"I mean that I met the man once, at his office, and he was roaring drunk. There was a bottle of Scotch on his desk as we spoke."

"When was this?"

"Late last week — Thursday or Friday."

"You were in his diary for Friday morning."

"That was it, I guess. I suppose this visit must be about his death."

The cop regarded him for a moment before speaking. "And how is it you come to know of his death, Mr. Vincent? He only died this morning."

"I spoke with Mr. Moriarty about acquiring the film rights to a novel called *Pacific Afternoons*. He controlled the rights, but as I said, he was drunk. He did manage to explain that all the rights to the work had been bequeathed to Carlyle Junior College, so earlier today I met with the chairman of their Board of Trustees, a lawyer named Wallace Merton. He told me that Mr. Moriarty had been run down by a hit-and-run driver."

"I see," the cop said, sounding disappointed.

"So, gentlemen, you now have my entire knowledge of Mr. Moriarty."

"Just one other thing, Mr. Vincent," the policeman said. "Did Mr. Moriarty refuse to sell you these rights?"

"He may have; it was hard to ascertain his meaning, given his condition. In any event, it seemed to me that if I was going to get anywhere, I'd have to talk with Mr. Merton."

"Were these rights very valuable to you, Mr. Vincent?"

"Not in a major way. The book was published in the nineteen-twenties and is little known today. A friend gave it to me to read last year sometime, and it occurred to me that it might make a film. I finally got around to looking into the rights. I didn't even know who controlled them until last week. If you don't mind my saying so, it seems that interviewing me is quite a long way from a hit-and-run incident."

"It was more than that," the policeman said. "Mr. Moriarty wasn't actually killed by the car. The driver got out and knifed him, just to be sure."

"Good God!" Michael said. "That's pretty brutal."

"Yes, it is."

"So I suppose you're interviewing anybody who had anything to do with him."

"That's right, and there are surprisingly few people who had anything to do with him."

"It's really ironic that he should be murdered," Michael said. "Wallace Merton told me that Moriarty was a dying man — a bad liver."

"That's what we learned from his part-time secretary. Mr. Vincent, can you tell me where you were between eight and nine o'clock this morning?"

Michael didn't miss a beat. "Of course. I got up later than usual this morning. I didn't leave the house until around nine-thirty, and I was in the office before ten."

"Is there anyone who can corroborate that?"

"Yes, my secretary can tell you what time I arrived here this morning, and the woman I live with can tell you when I left the house."

"And her name?" His notebook was poised.

"Vanessa Parks." He gave them the phone number.

"What kind of car do you drive, Mr. Vincent?"

"A Porsche Cabriolet."

"Color?"

"Black."

"Do you know anyone who drives a red Cadillac?"

"No. Everybody in this business seems to drive a foreign car — just take a look in the lot outside."

The policeman smiled. "I noticed." He looked around the room. "This looks like a room I saw in a movie once."

"This was the study in a nineteen-thirties movie called *The Great Randolph*."

"That's it! I knew I'd seen it somewhere."

"You're a movie fan, then?"

"Absolutely."

"Would you like a little tour of the lot?"

"I'd love it some other time, Mr. Vincent,

but we've got a lot on our hands this afternoon."

"Call my secretary anytime, and she'll arrange it for you."

"And when can I expect to see *Pacific Afternoons* on the screen?"

"Oh, that's hard to say. I only bought the rights today, and a screenplay has to be written. I'd say a year, at the earliest."

"So you did get the rights after all?"

"Mr. Merton and I reached agreement very quickly. I don't think he'd ever had another offer. By the way, would you like his number?"

"Thanks, we already have it."

Michael stood up. "Gentlemen, if there's nothing further . . ."

The policemen rose, then stopped at the office door. "There were two men in the Cadillac," Rivera said.

"Oh? Any leads?"

"One or two. It was a professional job; we know that much."

"Sounds interesting. Tell you what, Sergeant, when you've made an arrest give me a call, and let's talk about it. Might be a movie in it."

"Maybe I'll do that, Mr. Vincent," Rivera said.

"Don't wait until you're ready to go to trial,

though. Call me the minute you've made an arrest, before there's a lot of publicity." He smiled. "I wouldn't want to get into a bidding war."

The cop laughed and shook his hand. "A bidding war sounds good to me." He gave Michael his card. "Call me if you think of anything else I should know."

Michael gave him his card. "Same here. True crime stuff is always good for the movies." He waved and went back into his office.

He waited until he was sure they'd left the building, then called Vanessa.

"Hello?"

At least she was awake. "Hi, babe. You remember our conversation of this morning?"

"Yes," she said exasperatedly, "we made love and took a shower together, and you didn't leave until nine-thirty."

"You'll be getting a call from a policeman who'll ask you about that."

"What's this about, Michael?"

Stick close to the truth. "Last week I tried to buy the screen rights to *Pacific Afternoons* from a lawyer named Moriarty. He wouldn't sell them to me, so I went to the lawyer who represents the college that owns the rights, and he sold them to me. Then Moriarty gets run down by a car — murdered apparently — and the cops came to see me, since I was in Moriarty's diary."

"So where were you this morning?"

Michael stopped breathing. "Didn't you wake up at all when I got up?"

"No."

He relaxed. "Well, I was right there, babe. I fixed myself some breakfast as usual, and I decided to read a script before leaving for the studio. That's why I was late."

"So why didn't you just tell the police that?"

"Because you couldn't back me up if you were asleep."

"Oh."

"See you later, babe. We'll drive out to Malibu for dinner, okay?"

She brightened. "Okay."

"I gave the cops the number; they'll call."

"Okay, I know what to say."

He hung up. "Margot," he called out, "get me Leo."

Leo took the call. "Yeah, kid?"

"Just wanted to let you know I've sewed up the rights to *Pacific Afternoons*."

"How much?"

"Twenty grand against forty."

"You're my kind of guy. See you." Leo hung up.

Michael hung up, too. He was thinking of growing his beard again.

* * *

On the way home, Michael stopped his car at a phone booth and called a number Tommy Pro had given him.

A recorded voice answered. "Please enter the number of a touch-tone phone where you can be reached at this hour." There was a series of beeps.

Michael tapped in the number of the phone booth, then hung up and waited nervously. Ten minutes passed, then the phone rang. He snatched up the receiver. "Tommy?"

"Where are you calling from?"

"A phone booth on Pico."

"How are you, kid? What's up?"

"Tommy, you very nearly got me hung up on a murder rap. What the hell were you thinking of?"

Tommy was immediately apologetic. "Listen, I'm sorry about that, kid. The guy was recommended to me highly; who knew he was going to be a cowboy? Don't worry, he's already out of the picture."

"Tommy, people *saw* me in that car with him. The cops have already been to my office."

"That's natural; after all, you had a meeting with the guy, right? Just be cool and everything will be okay."

"Tommy, I don't know how you could put

me in this position."

Tommy's voice hardened. "Your problem is solved, right?"

"Yes, but . . ."

"I gotta go." Tommy hung up.

Michael was left with the dead phone in his hand.

CHAPTER

26

Michael sat at a table at a McDonald's on Santa
Monica Boulevard and watched the door for
Barry Wimmer. He recognized the short,
bearded man from his own description and
waved him toward the table. Wimmer stopped
at the counter and picked up a Big Mac and
fries first.

Michael shook the man's hand as he sat
down.

"First meeting I ever took at McDonald's,"
Wimmer said.

"Morton's didn't seem appropriate."

Wimmer emitted a short, rueful laugh. "No,
I don't guess you'd want to be seen with me
at Morton's."

"Or any other industry hangout," Michael
said.

Wimmer looked ill for a moment. "Thanks

for reminding me," he said bitterly.

"When did you get out?" Michael asked.

"Four months ago."

"How are you making a living?"

"I've worked up a couple of budgets for friends," Wimmer replied, attacking the Big Mac.

Michael reached into the briefcase beside him and fished out a budget for *Pacific Afternoons*. "Tell me what you think of this," he said, handing Wimmer the document across the table.

Wimmer put down his burger and began leafing through the pages, chewing absently. He took his time. "This is as tight as anything I've ever seen," he said finally, "but it'll work if you can shoot outside L.A."

"I want to shoot in Carmel."

Wimmer nodded. "If you've already got a budget, why did you want to see me?"

"I've heard some good things about you."

"Not recently, I guess. My name's mud in this town."

"Very recently. I heard that you may have taken various studios for as much as five million dollars over the past ten years."

"I got sent away for two hundred grand," Wimmer said. "That's all I'll cop to."

"What did you do with all the money?" Michael asked. "I'm curious."

"I lived well," Wimmer said.

"You lived high, too, from what I've heard."

Wimmer smiled ruefully. "You could say that."

"Are you still using?"

"Prison didn't do much for me, but it got me off cocaine. There was a pretty good therapy program."

"Out of all the money you took did you save anything?"

Wimmer snorted. "If I had, do you think I'd have gone to jail for two hundred grand? I'd have made restitution."

"What are your plans for the future?"

"I was thinking of starting a private course for production management."

"That should buy groceries."

"And not much else."

"Are you interested in getting back into the business?"

"Doing what? Props?"

"As a production manager."

Wimmer stopped chewing and looked at Michael for a long time. "Don't fuck around with my head, mister."

"I'm quite serious."

"On this project?" He tapped the budget.

"On this project."

"You think you could trust me not to steal?"

211

Michael wiped his mouth and threw his napkin onto the table. "Barry, if you come to work for me, stealing will be your principal duty."

Wimmer stared at Michael, apparently stunned into silence.

"Let me ask you something," Michael said. "How did you get caught on the two hundred thousand?"

Wimmer swallowed hard and fiddled with his french fries. "I had a producer who was as smart as I was."

"I'm smarter than you are, Barry," Michael said. "And if you were stealing from my production, I would catch you at it."

Wimmer nodded. "I see," he said. "You won't catch me, is that it?"

"That's it," Michael said.

"We split what I can take?"

"Not quite. Not fifty-fifty."

"What did you have in mind?"

"I'll give you twenty percent of anything you can rake off the budget."

"What happens if we get caught?"

"Who's going to catch you, if not me?"

"Doesn't Centurion have any controls at all?"

"Of course they do, and very good controls, too. But from what I've heard, you're something of a genius at fooling the studios."

"You could say that," Wimmer agreed.

"What's the number at the bottom of that budget?" Michael asked, nodding toward the document.

"Eight million, give or take."

"What sort of budget would that be in this town?"

"Tight, under any circumstances; but who's your star?"

"Robert Hart."

Wimmer's eyes widened. "And your writer?"

"Mark Adair."

"Director?"

"A very bright kid from UCLA Film School."

"Then eight million is an impossible budget, even with a kid director."

"Would ten million be more in line?"

"Fifteen million would be more in line, if everything were cut to the bone and Hart took points instead of salary."

"Suppose we settle at nine and a half million. We shoot the picture for eight million, and you, employing your special genius, flesh it out to nine million five. You think you could do that?"

"For twenty percent? In the blink of an eye."

Michael smiled. "That's what I thought."

"What do I get paid for the picture?"

"You'll work cheap. Nobody will be surprised; at this point you'd take just about any job, wouldn't you?"

"I would."

"You've never, ah, collaborated with anybody on something like this, have you?"

"No."

"Well, we had better get a couple of things straight. First of all, there will never be any transaction of cash between you and me. Every week, you'll go to the local Federal Express office and send eighty percent of the rake-off to an address I'll give you. I want you to remember at all times that I'm smarter than you, Barry; that's very important to our working relationship."

"Okay, you're smarter than me. I can live with that."

"My share of the money is going to be untraceable; I'll help you see that your share is, too. It is not in my interests for you to get caught."

"What happens if I do get caught? I mean, if you're underestimating Centurion's controls?'

"I assure you that I'm not, but I'll give you a straight answer to your question: If you get caught, you'll take the fall. I'll testify against you myself; there won't be any way you can implicate me, and if you try, I'll make things even worse for you."

"You're a sweet guy," Wimmer said.

"Is anybody else in town going to hire you?"

"Nope."

"Then you're right; I'm a sweet guy — as long as things go smoothly. You fuck up, and you're back in jail; you fuck *me*, and — I want you to take this seriously, Barry — I'll see you dead. That's not a euphemism; it's a serious promise."

Wimmer stared at Michael.

"On the brighter side, you'll make some very nice money, and you'll be seen to rehabilitate yourself. I'm going to make a lot of pictures, and as long as our relationship works out, you'll have a job."

"That sounds good," Wimmer said.

"So we understand each other? I wouldn't want there to be any misunderstanding."

"We understand each other completely," Wimmer said firmly.

"Good." Michael extended his hand and Wimmer shook it. "Be at my office on the Centurion lot first thing tomorrow morning. I'll have a desk ready for you, and I'll leave a pass at the gate."

"Yes, sir," Wimmer said, smiling.

CHAPTER

27

Monday night at Morton's. The *crème de la crème* of the motion picture industry sat in the dimly lit restaurant on Melrose Avenue and displayed their standing to each other. Michael and Vanessa sat with Leo and Amanda Goldman at a table between that of Michael Ovitz, head of the talent agency Creative Artists Agency, and that of Peter Guber, head of Sony Pictures. Michael had been introduced to and had exchanged desultory chat with both men. Being in their presence, on equal terms, gave him a satisfaction he had not felt since he had made his deal with Centurion.

After dinner, when the women had adjourned to the ladies' room, Leo put his elbows on the table and leaned forward. "There's a guy I'd like you to consider to direct *Pacific*

Afternoons," Leo said. "His name is Marty White."

"I appreciate the suggestion, Leo," Michael said, "but I think I've already found a director."

Leo's eyebrows went up. "Who? How could you do that without my knowing about it?"

"Leo, I shouldn't have to remind you that I don't need your approval to hire a director."

"Jesus fucking Christ, I know that; what I don't know is why I didn't *know* about it. I know *everything* that goes on at my studio."

"So I've heard," Michael said.

"You couldn't take a meeting with somebody about that job that I wouldn't know about. Not with any director in town."

"This guy has never directed anything. That's why you don't know about him."

Leo leaned forward and made an effort to lower his voice. "You've hired some schmuck who *never directed a picture?*"

"Well, he's directed things at school."

"At *school!*"

"He's at UCLA Film School."

"You hired a *student* to direct this movie?"

"Leo, *I* was a student at film school when I produced *Downtown Nights.*"

"That's different."

"No, it's not different; it's exactly the same."

217

"I think you've gone crazy, Michael."

"Did you screen the reel?"

"What reel?"

"Leo, I sent you the kid's reel last Wednesday."

"I didn't get to it yet."

"Well, if you had gotten to it, your blood pressure would be a lot lower right now."

"So, what's on the reel?"

"A scene from a Henry James novel that was so good I couldn't believe it."

"Just one scene?"

"A scene of eight pages with a long tracking shot, an orchestra, and seven speaking parts."

"Who's this kid?"

"His name is Eliot Rosen."

"Well, at least he's Jewish."

Michael laughed.

"Are you Jewish, Michael? I could never figure it out."

"Half," Michael lied. "My mother."

"What was your father?"

"Italian."

"What did they do about your religious upbringing?"

"I was a lapsed Catholic by the time I was six."

"If you were Jewish, you'd be perfect."

"You're going to love Eliot Rosen. He'll probably drive you crazy, but you'll love him.

He may be the new Orson Welles."

Leo groaned. "You got any idea how much money was lost backing Orson?"

"Eliot is going to make you a lot of money; I'll see to it."

"Well, you're as tight with a buck as anybody I ever saw; if he works for you, he'll make money for me." Leo flicked the ash off his cigar. "I hear you hired a production manager from outside the studio."

"That's right, Leo; I wanted somebody who'd report to me instead of you."

"You hired Barry Wimmer."

"That's right."

"Michael, you gotta know he did time for stealing from a production."

"He was a cokehead. He's clean now."

"I'm worried."

"Leo, he's so grateful for the chance that he'll work three times as hard as anybody else would." Michael paused. "Cheap, too."

"I like that part. If he steals from me, I'll take it out of your end."

"Fair enough."

"What're you paying the kid Jewish director?"

"Two hundred thousand."

Leo smiled broadly. "Don't you let him fuck up."

"Leo, even if he fucks up he won't cost

you nearly as much as Marty White would."

The women returned to the table, and as they sat down, Amanda Goldman's foot ran down the back of Michael's calf. He gave her a brief smile and filed that move away for later consideration.

CHAPTER

28

Michael put down Mark Adair's first-draft screenplay of *Pacific Afternoons* and picked up the telephone.

"Hello?" a deep voice answered.

"Mark, it's Michael Vincent."

"What did you think?" Adair asked.

"I think it's wonderful. You've captured the book, both in structure and in intent, and you've made the book's dialogue work beautifully."

"But . . . ?"

"But nothing. I think it's shootable as is."

"No producer has ever said that to me," Adair said warily. "There has to be something else."

"There is something else, but it in no way detracts from what you've done."

"What is it?"

"Near the end, you've left out a crucial scene and substituted something that doesn't work nearly as well."

"Are you talking about the scene where the doctor sings to the girl and wins her heart?"

"I am."

"There are two reasons that could never work in this film, Michael."

"What are they?"

"First, it would come off as mawkish, sentimental, and unbelievable to a modern audience; second, you'll never get Bob Hart to do the scene."

"Mark, the scene is sentimental, I'll grant you that, but it is by no means mawkish — at least not the way we'll shoot it."

"Name me a picture where that sort of thing has worked."

"All right, *A Room with a View*."

Adair was quiet for a moment. "There was no singing in that."

"No, but the period was one that accepted sentimentality as normal; the period of *Pacific Afternoons* is much the same, *and* the characters are not very different."

"What about Bob Hart? How will you get him to do it?"

"You leave that to me. When the time comes, I'll want your support to help persuade him, though."

"I don't know."

"Tell you what, Mark; I'll make a privat
deal with you. Put the scene back in — just
as it is in the book — and if, when you've
seen it on film, you don't think it works, then
I'll shoot your substitute scene."

"You've made me an offer I can't refuse.
Now tell me what other criticisms you have
of my script."

"I can't think of a thing. I'm sure Bob Hart
— and especially Susan Hart — will have some
comments, and the director may as well, but
it won't be anything that damages what you've
done. I won't let that happen."

"Who's going to direct?"

"A young director named Eliot Rosen. He's
very smart and sensitive, and you're going to
love him."

"I'll get right on a second draft."

"Don't write a second draft; just insert the
scene, and leave everything else as it is."

"Bless you, my son." Adair hung up.

Michael replaced the receiver and reflected
on how well everything was going. His intercom buzzed. "Yes?"

"Michael," Margot said, "Sergeant Rivera
is here; I've told him you've got a tough morning, but he'd like to see you if you can manage
it."

A trickle of fear ran down Michael's bowels.

im in," he said, keeping his voice

ʌivera was alone this time. "Thanks for seeing me," he said, extending his hand. "I won't take much of your time."

"Glad to see you, Sergeant," Michael said, shaking his hand and waving him to a seat. He held up Mark Adair's screenplay. "The first draft of the screenplay of *Pacific Afternoons* is in, and it's great. Looks like we'll be shooting in the spring."

"Good," the sergeant said, easing into a chair. "I thought I'd bring you up to date on where we are on the Moriarty homicide."

"Great, I'm all ears. I haven't seen anything in the papers about it for a few weeks."

"I haven't released anything to the papers."

"Have you made an arrest?"

"No, and I'm not sure we will."

Michael guarded against feeling relief. "Why not?"

"Looks like a mob hit, pure and simple; a contract job."

"Moriarty had mob connections?"

"Maybe, maybe not, but somebody who's connected wanted Moriarty dead, I guarantee you."

"Tell me about it."

"The car was driven by a low-grade hood

from Vegas named Dominic Ippolito — 1
scum."

"How'd you find that out?"

"Some hikers found Dominic dumped in the
desert near Twenty-Nine Palms; his fingerprints were on file."

"Did you find the car?"

"Dominic was *in* the car. It was a mess —
down a ravine four or five hundred feet."

"Is that it?"

"Not quite; we found some other prints in
the car that were interesting."

Michael's heart nearly stopped, but he
didn't blink. "Yeah?"

"The car was stolen; there were the car
owner's prints, of course, and his wife's, but
the other set was unusual."

"Tell me."

"They belonged to somebody named . . ."
He took a folded sheet of paper from his
pocket and glanced at it, then handed it to
Michael. "Vincente Michaele Callabrese."

Michael found himself staring at his own
birth certificate. "Who is he?" he managed
to say. He put the paper on his desk so that
Rivera wouldn't see his hands shaking.

"He's the son of Onofrio and Martina
Callabrese, and he's twenty-eight years old.
That's all I know; that much was on the birth
certificate."

el, who had been imagining hand-
saw a glimmer of hope. "You weren't
.e to find out anything else?"

"Nothing, and that's very unusual. There
is apparently no other piece of paper in the
world on this guy — no Social Security number, no driver's license, no insurance — the
guy has never had a credit card or a charge
account. The only reason we know about him
at all is that he had an arrest when he was
eighteen, for car theft — the charges were
dropped for lack of evidence — and he got
himself printed. That put him in the FBI fingerprint files. There was no photograph on
file; I don't know why."

Michael remembered it well. "You mean
there's no way to track him down?"

"Nope. But he's almost certainly mobbed
up."

"Why do you say that? Because he's Italian?"

"No, it's just that it's nearly impossible for
anybody to live to be twenty-eight years old
in this country and not have a lot of paper on
him. The only people who have no paper on
them are people who've been using forged
or stolen paper all their lives, and that adds
up to mob."

"So what does all this mean?"

"It probably means something like this:

Moriarty has some dealings at some time w
somebody who's connected, and somethin
goes wrong; he makes an enemy. The enemy
talks to somebody, money changes hands, and
a contract is put out on the guy. Callabrese,
or whatever name he goes by, is probably the
mob contact. He was the second man in the
car. He, or somebody he knows, hires Ippolito
to make the hit, and Callabrese goes along to
make sure it's right. Then, when it's all over,
Callabrese puts a bullet into Ippolito and
dumps him and the car in the desert, thus
making it impossible for Ippolito to ever tell
anybody who hired him. Only Callabrese
wasn't smart enough to wipe his prints off
the car. That tells me something about him."

"What?"

"That he's not the brains behind all this.
Otherwise, he'd have taken more care to cover
his tracks."

"I see." Rivera was right; he'd been stupid.
But he'd been so frightened at the scene that
he hadn't thought about prints until later. "So
what's your next move?"

"I don't have a next move," Rivera replied.
"But one of these days this guy Callabrese will
make a mistake and get picked up. I've flagged
his prints, so if he ever gets arrested again
and is printed, I'll get a call from the FBI
inside of a week."

ant, I'll be frank with you; it doesn't ke we've got a movie here. This is all incomplete."

"I figured."

"But if you ever come across another case that looks good, I want to hear from you." Michael had meant this to dismiss the policeman, but Rivera didn't move.

"There's something I'd like to satisfy myself on," he said.

"What's that?"

"Well, it's interesting that this Callabrese guy has two names that are similar to yours — Vincente and Michaele."

"An interesting coincidence," Michael said. He was frightened again now.

"How old are you, Mr. Vincent?"

"Thirty."

"Do you have some paper that would document that?"

"Sure." Michael was ready for this; he opened the file drawer in his desk and rummaged through the personal file. "Here," he said, handing the policeman a birth certificate.

Rivera read it carefully. "You're thirty, all right, and Callabrese was born at Bellevue Hospital, whereas you were born at St. Vincent's." He looked up. "Are you Italian?"

Michael shook his head. "Jewish."

"I see you're growing a beard."

"I've had a beard off and on for ye.

"I wonder if you'd be willing to do a lin. for me."

"Are you kidding?" Michael said. "I saw a movie when I was a kid where a guy agreed to do that, and he got picked out, even though he was innocent."

"Well, you're within your rights," Rivera said, standing up.

"It isn't that I'm standing on my rights," Michael said, walking him to the door. "I just don't have the time for something like that. I'd waste half a day, and that's a lot of money in this business."

"Sure, I understand." He held out his hand. "I'll let you know if I come up with another case that might make a movie."

"You do that," Michael said. "And Sergeant?"

"Yes?"

"Could I have my birth certificate back?"

"Oh, sorry," Rivera said, handing back the paper.

"I'll be happy to make a copy for you, if you need it," Michael said.

"Oh, no, no; just an oversight."

Some oversight, Michael thought, as he watched the homicide detective go. The certificate was real, on file — Tommy Pro had seen to that years ago. But now Michael's

...ts were on it. He sat down at his ...d took a few deep breaths. He hoped God that Rivera was satisfied.

Margot came in with the mail. "This is everything that isn't junk," she said, placing the pile on his desk.

"Thanks." He rummaged around his desktop and through the drawers.

"What are you looking for?" she asked.

"My letter opener."

"You're always losing things; I'll find it while you're at lunch."

When Michael came back from lunch, the letter opener was on his desk.

Michael looked across his desk at his director. Eliot Rosen was tall, skinny, and ill-shaven. At this moment he was exploring a nostril for something.

"Eliot," Michael said, "promise me that when Bob and Susan Hart get here you won't pick your nose."

"Sorry," the young man said, blushing. Eliot blushed a lot.

"I've shown them your reel, and they're impressed, but they still want to meet you. There's a lot riding on this meeting, Eliot."

"I know that," Rosen said.

"Remember, you're not just talking to the actor but to his wife as well. Susan Hart is the hardest to handle of the two, and I don't want you to mess this up by kowtowing too much to Hart. Include her in everything you say, and if you can muster some charm, that would help, too."

"I'll do my best," Rosen said.

"If there's an argument about *anything,* follow my lead, do you understand?"

"Listen, I have opinions, too."

"Not at this point you don't. If you have an opinion that might spark some controversy with the Harts, express it to me first, and privately. If it's a point I think we can win, then I'll carry the ball, okay?"

Rosen nodded. "Okay," he said sullenly.

"Eliot," Michael said placatingly, "you're at the beginning of what I think is going to be a big career. Don't screw it up by alienating a powerful star and his influential wife. If they want something that's bad for the movie, I'll protect the movie, don't worry. And when we get to the part about the singing scene, don't say anything; just nod agreement."

"I've got a lot of problems with that scene," Rosen said.

"Eliot, we've already been over this; the scene stays in, and I don't want to hear another word about it."

"All right, all right, you're the boss."

"Don't resent it, Eliot; everybody has a boss around here, except Leo Goldman, who is, effectively, God. Leo has given me a lot of freedom, and I'm not going to let anybody compromise that, especially a first-time director."

"All right, all right."

"Don't worry, this picture is going to establish you." He smiled. "After *Pacific Afternoons* I won't be able to afford you."

Rosen smiled. "I like that idea."

There was a brief knock on the door, and Margot showed in Robert and Susan Hart.

Michael went to Susan first, giving her an affectionate hug and kiss, then he shook Bob's hand warmly. "I'm so glad to see you both," he said, "and I can't wait to hear your reactions to the screenplay. And may I introduce Eliot Rosen?"

The young director shook both their hands. "Your work has given me a great deal of pleasure," he said to Bob Hart. "I'm thrilled to be on this picture."

Hart accepted this praise graciously, and everybody took a seat on the facing sofas before the huge fireplace.

"I remember this set," Hart said. "I loved the movie, and I loved Randolph. I always wanted to play the part."

Michael smiled. "That's a very good idea," he said. "When we've finished *Pacific Afternoons*, we ought to explore the possibilities." He leaned forward on the sofa. "Now," he said, "tell me what you thought of the screen-play."

"I just loved it," Hart said.

"There are problems," Susan interjected.

Michael picked up a copy of the script from a stack on the coffee table. "I want to hear about every one of them, starting from the beginning."

Susan Hart, speaking without notes, went through the screenplay, scene by scene, noting criticisms large and small. Michael noted that nearly every one of them was aimed at increasing the size of her husband's part and augmenting his dialogue. He agreed with Susan immediately on more than half her points and promised to consult with Mark Adair on the rest, then get back to her.

"Finally," she said, "the singing scene has to go."

Michael did not react immediately, but turned to her husband. "Bob, how do you feel about that scene?"

"I can do it," Hart said quietly.

"But he won't," Susan said firmly. "Bob has devoted the past twenty-five years to building an image that has become solid gold. I won't allow him to do something that would shatter that image in the minds of his public; we'll back out of the film first."

"Let me tell you how I feel about that,

Susan," Michael said to her, then directed himself almost entirely to Bob Hart. "Bob is at a turning point in his career; he has mined the vein of police, western, and action movies brilliantly, and he has reached a point where to continue exclusively in that vein would simply be repetition. If he does that, even the fans and critics who have loved all of it are going to begin to fade away. Another thing: it has been a long time since a script has really drawn on all of Bob's talent as an actor."

"That's very true," Hart said. His wife glanced sharply at him.

"Bob has resources that his public has not seen yet, and this film is going to stun them, I promise you. Here we have a somewhat retiring but thoroughly masculine character with many, many facets. He proves his manhood when he stands up to the trainer who has been abusing horses, and he shows remarkable sensitivity in the scenes with his child patients. Still, he is unable to express himself to this woman he fears may be too young for him. *But,* in this one terribly moving scene, he wins her heart forever. Now what can be wrong with that?"

Susan Hart spoke up. "Certainly, what you say about the scene with the trainer and those with the children is true, and certainly, the doctor has to win the girl, but why the hell does he have to *sing?*"

"Because he is an incurable romantic, Sue, and this is an incurably romantic film. That is its great strength, and that is what is going to create enormous word of mouth for this film. What's wrong with singing?"

Susan drew herself up and began to reply, but she was, uncharacteristically, interrupted by her husband.

"It wouldn't be the first time I've sung," Bob Hart said.

Susan turned and stared at him. "What?"

"Long before we even met, darling, I was trained for the musical stage; in fact, that was where I thought my career would lead."

"You never told me that," she said, astonished.

"It never came up. Before I joined the Actors Studio I was concentrating mainly on finding a part in a musical. It was Lee Strasberg who saw the dramatic talent in me and who changed my direction."

"For which we can all thank him," Michael said. "Let me ask you, Susan, have you heard this piece of music?"

"No, and that's not the point," she replied.

"I want you to hear it right now," Michael said. He picked up the phone. "Margot, please send in Anton and Hermann."

Anton Gruber and Hermann Hecht entered

the room and everyone settled in to listen.

Anton played an introduction, then Hermann began to sing. Michael glanced surreptitiously at Susan Hart from time to time, but her face was a blank mask. When Hermann had finished, everyone applauded, then the musicians left.

Michael turned to Bob and Susan. "Well?"

"I can sing it," Hart said. "It's within my range. I'll have to do a lot of vocalizing; get back in shape."

"Susan?" Michael asked.

"I grant you it's beautiful," she said, "but why does it have to be in German?"

"Tell you what, Susan, let's shoot it, then decide," Michael said. "I promise you I'm not going to make a fool of Bob. If you don't like it when it's done, we'll shoot an alternative scene."

She turned to her husband. "Do you really feel comfortable with this?"

Hart shrugged. "Let's see how it goes."

"All right," Susan said, "we'll look at it on film, then decide. But nobody, and I mean *nobody*, in the industry sees the scene until we've approved its inclusion."

"That's fine with me," Michael said. "Eliot?"

"Fine with me, too," Rosen said. It was the first time he had spoken.

"I'll get back to you on the screenplay after I've talked to Mark," Michael said. The meeting adjourned.

When the Harts had gone, Eliot Rosen spoke again. "Do you really think she'll sit still for that scene?" he asked. "She looks like a pretty tough cookie to me."

"Trust me," Michael said. "Anyway, the scene is what kept her from getting around to questions about you."

"I'm beginning to like the scene," Rosen said.

CHAPTER

30

Michael stood in the center of Leo Goldman's enormous office and basked in the glow of adulation. A hundred of the film industry's movers and shakers — producers, studio heads, actors, directors, and journalists — filled the room. They had all just seen the first screening of *Downtown Nights*, and there was nothing but praise in the air.

Michael's beard had grown fuller now, and he felt reasonably safe in this crowd, although he had spent the first ten minutes of the after-screening party checking out every face in the crowd. None of them was the man in the Mercedes who had witnessed the murder of Daniel J. Moriarty, and none of them was the woman in curlers across the street.

He was receiving the congratulations of

one of the town's hottest directors when Leo's secretary tugged at his elbow.

"What is it?" Michael asked, trying not to sound irritable.

"The security guard at the main gate is on the phone and wants to talk with you. Apparently there's someone who claims he knows you trying to get onto the lot."

Michael excused himself from the conversation and went into the outer office to take the call.

"Mr. Vincent, this is Jim at the front gate. There's a man here named Parish who says he's the director of your picture; he wants to come to the screening."

"Chuck Parish?" Michael asked. This was inconvenient.

"That's the one."

Michael thought for a moment. "Jim, give him directions to my office; I'll meet him there."

"Yessir."

Michael hung up the phone and left the building. He walked quickly toward his office and arrived just in time to see Chuck Parish climbing out of a battered sports car. As Michael approached, Parish tripped getting out of the car and fell on his face. A briefcase that had been in his hand bounced and came to rest a few feet away.

Michael picked up the briefcase, then helped the young man to his feet. "Careful there, Chuck; you took a bad spill." He looked terrible, Michael thought.

"Goddamned car," Chuck said. "Can't get used to it; belongs to a friend."

"Come inside." Michael unlocked the door, turned on some lights, then led Chuck into his office. "That's a pretty bad scrape on your forehead," Michael said. "Let me get something for it." He went to the liquor cabinet, poured some vodka on a tissue, then returned and dabbed at Chuck's forehead until the scrape was clean. The smell of the alcohol blended in with whatever Chuck had been drinking.

"Do you think I could have some of that stuff in a glass?" he asked.

"Sure." Michael filled a glass with ice and poured vodka over it. "Tonic?"

"Just ice will do."

Michael gave him the drink and showed him to one of the facing sofas. "I didn't know you were in L.A. Why didn't you call me?"

"I've been here a couple weeks," Chuck said, taking a big gulp of his vodka. "Heard there was a screening of my movie tonight."

"There was, earlier," Michael replied. "It was over an hour ago. I wish I'd known you were in town; I'd have invited you."

241

"Bad timing, as usual," Chuck said. "How'd they like it?"

"The reaction was mixed," Michael lied.

" 'Mixed,' huh? So it's going nowhere?"

"Too early to tell."

"How's the lovely Vanessa?" he asked bitterly.

"All right, I guess," Michael replied, then changed the subject quickly. "How are things going? What are you working on?"

"I've written another screenplay," Chuck said, staring into the cold fireplace.

"Good; I'd like to read it."

Chuck opened his briefcase and tossed Michael some bound pages.

Michael looked at the cover. "*Inside Straight*. Nice title; what's it about?"

"I'd rather you'd read the whole thing without my telling you too much."

"All right; I'll try to get it read over the weekend."

"I can't wait that long."

"Beg pardon?"

"I want to sell it to you now."

"But I haven't read it yet."

"It's better than *Downtown Nights*," Chuck said. "You can trust me on that."

"I don't doubt it, Chuck, but I can't buy it without reading it."

"Why not? Don't you have any authority

around here? I can't imagine you making a deal, Michael, that didn't put you in the driver's seat."

"I have the authority, Chuck, but don't you think it's a little unfair to ask me to buy it sight unseen?"

"I need the money, Michael."

Michael was stunned. "Chuck, the last time I saw you, you had something like three quarters of a million dollars in cash. What do you mean, you need the money?"

"I just need it."

"Why?"

"There are a couple people pressing me."

"What sort of people?"

"Very insistent people."

"What happened to all the money, Chuck?"

"Well, there were a couple of bad investments and some slow ponies. And there was this very expensive lady," Chuck said. "She and I picked up this little habit."

"Coke."

Chuck nodded. "God, I just don't know how the money could have gone so fast."

"I would have thought that after seeing what happened to Carol Geraldi you'd have stayed away from coke."

"Look, it's nothing I can't handle. I'm going into rehab next week — got a spot nailed down at a clinic up the coast. I just need to pay a few debts and get myself tided over until I can start the program, you know?"

Michael flipped quickly through the screenplay. There was no way to judge it so quickly, but it looked well organized, at least. And Chuck Parish was a very talented writer.

"How much do you want for it?"

"Jesus, I don't know. I'm into a shark for over fifty grand, and there's a connection or two who's looking for another thirty or so."

Christ, Michael thought; he really was in deep.

"How about a quarter of a million?"

"Chuck . . ."

"I know, I know, you haven't even read it. Believe me, Michael, it's my best work. It's terrific."

"How soon do you need the money?"

"Now."

"Now? Chuck, it's nine o'clock in the evening; I can't get a check cut at this hour."

"First thing tomorrow morning, then?"

"I can't pay you a quarter of a million dollars for this sight unseen."

"How much?"

"You really owe eighty grand to these people?"

"At least."

"All right, Chuck, I'll give you a hundred thousand for it, sight unseen."

"I'll take it," Chuck said without hesitation.

Michael went to his desk and found a standard boilerplate rights contract, then came back to the sofa. He placed the contract on the table and handed Chuck a pen. "Sign right here," he said, pointing.

"There are a lot of empty blanks," Chuck said.

"I'll fill them in later."

"When do I get the money?"

"I'll get a check cut first thing tomorrow morning."

"I need cash, not a check."

"All right, meet me at the studio's bank at the corner of Wilshire and Beverly Glen at, say, eleven. No, make it noon."

"Noon. You promise?"

"Of course."

Chuck signed the contract.

Michael took the contract back to his desk and put it into a drawer. "Chuck, I'd like to talk longer, but I've got to be somewhere."

Chuck stood up. "I want to direct it," he said.

"I'd like you to direct," Michael said, "but I can't commit on that right now."

"Where's my copy of the contract?"

"I'll complete it and bring your copy to the bank. Now you'll have to excuse me, Chuck."

They shook hands and Michael walked him

245

to his car. "Noon tomorrow," he said. "Noon tomorrow."

Like hell, Michael thought. Not unless this is a real winner. He waved good-bye, went back to Leo's office to say good night to everybody, then went back to his office, found a legal pad and a pen, adjusted a reading lamp, and stretched out on a sofa. Now let's see if this thing is any good, he thought, opening the screenplay. If it's not, Chuck will have a long wait at the bank.

Two hours later, Michael put down the screenplay and leafed through his notes. Chuck had been right; it needed some work, work that he could do himself, but it was terrific. *Inside Straight* was going to be his next picture, right after *Pacific Afternoons*. He drove home feeling great.

CHAPTER

31

Michael got to the office early the next day and began working up Chuck's contract. As soon as Margot came in he gave her the signed copy and asked her to fill in the blanks, then he called Leo Goldman.

"Great screening, huh?" Leo chortled.

"It seemed to go well."

"Well? It went terrific, kid; I'm smelling Academy Award nominations!"

"I'm glad to hear it."

"How's *Pacific Afternoons* going?"

"Extremely well. We'll have a finished script very soon."

"By finished, do you mean approved by Susan Hart?"

"I do."

"Good going. She's not easy to handle, but you're doing a great job. Let me give you a tip about the Harts: Bob is a lot weaker than he seems. He's been through a couple of drying-out programs, and he does fine for a while, but as soon as he's faced with a role that scares him, he's back on the bottle. His particular weakness is fine French wines. Susan made him sell his cellar at auction earlier this year, and the sale brought over a million dollars. The man had the largest collection of 1961 red Bordeaux in the United States; he'd been collecting them for years. I bought some of them myself, before the auction, but I can't serve them when the Harts come over. The man is helpless in the presence of a Mouton Rothschild."

"He seemed quite confident at our first script meeting; very much in control, not yielding to her."

"The man's an actor, and a good one; remember that. Susan is not a monster, she just wants to avoid any situation that might get Bob drinking again. She puts a lot of effort into that. When you start shooting, whatever you do, keep Bob away from wine."

"I'll keep it in mind." He certainly would.

"Any idea what you'll do after you wrap *Pacific Afternoons*?"

"That's why I'm calling, Leo; I've bought a script — only last night, in fact."

"What is it?"

248

"It's called *Inside Straight,* and it's about a friendly weekly poker game where three of the players conspire to take one of the others for everything."

"Who wrote it?"

"Chuck Parish, the guy who wrote *Downtown Nights.*"

"Sounds good; what did you pay?"

"Two hundred thousand, and it would be worth half a million if some agent were shopping it around."

"Great!"

"One thing, Leo, Chuck is in some sort of a bind, and he wants his money in cash. I told him I'd meet him at the bank this morning with a check that he can cash right away."

"Have you got a signed contract?"

"Yep."

"Have you got the screenplay in a safe place?"

"I do."

"I'll call Accounting and get your check cut; I'll call the bank, too, and tell them you'll want to cash it."

"Tell them we'd like a private room for the transaction."

"You got it. Listen, kid, do you want me to read the screenplay before you do this?"

"I'd love you to read it when I fix a few things, but believe me, it's not necessary now.

I don't want to option it, either."

"I trust your judgment, kid. Your check will be ready in an hour."

Michael was at the bank at 11:30 with his own briefcase and a cheap plastic one. He sought out the branch manager and introduced himself.

"I'm glad you called ahead," the manager said. "We needed some time to put that much cash together." Michael handed the man both briefcases. "Ask your people to put a hundred thousand in each one," he said. "I'm expecting a Mr. Parish, and I'll give you the endorsed check as soon as he arrives."

"I'm glad you brought two," the manager replied, taking the cases. "We didn't have a lot of hundreds, so most of it is in twenties and fifties." He showed Michael to a conference room and left with the briefcases. He was back in five minutes. "I'll have to have the check, of course, before I turn the money over to you."

"Of course," Michael replied. "Why don't you keep the money at your desk until I get the check endorsed by Mr. Parish?"

"Glad to." The manager left with the two briefcases.

Chuck arrived at five minutes before the hour and was shown to the conference room;

he didn't bother with pleasantries. "Did you bring the money?"

Michael took an envelope from an inside pocket. "I've got the check right here; you'll have to endorse it." He took the check from the envelope, turned it face down on the conference table, and gave Chuck a pen. "Sign right here."

Chuck hurriedly signed the check; his hands were shaking, and he looked even worse than he had the evening before.

"I'll be right back," Michael said. He left the room and took the check to the manager's desk. "Here's your endorsed check," he said.

The manager examined it. "Do I have your assurance that you know this man to be who he says he is?"

"You have it."

The manager handed over the two briefcases.

Michael returned to the conference room with both cases. He entered, placed his own case on the floor beside the table, then put the plastic one on the table top. "I want you to count it," he said to Chuck.

Chuck opened the case, shuffled briefly through the money, then closed it. "Looks okay to me; I'll trust you."

"It's all there," Michael said. He took more papers from his jacket pocket. "Here's your copy of the contract with my signature." He handed the folded papers to Chuck, who put them in his own pocket. Michael produced another sheet of paper and placed it on the table. "I'll need you to sign a receipt, and then the money's yours."

Chuck signed the receipt without looking at it, then stood up. "Thanks, I'm out of here."

"Chuck, before you go, there's something you had better understand."

"Yeah?"

"The contract and the receipt state the amount as two hundred thousand dollars."

"What?"

"I've put that figure in for my own reasons, and for all practical purposes I have just given you and you have just received two hundred thousand dollars."

"I don't understand."

"Don't worry, it'll help you get your price up in this town. You can always show people a contract that says two hundred thousand instead of a hundred. And it would be in your own best interests, if anyone should ever ask, to say that you got two hundred thousand."

"Michael, are you stealing money from me?"

"Chuck, if you ever say anything like that

to me again — or to anybody else — you and I will have done business for the last time. Now, if you're unhappy in any way, you can put that briefcase back on the table, I'll give you back your contract, and we'll call it a day." He waited for an answer.

"I'm happy, Michael," Chuck said. "After all, who else would give me a hundred grand for a screenplay he hadn't even read?"

"That's right, Chuck," Michael said. He smiled. "Just remember, you and I are both going to be around for a long time; we've already made some money together, and we'll make a lot more."

Chuck shook his hand and left. Michael waited five minutes, then picked up his own briefcase and left, waving goodbye to the banker.

Michael got into the Porsche and drove downtown to his own bank, the Kensington Trust. Derek Winfield received him in his office.

"I'd like to make a deposit," Michael said.

"Of course," Winfield replied. "I'll just have this run through a counting machine to confirm the total." He left the room with the briefcase for a few minutes, then came back and handed Michael the empty case and a receipt. "Is there anything else I can do for you?"

"I'd like to know my current balance," Michael said.

"Of course." Winfield took a key from his pocket and inserted it into a computer terminal on his desk. He typed a few keystrokes, looked at the screen, then typed a few more strokes. A printer on a side table hummed and produced a sheet of paper. Winfield handed it to Michael. "Interest will be paid tomorrow on the past week's earnings," he said. "This amount doesn't include that."

Michael looked at the sheet of paper and smiled. "Thank you," he said. "I'm very pleased."

"I'm glad," Winfield replied. "And today's deposit will be earning from tomorrow."

Michael left Winfield's office whistling. It was difficult to know how things could be any better.

CHAPTER

32

Special Agent Thomas Carson of the Los Angeles office of the Federal Bureau of Investigation leaned over the counter and pressed his ear to a headset. Lined up along the twelve-foot counter were half a dozen Ampex reel-to-reel tape recorders, moving spasmodically.

"It's his second trip to the bank," the technician said, twitching the volume slightly so Carson could hear better.

"What happened the first time?" Carson asked. "Remind me."

"My memory is that he deposited a large sum of money, but you'll have to check the transcripts to be sure. Callabrese's name is in the log for that date, and the log should be cross-referenced by now."

"Thanks, Ken," Carson said. "I'll look up

Mr. Callabrese." He went to the files, found the name, and referenced the date; then he went to another filing cabinet and extracted the transcript. He sat down and read it thoroughly, then reread the file on the Kensington Trust. There was a weekly meeting with the bureau chief in a few minutes, and Carson was light on input; this would give him something to talk about. He went to the computer room and requested a profile on Vincente Callabrese, waiting for the printout. He was not the first, he noted in the logbook. An LAPD detective named Rivera had gotten in ahead of him. He called Rivera.

"This is Tom Carson over at the FBI," he said.

"Hi."

An unenthusiastic response. Why did cops hate the FBI so much? He had never understood it. "I just ran a guy named Vincente Callabrese through the system, and I saw you did, too. What have you got?"

"His fingerprints were on a car used in a crime. A mob hood from Vegas named Ippolito stole a car and ran a guy down with it. Contract job. Callabrese's prints were on the dashboard."

"And what do you surmise from that?"

"I surmise he was in the car. A witness said there was a second man."

"Where do you go from here?"

"Nowhere," Rivera replied. "The guy's a complete zero in the system; no paper of any kind. All I can do is put a flag on his record and wait for him to get arrested. It'll happen sooner or later; it always does."

"Right, Detective Rivera," Carson said. "Thanks for your help."

"Hey, wait a minute," Rivera said. "I showed you mine; now you show me yours."

"Oh, we've got even less than you have," Carson said. He could hear Rivera swearing as he hung up the phone.

Carson stopped by his desk to check his messages, then tucked the file under his arm and walked down the hall toward the large corner office that housed his chief. There were two other department heads present — personnel and investigation; Carson was head of surveillance.

Carson endured the personnel report in silence and the investigation report with interest, then it was his turn.

"What have you got for me, Tom?" the chief asked.

"You'll recall, chief, that we've had a tap on the offices of the Kensington Trust since last May."

"No, I don't," the chief replied curtly. "What the hell is the Kensington Trust?"

Carson was going to have to make this good. "They're an investment bank based in London, with offices around the world; what the Brits call a merchant bank."

"So?" The chief looked at his watch. The man had come out of the major crime side of the Bureau, and financial stuff bored him. He liked mob stuff, though; Carson knew that.

"We've suspected them for a long time of a major laundering operation, but they're very slick, and it's been hard to nail down anything. However," he said quickly, before the chief could interrupt, "now we think there's a significant connection with La Cosa Nostra."

Suddenly the chief was all ears. "Oh? Tell me about it."

"A few months ago, a new face turned up at Kensington's offices, name of Callabrese."

"And he's mob?"

"We believe him to be." Carson had precious little evidence to support this conclusion, but he had the chief's interest for the first time in weeks, and he wasn't going to let this opportunity pass. "In the first of his two visits to the Kensington offices Callabrese opened a new investment account with seven hundred and sixty thousand dollars. A hundred thousand was in cash, and the rest was in a cashier's check on a New York Bank."

"Which bank?"

258

"We don't know that, and we'd have to subpoena their records to find out. I don't think it's worth doing just yet."

"Go on."

"Callabrese specifically requested that his money go, and I quote, 'on the street.' "

"Jesus, Carson, that could mean Wall Street. What's the big deal?"

"You'd have to listen to the tapes to get the nuances, chief, but I don't think he meant Wall Street. He said he expected a return of three percent a week, and Kensington's L.A. manager said he thought he could manage that."

The chief nodded. "That sounds like loan-sharking," he said, "but we don't have enough evidence to prove it, do we?"

"Not yet, chief, but even if we did, I wouldn't want to go after Kensington. I think the bank is important because it could lead us to some really big-time stuff. It's more important as a conduit of information for us than as a target for a bust."

"I see your point," the chief said, nodding. "How much longer have we got on the court order?"

"Three weeks," Carson replied.

"Have we got a cooperative judge?"

"Cooper; he's pretty good."

"Wait two weeks and then go back for a

six-month extension," the chief said. "I'll sign the request."

"Yessir," Carson said happily; this had been exactly what he had wanted. He hated to see a wiretap order expire; it made him look bad.

"What happened on Callabrese's second visit?" the chief asked.

"He brought another hundred thousand in cash."

"Well, he's got to be mob; nobody walks around with that much cash."

"On his first visit, he mentioned a New York connection, but no names. I'd give odds he's connected, though."

"With a name like Callabrese? Sure he is. Did you run him through the system?"

"Yes, and he's there, but it's a low-grade presence. He was printed on a juvenile arrest eleven years ago, but nothing since. An L.A. homicide detective had run a request recently; I talked to him about it. Turns out Callabrese's prints turned up on a car that had been stolen by a Vegas mob guy and used in a hit-and-run murder. This guy came up dry on a background check — there's no paper at all on Callabrese."

"Then he's mob," the chief said, excited now, "and it doesn't sound like he's just passing through. Did you order a photograph?"

"There isn't one on record. The local precinct must have screwed up. I've flagged his file, though. If he gets arrested, I'll hear about it."

"Add Callabrese to the watch list," the chief said. "I want the name cross-referenced to both banking and loan-sharking."

"Yessir."

The chief stood up. "Thank you, gentlemen. Next week at the same time."

Carson went back to his desk feeling pretty good. Odds were he wouldn't hear from Callabrese for a while, but it was a name he could use in weekly meetings for weeks to come. "Thank you, Vincente Callabrese," he said, "wherever you are."

CHAPTER

33

The ringing telephone woke Detective Ricardo Rivera. He rolled over and looked at the bedside clock: 6:30. And he didn't have to be in until 11:00. Shit.

"Hello?"

"Hello, Ricky."

He should have known. "Cindy," he said, exasperated, "why the hell are you calling me at six-thirty in the morning?"

"I guess you know why," she said.

"Goddamnit, I'm not on until eleven; I could have slept another three hours." She had lived with him long enough to know that once he was awake he couldn't go back to sleep.

"Sorry, I wanted to be sure and catch you."

"How's Georgie?" He'd always hated the name, but she had insisted on naming him after her father. George Rivera just didn't work for him.

"He broke a finger playing football yesterday."

"Are you sure it's broken?"

"Sure, I'm sure; they put a cast on it in the emergency room. He'll have to wear it for six weeks."

"Badge of honor," Rivera said, smiling in spite of himself. He'd had a cast on his arm once, and he'd gotten a lot of mileage out of it with the girls.

"I had to write a check for the hospital," she said. "We hadn't used up the deductible yet."

He cringed inside. "How much?"

"Three hundred and twenty dollars."

"Christ! You'd think he'd broken his back!"

"They had to x-ray and everything. It's not really out of line, considering what medical stuff costs these days."

"Did you have that much in the bank?"

"That's why I'm calling. I've got to make a deposit today to cover the check, and I haven't got it."

"Let it bounce once," he said. "Payday's the day after tomorrow."

"I can't do that, Ricky," she said. "I'm not screwing up my credit record now that I'm on my own. The order says you pay for medical."

"All right," he said. "I'll stop by a branch this morning on the way to work."

"Thanks," she said. "And Ricky?"

"Yeah, your check will be on time; don't worry."

"Is that the truth, Ricky?"

"Yes, it's the truth."

"Because you've been late three times, and it's really screwed up my life every time, you know?"

"It'll be on time."

"My lawyer says that if you're late again I shouldn't let you see Georgie this weekend."

"So you're going to hold me up with the kid?"

"Not if I get the check on time," she said.

"It'll be on time, I promise."

"And you promise to make the deposit this morning?"

"Yes, I promise."

"Thanks, Ricky; I'll see you this weekend."

Rivera got out of bed and rummaged in the bedroom desk for his checkbook; his balance was three hundred and thirty-one dollars. He'd have eleven bucks left after he wrote her the check. He looked in his trousers pocket; twelve bucks there. It was TV dinners until payday. He sat down at the desk, took a fistful of bills from the top drawer, and added them up on the calculator. After the bills and

Cindy's check, he'd have just under a hundred dollars to last him until the next payday.

Ever since the divorce, over a year ago, he'd had no money. Even his small part of their savings had been frittered away paying the most basic bills. He wasn't making it, and that was a fact.

They'd lived decently when they were married; there was a pretty nice house in the Valley and two cars. She'd gotten the house and the station wagon, but he was making the payments on both, of course. They'd accumulated some savings, but the judge had given her most of it. He knew her well; if he didn't keep up the payments, she'd go for sole custody of the boy, and she'd probably get it, too.

He sighed heavily. His life was in the toilet, and he didn't like the swim.

He stopped at the bank and deposited the three hundred and twenty dollars into her account, and he arrived at his desk early. There was a message to call Chico; he walked over there instead.

Chico was bent over a photographic negative of a thumbprint, inspecting it carefully with a magnifying glass. Rivera waited until he straightened up to speak.

"How you doing, *amigo?*" he asked.

"Ricardo, my boy, how you?"

"Okay. You got something for me?"

"Yeah; sorry I took so long."

"That's okay, there was no rush. It's off the books, anyway; I'm just satisfying my own curiosity."

Chico poked through a drawer and came up with a plastic Ziploc bag containing an elongated silver object. There was a fingerprint card stapled to it. "I got a match on the right index," he said. "That what you wanted?"

"Well, it confirms my guess," Rivera replied wearily, "but it doesn't get me anywhere, really. I can't prove when the prints got where they did."

"That's the way it goes," Chico said, handing him the bag.

Rivera accepted it. "Thanks, *amigo;* I owe you one." He walked back to his desk, and his heart was beating faster. He had the sonofabitch, he had him cold. Now he had enough for an arrest and a lineup.

He sat down at his desk and thought carefully about this. If he played his cards right, there was light at the end of his own particular tunnel. He picked up the telephone and dialed the number.

"Hello," he said. "This is Detective Rivera, LAPD. I'd like to see him as soon as possible."

"Please hold," the woman said.

"Michael, that Detective Rivera is on the phone again. He wants to see you as soon as possible."

Michael thought for a moment. "Margot," he said, "remember when I lost my letter opener a while back?"

"Yes," she replied.

"Where did you find it?"

"I didn't. I just went over to Supply and got you a new one."

"I see," he said. "Ask Detective Rivera if he's free for lunch."

CHAPTER

34

Michael got to the beach half an hour early. He'd borrowed Margot's little BMW, and he parked it at the extreme northern end of the parking lot, by itself. He got out and trudged through the sand toward the sea, then stopped halfway and looked back toward the highway. The beach was lightly populated at this hour on a weekday; that was good. A couple of hundred yards to the north was a small concrete block building containing toilets. He walked over to it and checked the men's room: Three urinals, two stalls, and a sink. He reached behind him and made the pistol stuck in his belt more comfortable; then he left the building and returned to the parking lot.

Rivera was on time. Michael watched him park his car and approach; he smiled and extended his hand. "Good to see you, and thanks for meeting me out here; it was a lot more convenient for me."

Rivera shook his hand but didn't speak.

"Let's take a stroll while we talk," Michael said. He started up the beach toward the toilets, and Rivera kept pace with him. The wind was at their backs. "What's up?" Michael asked. "Made any progress on your case?"

"Funny you should ask," Rivera said. "It's solved; I wrapped it up this morning."

Michael felt nauseous. "Congratulations! Tell me about it."

"You want me to lay the whole thing out for you, or you just want the results?"

"Lay it out for me," Michael said. Another hundred yards to the toilets.

"It went something like this," Rivera said, puffing a little; it was hard walking in the soft sand. "Our man Callabrese was some sort of a mob guy in New York. Mob guys always have false I.D.'s — Social Security cards, driver's licenses, that sort of thing — that's why there was no paper anywhere on Callabrese under his own name. So, anyway, Callabrese gets the hots for L.A. He comes out here and goes into a legitimate business, and he's doing pretty good. Then Moriarty gets in his way. The lawyer has something Callabrese wants, and Moriarty won't sell it to him. Callabrese doesn't like this, and he

269

reverts to type. He calls somebody, who calls somebody in Vegas, who sends Ippolito down to L.A. to deal with Moriarty. Ippolito steals a car, meets Callabrese somewhere, probably so he can ID the guy, and they park on Moriarty's street and wait for him to surface. He comes out of the house to get in his car, Ippolito runs him down, then gets out of the car, goes back, and puts a knife in him. Callabrese watches all this from the car, and two neighbors get a good look at him."

Fifty yards to the toilets. "Yeah, go on."

"Then Callabrese and Ippolito part company, and somebody, a third party, probably, takes Ippolito out to the desert and whacks him, so he can never finger Callabrese. But Callabrese has made a stupid mistake; he has left some fingerprints in the car."

"So how do you find him?" Michael asked. Twenty yards to the toilets. Nobody near.

Rivera stopped and turned toward Michael. "I think I know where to put my hands on him."

Michael took him by the arm and propelled him gently forward again. "I've got to take a leak," he said.

Rivera began walking and continued talking. "All I've got to do, see, is pick this guy up, fingerprint him, and put him in a lineup. I'll have firm fingerprint evidence, which puts

Callabrese in the car, and two eyewitnesses who'll put him at the scene. Bingo! A first-degree murder conviction. Remember, we've still got the death penalty in California."

Ten yards to the toilets. "I've got to stop in here for a minute," he said. He walked into the toilet and stood at a urinal. Rivera followed him and did the same. Good. This was reckless, Michael knew, but there was no other way. He finished at the urinal, zipped up his fly, and took a step backward. His right hand went to the small of his back.

There was a scraping noise from the door, and a man and a small boy entered. Where the hell did they come from? Michael pretended to be stuffing in his shirttail. Rivera stepped to the sink, rinsed his hands, and walked out of the restroom. Michael followed. What was he going to do now? He started back toward the parking lot. It would have to be in the car; maybe that was best anyway.

The two men trudged silently through the sand for a moment, then Rivera continued.

"So, I've got my man," he said. "You think there's a movie in this?"

"Maybe," Michael said.

"I've always been interested in the movie business," Rivera said.

"Yeah? What in particular interests you?" Maybe there was another way.

"Oh, production, development, that sort of thing."

"You might be very good at it, ah . . . what's your first name?"

"Ricardo; my friends call me Rick."

"Well, Rick, there's always room in the movie business for fresh talent."

"I thought there might be, Michael," Rivera replied. "In fact, I noticed there are a couple of empty offices in your building."

"That's right; I'm still staffing up. I'm going to need a production assistant and maybe an associate producer. You interested?"

"I might be," Rivera said.

"What do you think you could bring to the job?" Michael asked.

"Well, I've worked on lots of interesting cases that might make movie material," Rivera replied. "And I could serve as a technical consultant on cop films."

"That's very interesting," Michael said, "and you're obviously a bright guy. You might do very well in the movie business."

They were nearly to Rivera's car now. "Is that an offer?" he asked.

"I'd have to be sure of what I'm getting," Michael replied.

"Shall I be absolutely frank?" Rivera asked.

"Of course. I appreciate frankness."

"You'd still be in the movie business, for

272

one thing," Rivera said.

"How would I know I was secure in my position?" Michael asked.

"You'd have my personal guarantee," Rivera said.

"But how can you guarantee such a thing?"

"Well, you see, I would ordinarily have my partner involved in a case like this — you met him the first time we came to your office — but he's on his two-week vacation, so I've developed this evidence on my own."

"I see; and where is this evidence?"

"Right this minute it's in a safe in my lawyer's office. That's so if I should die from anything other than natural causes, my lawyer could take the appropriate action."

They were approaching Rivera's car. He was probably lying, Michael thought, but he couldn't take the chance. "Rick, I think you might be very useful to me. Let's make a deal." How much did a detective make, fifty, sixty grand? "Why don't you come to work for me as an associate producer. I'll give you an office in my building, and you can develop cop stories for me."

"Sounds good," Rivera said. "And I could provide, ah, security for your productions, too."

"Good idea. How about a hundred grand a year?"

"How about a hundred and fifty?"

Michael laughed. "You drive a hard bargain." He had to make a decision; he was either going to have to blow the cop's brains out right now or bring him on board. What was it Lyndon Johnson used to say? It was better to have an enemy inside the tent pissing out than outside the tent pissing in.

"I think I'm a pretty good bargain," Rivera said. "After all, if I take this job, I won't be in a position to make that evidence available to the department, not without compromising myself. I think having me aboard would be very good insurance, and a hundred and fifty grand isn't big money in the movie business. I'd want more, of course, when I'm worth it."

"Of course," Michael said. "The sky's the limit in the movie business." He made his decision. "You've got a deal, Rick; when can you come to work?"

"Almost immediately," Rivera said. "I'll put in my retirement papers as soon as we've signed a contract."

"I'll get something drawn up today," Michael said.

"Oh, I would like a little something up front, just to seal our deal," Rivera said. "How about twenty-five thousand in cash, under the table? Let's call it a signing bonus. I wouldn't like to have to pay taxes on it."

"I think we can arrange that," Michael said, shaking his hand. "Why don't you come around tomorrow about five, and I'll have a contract for you. You can start as soon as you can get out of the police department."

"That sounds good," Rivera said, sticking out his hand. "As Bogart said to Claude Rains, I think this could be the beginning of a beautiful friendship."

Michael took the hand. "I certainly hope so," he said. *Right up until the moment I see you dead,* he thought.

CHAPTER

35

Michael shifted the Porsche down into second gear and turned off Sunset onto Stone Canyon. He glanced at Vanessa, who sat silently in the passenger seat.

"Look, this is supposed to be a celebration tonight; do you think you could try and cheer up a little?"

"Some celebration," Vanessa said sullenly.

"*Downtown Nights* got a nomination for best picture, for Christ's sake! Can't you be happy about that?"

"Yeah, and so did Carol Geraldi! In *my* role! I could have had that nomination!"

"Are you blaming *me* for that? It was Chuck who dumped you from the part."

"That's not the way I hear it," she said through clenched teeth. "In fact, I hear it quite differently."

"I don't know what the hell you're talking about." They passed the Bel-Air Hotel; they were nearly at the Goldmans' house.

"I just happened to run into Chuck at the Bistro Garden," she said. "You didn't even tell me he was out here."

"Chuck. Great. The idiot has blown three quarters of a million dollars since we made the picture, and he's turned himself into a junkie. I'm surprised he can afford the Bistro Garden."

"He's looking very well, as it happens; he's just out of rehab and seems very together."

"Swell; I'm glad to hear it."

"You didn't tell me you'd bought his screenplay."

"I haven't told anybody; I'm still working on it."

"He seems to think you've cheated him somehow."

Michael slammed on the brakes and brought the car screeching to a halt. "*Cheated him?* Let me tell you the truth about that. Chuck came to me in dire need of money; he had blown all the money he'd made on *Downtown Nights,* and he was into the loan sharks and pushers. I gave him *two hundred thousand dollars* for his screenplay, *sight unseen,* because I respect his talent and wanted to help him.

Do you think there's anybody else on the face of the earth who would have done that?"

"He also told me about how you brought Carol Geraldi into the movie, and how I got dumped."

"All right, I'll tell you exactly what happened. Chuck came to me at lunchtime one day during rehearsals and said that he didn't think you could hack the part, that you weren't right for it. I said I thought that you weren't superficially right, but that you were a good enough actress to carry it off. He insisted that we find somebody else for the part; he was the director, and I couldn't really argue with him, so I went out and found Carol Geraldi, who was down and out, and I convinced Chuck to use her.

"I hardly knew you; you were nothing to me at the time, and the director wanted another actress. If Chuck has told you anything else, he's lying."

Vanessa said nothing.

He reached over, took her by the shoulders, and turned her toward him. "Listen to me," he said. "I've taken you out of a modeling career and given you the role of a lifetime in *Pacific Afternoons*, playing opposite one of the biggest stars in the world. I've installed you in a beautiful apartment, directed your career, and I'm paying you five thousand dollars a week, which, I might add, you're blowing on clothes and an expensive car. I've done all this on nothing more than instinct that you'll make a fine actress and because I love you, and what I'm getting back is that you're angry with me because a director dropped you from a part you weren't really suited for and gave it to another actress who could turn it into an Academy Award nomination." He reached around her and opened the passenger door. "It's time for you to decide where your true interests lie, Vanessa; it's time to decide whether you want to be with me or with Chuck Parish; it's time to decide whether you really want the part in *Pacific Afternoons.* There's the door; either get out and go your own way or close it and apologize to me."

Vanessa hung her beautiful head for a moment, then reached over and pulled the car door closed. She turned back to him, snaked an arm around his neck, and kissed him. "I'm sorry, Michael," she said.

"How sorry?" This was an old game with them.

Her hand went to his crotch and began massaging. "I'm an ungrateful bitch. You've been wonderful to me, and I want you to know how much I love you for it." She unzipped his trousers and pulled him free. Her head

279

went down into his lap, and her lips closed over him.

Michael leaned back against the headrest and ran his fingers through her hair. "Sweet girl," he said.

Vanessa concentrated on her work, moving her head up and down, making little noises.

It had been a long time since she had done this, and Michael had almost forgotten how good she was at it, how much she knew about pleasing a man, how much she could do with lips and tongue. He came violently, but she held onto him, sucking, kissing, stroking, until his spasms ceased.

She tucked him back into his trousers and zipped him up. "Am I forgiven?" she asked, kissing him lightly on the ear.

"You're forgiven," Michael replied. He put the car in gear and drove up Stone Canyon toward the Goldman house and the adulation that awaited him.

CHAPTER

Michael eased the Porsche into the turnaround of the Goldmans' driveway and handed the keys to the valet parker. Cars were lined up in the driveway waiting their turn.

They were greeted at the door by an English butler. "Everyone's out around the pool, sir," the man said.

They followed the music outdoors and joined a crowd, the core of which was the Monday night mob at Morton's, where Michael was now a regular. Amanda Goldman broke away from a group, hugged Vanessa, and planted a firm kiss on the corner of Michael's lips. For an instant her tongue found its way surreptitiously into his mouth. She seemed to get just a little hotter each time he saw her. "You both look wonderful," she gushed, "and congratulations on your nomination, Michael." She turned to Vanessa. "I know that this time next year we'll be giving a party for you. I can't *wait* to see *Pacific Afternoons*."

Michael thanked her. "Where's Leo?" he asked.

"At the other end of the pool, I think," Amanda replied. Vanessa saw one of her girlfriends and wandered off.

Amanda took Michael's arm and tugged him toward the house. "Before everybody gets hold of you, come inside. I've never shown you the wine cellar, have I?"

"The wine cellar?"

She towed him quickly down a hallway, then down a narrow flight of steps; at the bottom, she flipped a switch, and a room about fifteen feet square opened before them. The walls were stacked from floor to ceiling with rows of bottles, and the contents of each rack were clearly labeled.

"Amanda, this is very impressive, but what the hell are we doing down here?"

"I just wanted a moment alone with you," she said, stepping close to him and putting her arms around his waist.

"That's a very nice thought," he said, smiling. "And just why did you want to be alone with me?"

"I've wanted to be alone with you since the

first moment I set eyes on you, at Barbara Mannering's in New York."

"That's the nicest thing anybody has said to me all day."

"Every time you're around, all I can think about is getting you into bed."

"Now, Amanda," he said, "don't you think that would be a little dangerous in the circumstances? After all, I work for your husband."

"Let's get something straight," she said. "I have no interest in leaving Leo for you, so you're not under any pressure. All I want is to be fucked crazy now and then. If we can keep it on that level I think we can enjoy ourselves quite a lot."

"I like the idea, I must admit. And I like the terms."

"Don't call me, I'll call you," she said. "And I mean it, I *will* call you."

"Not at home, and when you call the office, use this number." He took a pen and wrote it on the palm of her hand. "Margot doesn't answer that line; it goes straight to my desk."

"Ah, the lovely Margot," she said cattily. "Have you fucked her yet?"

"Certainly not," Michael replied with mock sternness. "Margot's a little too close for comfort."

"That never stopped her before," Amanda said.

"It's strictly business with Margot and me," he said.

She turned to the rack behind her and extracted a bottle. "Here's a little reminder of our bargain," she said, handing him the bottle.

"Château Mouton Rothschild, 1961," Michael read from the label. "One of Bob Hart's favorites, Leo tells me."

"Poor Bob," Amanda said, pouting. "Can't drink anymore. Leo bought that wine from him, you know." She took his hand. "Now let's go socialize before they search the house for us."

She took him from group to group, introducing him, while he accepted congratulations. Finally she put him with a writer from the *Los Angeles Times*. "Michael, this is Jack Farrell. Be nice to him, or he'll say something awful about your pictures." With a squeeze of Michael's hand, she left them alone.

"I thought *Downtown Nights* was wonderful," Farrell said.

"Thank you; we worked hard on it."

"What's happened to the director — what's his name?"

"Chuck Parish," Michael said. "Are we off the record here?"

"Of course; this is a social occasion."

"Chuck's had a bad time, I'm afraid; the

money he made on the movie is all gone — fast women and white powder. He turned up at Centurion a while back, desperate for money, and wanted to sell me his new screenplay."

"You didn't buy it?"

"I did buy it, and sight unseen."

"That's incredible; what did you pay him for it?"

"Two hundred thousand."

"Christ, did Leo know you hadn't read it?"

"That's between you and me," Michael said.

"So where's Parish now?"

"I got him into a rehab program, and to his credit, he finished it. I hope he can keep it together this time, but . . ." Michael shook his head regretfully. "I've had to tell him that I can't buy treatments from him, only finished work. That way, you know, he produces. The worst possible thing you could do to a guy like that would be to give him money up front. It would go to some pusher, and he'd never finish anything."

"I see your point," Farrell said, looking sympathetic. "I think it's a fine thing that you would help him when he's in that kind of shape. In this town, people just dump junkies, write them off."

Michael spotted Leo at the other end of the

pool. "Excuse me, will you? I want to catch up with Leo."

"Sure. Listen, can I call you sometime and get the latest on your projects?"

"Of course, any time."

"I'll call you."

Michael waved, then walked over to the bench where Leo was sitting, blowing smoke rings from his cigar toward the high hedge. "How goes it, boss?"

Leo slapped him on the knee. "Just the man I'm looking for. First of all, a formal congratulations on your nomination."

Michael held up the bottle of wine. "I've already been rewarded by your lovely wife."

"She showed you the cellar, huh?"

"I was very impressed. I'll save this bottle for a special occasion."

"Good, there are going to be a lot of them. By the way, I was very impressed with your presentation of *Pacific Afternoons*. Script, storyboards, costumes, production design — it all looks great. And on a nine-and-a-half-million-dollar budget, too. It's a fucking miracle!"

"It's the way I plan to shoot everything, Leo. I think too much money gets spent in this town."

"My philosophy exactly, kid. We're going to make beautiful music together."

"You bet," Michael replied.

"Listen, kiddo, I think the studio owes you a little reward. Why don't you find a house for yourself, something nice. The studio will buy it, then sell it back to you for fifty cents on the dollar."

"Leo, that's very generous."

"No, it's not; it's good business. You and I are going to make a lot of money together, kid."

"I believe we are."

"You start looking for a house tomorrow. Call Marie Berman, she's the best real estate lady in town." He scribbled the name on the back of his card. "Remember, now — something nice. You can go to, let's say, five million."

"You're a prince, Leo."

"I'm a king, kiddo; *you're* a prince."

Michael liked the sound of that.

CHAPTER

37

Michael was already dressed when Vanessa woke up. "It's Saturday," she said. "What are you doing?"

"I've got some things to clear up at the studio before we leave for Carmel tomorrow," he said, brushing his hair briskly.

"I thought we'd have lunch today," she said, pouting.

"Not today, Vanessa."

"Where did you and Amanda disappear to at the party last night?" There was petulance in her voice.

"She wanted to show me Leo's wine cellar." He slipped into a linen jacket and inspected himself in the mirror.

"Did you screw her?"

Michael looked at her. "In a wine cellar?"

"That wouldn't matter to you; it wouldn't

matter to her, either."

"Vanessa, you're beginning to sound like a wife." He had considered and rejected this option long ago.

"So? What's wrong with that? I want to be a wife."

"Vanessa."

"Why not, Michael? We'd be the golden couple of Hollywood."

"We can be that without being married."

"If you're working today, why are you all slicked up?"

"I'm casually dressed, Vanessa; it's a Saturday, remember?"

"I want to go to the studio with you."

"And what would you do at the studio but keep me from working? You'd be bored stiff."

"I want to go."

"No. I'll see you later." He walked out of the bedroom before she could reply. The place was a mess, he noticed on his way to the front door, and the maid had come only yesterday. Vanessa would live like a pig if he'd let her. She really was beginning to be a pain in the ass.

He gave the Porsche to the doorman at the Beverly Hills Hotel and found the coffeeshop. Marie Berman was waiting for him. He sat down and ordered a Danish and coffee.

"So," the real estate agent said, "you want to see houses in the four-to-five-million-dollar bracket?"

"I've thought about it, and I've changed my mind."

"What do you mean?"

"I don't want to look at houses; I want to look at one house."

"One house?"

"Just one. Sift through your mental files and find the best house in town for under five million."

She looked thoughtful. "What do you want, exactly?"

"I want big rooms, sunshine, nice gardens, a pool, and a tennis court. I'd like the guest rooms to be away from the master suite."

"How do you feel about the beach?" she asked.

"Love it."

"Finish your breakfast."

He followed her car out the Pacific Coast Highway through Malibu. He kept expecting her to stop at one of the hundreds of beach houses, but she kept going. Finally, she turned left and stopped at a security guardhouse. The guard raised a gate, and they drove in.

He followed her past a number of beautiful homes, then she turned into a circular drive and stopped before a very impressive contemporary house. They got out of their respective cars.

"Do you know where we are?" she asked.

"I'm fairly new in town; tell me."

"You're in Malibu Colony. This little peninsula contains the biggest and best houses; it has the best beach and the best neighbors."

"Looks good," Michael said. "Let's see the house."

She fiddled with a key safe hanging on the front doorknob, then opened the door. Inside, the hallway ran straight through the house to the beach. They walked through, her high heels clicking on marble floors. On the ground floor there was a huge living room, kitchen, dining room, and, best of all, Michael thought, a large library. It would make a spectacular home office.

She led him down a stairway. "Wine cellar through there, temperature-controlled year-round, and here —" she threw open a set of double doors. Beyond was a screening room with two dozen seats and the latest projectors.

Upstairs there was only one enormous suite, with bedroom, sitting room, kitchenette, two dressing rooms, and two baths; there was also a sauna, and a big whirlpool tub on a high deck overlooking the Pacific.

She led him back downstairs and outdoors.

Enclosed by a high wall were a two-suite guesthouse, a pool, and a tennis court. Michael had never played any sport except for stickball and handball, but tennis appealed to him. He liked the clothes, for one thing, and he liked to watch beautiful women play.

"There are servants' quarters on the other side of the house, off the kitchen," she said.

"How much?" Michael asked.

"This house cost seven million dollars to build three years ago. The owner was a studio head who got chopped. It's been vacant for nearly a year."

"Sounds too rich for me," Michael said regretfully.

"Leo Goldman is a good friend of mine," she said. "I'd like to do him a good turn. I happen to know that the bank that holds the mortgage wants out very badly. The market in big houses has gone to hell in this recession. If I make them an offer that covers most of the mortgage and my commission, I think they'd be willing to take a loss."

"What would it take?"

"You're not going to be able to get a mortgage for this place in today's climate," she said. "It would have to be all cash on closing."

"How much?"

"Offer them four million six," she said, "and a quick closing."

"Make the offer," Michael said. "I can close immediately."

"I'll call the bank president at home." She walked into the kitchen and produced a small cellular phone from her handbag.

Michael walked around the pool, peeked into the cabana. He walked onto the tennis court and inspected the surface. Perfect, like everything else about the house. He looked back toward the kitchen and saw Marie Berman gesticulating, pacing the floor. He glanced at his watch; she had been on the phone for five minutes. She hung up.

Michael watched as she came through the sliding doors toward him. *It didn't work,* he thought.

She stopped in front of him. "If the studio will close on Tuesday, you've got a deal."

Michael's heart leapt. "I'm delighted to hear it," he said, smiling broadly.

She handed him the keys. "As far as I'm concerned, the place is yours from this moment. Who's going to decorate it for you?"

"Who's the best?"

"James Fallowfield," she said. "*If* you're willing to spend at least half a million." She dug into her purse. "Here's his number."

"Does he work on Saturdays? I'm leaving town tomorrow for three weeks."

"Maybe."

Michael handed her back the card. "Call him for me. Tell him I'll spend a million dollars if he's here in an hour."

She whipped out her little phone and dialed. "James? It's Marie. Good, and you? Glad to hear it. Listen, I have a new client for you, but he's in a hurry. No, listen to me, James; it's a million-dollar budget. Right. Malibu Colony in an hour; there's a black Porsche parked out front. Your client's name is Michael Vincent." She hung up. "He's on his way."

"Thanks, Marie, I appreciate that."

"Don't mention it; I appreciate the commission. Should I call Leo about the closing?"

"If you would. He'll know where to reach me if you need to talk to me. And Marie, I don't want *anyone* to know about this but Leo and me. I don't want to read about it in the trades."

"I understand. If you don't need me further, I've got a house to show in Bel-Air."

"I'll be fine, thanks."

They shook hands and she left the house.

While he waited for the designer, Michael toured the house again. It looked even better than before.

James Fallowfield arrived half an hour later. "The budget is one million dollars, and not a penny more — and that includes your fee," Michael told him.

"My fee is ten percent of whatever you spend, and I'll get you a lot of stuff at cost plus ten."

"Okay. Six weeks from now, I want to walk in this house and find it furnished to the hilt — dishes in the cupboards, towels in the baths, books on the shelves, pictures on the walls. I don't want to have to go shopping for a thing."

"No problem," Fallowfield said. "Any preferences as to style?"

"Rich, elegant, subdued; soft, comfortable furniture. I'd like a Steinway grand in the living room. Don't buy everything new; I want the place to feel lived in. I want to walk in and feel that I've always lived here."

"Will there be a woman living here?"

"Yes, but she won't be involved in the decorating."

"I won't have to get a woman's approval on anything, then?"

"No, just mine." It was easier this way; he'd surprise Vanessa when *Pacific Afternoons* wrapped.

"That will save an enormous amount of time."

Michael wrote in his notebook, then tore out the page and handed it to Fallowfield. "I'm going to Carmel tomorrow; this is where I'm staying. Send me sketches of what you're doing; the bills go to my office, to Margot Gladstone. I want a detailed accounting of everything as you go, then Margot will check everything off as it's delivered."

Fallowfield looked at his watch. "I'd better get started," he said.

"You do that."

The man left, and Michael walked around the house again. Perfect.

Michael stood on the beach at Carmel and watched Robert Hart approach on horseback. Vanessa waited for Hart in the foreground of the shot. The sun was a huge red ball sinking into the Pacific behind them, lighting the scene to perfection. Hart dismounted, kissed her lightly, then took her hand and led her and the horse down the beach toward the façade of the cottage that George Hathaway had designed.

"Don't cut," Michael whispered to Eliot Rosen. "Shoot whatever's in the camera; we can use this footage behind the titles."

Eliot nodded. "Good. It's perfect, isn't it?"

"Couldn't be better."

"That's it," the camera operator called out. "Want to do another one before the light goes?"

"Print that and wrap," Eliot called back. The man gave a thumbs-up sign.

Michael took Eliot's arm and walked him down the beach toward the cottage. "You've done a fine job up here; I want you to know that."

Rosen blushed. "Thanks."

"When we start the interiors at the studio next week I want you to deal a little differently with Bob Hart."

"What do you mean?"

"All during the exteriors you've been properly deferential to Bob, and that's good, given your relative positions in this business. Also, most of the exteriors have shown the doctor in charge of things, confident. But in the interior scenes, the doctor is less certain of himself, because he doesn't know if the girl can ever want him. Bob, given his natural mien, will appear confident and in charge in almost any scene, and you cannot let him do that in the interiors. I want you to crack the whip with him, rattle him; don't let him get away with a thing; do an extra take or two, even when it's unnecessary."

"I don't know if I can treat Robert Hart that way," Eliot said. "Do you think he'll sit still for it?"

"He will, because he knows he should. Susan won't."

"Oh, shit," Eliot said. "I have to tell you, I'm scared to death of her."

"And it shows. I'll keep her off your back as much as I possibly can, but if she starts getting to you, just tell her, as calmly as you can, that you're the director, and what you say goes. If she won't take that, tell her to see me. I'll back you all the way."

"All right, if you say so," the young man said. "Michael, I haven't told you this, but Susan has been at me about the singing scene. She really doesn't want Bob to do it."

"I know, and nothing you or I can say to her will change her mind. But we *are* going to shoot it."

"I'm worried that her attitude will erode Bob's confidence in his ability to do it."

"That can work to our advantage, Eliot. The doctor begins the scene shakily anyway, then gains confidence. Bob can bring it off; I'll see to it."

"I don't know how you're going to do that," Eliot said, "but I wish you luck."

"You crack the whip on everything else; leave Bob in that scene to me."

When the crew moved back to L.A., Michael's offices were a hornet's nest of activity. Besides himself, Margot, and Rick Rivera, Michael had two production assistants

299

on board, and he was working every day in the editing room with Eliot Rosen, the film editor, and her assistant, editing the exterior footage. The business of making *Pacific Afternoons* exhilarated Michael, and his concentration was complete.

But when he finally left the studio late in the evenings, he had Vanessa waiting for him at home. She hadn't had a lot to do in the exteriors, and she had been fine then, but now that the burden of shooting rested as much on her as on Robert Hart, she was nervous, tense, and bitchy. Michael had read lines with her for a while, but finally, when her insecurity had driven him nearly mad, he'd hired one of the supporting actresses, an old pro, to work with her, and he took to sleeping in his office.

Leo always sat in on the dailies with Michael, Eliot, and Margot, who took notes. He was protecting his investment, and he seemed pleased. Near the end of shooting, he asked Michael to stay behind in the screening room when the others left.

"Michael, I think it's going beautifully," Leo said.

"I'm glad you think so, Leo." He thought he knew what was coming, and he was not wrong.

"Kiddo, Susan Hart came to see me this morning."

"Right on schedule," Michael said, smiling.

"I think she may have a legitimate concern, Michael. She really doesn't think Bob can bring off the last scene, and God knows, she knows him better than anybody. She was frantic this morning; I've never seen her like that."

"She's been getting short shrift from Eliot, and I haven't been very sympathetic, I guess. I'll try to placate her."

"I don't think you can do that, not if you shoot that scene."

"For Christ's sake, Leo," Michael said irritably, "I made a deal with her; I told her that if she and Bob weren't entirely happy with the scene, I'd shoot an alternate. What more can I do than that?"

"Maybe you ought to just shoot the alternate and forget the singing scene."

"No, absolutely not."

Leo lit a cigar and blew smoke at the screen. "I think the problem is, she doesn't want footage to exist in which Bob makes a fool of himself. She's worried that it might get around town. When Bob was drinking, he wasn't exactly everybody's sweetheart; he has enemies."

"I see."

"I hope you do. You're going to have to find a way to get past Susan on this, or she's not going to let Bob do the scene."

"I'll work on it."

"You better, kiddo."

Michael sat in a rehearsal studio and listened to Robert Hart sing *"Dein ist mein ganzes Herz."* Anton was at the piano, and Michael thought it went well. Hart, in fact, sang better than Michael could have hoped. His voice was a light baritone and quite pleasing. Anton liked it too, he could see. Susan Hart was there, and she motioned Michael outside.

"Michael," she said when they were in the hallway, "I don't want Bob to do this scene."

"Susan, we have a deal."

"Not anymore, we don't. The scene is driving Bob crazy. You don't see it, but I hear about it when we get home. I won't let him do it, and that's final."

"Didn't you think he sang well?" Michael sighed. "All right, Susan. We wrap the day after tomorrow. I'll cut the scene; we'll shoot the alternate."

"Good," she said, pecking him on the cheek. "When do I see it?"

"I want Mark to do a polish first. How about ten o'clock Friday morning, my office? We have to do a set change, and we won't be ready to shoot until after lunch."

"You promise?"

"I promise. The scene will be waiting for you."

She gave him a big smile, then walked down the hall toward the ladies' room.

Michael watched her go. He was thinking hard.

CHAPTER

39

Michael slept in his office again on Thursday night, and on Friday morning, the last day of shooting on *Pacific Afternoons*, he held an 8:00 A.M. meeting with Eliot Rosen and the production manager, Barry Wimmer.

"Barry, I want you to go now and get the set ready for the drawing room scene."

"Which drawing room scene — the singing one or the alternate?"

"We're going to do them both — the alternate first."

"Has anybody told Bob Hart?"

"Leave that to me. I want Eliot to be able to light the set in an hour. We shoot at ten-thirty. Eliot, the schedule calls for three cameras for today, right?"

"That's right. I wanted to get Bob on one, then use the other two for simultaneous reaction shots from Vanessa and the little audience."

"In the singing scene, we'll use all three cameras on Bob, then shoot the reaction shots later. Tell the operators, Barry."

"Whatever you say," Barry said, rising.

"Make sure Bob doesn't hear about it until I'm ready to tell him."

"Right." Barry left.

Eliot looked frantic. "Have you told Susan about this?"

"She's due here at ten, and she'll be fifteen minutes early. I'll break it to her then."

"You'll keep her off my back?"

"She won't be at the shooting."

"How are you going to keep her off the set?"

"Leave it to me, Eliot. Now go talk with your people and make sure the cast and crew are ready at ten-thirty sharp. Have Anton standing by to play piano; find him a costume."

Eliot left, shaking his head.

Michael went to his briefcase, found a small bottle of Valium, and shook two into his hand. Reconsidering, he added a third. He found a coffee cup in the wet bar and, using the butt of his fat Montblanc fountain pen, crushed the pills into a fine powder. He added a few drops of hot water from the tap and stirred until the tranquilizer had completely dissolved; then he poured the liquid into a bar glass and returned it to its place on the shelf. If this didn't work, he'd slug her, if he had to.

At a quarter to ten, Margot showed Susan Hart into Michael's office. He put her on the sofa and gave her the pages to read. "Hot off the fax machine from Mark," he said. These were the pages he had removed from the first draft of Adair's script. She began to read.

He went to the wet bar. "Something to drink?"

"No thanks," she said, reading rapidly.

"Fruit juice? Perrier?" Come on, lady, he thought; the alternative is a quick chop to the neck.

"Oh, all right, I'll have a V-8."

He took down the prepared glass, opened the juice can, and poured the contents into the glass, giving it a quick stir with a spoon. Then he poured himself a Perrier and went to the couch. "Here you are," he said, placing the glass in her hand.

Susan sipped the juice idly and continued to read. Finally, she put down the pages and smiled. "I think it's so much better than the singing scene, don't you?"

"If you say so, my darling."

She drank more of the juice. "What time are we shooting?"

"One o'clock sharp. They're putting the new set together now."

"Why don't we go over and take a look at it?"

"I promised George Hathaway we wouldn't see it until it was done. If you have any objections, there'll be time to make changes."

"Good." Susan yawned. "Sorry, I didn't sleep very well last night."

You'll sleep well today, Michael thought. "Relax. I'd like you to read something, if you have time."

"Sure. Something for Bob?"

"Not really. I'd just like another opinion." He handed her the screenplay for *Inside Straight.* "You're the first to read it — not even Leo has seen it."

She took the script. "I like the title."

"Just read the first act, and tell me what you think."

"Sure."

"If you'll excuse me for a moment, I've got to attend to something."

"Go ahead, I'll read." She sipped the V-8.

"More juice?"

"No, this is fine."

Michael left the office and closed the door.

He waited ten minutes, then returned. Susan Hart sat on the sofa, her head on her chest, snoring lightly. Michael put a cushion at the end of the sofa, lowered her head gently onto it, then lifted her feet onto the couch.

He went to a cupboard, removed a gift-wrapped box, and left the building. He walked quickly down the street to the bungalow occupied by Robert Hart as a dressing room, knocked, and was invited to enter.

Bob Hart was sitting at his makeup mirror reading a newspaper. "Come in, Michael," he said. "We ready to shoot?"

"In a few minutes, Bob." He held out the package. "This was on your doorstep."

"Who from?" Hart asked, accepting the package.

"I don't know. Go ahead and open it."

"I hear we're shooting the alternate," Hart said. He tore away the ribbon and foil wrapping, then opened the box.

"That's right."

"Where's Susan?"

"She's in my office, reading a script."

The actor looked into the box, gave a little gasp. "Jesus H. Christ," he said, "look at this." He held up a bottle of wine.

"I don't know much about wines," Michael said. "Is it something good?"

"It's a Château Mouton Rothschild 1961; a lot of knowledgeable people would say it's the greatest wine of this century."

"I've certainly never tasted anything like that," Michael said. "I suppose you'll save it for a special occasion."

Hart removed two glasses and a corkscrew from the gift box. "Have some right now," he said. "Taste it for me; tell me what you think."

"I'd love to," Michael said. He watched as Hart lovingly removed the cork, wiped the lip of the bottle, and poured a glass. He swirled the red liquid in the glass and sniffed it deeply.

"Magnificent nose," he said. He handed the glass to Michael.

Michael accepted it, held it to the light. "Beautiful color," he said. He sniffed the glass. "You're right; it has a wonderful bouquet." He tilted the glass back and sipped the wine. "My God," he said. "I've never tasted anything like it!"

"Is it truly wonderful?" Hart asked, his envy obvious.

"You know, Bob," Michael said, "in this scene the doctor is supposed to have had a couple of glasses of wine."

"I shouldn't," Hart said regretfully. "I'm on the wagon."

"Of course," Michael said, watching the actor closely.

"Still, if it would help the scene, I don't suppose half a glass would hurt."

Michael picked up the bottle and filled the second glass. "I don't see how it could possibly hurt," he echoed.

Hart sniffed the glass again, then took a sip, sloshing it around his mouth. "Perfectly wonderful," he pronounced. "A hint of blackcurrants, wouldn't you say?"

"I would." Michael had no idea what blackcurrants were.

Hart took another sip. "Fills the mouth; and a very clean finish. God, what memories this brings." He took another, deeper draught of the wine. "Ahhhhhh," he breathed. "You know, Michael, I have been more worried about the singing scene than I may have let on."

"Oh? It certainly never showed."

He drank from his glass, and Michael refilled it. "Yes, I'm afraid I let Susan carry the can on that one. I mean, it went well enough in rehearsal, but I was worried. It's been thirty years since I sang in front of an audience — even an audience of actors."

"Well, nothing to worry about now."

"I know, but I really would have liked to see it on film. I mean, I wouldn't like for anyone else to see it, but I would have found it interesting."

"If you like, one of these days we'll shoot a test."

"Yes, maybe." Hart emptied his glass.

Michael walked onto the set with Bob Hart and called Eliot Rosen over. "Do one quick take of the alternate," he said. "No more."

"All right, everybody," Rosen called to the cast and crew. "Let's shoot one; this is not a rehearsal."

They went through the scene: the doctor interrupted a recital, with Vanessa at the piano, and made his speech to her.

"Cut!" Eliot called. "Print it! That's a wrap, it's all we need."

There was a buzz as the actors rose from their seats.

Michael walked onto the set. "Just a minute, everybody!" He turned to Hart. "Bob, I wonder, just as a little treat for us all, if you'd sing *Dein ist mein ganzes Herz*' for us."

"Yes, yes," some of the supporting cast cried.

Hart, who was showing a little pink under his makeup, looked around as if to see if his wife were present. "Well, all right; I'd love to. Just give me a moment." He walked out of the lighted area.

Michael was waiting for him. He handed the actor a glass of wine, then raised his own. "Your good health."

"Thank you, Michael," Hart said, raising his own glass. He emptied it, then turned back to the set. As he walked on, there was a round of polite applause from the supporting players.

Michael looked at Eliot Rosen, who nodded. All three cameras were trained on Hart. "Just for fun, let's shoot it," he said.

"Whatever you say," Hart replied with a wave of his hand.

Anton, dressed in period costume, took his place at the piano.

"Quiet, please!" the assistant director called out. A hush fell on the stage.

"Roll cameras," Rosen said quietly.

"Speed," each operator called back.

"Action."

Hart waited a moment, then made his short speech. He nodded to Anton, who played a short introduction, then the movie star began to sing.

Michael stood entranced. The music had the same effect on him as it had the first time he'd heard it, and as he looked around, it was clear that the audience of supporting actors was rapt too. Hart, as the doctor, played the scene expansively, singing his heart out, and as the song drew to a close, tears could be seen running down his cheeks. The little audience burst into spontaneous applause, something that had not been in the script.

Eliot Rosen waited a full minute before calling, "Cut! Wonderful, Bob! For all of us, thank you so much."

Michael took him aside. "Shoot the reaction shots now, to playback. Wrap it as soon as you can, and get the film to the processors. I want to work on this tomorrow." He went forward, separated Bob Hart from the little throng of actors who were fawning over him, and walked him toward his dressing room.

"Bob," he said, "that was a thrilling moment for me. I only wish your public could have seen that scene."

"I only wish Susan could have seen it," the actor replied. "But don't tell her I did it."

"Don't worry, Bob. Mum's the word." Michael left Hart at his dressing room door and began walking toward where his car was parked. As he got into the car he glanced back and saw Vanessa knocking at Hart's door. Hart opened the door, and she went inside.

Michael was unaccustomed to being cuckolded. He drove back to his office in a quiet fury.

CHAPTER

40

Michael watched as Bob Hart leaned over his wife and kissed her on the lips. "Come on, sleeping beauty, wake up."

Susan Hart opened her eyes and looked at her husband. "Hello. Is it time to shoot?"

"We've already done it," the actor said. "Got it in one take; I think it'll be good."

She sat up, rubbed her eyes, and looked at Michael. "Why didn't you wake me?"

"You were exhausted; I didn't have the heart."

"You didn't sleep well last night, you know," Hart said to her.

"That's right; I was so tense about this last scene. When can I see it?" she asked Michael.

"Not until Monday," he replied. "I've told everybody to go home and relax. We're on schedule, so there's no need to work this weekend."

She suddenly looked sharply at her husband. "Bob, have you been drinking?"

"Just a glass of wine," the actor replied. "A fan sent a bottle."

"You shouldn't have," she said worriedly.

"It's all right. Come on, let's go home."

Michael saw them to their car. When he got back, Rick Rivera was waiting for him. "I hear it went well," the former detective said.

"It did. What did you want to see me about, Rick? I'm very busy."

Rivera laid some pages on Michael's desk. "I've done a treatment based on a case I had a couple of years ago. I'd like your reaction."

"I'll get to it as soon as I can," Michael said. "Now if you'll excuse me . . ."

"Sure." Rivera left Michael's office.

Michael glanced at Rivera's treatment, then dropped the pages into a drawer.

The phone rang. "Michael," Margot said, "it's James Fallowfield; will you speak to him?"

"Yes." Michael was excited about the call. After weeks of looking at photographs of furnishings, of approving fabric and paint samples, the new house was approaching completion. "James? How are you?"

"I'm extremely well, Michael. Let's see, it was six weeks ago tomorrow that you gave me the assignment, wasn't it?"

"That's right."

"It's finished. When do you want to see it?"

"I can be there in an hour." Michael hung up and walked out of his office to Margot's desk. He handed her a key. "Margot, I'd like you to find a couple of men and a van on the lot, then go over to my apartment and remove my clothes and take them to the new house."

"It's ready?" Margot asked.

"It is."

"Shall I move Vanessa's things, too?"

"No."

Margot looked surprised. "As you wish." She found her purse and left the building, passing Barry Wimmer on the way out.

"Barry, my office," Michael said. Once inside, he closed the door. "How much?" he asked.

Barry dug a piece of paper from his pocket and handed it to Michael. "A little over a million three," he said. "I kept twenty percent as agreed and shipped the rest as you instructed."

"It should have been a million five," Michael said.

"I could have done it, but it might have

been noticed," Barry said. "I used my best judgment."

"All right," Michael said. "Is Eliot still shooting the reaction shots?"

"Yes. He's done the supporting cast; Vanessa's shots are next."

"Go and see Eliot. Tell him to keep Vanessa working for another couple of hours."

"She's a quicker study than that."

"Just do it."

"All right. By the way, we're throwing a little wrap party when Eliot finishes Vanessa's shots. Will you come?"

"Thanks, but I can't. Give my best to everybody, and send me the bill."

"Right; thanks."

Michael took Rick Rivera's treatment from his desk drawer. "Read this over the weekend, will you?" he said, handing Barry the pages. "I want to know what you think."

"Sure, I'll be glad to."

"Barry?"

"Yes?"

"Has Rick ever shown any interest in the budgets?"

"He asked me what we were spending for *Pacific Afternoons.*"

"Did you tell him?"

"It was no secret."

"If he ever asks you about budgets again,

I want to know."

"Sure."

"That's all."

The production manager left.

As he drove toward Malibu Michael felt the same thrill of anticipation that he had felt when he was on his way to L.A. for the first time. He had never owned anything but clothes and a car; now he was about to become a homeowner.

The guard at Malibu Colony admitted him quickly, and Michael drove toward his new house. He parked in the circular drive and opened the front door with his key. Although he had approved of everything that had gone into the house, Michael had made a point of not visiting the place while James Fallowfield was doing his work, so it was as if he were entering the place for the first time.

The designer met him in the hall and walked him through the house. Michael followed him silently, drinking in the atmosphere of his new home. Everywhere there was handsome, comfortable furniture, plush rugs, good pictures. Already the house seemed an extension of him.

When they had finished, Fallowfield faced him anxiously. "You haven't said a word," the designer said.

"It's absolutely wonderful, James," Michael said. "You've done exactly what I asked you to do."

Fallowfield exhaled sharply. "Thank God. You scared me badly there. I've never had a silent client."

Michael walked the man to the front door and stuck out his hand. "Thank you so much," he said.

"There's champagne in the fridge," Fallowfield said, then left.

As Michael was about to close the door, a van pulled up, followed by Margot's BMW. Michael showed the men where to put his clothes, then came back downstairs. He looked through the house until he found Margot standing in his study, staring.

"It's very beautiful," she said. "In a strange sort of way, Fallowfield has made the place like you."

"How so?"

"I don't know — it's very handsome, even sexy, but it tells me very little about you."

Michael liked that. "Excuse me, I have to make a call; don't leave." He picked up a phone, dialed the studio, and asked to be connected to the soundstage where Eliot was still shooting. When the director was on the phone, Michael asked, "Are you finished?"

"Only just," Eliot replied.

"How did it go?"

"Beautifully. Vanessa was very good."

"I want the film back tomorrow morning, and I want a rough cut by Monday at nine."

"We can do that," Eliot said.

"Congratulations; you did a fine job."

"Thank you, Michael. You were very supportive."

"I won't be at the wrap party. Please thank everyone for me; tell them they did a superb job."

"All right."

"And let me speak to Vanessa."

Vanessa's voice was tired but happy. "Hello, Michael? Where are you?"

"I had to leave the studio. You've done a good job, Vanessa; you'll get a lot of offers when the film starts to screen."

"Aren't you coming to the wrap party?"

"No. I'm otherwise occupied, I'm afraid."

"Michael, you sound funny."

"It's time for you to do Hollywood on your own, my dear."

"What?"

"I've moved out of the apartment."

"Michael, I don't understand."

"You and I don't need each other anymore. You'll do just fine on your own."

"Michael . . ."

"The lease on the apartment has another

six weeks to run; that'll give you time to find a new place. I'm doubling your salary under our contract. If you need anything, call Margot."

"Michael . . ."

"Good-bye, Vanessa." He hung up. When he turned, Margot was staring at him oddly.

"That was . . . very strange," she said.

"Come into the kitchen," he said. He led the way, then found a bottle of champagne in the refrigerator. He began opening it. "There's a lot of food in the icebox," he said. "Will you join me for dinner?"

"Michael, what exactly does this invitation mean?"

He found two glasses and poured the wine. "Nothing profound; just a good dinner and an evening of uninhibited sex between two people who know each other well. By Monday morning, we'll have forgotten all about it."

She smiled. "In that case, I'd be happy to accept."

He handed her a glass. He'd always enjoyed older women, and he'd always wondered what she'd be like in bed.

CHAPTER

41

Michael went to the studio on Saturday, leaving Margot lying by the pool, and saw the dailies of the last day of shooting. He was astonished at how powerful Bob Hart's performance was in the singing scene, even without reaction shots. The editor, Jane Darling, and Eliot Rosen watched with him.

"It's extraordinary, Michael," Eliot said. "You were right."

"Jane, I want you to keep the reaction shots of the supporting cast to a minimum," Michael said. "I don't want anything to detract from the performance we've just seen."

"What about Vanessa's shots?" Eliot asked.

"They're important to the scene, of course, but the scene is Bob's, not Vanessa's, so don't use any more of her than is necessary to convey his conquest of her."

"Conquest?" Jane Darling said. "I hadn't thought of it that way."

"It's a conquest pure and simple," Michael said.

"The male point of view, I suppose."

Michael laughed. "Exactly that. Jane, how close are you to a rough cut?"

"Close. All that's left to do is organize this scene."

"Can I screen the whole thing Monday morning?"

"Oh, I guess I can work tomorrow," she said.

"I'll send you large amounts of flowers if you do."

"How can I resist?" she said dryly.

When he got back to the new house, Margot was gone.

Michael arrived at his offices at nine o'clock sharp on Monday morning. He exchanged greetings with Margot as he usually did, and there was not a hint of anything other than business in her mien. That was the way he wanted it. "Get me Leo," he said.

"Morning, kiddo," Leo yawned.

"Rough night, Leo?"

"A late one. Poker with the boys."

"You up for a screening of the rough cut

of *Pacific Afternoons*?"

"Already? You better believe I'm ready. Eleven o'clock in Screening Room A?"

"See you then." He buzzed Margot. "We're screening the rough cut at eleven in A. I want you to round up enough people to fill the room, and go heavy on the secretaries."

"Can I come?"

"I wouldn't do it without you. And get the Harts for me."

Susan Hart sounded tired. "Hello, Michael."

"Good morning, Sue. Can you and Bob make a screening of the rough cut at eleven?"

"Bob's, ah, not very well," she said. "I'll be there, though. How does it look?"

"We'll see it together. I'm sorry Bob isn't well."

"Michael, what exactly happened on Friday?"

"What do you mean?"

"I mean, I fall asleep, which I never do in the daytime, and Bob ends up drinking wine with you."

"Bob invited me to have a glass," Michael said.

"Where did he get it?"

"It was delivered to his bungalow. Some fan sent it, he said."

"That's what he said."

"Susan, is there something wrong?"

"Didn't you know about Bob's, uh, problem?"

"I'm sorry?"

"Bob can't handle alcohol. He'd been on the wagon for months."

"He did say that, but I didn't infer that he had a problem."

"All right, I'll see you at eleven."

"Screening Room A." He hung up.

Barry Wimmer appeared at the door. "Got a minute?"

"Just about that. Come in."

Barry handed him some pages. "I read Rick's treatment over the weekend."

"And?"

"It's interesting stuff; certainly worth your time to read. To tell you the truth, I could never figure out what Rick does around here. He's looking better to me now."

Michael tapped the pages. "This is what he does; he's my resident expert cop."

"Well, I like it. A good writer could whip it into something really taut and exciting."

"I'll read it first chance I get." As Barry left, Michael reflected that maybe Rick Rivera wouldn't be a total liability after all. Certainly this treatment, if it was as good as Barry said, could help justify having Rick on the payroll. Leo had been asking questions about that.

★ ★ ★

Michael picked up Leo at his office and walked him to the screening room. Margot had done her job well; the room was packed.

"What is this, a sneak preview?" Leo asked as he entered the room.

Everybody laughed.

Michael looked around for Susan Hart, then saw her in the fourth row, where Leo liked to sit. "Leo," he whispered.

"Yeah?"

"If Susan tries to talk before it's over, shut her up, will you?"

"Yeah, okay."

Michael followed Leo into the row and sat down. The fourth row had little writing desks attached to the soft seats, and Leo sat down and picked up a pencil. Michael pressed a button on the arm of his chair and said, "All right, roll it."

Five minutes into the film, Michael got up and stood against the wall, watching the faces of his audience. He didn't need to see the film; he needed to see their reactions. The audience was very still.

He stood against the wall for most of the film's running time, and he knew from the faces that he had made a good film. What he didn't know was if he had been crazy to force a bigtime movie star to do a scene that might make laughingstocks of them all.

As the scene began, Susan Hart looked over at him with an expression of pure hatred. She whispered something to Leo and started to get up.

Leo put his hand on her arm and pressed her back into the seat, holding a finger to his lips. On the screen, Robert Hart began to sing.

Michael looked up the rows of viewers, mostly women, and watched their faces as Bob sang. There was a look of pure wonder on each of them, but Michael's great surprise was Leo Goldman as Hart finished his song. Leo's face was shiny with tears.

The editor had cleverly put a piano track of the song under the final scene, when Bob and Vanessa walked down the beach toward the cottage, and as the screen went dark, the little audience stood and applauded.

It took Michael a few minutes to get to Leo, as they were both crowded by women who wanted to congratulate them. He caught a glimpse of Susan Hart's face through the crowd, and it was stony with anger.

Finally, only Michael, Leo, Susan, Eliot, and Jane, the editor, were left in the screening room.

"Michael," Susan Hart said, "I want to see the alternate scene."

"There is no alternate scene," Michael said.

"You shot it, I know you did."

"I burned the negative this morning."

She turned to Leo. "Are you going to let him get away with this?"

"Susan," Leo said, "am I crazy or something? Didn't you just see the movie I saw?"

"Of course I saw it."

"Didn't you like it?"

"I didn't like the singing scene."

"Didn't you hear the reaction of those women?"

"Michael packed the screening."

"So what? Those secretaries are people; they go to the movies."

"I've been tricked," Susan said. "I don't know quite how it was done, but I won't be made a fool of."

Leo put his arm around her shoulders. "Susan," he said firmly, "thank Michael."

CHAPTER

42

From an article in *Vanity Fair*:

As Academy Award time approaches again and the usual prognostications paper the trades and the daily newspapers, more than a little attention is being paid to a "little" film and its rather mysterious producer, relative newcomer Michael Vincent. The film is *Pacific Afternoons*, adapted by Mark Adair from an obscure 1920s novel of the same name by a spinster named Mildred Parsons.

The movie has received four nominations, for Best Picture, Best Actor, Best Actress, and Best Screenplay Adapted from Another Medium. Not since *Driving Miss Daisy* has a low-budget film attracted such rave notices or, for that matter, such box office.

Variety reported last week that the picture has had a domestic gross of more than $70,000,000, and if it does well at the Awards, insiders say it could end up doing more than $150,000,000 worldwide. This is especially good news for its producer, because if sources at Centurion Pictures are correct, his contract gives him ten gross points if he keeps his budgets under $20,000,000. *Pacific Afternoons* is reported to have cost less than $10,000,000 to shoot, plus as much again for prints and advertising.

Michael Vincent arrived in Hollywood a couple of years ago with only one movie under his belt, the much-lauded *Downtown Nights*, which was nominated for Best Picture but didn't win, and for Best Actress. The late Carol Geraldi, who died of a drug overdose shortly after completing work on the film, won a posthumous Oscar with a performance that everyone said would have revived her moribund career if she had lived. *Downtown Nights* was written and directed by a New York University Film School student named Chuck Parish, but it was the film's producer who has, unaccountably, received all the praise. Vincent sold the just-completed film to Centurion's Leo Goldman and simultaneously made a production deal for himself with the studio.

Vincent is currently shooting *Inside Straight*, another screenplay by Chuck Parish, and his next project is said to be a cop drama brought to him by an ex-homicide detective who is now an associate producer with Vincent. This time, Vincent is directing.

Leo Goldman, who could be said to have discovered Vincent, is bullish on the thirty-one-year-old producer. "He's another David Selznick," Goldman said in a telephone interview. "I've never worked with a young producer who had so great a grasp of what goes into making a movie — *and* he keeps costs down. I don't think anybody else could have shot *Pacific Afternoons* on the budget Michael did."

True enough, Vincent is adept at shooting on a shoestring. His secret seems to be to get good people to work for very little. For instance, Robert Hart, whose usual fee these days is in the $3,000,000 range, is said to have done *Pacific Afternoons* for under half a million, because Mark Adair was writing the screenplay, and because the part gave him an opportunity to do something strikingly different. Adair, too, is said to have worked for a fraction of his usual fee.

Neither man would comment on what he was paid.

Another way Michael Vincent is able to keep costs down is by using unknown talent. He picked Eliot Rosen, the director of *Afternoons*, right out of UCLA Film School, on the strength of an eight-minute scene Rosen shot for a class. And Vanessa Parks, the beautiful young actress who has been nominated for her work in the film, was a little-known model when Vincent met her. He placed her under personal contract to him on a salary of $5,000 a week, and after *Afternoons* he doubled her salary. He also moved her into a Century City penthouse with him.

So it would seem that everybody is delighted with Michael Vincent — Centurion and all the people who have worked with him. Except that isn't the case. It seems that almost everybody who works with Vincent does well out of it in one way, but loses out in another. Witness the salaries Vincent paid Hart and Adair, compared to the money Vincent himself has made on the film. Vincent also seems to leave human wreckage in his wake. Carol Geraldi, who was, during the time she worked on *Downtown Nights*, a serious heroin and cocaine junkie, is now dead; Robert Hart, who had been on the wagon for some months after years of a drinking problem, was back at the Betty Ford Clinic for a tuneup three days after completing his outstanding work on *Pacific Afternoons*.

Vanessa Parks is another such case. While $5,000 a week sounds like a lot of money, it is only about a quarter of a million dollars a year, and even though Vincent has doubled her salary, her performance in *Afternoons* and her nomination have pumped her asking price up to two million or more. She has the fastest-developing career of any actress since Julia Roberts, but Vincent stands to gain the most from her success, since he owns her contract and negotiates all her deals.

Is this all just good business on the part of Vincent? Well, consider this: When Vanessa Parks signed her contract with Vincent, he took all her living expenses — clothes, a new Mercedes, everything — out of the weekly salary he was paying her. Then, during the shooting of *Pacific Afternoons*, he bought a fabulous new house in the Malibu Colony without mentioning it to Parks, and minutes after she finished shooting her part in the film, he called her and told her that he had moved out of the Century City apartment, and that she had only a few weeks to find a new place to live. After that, he declined to take her phone calls unless the subject was strictly business. Parks is now back with Chuck Parish, who was her boyfriend when she met Vincent.

But earlier in this piece it was said that Michael Vincent was mysterious. Consider this: Vincent is happy to give interviews to the press, on the condition that no photographs are taken of him, his office, or his house, and that there be no discussion of his personal life. The only photograph extant of the producer is the illustration for this article, and that was taken from the TV screen when he accepted Carol Geraldi's posthumous Oscar. His acceptance speech — "I didn't know Carol Geraldi before shooting *Downtown Nights* and I never saw her again afterwards, but she touched all our lives with her talent" — is the Gettysburg Address of acceptance speeches, and he dodged the usual photographs and interviews after the ceremonies, heading straight for Swifty Lazar's after-Oscar party at Spago, where he felt he had to be seen.

When one looks into Michael Vincent's background independently, one finds nothing; a blank. It is known that he is a native New Yorker, but no one knows where he attended school and college, except for his part-time stint as a student at the NYU Film School, or where he worked before joining Centurion. His parents, whose names appear on his birth certificate, a public record, are apparently dead, since they cannot be located.

So the mysterious Mr. Vincent lives silently in his Malibu Colony mansion (practically a gift from Centurion), and the only person in whom he seems to confide even a little is his executive assistant, Margot Gladstone, a beautiful, fiftyish former actress who also once worked for Leo Goldman. Gladstone guards the gates, and she is effective.

Leo Goldman and Centurion, as might be expected, are deliriously happy with Michael Vincent, as the total grosses on his two completed films are well over a hundred million dollars, on an investment of less than thirty-five million. Recently Goldman invited Vincent to join Centurion's board of directors. "Except for me," Goldman says, "our board was financial people and captains of industry. I felt it was time we had another filmmaker on the board."

So the mysterious Vincent sails on toward major Hollywood success, perhaps even immortality, and who cares about the jetsam left in his wake? Granted, it's an industry of sharks, but Michael Vincent is, even in Hollywood, something special.

CHAPTER

43

Michael put down the magazine and stared out at the sea. He kept telling himself that this was part of the business, but he could not put down the fear inside him. They had been checking out his background, and that was very frightening indeed. They hadn't found much, because he had anticipated such an inquiry, but if anybody smart ever had a reason to find out about him, the truth would eventually be known.

He turned his mind toward the past and observed Vinnie, the mob collector, on his rounds — breaking fingers and noses, forcing money out of people, getting blood from turnips. That had been his job. Vinnie was another person from another time; he in no way resembled Michael, who was everything Vinnie had ever wanted to be.

The phone rang, startling him. He was doing a lot of his work at home now, and Margot could ring him directly and put any caller through. Only a handful of people had his home number.

"Hello?"

"Hiya, kid," Leo said. "I know you don't deign to come into the office these days, but I trust you will show up for the board meeting at two."

"I'll be there, Leo."

"I'm looking forward to introducing you to the guys, and they're looking forward to meeting the producer who is putting so much money in their pockets."

Michael had never been to a board meeting; he had no idea what happened in one. "What am I supposed to do, Leo?"

"Just agree with me, kid; vote my way."

"Is there something to vote on today?"

"You'll hear about it at two. See ya." Leo hung up.

Almost immediately the phone rang again, and this time it was the special ring that identified a call from the front gate.

"Mr. Vincent, there's a lady here to see you," the guard said.

"A lady?" Michael was irritated. He had been dating half a dozen starlet types, but he didn't like them showing up at the house unannounced. "What is her name?"

"She said to tell you Amanda."

Suddenly Michael wasn't irritated anymore. "It's all right; send her in." He walked quickly through the house to see that everything was neat. It was; it was always meticulously organized.

The front bell rang, and he went to the door. Amanda Goldman stood there in a wisp of a silk dress, her blonde hair falling around her shoulders, looking very beautiful.

"Good morning, sir," she said. "Is it too early for deliveries?"

"Deliver yourself inside," Michael said, smiling and kissing her softly. "You've been a long time coming."

"I thought the anticipation would do you good," she said. "Show me your house."

Michael led her around the ground floor, down to the screening room, out to the pool and tennis court.

"Now show me upstairs," she said.

Michael showed her upstairs.

Amanda nodded with approval as she walked around, then, when he showed her the upstairs deck with the hot tub, her eyes brightened. "Now this is what I'm in the mood for," she said. She reached behind her neck, undid something, and the little silk dress fell around her feet. She was wearing nothing underneath.

Michael was immediately thankful for the Southern California female's obsession with beauty and fitness. Amanda Goldman, in her early forties, must have looked much the same fifteen years before, he thought.

"Join me?" she asked, stepping into the hot tub.

Michael joined her.

The board of directors of Centurion Pictures convened at a little after 2:00, after some desultory chat among the participants. Michael had shaken hands with all of them before entering the boardroom, but Leo, nevertheless, made a formal introduction.

"It is my great pleasure to welcome today our newest director, Michael Vincent. I expect Michael to bring to this board the intelligence and creative thinking of a first-rate film-maker, and, in addition, a lot of good old horse sense."

There was a round of polite applause.

Leo remained standing. "Gentlemen, this is a special rather than a regular meeting of this board; I have called this meeting to consider a takeover offer."

Michael was startled, but he immediately began thinking what this might mean to him; he didn't think he liked it. It was plain from the expressions on the faces of the other directors that they were surprised, too.

"I would be very surprised," Leo said, "if none of you had heard this was in the wind. These things have a way of getting around."

A gray-haired man at the opposite end of the long table spoke up. "Well, I sure as hell haven't heard anything about it, Leo, and I think I'm as well-connected as anybody else here."

"Harry," Leo said, "if you haven't heard about it, nobody's heard about it."

There was a murmur of amusement around the table.

"The offer comes from the Yamamoto Corporation of Tokyo," Leo said. He mentioned a very large figure.

Michael suddenly wished he owned some Centurion stock.

"Yamamoto?" a director asked. "I tend to get these Japanese companies mixed up."

"The Yamamoto Corporation has wide interests — electronics, of course, real estate in this country and Europe, a car-manufacturing operation in Thailand, pharmaceuticals and the record business in Europe. They seem to think that a major American film studio would be compatible with their other holdings."

"If they're offering that, they'll offer more," Harry said from the other end of the table.

341

"I move we tell them to stick their offer up their sideways Oriental asses."

"There is a motion on the table to decline the offer," Leo said. "Do I hear a second?"

"Second," a voice said from down the table.

"All in favor," Leo said.

There was a chorus of ayes.

"All opposed?"

Silence.

"Harry's motion is carried unanimously," Leo said.

"Leo," Harry said, "just because I don't like their offer doesn't mean that I couldn't be persuaded to like the right number."

"Harry," Leo said, "I want you and every member of this board to know that I will never accept an offer from a Japanese company. I don't mean to sound racist, but the little bastards already have Universal and Columbia, and anyway, Centurion is just not for sale."

"Everything's for sale, Leo," Harry said, "even Centurion."

"Not as long as I control fifty-four percent of the voting shares," Leo said.

Harry said nothing.

"Now, gentlemen, there being no other business before this board, we are adjourned. Scatter to the four winds this afternoon, but remember, dinner is on me tonight. My house at seven."

The directors stood and shuffled from the room, chatting among themselves.

Ten minutes later, Michael was alone with Leo in his office. "Tell me something, Leo," he said. "Those men have come from all over the country for this meeting, haven't they?"

"They have."

"I know you must have a good reason for this, but I think if I were one of them and I were summoned out here for a five-minute board meeting, I would be somewhat pissed off."

"I do have a reason," Leo admitted. "This is not the last we're going to hear from this Yamamoto bid. This particular group of Japs is one tough bunch of sonsofbitches. I wanted my board to know that I am not going to brook any leaning toward accepting such an offer. Not as long as I control fifty-four percent of the stock."

"Why not, Leo?"

"Because this studio is me. It is my life. It is what I do and who I am. I'll sell when I'm on my deathbed — if the offer is stupendous."

"I see."

"Good, because I'll want you on my side, finding good business reasons to hang on to this studio."

Michael walked to the door. "I'll keep that in mind."

"See you at my house tonight," Leo said, giving him a little wave with his cigar.

CHAPTER

44

Rick Rivera sat by the pool behind the house in West Hollywood and regarded the young woman who slept, naked, on the chaise next to him. She was slim, brown everywhere, and oily to the touch. It was only five o'clock on a Saturday, he reflected, and he had already banged her twice.

Rick lay back and reflected on the changes in his life since he had come to know Michael Vincent. He was only renting the house, sure, but he had an option to buy if he could come up with a substantial down payment. Cindy and the kid were taken care of now; no more squawks from her at alimony time, although she had been dropping big hints about a new car.

His sex life was athletic, thanks to his position in the movie business. The starlet as a life form would outlive the cockroach, he thought. As long as there were movies, there would be pretty women who wanted parts. If a hydrogen bomb fell on L.A. and wiped out all the studios, the next day those girls would be drifting in from Nebraska and Alabama, picking among the ruins, looking for a producer to fuck for a walk-on. He heaved a sigh of great contentment.

The cordless phone rang.

"Hello?"

"Mr. Rivera?"

"Yes."

"This is Miss Callahan at the Bank of America."

A little knot of tension formed inside his stomach.

"Yes?"

"You're a month late on your Visa payment," she said. "When may we expect payment?"

"Oh, I'm sorry about that," he said. "My secretary must have overlooked it. I'll see that she gets you a check next week."

"By that time you'll be into the next billing cycle, Mr. Rivera. If you're going to go on using the card, I'll have to have a payment by the close of business on Tuesday."

"Sure, sure, no problem. Sorry about being late."

"Given the way the mails are these days, perhaps it would be best if your secretary took your payment to a branch."

"I'll see that she does," Rivera said. He hung up the phone. Payday wasn't until next Friday; he'd have to take the payment to a branch at the last minute and hope the check didn't clear before he got his paycheck into his account.

The afternoon was ruined for him. A whole Saturday of sex and contentment ruined by a bill collector. It was amazing, he thought: when he'd been on the force, he'd been living from paycheck to paycheck, just barely getting by. Now he was pulling down a hundred and a half a year, and he was *still* living from paycheck to paycheck. At a different level, of course; he was driving a BMW instead of a Toyota, and his current address was a better one, but still, he was living right at the line. What he needed was to pump up his income, say, another fifty thousand a year. That would do it; that would put some money in the bank every month after the bills were paid.

Michael was spending one of his rare days at the office, working through a pile of phone messages and mail that had built up over the past weeks. He had cut the negative on *Inside*

Straight, and it was good. It might not pull down a nomination for best picture, but it would make money and, with his points, and with the money Barry Wimmer was skimming off the top for them both, he'd be richer next year. The phone buzzed.

"Yes?"

"Rick would like to see you," Margot said. "He says it's important."

He sighed. "All right, send him in." Rivera was a pain in the ass.

Rick came bustling in and laid a fresh script on Michael's desk. "Just back from the typists," he said. "A shooting script, I reckon. When do we go?"

"We've wrapped on *Inside Straight*," Michael replied. "I'll put it into preproduction next week, if the script's right."

"Who's going to direct?"

"I am."

"Good, good. From what I've seen on the dailies of *Inside Straight*, you're going to be a top director."

Why did he have to sit here and take this syrup from this annoying ex-cop, Michael wondered. He'd like to give him the chop right now. Granted, he had finally gotten a shootable script out of Rivera's treatment, but that was the only productive work Rivera had done since he had crowbarred his way into

Michael's offices. "Thanks, Rick. Was there anything else?"

Rivera got up and closed the door, then sat down again. "I got this call over the weekend," he said.

"Yes?" Michael asked irritably.

"From an FBI agent in the L.A. office," he lied.

Now Michael worried, but he tried not to show it. "And?"

"This agent says he did a records search on a guy named Callabrese, and he found out that I had done the same a while back."

"Why would he do that?" Michael asked, alarmed now.

"He wouldn't say, exactly; he just wanted to know if I had found out anything else about this guy — something that might not be in the FBI records."

"Come on, Rick, don't string this out; what do you think the guy has got?" There couldn't be anything, Michael told himself. He had never committed a federal crime; he had never done anything that would bring him to the attention of the FBI, not in L.A.

"Well, I happen to know that this particular agent runs the wiretap operation in the L.A. office," Rivera said. "I think he might have picked up the Callabrese name that way."

"What else?" Michael asked.

"That was it," Rivera replied. "He said to call him if I ever heard anything."

"Fine; don't worry about it. I've got some calls to make, Rick."

"Ah, Michael, I was wondering — you're going into production on my movie pretty soon. Doesn't that rate a raise?"

"Listen to me, Rick. You've been on board here for a long time; I've paid you a lot of money, and you've come up with exactly one treatment. All you do is hold casting sessions for nonexistent films and screw whoever will go for your line. You might just give some thought to what you'd be doing now if you weren't working for me, if I weren't around to prop you up."

"Listen, Michael, I didn't mean . . ."

"Sure you did, Rick; you thought you could hold me up for even more money, didn't you? Well, if you want to keep making what you're making, you'd better start coming up with some filmable ideas, do you understand me?"

"Sure, Michael, I'll get right on it."

"See that you do, and I don't want to see any more bimbos in your office. Run your casting scams somewhere else, you got it?"

Rick was backing out of Michael's office. "Sure, Michael, whatever you say. And listen, there was this case I had a few years back . . ."

"Write a treatment and have it on my desk by the end of the week," Michael said.

"Sure thing, Michael."

"And if you hear from this FBI agent again, I want to hear the conversation."

"I'll report to you right away, if I hear from him."

"Put a recorder on your phone. I want to hear the tape."

"Sure, Michael, right away." Rivera backed out and closed the door.

Michael sat and thought. After a moment, he knew that there was only one place he'd ever used the name Callabrese in L.A.

He left the office, got into his car, and drove until he found a working pay phone. He looked up a number in his pocket address book and dialed. The phone was answered by a beeping noise.

"Message for Mr. T.," he said. "Call V. tonight from a good phone."

He hung up, got into his car, and drove back to the studio.

CHAPTER

45

Michael stood at the front door and watched the stretch limousine follow the road from the security gate to his driveway. The car stopped, and the chauffeur leapt out and held the door for Tommy Pro, followed by a blonde.

Michael met them on the walk and hugged Tommy. "Jesus, man, you've slimmed down!" He held Tommy back and looked him up and down. "A new tailor, too; you look great!"

Tommy grinned. "Two grand a pop, *paisan*." He turned and introduced the blonde. "This is Sheila."

"Hi, Sheila," Michael said.

"Hello," the girl said. She was nervous and looked a little sick.

Michael turned to the chauffeur. "Take the bags in and to your left and out to the guesthouse by the pool."

"Hey, hey," Tommy said, looking around the house. "This is a number one pad; this is better than the Bel-Air Hotel!"

"I thought you'd enjoy staying with me," Michael said, starting the tour of the house.

"Tommy," Sheila whispered, tugging at his sleeve.

"Oh, yeah," Tommy said. "Vinnie, did a messenger bring a package for me?"

"Right here," Michael replied, reaching for a fat brown envelope on a hall table.

Tommy took the package and held it out toward the girl, then snatched it back. "Don't overdo it," he said. "We're going to the Academy Awards, and you're not going to be stoned out of your tiny mind."

"I won't, Tommy," she said meekly.

He handed her the package, and she trotted toward the guesthouse after the chauffeur. Tommy shook his head and laughed. "Junkies gotta have their junk."

"Is she going to be okay, Tommy?" Michael asked.

"Sure, sure. She just had a long trip; she'll be fine when she's fixed." He looked at Michael's worried face and laughed. "Don't worry, baby, I'm not gonna stick you with another bummed-out broad."

Michael gave him the tour of the house,

and after suitable praise from Tommy, he took him out onto the terrace overlooking the ocean. A man in a white jacket materialized.

"May I get you something, gentlemen?" he asked.

"Just a vermouth on the rocks," Tommy said. He turned to Michael. "I gotta stay off the hard stuff; my weight, you know."

"I'll have a Pellegrino," Michael said.

"You too, huh?" Tommy laughed.

"It's not a booze town," Michael explained. "After a while you get used to paying five bucks for water."

They settled into wicker chairs and looked out over the Pacific Ocean.

"This is really something," Tommy said, shaking his head. "A whole ocean at your doorstep. A *blue* ocean, too. You know what you gotta do to get by the ocean on Long Island these days? Millions, and then all you get is the grey Atlantic."

"You're looking really well, Tommy," Michael said. "I've never seen you so skinny."

"Well, you gotta make an impression these days, you know?" He leaned forward. "I got a personal trainer comes to the house three times a week. Maria can't believe it."

"How is Maria?" Michael asked. "And the kids?"

Tommy waved a hand. "Ah, she's Maria,

always bitching, you know? The kids are great. Little Tommy got himself busted," Tommy said, laughing.

"What?"

"Went joyriding in somebody's Mercedes. Imagine, a twelve-year-old kid stealing a Mercedes!"

"That's good," Michael said, remembering that his own car-stealing record was why this meeting was taking place.

"Listen, I'm really looking forward to this Academy Awards thing. How'd you swing it?"

"I'm a member of the Academy now," Michael said. "Your seats won't be down front, though. That's reserved for the nominees. You'll be in the rear third of the orchestra."

"Listen, that's just great. I don't want to be anywhere near you, anyway. I don't want you and me connected just yet, you know?"

"Tell me how it's going in New York," Michael said.

"It couldn't be going better," Tommy replied. He took his drink from the silver tray and waited until the butler had left. "English?"

"Irish; they're the best."

"I'm impressed, boy."

"So tell me about New York."

"Well, you must have read in the papers, even out here, that we had kind of a shakeout in the family."

"Yeah, I saw that Benny Nickels and Mario B. got it."

"Coming out of a restaurant on Park Avenue, no less."

"And you profited from this event?"

"Did I ever! I pulled all of Benny's people and about half of Mario's into my operation. The Don is very, very happy with me these days."

"And how is the Don?"

"Ailing. His liver, you know? He always drank too much."

"What happens when he goes?"

Tommy smiled tightly. "I happen."

"That sounds great."

Tommy looked around. "You do what I tell you about this place?"

"Yes, it was swept this morning. Nothing, believe me. Nobody has a handle on me out here."

"Except the FBI," Tommy said.

"Not even them. My source says that the agent that runs the wiretap unit in L.A. picked up on Callabrese. Like I told you on the phone, there's only one place in this town where that name was ever used."

Tommy nodded. "The bank. I had somebody talk to Winfield. He's taking precautions."

"Tommy, I don't know whether to leave my money with that guy. What do you think?"

"How much you got with him?"

"About three million, four."

"Hey, that's good. You left the interest in, huh?"

"Nearly all of it. Once in a while I need a little untraceable cash, you know?"

"Don't I know?" Tommy laughed.

"Anyway, you're secure here. Malibu Colony is a very, very private place."

"Good, good." Tommy leaned forward again. "Listen, I'm so proud of you, kid; you're doing just great. I read about you all the time."

"You saw the *Vanity Fair* piece."

"Yeah; that was a little rough."

"Things are quieting down. I gave a quarter of a million to an industry AIDS charity — anonymous, you know? It was in the trades the next day."

Tommy's jaw dropped. "You *gave* away a quarter of a million?"

"A cheap investment. Now I'm known in the business as a philanthropist. Only trouble is, every charity in town has come out of the woodwork. I give ten grand here, twenty grand there."

"You can afford it, baby, with three and a half mil on the street."

"Tommy, that's the smallest part of it. I've made nearly fifteen million on my points on three movies, and there's more to come."

"How much of it you got left?"

"Well, after taxes, expenses, you know; maybe four million in the market, besides what's on the street."

"Taxes," Tommy said, shaking his head. "Imagine you and me paying taxes."

"You, too?"

"Listen, I've got a very nice line in legitimate stuff now. I run a dozen little businesses out of a holding company. We got offices in an office building — everything. And we pay taxes! It's driving the feds nuts."

"That's got to be the future," Michael said. "Legitimate."

"I'm always looking for an investment," Tommy said. "In fact, some friends of mine have brought up the subject of Centurion Studios."

Michael nearly dropped his drink. "Centurion?"

"Yessir. I've made some contacts in Japan. They've got their own little *Cosa Nostra* over there, only they call it the *yakuza*."

"That's very interesting," Michael said.

"In fact, they've got the jump on us in going legit. For years they've been working their way into big, big corporations over there. Just between you and me, they've got Yamamoto sewed up tight."

"Yeah?"

"And they think there's a lot of money to be made in the movie business."

"They're right about that," Michael said. "Universal and Columbia are already in the Japanese bag."

"My friends think they can make even more money than those studios by using, shall we say, tried and true methods?"

"That's very interesting," Michael said.

"And you're on the Centurion board."

"Went to my first board meeting the other day."

"And?"

"Leo Goldman let the board know that he would never sell, especially to the Japanese. He owns fifty-four percent of the voting stock, you know."

Tommy smiled slightly. "Not owns; *controls*. Big difference." He got up. "Well, I'd better freshen up. We'll talk some more about this later." Tommy went back into the house, leaving Michael alone.

Michael sat and watched the waves break on the beach, trying to figure out what this could mean for him.

CHAPTER

46

Michael was picked up by a studio limousine in the afternoon and driven to the Dorothy Chandler Pavilion for the Academy Awards presentations. Leo had tried to get him to escort an actress starring in one of Centurion's films, but Michael insisted on going alone.

His car had a pass taped to the front window that allowed it to drop its occupants at the front door, where the television cameras were. Michael made his entrance right behind Meryl Streep and her husband, and the television interviewer in front of the stands didn't recognize him. He liked that. Since the *Vanity Fair* piece, he had thought it good to cultivate the "mystery man" image, while doing anonymous good works that were always made public.

Once inside the Pavilion he met Leo and Amanda and worked the crowd, with Leo introducing Michael to half the stars in town. Shortly an announcement was made.

"Ladies and gentlemen," an amplified voice said. "Will you please take your seats; we go on the air in twelve minutes."

Michael sat with Leo and Amanda ten rows back from the orchestra. As the music came up for the beginning of the telecast, he put on his heavy black-rimmed glasses. Even with Rick Rivera neutralized, he was terrified of being recognized by a witness to Moriarty's murder.

Michael looked to his right and saw Vanessa Parks and Chuck Parish sitting directly across the aisle. He nodded, but both of them ignored him.

After ten minutes of monologue by the master of ceremonies and another ten of dancing and singing, the awards began. There were only four that Michael had the slightest interest in: the nominations that *Pacific Afternoons* had earned — Best Actress, Best Actor, Best Picture, and Best Screenplay (Adapted). In fact, he cared deeply only about Best Picture, because the Oscar would come to him.

Leo leaned across Amanda and whispered, "I don't know if you noticed this last year, but it always seems to take longer here than it does watching it on television."

361

Michael could but agree. He was intensely bored with the pageant unfolding in the huge auditorium. His mind ran from his banking relationship with the Kensington Trust to the coming screenings of his new film to Tommy Pro's surprise announcement of his involvement with the Japanese who were bidding for Centurion. He wondered what Tommy meant by his statement that Leo controlled, but did not own, a majority of the studio's shares.

He was startled from his reverie by the reading of Vanessa's name, and he watched as a scene from *Pacific Afternoons* was projected onto a huge screen. There was the usual business with the envelope, and another actress's name was read out. He glanced across the aisle at Vanessa and saw her pale and rigid, clapping noiselessly for the winner. As soon as the winning actress had made her speech, Vanessa and Chuck got up and left the auditorium. Graceless, Michael thought; that would be written about, and he hoped it would not reflect badly on the film.

More dancing and singing, more hilarity from the emcee, then the award for Best Actor was announced. Michael looked around and found the back of Bob Hart's head three rows in front of him. He knew well how controlled the expression on the actor's face would be as the nominees' names were read and the clips of their performances shown. Bob's was shown last, and there was a burst of applause at the end of it. That must mean something, Michael thought. The people clapping were the ones who had voted.

A willowy actress, winner of last year's Oscar, read: "And the winner is Robert Hart for *Pacific Afternoons*." The name of the film was drowned out in the roar of approval from the audience. Hart made his way down the aisle and up to the podium.

"I will be as brief as my conscience will let me," the actor said to the audience. "First of all, I must thank my wife, Susan, without whom I never make a move, as you all know." There was applause for Susan, then Hart ran down a long list of names. "Finally," he said, "I must thank the man without whose foresight and wise guidance *Pacific Afternoons* could not have been made." He drew a breath.

Michael suddenly felt all warm inside. He was smiling in spite of himself.

"Leo Goldman," Hart said, then, holding the Oscar aloft, he left the stage in triumph.

Michael was stunned. Amanda's hand gripped his arm, and Leo leaned across her. "That was a shitty thing to do," Leo said.

Michael took a deep breath and tried to keep a pleasant expression on his face. His impulse was to flee the theater, but he calmed himself and waited.

Finally, finally, the award for Best Picture was up, and Michael watched through glazed eyes as the clips from the films were shown. He had just endured a personal insult witnessed by a billion people all over the world, and his mind was on how he could possibly get out of the auditorium without meeting the eyes of anyone present.

"*Pacific Afternoons*, producer, Michael Vincent," someone said. Michael continued to stare at the back of the seat in front of him. Suddenly Leo was banging him on the back and shouting, "Get up there, kiddo, you won!"

Michael stood, dazed, and a shove from Amanda started him down the aisle. He climbed the steps to the stage slowly, as if exhausted, and accepted a peck on the cheek from an actress he had admired all his life.

The applause died down as he stepped to the podium and cleared his throat. "I have already thanked repeatedly and profusely everyone associated with the marvelous experience that was *Pacific Afternoons*, including the perfectly wonderful Leo Goldman, so it only remains to thank all of you for conferring this award, and the Academy for presenting it. Good night." Someone took his elbow and guided him offstage.

Weak and perspiring from the double shock of Bob Hart's insult and winning the Oscar, Michael suddenly found himself in a backstage room with what seemed like a thousand photographers. Bob Hart was just concluding his remarks before a bank of microphones, and, collecting his wits, Michael strode across the room and flung his arms around the astonished movie star. "Take that, you son of a bitch," he whispered into Hart's ear; then he stepped back and pumped the actor's hand while a thousand flashguns recorded the event.

The bemused Hart was led away from the microphones by someone, and Michael found himself facing more press than he could ever have imagined existed.

Michael ignored their shouted questions and raised his hands, one of them clutching the remarkably heavy statuette, for quiet. "Ladies and gentlemen," he said. "I am too stunned to answer questions, so I will just say that this award was made possible by superb performances by Vanessa Parks and Robert Hart and a wonderful job by a new director, Eliot Rosen. Without their work, I would not be clutching this Oscar, never to let it go."

He left the microphones and pushed his way through the mob, saying "thank you" repeatedly. There was no point in returning to his seat, since the Best Picture award ended the ceremonies, and he could hear the final music rising. Instead, he looked for the stage door that led to where the limousines were parked. He spotted an exit sign and headed for it, but someone took his arm and pulled him into what must have been the stage manager's office. Michael was prepared to fend off another reporter, but instead a man held up a wallet with an identification card.

"Mr. Vincent, I am Special Agent Thomas Carson of the Federal Bureau of Investigation." He nodded at the other man. "This is Special Agent Warren. We'd like to talk to you."

"What the hell is this?" Michael asked angrily.

"Perhaps I should say Vincente Callabrese?"

Michael was terrified, but he maintained his composure. "What are you talking about?"

"That is your real name, isn't it?" the agent asked.

"My name is Michael Vincent," he replied, "and I resent this intrusion."

"Are you refusing to talk to us?" the agent said, and there was something threatening in his voice.

"I most certainly am," Michael replied, uncowed. "If you wish to speak to me you may call my office during business hours. Is that perfectly clear?"

"Perhaps you'd rather come down to our offices to talk?"

"Am I under arrest for something?" Michael demanded.

"Not exactly."

"Then get the hell out of my way," Michael said, brushing past the two men and out into the hallway. He spotted the exit sign again and headed for it.

Outside there was a sea of limousines; Michael searched frantically for his, but they seemed to be identical.

"Mr. Vincent?" a voice called out, and Michael spotted his chauffeur.

"Yes, yes," Michael said, heading for his car.

"Congratulations, sir," the chauffeur beamed.

"Let's get out of here," Michael said, diving into the back seat of the car. "Take me home."

The chauffeur turned and looked over the seat. "Don't you want to go to the Lazar party at Spago?"

Michael hesitated. If he didn't show for the party, the papers would be full of it the next morning. He had to brazen it out. "All right, take me to Spago, but drive around a little; I don't want to be the first one there."

He sank back into the seat and tried to get ahold of himself.

CHAPTER

47

Michael was home before midnight. He said good night to the chauffeur, tipped him a hundred dollars, and let himself into the house. The servants were asleep in their quarters, and the lights were off in the guesthouse.

He had barely managed to be civil to his hosts and the other guests at the Lazars' party; his mind had been racing the whole time, working on the FBI angle. They knew his real name, and they knew that Rick Rivera knew his name; they must also know why Rick knew it. He did not have much time.

He walked out to the pool and past it to the guesthouse, knocked on the door, and entered. Tommy and Sheila were still out. It did not take him long to find what he was looking for; he grabbed the brown envelope and stuffed it into a pocket. He went to the kitchen, rummaged around until he found some plastic freezer bags, then took two of them out to the beach, put one inside the other, and filled it with sand. Back in the house, he rolled the bag into a sausage shape and taped it closed. Under the sink, he found a pair of rubber kitchen gloves and put them into his pocket.

The security guard went off at midnight, and the gate opened automatically as the Porsche approached. He drove slowly into L.A., taking the freeway and exiting at Sunset. Soon he was in West Hollywood, searching for the address. He found it a little past one o'clock.

The block was dark and quiet as he drove past the address and parked at the end of the street. He walked back to the house and stopped on the front porch; no lights were on. He rang the bell.

Shortly a light went on somewhere at the back of the house, and a moment later a bleary-eyed Rick Rivera opened the door.

"Michael? What the hell?"

"I need to talk to you, Rick."

"Sure, sure, come on in. Congratulations on the Oscar; that's really great. Can I get you something to drink?"

"Are you alone?"

"Absolutely."

"No girls in the house?"

"Not a one." Rick turned toward the bar.

"Nothing for me," Michael said. "You have something."

"Well," Rick said, pouring himself a stiff bourbon, "with what I've already had tonight, another one can't hurt."

"I won't take much of your time, Rick; there's something I have to know."

"Right."

"I heard from the FBI tonight, backstage at the Academy Awards."

"No kidding?"

"What have they got on me, Rick?"

"I told you, I think they picked you up on a wiretap."

"What, exactly, did they pick up?"

"I don't know. I just know that the agent who called me, Carson, is head of the wiretap unit."

"What did they ask you, exactly?"

"They asked me why I had run a check on Callabrese."

"And what did you tell them? Exactly."

"I told them that I had found the Callabrese prints on the car that ran down the lawyer."

"What else?"

"That was it."

"Rick, you said that you took the fingerprint

evidence with you when you left the force, is that right?"

"That's right." Rivera spread his hands. "Look, Michael, I'm not going to give you up; it's insurance, that's all."

"What, exactly, does the evidence consist of?"

"The fingerprint card showing the prints lifted from the car, and the card with the file prints faxed in by the FBI."

"Is the card showing the prints lifted from the car the original?"

"Yes."

"Are there any copies?"

"No."

"Is there any other record showing the evidence you found on the car?"

"No."

"Your partner doesn't know about it?"

"No. He was on vacation when this came up."

"And where is the evidence now?"

"I told you, it's with my lawyer."

"I see." Michael walked over to the door and opened it. "Come over here; there's something I want you to see."

Rivera walked to the open door and peered out into the dark street. "What?"

Michael took a good backswing and, remembering his early experience, caught Rick

371

across the back of the neck with his homemade cosh.

Rick's knees buckled and he fell in a heap. Michael dragged him away from the door, closed it, then massaged the ex-detective's neck to help prevent any bruising.

Michael made a quick tour of the house, switching on lights as he went, then switching them off behind him. He went back to the living room, heaved Rivera onto a shoulder, carried him to the bedroom, and dumped him on the bed. He stripped off Rivera's bathrobe, leaving him dressed only in jockey shorts, then tucked the man into bed.

He removed Sheila's brown envelope from his pocket, donned the rubber kitchen gloves, and opened the package. Two pharmaceutical vials of morphine were inside, along with half a dozen disposable syringes and a length of light rubber hose.

Rivera made a gurgling sound, and his eyelids fluttered. Time to hurry. Michael completely filled a syringe with morphine, then stood behind Rivera, winding the rubber hose around his arm from the same direction that Rivera would have done himself; the vein came up nicely. Rivera jerked and opened his eyes, staring at Michael.

Quickly, Michael inserted the needle into the vein and emptied it. Rivera opened his mouth as if to speak, then his eyes glazed over, and his head rolled to one side. Michael left the needle in the vein, took Rivera's other hand, and put his fingerprints on the syringe. He put Rivera's prints on the other syringes and the morphine vials, too, then put them into the bedside drawer.

Still wearing the rubber gloves, Michael began a systematic search of the house. After ten minutes he got lucky; in a small desk in the den he found an interoffice mail envelope marked LAPD, and inside were two fingerprint cards and Rivera's notebook, the kind carried by all police officers. He closed the drawer, turned off the light, and returned to the bedroom. He rearranged Rivera's body to look more natural, then, as a final touch, he turned on the TV to a late movie. Leaving the bedroom light on, he retraced his steps to the front door, making sure that he had left no trace of his visit; then, looking up and down the empty street, he closed the door behind him and heard the latch grab.

Slowly, he walked back down the street to the Porsche, got in, and started the car. Before switching on the lights he checked the rearview mirrors; not a light on in any house on the street. Taking care to remain inside the speed limit, he drove back to Malibu.

He let himself in through the security gate

with his card and drove to the house, parking in the garage. The lights in every house in the Malibu Colony were out, he noted.

Inside, he went to the kitchen, replaced the rubber gloves under the sink, and found a packet of matches. He walked out the back of the house and along the beach in the moonlight, emptying sand from the plastic freezer bag as he went. A hundred yards down the shore, he walked to the water's edge, made sure he was alone, struck a match, and lit the police envelope. He held it carefully as it burned, and when it was down to ashes, he dropped it into the water. The tide was ebbing, and fragments of ashes went out with it.

He walked back to the house and, as he was about to go upstairs, Tommy let himself into the house with his key, Sheila trailing him. He walked over to Michael and gave him a big hug.

"You sonofabitch, you did it!" Tommy cried, shaking Michael like a rag doll.

"Congratulations, Michael," Sheila said. "Tommy, I want to go to bed now." She looked ragged.

"Go ahead, sweetheart, I'll be there in a minute." The two men watched the blonde twitch out of the house.

"Tommy," Michael said, "I'm afraid I borrowed Sheila's stash; a friend was in need."

"All of it?" Tommy asked, surprised.

"His need was great. I hope you can replace it without too much difficulty."

"No sweat, *paisan*," Tommy said. "I'll fix it in the morning."

"I'm bushed, Tommy. Let's talk at breakfast in the morning."

"Right." Tommy planted a big kiss on Michael's cheek and headed for the guesthouse.

Michael trudged up the stairs, drained of adrenaline and energy, sure of having covered his tracks.

CHAPTER

48

Michael had already finished breakfast on the terrace overlooking the Pacific when Tommy came out of the guesthouse, still in pajamas and a silk robe.

"Good morning, Vinnie," he said.

"Morning, Tommy."

The Irish butler appeared, and Tommy ordered breakfast. When he had gone, Michael put his hand on Tommy's arm.

"I need your help," he said.

"Sure, anytime. What do you need?"

"Two things: I need an alibi from the time I got home last night a little before twelve until about two-thirty. How about, you and Sheila got home at, say, twelve-thirty, and you and I talked until two-thirty, then we both went to bed."

Tommy shook his head. "You don't need

me in this; the cops hear my name, and they're all over you." He thought for a moment. "Here it is. Your houseguests were Sheila Smith and Don Tanner from New York. It happened the way you just said."

"Who is Don Tanner?"

"Straight guy, as far as the cops are concerned; works for me in a legitimate business. Don't worry, he'll play."

"All right, that sounds good."

"What else?"

"Can you get a message to Winfield at the Kensington Trust without the feds overhearing?"

"Sure; what's the message?"

"Tell him it was like this: I deposited over three quarters of a million with him two years ago, then pulled it out last April. Then tell him to pull everything I've got off the street and wire it to his branch in the Cayman Islands."

"Consider it done. Listen, Vinnie, I talked to you a little yesterday about our thing with the Japs."

"Yeah."

"It boils down to this: How would you like to be the head of a major studio?"

"Of Centurion?"

"That's the one."

"That's a very interesting idea, Tommy."

"Well, you are what I've got in mind. With an Academy Award under your belt, and with your record on keeping costs down, I can sell you to the Japs, no problem."

"What about Leo's control of the voting stock?"

"This is how it is: Goldman owns less than ten percent of the stock personally. His wife is the key. She's an heiress — her old man was into everything, and before he died, he set up a trust for her. That trust owns forty-five percent of Centurion's voting stock."

"Yeah, but Leo controls it."

"Here's the thing — there are three trustees who control Mrs. Goldman's trust; they appoint a representative who sits on the board and votes the stock. Mrs. Goldman has a big say, too; that's why Leo Goldman is the trust's representative."

Michael nodded. "Go on."

"Now the guy who heads the trustees is named Norman Geldorf. He's an investment banker who was a friend of Mrs. Goldman's father; he's also into some stuff with us."

"What kind of stuff?"

"Doesn't matter; it's all legitimate; Geldorf is a very legitimate guy. Thing is, though, the family has a *lot* of legit money invested with him, so I have his ear, and if I can show him how Mrs. Goldman's trust can benefit from a takeover of Centurion, he's in the bag."

"But won't he listen to Amanda Goldman? Won't he consider her wishes?"

"That's a consideration, sure. She has to be made to see the light." Tommy smiled and spread his hands.

Michael blinked. "You mean you want *me* to talk Amanda into voting her stock against Leo?"

"That would be very helpful."

Michael shook his head. "Listen, Tommy, you're getting into the realm of the impossible here."

"Impossible? Not with your talent with women. Jesus, Vinnie, with your yen for dames, I'd be surprised if you weren't banging her already."

"That's beside the point," Michael said quickly. "And have you considered Leo's pull with the board? It's a closely held corporation. If the trust owns only forty-five percent of the stock, that means Leo and the other board members together control a majority, and Leo handpicked every one of those guys."

"You let me worry about that," Tommy said smugly. "You get on the good side of Amanda Goldman and start creating a few doubts about how Leo is running the store. Just a few. If you can gain her confidence then, worse come to worse, if we have to, ah, displace Goldman, then you'll be the only game in town."

Michael looked sharply at Tommy. "Wait a minute; Leo Goldman has taken pretty good care of me. I'm not about to pour a pair of cement shoes for him so you can drop him in the Pacific."

"Easy, kid," Tommy said. "It's never going to come to that. But you have to remember something: Leo Goldman is a Jew; he's not one of us, he's out for himself. The only reason he's backing you is because he knows you'll make money for him. Those people are just like us; they only care about their own kind. It's human nature."

"I don't want anything to happen to Leo," Michael said.

"Then get him to see the light."

Michael put down his coffee cup. "I've got to get to the office; I'm expecting the feds to call on me."

"Yeah?"

"Something to do with the bank, I think."

"Tell them Don Tanner sent you there, that the company he works for does some legitimate business with them. He's in town for the awards show."

"Tell me more about Tanner, in case they ask."

"He's corporate counsel for a film distribution company, small time, nothing you'd know about, but you can tell the feds that's how you met." He took a pad and pen from the table and wrote down Tanner's address and phone number in Los Angeles.

"Will I see you tonight?"

Tommy shook his head. "Nah, this was a one-nighter for me; I've got to be back at business in the morning. We're getting a noon plane."

The two men stood up and embraced.

CHAPTER

49

It was after lunch before the two FBI agents showed up at Centurion Pictures. Michael showed them into his office.

"All right, what can I do for you?" he asked.

"We need your help," Carson said.

"If you needed my help you shouldn't have approached me last night," Michael replied. "I did not appreciate that."

"Tell you the truth," Carson said, "I don't much give a shit whether you appreciated it or not. You're between a rock and a hard place, mister, and you're going to help us whether you like it or not."

Michael glanced at his watch. "I'm going to give you just one minute to start making sense, and if you don't, then you can talk to my lawyer."

"I'll lay it out for you, Callabrese."

"My name is Vincent. It was legally and properly changed in New York State six years ago, for personal reasons. Lots of people change their names."

"All right, you're Vincent, but I know a homicide detective can put you away on a murder one charge; all it takes is a word from me."

"You're insane."

"You left your fingerprints all over the car when you ran down Moriarty."

"The lawyer? Detective Rivera told me he was killed by some Mafia hoodlum. They found him dead somewhere."

"Rivera didn't mention the Callabrese prints, I guess, because he didn't know you were Callabrese. When I tell him, he'll know, and I'll tell him unless you cooperate with me."

"Cooperate with you on what?"

"Bringing down the Kensington Trust."

"What has the Kensington Trust got to do with me?"

"You're doing business with them; they're funneling your money to the street sharks."

"You make less and less sense, Carson, and I'm running out of patience."

"Then I'll have a word with Rivera," the agent said, rising, "and then we'll see about your patience."

"Let me make it easy for you," Michael said.

He pressed a button on the speakerphone. "Margot, will you please go to Rick Rivera's office and ask him to come and see me right away?"

"Yes; Mr. Vincent," Margot said.

"Wait a minute," Carson said. "You mean to tell me Rivera works for you?"

"And has for about a year and a half," Michael said.

"Doing what?"

"He's an associate producer, specializing in police stories."

"Horseshit. You bought him."

"I go into production next month on his first story," Michael said. "He's a valued associate."

Margot buzzed back. "Mr. Vincent, I'm afraid Mr. Rivera isn't in yet."

Michael sighed. "I'm afraid that's not unusual," he said. "He's been out of the office a lot recently."

"Let's get back to the Kensington Trust," Carson said. "What business have you done with them?"

"When I first came out here a couple of years ago, I deposited something over seven hundred thousand dollars with them."

"Where'd you get the money?"

"I earned it. On a film called *Downtown Nights*."

"What else?"

384

"Sometime later I deposited another hundred thousand with them, then in April of last year I withdrew all my funds and closed my account."

Carson looked surprised. "Why?"

"I wasn't terribly happy with the service. I moved my funds to two brokerage accounts. Would you like the names of my brokers?"

"Yes."

Michael took a legal pad from his desk and wrote down the names. He wondered if they knew yet that Rivera was dead.

"Another thing," Carson said, "where were you between midnight last night and two A.M. this morning?"

They knew. "At home. From the Awards ceremony, I went to Irving Lazar's party at Spago, but I left early; I was home before midnight."

"Can you support that statement?"

"Of course; I had houseguests. They were already home when I got there, and we stayed up talking until about two-thirty."

"Who were these guests?"

"Don Tanner, a lawyer for a film distributor, and his girlfriend, Sheila Smith. Would you like their number?"

"I would."

Michael wrote down Tanner's number on the pad, then shoved it toward Carson.

"That's it, gentlemen; I don't have any more time for you."

Carson and Warren stood up. "We'll be back," Carson said.

"No, you won't," Michael said, remaining seated. "Not unless you have a warrant for my arrest. Otherwise, we'll meet at my lawyer's office."

"You're a slick number, Callabrese," Carson said, "but we're on to you now."

"The name is Vincent," Michael said. "Get out."

The two agents left, and after they had gone Michael lowered his forehead to the cool glass top of his desk. He was covered. They had nothing.

CHAPTER

50

Michael and Amanda Goldman lay naked on the upstairs back deck of the house, baking in the midafternoon sun. They had already made love once. Michael dribbled oil on her back and rubbed it in gently.

"Mmmmm," Amanda sighed. "I don't think I've ever known a man who knew women so well, Michael. You never miss an opportunity to please."

"I'm glad you think so," Michael said softly.

"If I weren't married, you'd be dangerous."

"You mean to Leo specifically, or just married?"

"I mean to Leo. If I were married to anybody else, I'd be thinking about leaving my husband for you."

"I'm glad you couldn't leave Leo for me.

I love the man; he's been absolutely wonderful to me."

"Don't take it too personally," she said. "It's not as if he isn't making a lot of money out of the relationship."

"Funny, another friend of mine pointed that out not long ago."

"Who?"

"Just a friend; somebody who doesn't know Leo, who was just making an objective observation."

"Your friend is a shrewd judge of character. People like Leo get as good as they give."

"Leo has always struck me as generous."

"Generosity is a two-way street. Surely you aren't naive enough to believe that anybody in this town, in this industry, has the slightest whit of unrequited generosity in his soul. You read in the trades about somebody who's made some big donation to some charity. Chances are he's doing it because somebody he wants to do business with is involved with the charity."

"So what do you and Leo give each other? How do you reciprocate?"

"Well, let's see; Leo gives me a status in this town that only two or three other men could. There's hardly anybody in the country that I couldn't have at my dinner table on a couple of days' notice — right up to, and including, the president of the United States."

"What could you offer the president of the United States, besides a good dinner?"

"Leo could put together a million dollars in campaign contributions to the party in a week, and with his left hand. Every politician in the country knows it."

"What else does Leo do for you?"

"Status is everything in this town," she replied. "I can pick and choose among our invitations — and we're invited everywhere. I can lunch with a Nobel laureate; I can give a boost to any charity I choose. Leo makes all that possible."

"And I suppose his money doesn't hurt."

"Money has nothing to do with what Leo does for me. I'm richer than he is."

"I didn't know."

"Leo is the perfect man for a rich woman to be married to, you know; he's an excellent tender of my money. Since we've been married, he's increased my fortune many times over. If we were divorced, I'd have to pay him alimony."

"How did he do this?"

"With the studio."

"Your money is invested in the studio?"

"My money practically controls it. The trust my father set up for me owns nearly half the stock, and Leo's bit puts us over the fifty-percent mark. Not many people know that; Leo likes for the town to think that he's in personal control."

"I guess that must keep him in line."

She laughed. "It certainly does. I can promise you, in all the years we've been married, Leo has never slept with another woman. He knows that if he did and I found out about it, I could cut his dick off, and the size of a man's dick is everything in this town." She laughed even louder. "A woman I knew, who before she died was a very important hostess in this town, was being wheeled into the operating room for surgery, and she said to her husband, who was walking along beside the gurney, 'Whatever they do, don't let them cut off my dick.' "

Michael laughed appreciatively. "And what is it you give Leo, besides money?"

"I'm the smartest and best hostess in this city, maybe the country. You should know; you've been to my house often enough. I make Leo look like the king he likes to think he is. I cater to his every vanity. I order his clothes, I choose his food and wines, and of course, there's the sex."

"How is that?"

"Well, we've been married a long time. Leo is happy with an occasional blow job, and I'm an ace at that, as you well know."

"I know. Doesn't he do anything for you?"

"Why do you think I'm fucking you?"

"I'm glad to be of service."

She rolled over. "I didn't mean to sound hard; it's more than just sex. If I let myself, I could fall very much in love with you." She shrugged. "Hell, maybe I already am."

"That's the nicest thing I've heard since I came to L.A."

"I'm glad you think so."

"What do you think of me?" Michael asked. "I'd really like to have your blunt opinion."

She looked up at him. "I think you're more than just a young man on the make. I think that, in a few more years, you could become a legendary moviemaker, right up there with the best of them. I think, if you play your cards right, you could rule this industry."

"Thank you, I have to agree."

They both laughed.

"Amanda, apart from loving me, do you like me?"

She smiled. "I do."

"That's a relief," he sighed. "I'd like to think I'm more to you than a good fuck."

"You are."

"Do you trust me?"

"Probably as much as I trust anybody."

"Then there's something I have to tell you."

"What?"

"I wouldn't have brought this up, but I had no idea about your financial involvement in the studio."

"What is it, Michael?"

"I think there's major trouble brewing at Centurion."

"What kind of trouble?"

"Has Leo told you about, the Japanese offer?"

"Yes. He said it was inadequate."

"Suppose they made it good enough? What do you think Leo would do?"

"I hope he would take it."

Michael shook his head. "I don't think he would take it under any circumstances."

"*Any* circumstances?"

"I think Leo likes running the studio so much that he's too emotionally involved to make a good business decision."

"God knows, he loves running the studio," she agreed.

"There's more to this. Leo is getting into a couple of very expensive projects — the sort of thing that he's always saying he doesn't like."

"You mean the science fiction film?"

"Yes. I'm alarmed at the amount of development money that's gone into it without a finished script. Then there's the Vietnam movie; it would have to be shot in the Philippines, and you know how shaky the political situation is there."

"Well, he's always felt strongly about Vietnam, but that does sound risky."

"I think there's some restiveness among the board members about those two films and about the Japanese offer."

"How much restiveness?"

"It's hard to say. I'm operating on instinct here."

"And what do your instincts tell you?"

"That the potential exists for a major debacle. If Leo proceeds with both these projects, while at the same time refusing even to consider an offer for the company that interests the board, then . . ."

"Then, what?"

"Then there could be a boardroom rebellion."

"So what? Leo and my trust together have an absolute majority."

"That's not the only consideration. Centurion borrows to finance its films, just like all studios. In fact, its debt is heavier than most. If several board members decided to sell their stock to the Japanese outfit, the banks are going to take it as an indication of a lack of faith in Leo's management, and things could get very shaky indeed."

"Are you seriously worried about this,

Michael?" She looked very worried indeed.

"Look, I'm sorry; Leo's no fool; he can handle the situation. I shouldn't have brought it up."

"No, no, I'm glad you did. I should know about these things, and Leo isn't telling me."

"For God's sake, don't bring this up with Leo. He might figure out where you got the information."

"I've got to do something," she said.

"Don't say a word to Leo, whatever you do. I'll keep you posted on developments. Then, if things get serious enough, you can say that you were approached by some of the board members, who gave you the information."

"That's very sweet of you, Michael," she said, stroking his cheek. "I know how loyal you are to Leo. I know you would never do anything to hurt him."

"Of course not. I'd like to keep him out of trouble, but he's just not willing to take anybody's advice about the situation. I hesitate to say it, but I think there's a touch of megalomania in Leo these days."

"There always has been," she said.

"Let's change the subject."

"What subject did you have in mind?"

He leaned over and bit a nipple lightly.

"Ooooh," she moaned. "*That* subject."

CHAPTER

51

Michael sat in Leo's private screening room, adjacent to his office, and watched the studio head's latest personal production, *Drive Time,* a comedy.

"What do you think?" Leo asked when the lights came up.

"I think it's going to do business," Michael said.

"Is that it?"

"Leo, I won't bullshit you; it's like *Inside Straight* in that it's not going to pull any nominations, but it's going to do business. It's a good movie; I liked it."

"Good," Leo said, sounding relieved. "I'm getting some flak from Harry Johnson about my personal stuff. He and I have never agreed on movies; now he's hoping I'll fall on my face with the sci-fi movie." He beckoned to

Michael. "Come on in my office for a minute."

Michael followed Leo into his huge private office. The storyboards for the science fiction movie were stacked against a sofa. The movie still had no name.

"Have you seen these, Michael?" Leo asked, waving his cigar at the storyboards.

"Of course, Leo; I was at the presentation yesterday, remember?"

"Oh, yeah, yeah. I want your honest opinion. If I can make the movie that's on these storyboards for, say, eighty million — and that figure is strictly between you and me — what do you think it'll do in the U.S.?"

"Leo, have you ever known me to be over-optimistic about grosses?" Michael asked.

"No, never."

"Good. So believe me when I say I think it'll do a hundred and seventy-five million domestic. God only knows what it'll do world-wide, maybe two hundred fifty million?"

Leo's eyes lit up. "That's what I think," he said. "You know damned well I'm down on blockbusters, but this one I'm willing to bet the farm on."

"You may have to, Leo."

"You mean the board? They'll bitch and moan until they see the grosses, then I'll be their hero again."

"I think you're right, Leo. If I were in your

shoes, I'd go the whole hog."

"Well, that's something coming from you, kiddo, stingy as you are with a budget."

"You can't do low-budget sci-fi," Michael said.

"I'm thinking of putting the Vietnam film into turnaround," Leo said.

"Why?"

"Well, you know how nuts the Philippines have been, politically."

"They've had a successful election," Michael said. "The right man won; the communists seem to be in retreat. It might be a good time."

"You think so?"

"Do you know anybody in the State Department?"

"Yeah, as a matter of fact."

"Call him; ask him to talk to somebody on the Philippines desk; see what's happening."

"Good idea. I'd really hate to stop work on the film; I think it could be great."

"So do I. It would be worth a little hassle in the Philippines to get a great movie made."

"Johnson, that cold-eyed Scandinavian son of a bitch, was on the phone this morning about these two films. I don't know what's got into the old bastard; he always used to back me on everything. It's not like we're losing money."

"Fuck him," Michael said. "Make the movies you want to. Why else be the head of a studio?"

"You're right about that, kid," Leo said with vehemence. "That's why I could never sell this place. Do you have any idea what it's like to be able to make any movie you want, and without *anybody's* permission?" He walked over and sat down at his desk.

"Almost," Michael said. "You've been that good to me."

Leo reached into his top desk drawer and removed a small revolver, gold-plated. He flipped the cylinder open and showed Michael that it was loaded. "You know what I'd do if I had to let somebody like Johnson tell me what movies I could or couldn't make?" He held the pistol to his temple.

"Leo . . ." Michael said.

Leo pulled the trigger.

Michael was halfway out of his chair before he realized that the gun had not gone off.

"Heh, heh," Leo chortled. "Had you going, didn't I?" He tossed the revolver across the desk to Michael.

Michael opened the cylinder and extracted a cartridge. It looked real enough, though it felt a little light.

"Special effects made them for me years

ago," Leo said. "The pistol is one of only two made special by Smith & Wesson. Eisenhower owned the other one."

Michael took the silk handkerchief from his breast pocket and carefully wiped the pistol. "It's beautiful, Leo." He placed the weapon on Leo's desk.

"Oh, I've got the real ammo, too," Leo said, holding up a handful of loose cartridges, then dropping them back into the drawer with a clatter. "If ever some nutcase gets through security and into this building, I'd like to have a piece nearby, you know?" He put the weapon back into the drawer.

"I hope you have a permit, Leo."

"Sure I do; I can even carry it as a concealed weapon, but I'm not as paranoid as all that."

"I'm glad to hear it. Guns are dangerous."

"You're right, of course. I mean, I'm no NRA enthusiast like Chuck Heston, for instance, but I think a man ought to be able to own a piece for his own protection."

"A responsible man, yes," Michael replied. He looked at his watch. "I'd better get back to my office; I'm due to look at the first advertising ideas for *Inside Straight*."

"Let me know when they're ready for me to see," Leo said.

"Sure," Michael replied. He left Leo's office wondering what it would be like not to have to go to anyone for approval of anything, ever.

Margot gave him his messages. "I put the ad people in your office," she said.

"Right," Michael replied, flipping through the messages.

"How did the screening go?" Margot asked.

"I thought it was okay. Leo put a gun to his head when it was over."

Margot laughed. "The gold-plated one?"

"That's the one."

"He's been doing that for years, every time he wants to make a point."

Michael looked at her. "Why don't you come over this weekend and cook you and me dinner?"

"Why not?" Margot said, smiling.

Michael was spending a lot of afternoons with Amanda, but he still enjoyed Margot on a Saturday night.

52

Michael walked into the Beverly Hills Hotel, through the main lobby, and out into the rear gardens. A housemaid directed him to Bungalow Four. A Japanese answered the door.

"I am Michael Vincent."

The man bowed, then ushered Michael into a living room. At one end of the room a large dining table was surrounded by several men, all but three Japanese. Harry Johnson stood up and approached Michael, his hand out.

"Hello, Michael," he said, beaming. "Thank you so much for coming."

Michael nodded noncommittally.

"Please let me introduce you to these gentlemen."

Everyone at the table stood.

"This," said Johnson, indicating a white-haired Japanese man, "is Mr. Matsuo Yamamoto, head of the company that bears his name."

The Japanese bowed. "How do you do, Mr. Vincent," he said, and his English was vaguely British.

"How do you do?" Michael replied, bowing slightly as he had been told to do.

"This," Johnson continued, "is Mr. Yamamoto's consultant, Mr. Yasumura."

A stocky, low-browed man standing next to Yamamoto bowed, but said nothing.

There were three other Japanese, two of whom seemed to be management types; the third seemed somehow less business-oriented. Johnson then introduced the two Caucasians standing at the table.

"This is Norman Geldorf, chairman of Geldorf & Winter, investment bankers."

Geldorf shook Michael's hand but seemed very reserved.

"And this is Mr. Thomas Provensano, an associate of Mr. Geldorf."

Tommy Pro stuck out his hand. "I'm very glad to meet you, Mr. Vincent; I've heard a great deal about you."

Johnson indicated a chair. "Please sit down."

When Michael had done so, he waited for Johnson to speak again.

"I've asked you to come here, Michael, to

help resolve some concerns expressed by some of the board."

Michael finally spoke. "Harry, you are the only board member I see here."

"I am, Michael, but Mr. Geldorf is the chief trustee of a private trust which owns forty-five percent of Centurion stock."

Michael looked surprised. "I was not aware that anyone but board members owned any Centurion stock."

"That is probably what Leo Goldman wished you to think," Johnson said.

"I was under the impression that Leo owned a controlling interest."

"Not exactly. Leo *votes* a controlling interest, but, you see, he currently votes the trust-owned shares, in addition to his own."

"I see," Michael said, taking care to look surprised.

"This meeting was called so that I could present Mr. Geldorf and Mr. Provensano with an up-to-date account of the present condition of Centurion."

"I see. Is Mr. Yamamoto to be given this information, as well?"

"Now, Michael, Mr. Geldorf and I represent between us voting control of Centurion, and we felt it altogether proper for Mr. Yamamoto and his associates to share this information."

"Does Leo know about this?" Michael asked.

"He does not; Leo is in New York today. Mr. Geldorf and I thought it best to consult with Mr. Yamamoto in Leo's absence."

"Well, I suppose you have that right," Michael said.

Geldorf spoke for the first time. "Mr. Vincent, on behalf of the trust I administer, I would like to know your opinion of the current production schedule of Centurion. Excepting your own productions, of course. I have been very glad to hear of their contribution to the studio's profits."

"My opinion?" Michael asked.

"Please. You are the only active production executive on the board besides Mr. Goldman, and we would like to have your views."

Michael hesitated artfully.

"Michael," Harry Johnson said, "I know very well the loyalty you must feel to Leo, but surely you feel a loyalty to the studio as a whole."

"Of course," Michael said. "Centurion has made it possible for me to do successful work."

"Then please believe me when I tell you that it is entirely in the studio's best interest that you be as frank as possible in your opinions of the production schedule."

Michael looked at Johnson and Geldorf. "Do I have your absolute assurance that what I say will be held in the strictest confidence?"

"You do," Geldorf and Johnson said together.

Michael looked at his reflection in the polished table. "I . . . have some concerns about the direction the studio is taking," he said.

"What concerns?" Geldorf asked.

Michael looked directly at him. "From what I know of Centurion's history, its reputation and its success have been built on reasonably priced but high-quality motion pictures, pictures that have earned more than their share of Academy Award nominations and an excellent profit for the studio."

"That is correct," Johnson said.

"I'm afraid that seems to be changing," Michael said.

"How so?" Geldorf asked.

"The current production schedule contains two projects that are very high-budget, indeed, and not, I'm afraid, what I'd consider high-quality."

"Which are those?" Geldorf asked.

"Two untitled projects — a science fiction film and one about the Vietnam War."

"Have you read the scripts of these productions?" Johnson asked.

"I have."

"And have you seen the budgets and production schedules?"

"I have."

"And what is your opinion of the chances for success of these productions?"

"Well, of course, both pictures could conceivably make a lot of money . . ."

"In your considered opinion, will they?"

"I think that both these projects are highly risky at best — more than the risk that usually runs with making motion pictures."

"Why?" Geldorf asked.

"The science fiction film has a derivative script, and the opportunities for budget overruns are prodigious. Mr. Goldman expects to make this film for, I think, around eighty million dollars . . ."

"Which is twice the budget of Centurion's most expensive productions, is it not?" Johnson asked.

"Yes, it is."

"And do you think the film has a chance of coming in on budget?"

"A chance, perhaps; no more."

"If you were producing this film, Michael, what budget would you realistically expect to need?"

"I don't believe I could shoot it for less than a hundred and twenty-five million," Michael replied.

"And what sort of domestic gross would you anticipate?" Johnson asked.

"Well, of course, it could go through the roof, but I think it would be unwise to count on more than a hundred and fifty million."

"And would that figure cover production, prints, and advertising?"

"Not much chance of that."

"So Centurion might be facing a loss on the film?"

"It very well could."

"Michael, what do you think the chances are of the film doing as much as a hundred and fifty million?"

"Not good," Michael replied.

"So Centurion could be facing a very great loss indeed on the film?"

"Quite possibly."

"What about the Vietnam film? What do you think of that?"

"I think it's a very serious look at the political consequences of that war."

"Is there a demand for such a serious film at this time?"

"Possibly; I'm not at all sure."

"Are there any other risks associated with this film?"

"It is to be shot in the Philippines, and although there has been an election recently, the communist insurgents are still very active, and there are many other difficulties associated with shooting that far from the studio."

"I see. Have any other major productions been filmed in the Philippines?"

"Francis Ford Coppola's film *Apocalypse Now* was shot there."

"And what happened to the budget on that film?"

"It went completely out of control. There was a hurricane, illness, every sort of disaster."

"Has that film ever made money?"

"I don't know; I doubt it."

"Michael, have you recently attended a screening of a new production called *Drive Time*?"

"Yes."

"What did you think of it?"

"I don't think it will be a great success."

"Why not?"

"I think they began shooting with less than a good script."

"This was Leo Goldman's personal production, was it not?"

"Yes."

"Mr. Vincent," Geldorf asked, "what sorts of films do you believe Centurion should be making at this moment in time?"

"I'm personally making the kind of movies that I think we should concentrate on,"

Michael said. "Very tight budgets, no highly paid stars, high-quality writing. Films with low risk and high profitability."

Geldorf continued. "Do you have an opinion as to whether Centurion could continue to make such films if under new ownership?"

Michael looked at Yamamoto, who smiled slightly.

"If good management were allowed to make good films without hindrance, yes."

Harry Johnson stood up. "Michael, we are all grateful to you for your candor. Please be assured that your remarks will be held in the strictest confidence." He shook Michael's hand. Everyone stood.

Michael understood that he was dismissed.

An hour later, Michael was parked on a side street off Sunset when a limousine pulled up next to his car and the rear window slid silently down. Tommy Pro beamed at him from the rear seat of the big car.

"Aces, *paisan*," he said. "Now Norman Geldorf will go and see Amanda Goldman."

"Good," Michael said.

"When does Goldman get back from New York?"

"Tomorrow afternoon."

"Schedule a meeting in his office, okay?"

"All right," Michael said.

The window slid up and the limousine moved away.

Michael drove back to Centurion and parked in front of the Executive Building. He ran up the stairs to Leo's office. Leo's secretary was sitting at her desk.

"Hi," he said. "What time should Leo be back in the office tomorrow afternoon?"

"He always comes straight from the airport," the woman said. "He should be here by four."

"Good. Would you schedule a meeting for me at that time? It's important that I see him the moment he gets back. Tell him I won't take no for an answer."

She flipped open a diary. "Four it is."

Michael put a hand on the doorknob of Leo's office. "Oh, there's something I left in here yesterday; it's on Leo's desk."

"Sure, go ahead," she said.

Michael stepped into Leo Goldman's office and closed the door behind him.

CHAPTER

53

Michael looked up into the glazed eyes of Margot Gladstone and gave a little thrust. Margot's eyes closed, and she whimpered.

"Again," she said.

Michael complied.

Margot dissolved into a series of whimpers, climaxing quietly, as she always did. She collapsed onto Michael.

He held her against him, rubbing her back and shoulders while she continued her orgasm. It occurred to Michael that perhaps his secret in bed was that he derived his greatest pleasure from making women come, then come again and again. He rolled onto his side but remained inside her.

"That was a wonderful bit of weekend recreation," Margot said, sighing. "I lost count of how many times I came."

"Six or seven," Michael said.

"Stop bragging," she laughed.

"I'm hungry."

"All right, all right, I'll finish dinner."

He had interrupted her in the kitchen and had taken her on a double lounge at poolside. Margot rose, pushed back her hair, and dove into the pool. She swam gracefully to the end, picked up a terrycloth robe, and strode toward the kitchen, dripping as she went.

He watched through the glass wall between the kitchen and the pool as she went about preparing their dinner.

When they had finished dining, Michael leaned back in his poolside chair and gazed at the stars. "That was wonderful," he said. "What was it?"

"It was a caesar salad, chateaubriand with béarnaise sauce, *pommes soufflé, haricots verts,* and Stock Exchange Pudding."

"It was the last one I meant. What was it again?"

"Stock Exchange Pudding. When I was but a slip of a girl I had a job conducting guided tours of the London Stock Exchange. There was a corps of us girls, and we cooked lunches for ourselves — quite elaborate ones, sometimes. That's where I got the recipe for the pudding."

"It was superb."

"So were you."

"What would I do without you?" he asked.

"Funny you should mention that."

"What?"

"Michael, you must remember that when I came to you I said I was serving out my time until my pension matured. You do remember."

"Vaguely," he replied.

"Well, next month I'm off."

Michael was alarmed. "You can't do that," he said. "I can't do this without you."

She shrugged. "I was thinking of Mexico. I might buy a little place somewhere around Puerto Vallarta."

"I won't let you go. I can't."

"Michael, it's been fun, but I can't go on doing that job the rest of my life. I'll be sixty in fewer years than I care to think about."

Michael was genuinely panicked at the thought of losing Margot. She made his life work; she was the closest thing to a confidant he had ever had. "Suppose you were doing a different job," he said.

"What do you mean?"

"I mean something better."

She shook her head. "I wouldn't derive the pleasure from producing that you do. Really, I wouldn't."

"Something bigger."

She looked at him closely. "Why don't you tell me what's going on? I know something is; I can always tell."

Michael sat back and sipped his wine. He was a little tipsy — rare for him — and he was enjoying her company greatly. He was not enjoying the idea of having to replace her. He made a decision.

"All right, I'll tell you."

She curled up in her chair and waited.

"In a day or two, Leo will be out."

Her eyes widened.

"And I'll be running the studio."

"Michael, you shouldn't underestimate Leo's influence with the board."

"The board came to me. They're worried about Leo — especially that he won't consider an offer from the Japanese."

"That I had heard about," she said, "but do you know that Amanda's trust has the biggest chunk of stock?"

"I do. The head trustee, Norman Geldorf, is in town right now. I met with him and Harry Johnson and . . . some other people this afternoon."

"The Japanese?"

Michael nodded. "And a friend of mine."

"Tommy?"

"You do keep up, don't you?"

414

"I read the papers, and I hear more than you think at the office."

"What do you hear?" he asked, a little worried.

"Oh, come on, Michael; you don't have any secrets from me. We're too close for that."

"I have some secrets from everybody," he said.

"Not from me."

"Just which of my secrets do you know?"

"All of them," she said. "I know how much money you have, where it is, and how you made it."

"Where is it?"

"Well, you've moved it out of the Kensington Trust, but I know how it was invested there. What was it, three percent a week?"

Michael was taken aback. "What else do you know?"

"Oh, I've put the pieces together. I know about Callabrese and Moriarty. I'm damned sure you got rid of Rick Rivera, but I'm not quite sure how."

Michael was flabbergasted, but he kept his composure.

"Oh, come on, Michael; that poker face won't work with me. You know I know."

"Well, this is an unexpected turn of events," he said.

She held up her hands. "Now, Michael, you

have nothing to fear from me, so don't start thinking about somehow getting rid of me. I've watched you operate with total admiration. I mean, I've seen some operators in this town, but you are truly something special. You have the single most important quality that a successful producer can possess in this town: you are a complete sociopath."

Michael stared at her silently.

She held up a hand again. "Please don't take that as a criticism. I simply mean that you have no conscience whatever and that you will do anything necessary to get what you want." She smiled at him. "Am I wrong?"

He smiled back. "You know me better than I thought."

"It has been thrilling to watch," she said. "If I had met you when I was twenty-five, you and I could have ruled this town together."

"We still might," Michael said. "How would you like to be chief operating officer of Centurion?"

Her eyebrows went up. "That's a big leap from executive assistant," she said.

"Honestly, Margot, do you think there is anyone in administration at the studio whose job you couldn't do better?"

She laughed. "Michael, *you* know *me* better than I thought."

"I do."

"But there's a problem here."

"Nothing we can't overcome."

"So you get your way; you get Leo's job, and you're running the studio. Then Geldorf and Johnson sell out to the Japanese, and suddenly you're not in charge anymore. You'd be working for them, just as you're working for Leo now. And I don't think you'd like that."

"You're right, I wouldn't. I understand what Leo loves so much about running the studio. As he put it himself, he has the ability to make any movie he wants, without asking anybody."

"The Japanese wouldn't let you do that; not for long."

"You're right."

"So what are you going to do?"

Michael smiled. It was wonderful telling somebody this. "I'm going to take Leo's job, and then I'm going to fuck the Japanese."

"And Tommy?"

"Tommy is my closest friend. He and I can work something out."

"If you can do that, I'm with you," Margot said.

"Then you're with me."

CHAPTER

54

Michael waited impatiently for the call from Leo's secretary, and when it came, he made his own call. "Leo's ready," he said.

"We're right behind you," Johnson replied from his car phone. "We're already inside the gates."

Michael left his office and walked toward the Executive Building, taking his time, waiting for Johnson. As he mounted the steps to the building, the limousine hove into view. He continued through the lobby and up the stairs to Leo's office.

"Hi," he said to Leo's secretary.

"He's expecting you," she said.

Michael knocked, then opened the door. Leo was sitting at his desk shuffling through some papers. He looked up. "Hiya, kiddo."

"How was your trip?"

"Pretty damn good. I got some new distribution — sixty screens for first releases."

"Congratulations."

"What did you want to see me about?"

Before Michael could speak, Leo's phone buzzed and at the same time, the door to his office opened. Harry Johnson entered, followed closely by Norman Geldorf.

Leo looked at them, puzzled. "I didn't know you guys were in town," he said. "Why didn't you call?"

"There was no time, Leo," Johnson said. "We have to talk."

"Sure." Leo waved them to chairs in front of his desk, and Michael sat down near Leo's right hand.

"I'll come right to the point," Johnson said.

"Good," Leo replied. He seemed unconcerned.

"Leo, the board is unhappy. We've met in your absence, and we've decided that it's time for you to step down."

Leo stared at Johnson. *"What?"* he demanded.

"Board members with a large majority of shares concurred in this decision."

Leo looked at Geldorf. "Did you buy into this?"

"I did," Geldorf said.

"What about Amanda? What did she have

to say about it?"

Geldorf looked away. "It is not her decision. As head trustee, it is mine alone."

"You're out of your fucking minds, all of you." He turned to Michael. "You hear this? I've made these bastards richer and richer by the way I've run this studio, and now they're stabbing me in the goddamned back."

Michael looked down.

"Not a moviemaker among them," Leo said, and his face was becoming very red. "How do they expect to run this place without me?" He looked at Johnson. "Or do you just expect to sell the joint to the Japs?"

"Maybe," Johnson said. "They've made us another offer."

"So why didn't you consult me about it?"

"Because you've made it plain that you wouldn't accept under any circumstances."

Leo stared at him for a moment, then reached into his top right desk drawer and took out his gold-plated revolver. He put the gun to his head. "You know something? If I thought I couldn't run this place better than the bunch of you and the Japanese put together, I'd blow my brains out right here and now."

"Oh, come on, Leo," Johnson said, exasperated, "don't start with that old routine; I've seen it half a dozen times."

Leo took the gun away from his head and pointed it at Johnson. "Okay, instead of me, I'll do you."

Johnson shook his head. "Leo, stop behaving like a child."

Leo pulled the trigger. The gun went off, and Johnson spun sideways out of his chair.

"Jesus Christ!" Geldorf shouted. He pushed his chair aside and knelt beside Johnson.

Leo was standing, looking first at Johnson, then at the gun, a look of amazement on his face.

Michael saw his chance. He stood up, grabbed Leo by the wrist with one hand, then closed his other hand over Leo's, running his finger inside the trigger guard. "Don't do it, Leo!" Michael shouted. Then he jerked Leo's hand around toward his head and pressed Leo's trigger finger.

The gun roared again. The bullet entered Leo's head just under the temple and exited above his right eye, knocking Leo back into his chair and spattering Michael with gore.

Geldorf looked up from attending to Johnson. "Michael, are you shot?" he yelled.

Leo's secretary burst into the office, and, seeing Johnson lying facedown on the floor and her boss in his chair with part of his head missing, fainted.

Michael hesitated only a moment, then

picked up Leo's phone, got an outside line, and dialed 911. "An ambulance," he said to the operator, giving her the address. "There's been a shooting." He hung up and dialed the Legal Department. "This is Michael Vincent," he said. "Leo Goldman has just shot another man and himself. Get the best lawyer you can find up to Leo's office at once."

Michael and Geldorf sat on facing sofas before the fireplace in Leo's office. The swarm of ambulance men, policemen and crime technicians was thinning out; only two detectives, Michael and Geldorf, and the Centurion lawyer remained.

"All right, let's go through it once more," a detective said.

"No," Michael replied. "You've heard it again and again. Do you have any doubt what happened?"

"We've told you the truth," Geldorf said. "Surely you don't think that Mr. Vincent and I murdered two men in this office."

The other detective put down the phone. "There hasn't been a murder," he said. "They're both still alive."

Michael looked at the man. "That's wonderful," he managed to say. "How are they?"

"Johnson wasn't hurt bad. The bullet missed the lung and exited the shoulder; broke

422

his collarbone. He'll be out of the hospital in a couple of days."

"What about Mr. Goldman?" Geldorf asked.

"He's alive; that's about it. You can talk to his doctor when we're through here."

"We're through here," Michael said, rising. "I'm going to the hospital." He stopped. "Jesus Christ, has anybody called Amanda?"

"Mrs. Goldman?" the detective asked. "His secretary called her; she's at the hospital."

"Are you coming, Norman?" Michael asked.

"Yes, of course. Amanda will need us."

The group started to shuffle out of the office, but one detective pulled Michael back.

"Do you remember me, Mr. Vincent?"

"I'm sorry, I don't."

"My name is Hall; I was Rick Rivera's partner. We met when Rick and I came to see you about the Moriarty murder."

"Oh, yes, I remember."

"People around you keep dying or getting hurt," Hall said.

"I beg your pardon?"

"Moriarty dies right after you see him; Rick dies after he comes to work for you — and Rick was never a junkie. And now these two."

"What are you getting at, Detective?"

423

"The shame of it is I'm not getting anywhere," Hall said. "But I want you to know that I'm not through rooting around in your life. Rick was my friend, and . . ."

"That's about enough out of you," Michael interrupted. "You're implying that I had something to do with all these things, and you're wrong. You just do your job, and you'll find out that I'm nothing more than an innocent bystander. Go too far, and you'll find that this studio has more than a little influence with the government of this city." Michael turned and stalked out of the room.

Michael and Amanda sat in a corner of the large, sunny hospital room occupied by Leo Goldman. Geldorf waited outside. Leo lay on his back, his head swathed in bandages, his left eye open and staring.

"I can't believe any of this," Amanda was saying. She was composed now, and coming to terms with what had happened. "What happened in that office?"

"Leo was arguing with Johnson. He pulled a gun out of his desk and pointed it at his head. Johnson seemed to have seen the gun before; he told Leo to put it down and stop acting like a child. Leo shot Johnson and then put the gun to his own head. I tried to stop him, grabbed at his arm, but it went off."

"Had Johnson and Geldorf told Leo that he was finished at the studio?"

"Yes."

"Did you know this was coming?"

"I was called to a meeting with them yesterday. I defended Leo as best I could. I scheduled a meeting with him as soon as he returned to warn him of what was happening, then Johnson and Geldorf showed up."

"The worst part of it is, he's going to live and be a vegetable," Amanda said. "He'd rather be dead, believe me."

"Amanda, you aren't obliged to keep him alive artificially under these circumstances."

"Don't worry, I won't." She began to cry.

"There, there," he said. "Don't cry; Leo isn't in pain."

"That's not why I'm crying," Amanda sobbed. "I'm crying because right now, all I can think about is wanting you."

CHAPTER

55

Michael looked around the hospital room. The entire Centurion board of directors was gathered around Harry Johnson's bed, and Harry, his arm and shoulder in a cast, was speaking.

"All right," he said, grimacing with pain. "You've all heard from Norman, Michael, and me what happened in Leo's office yesterday. Now we've got some business to conduct, and I want to get on with it so that I can have a painkiller. Norman, do you have a motion?"

Geldorf nodded. "I move that the board appoint Michael Vincent as president and chief executive officer of Centurion Pictures, with full operating authority, at a salary and with benefits to be negotiated between representatives of the board and Mr. Vincent."

"Do I hear a second?"

"Second," another board member said.

"All in favor?"

"Aye," rumbled from the group.

"Opposed?"

Silence.

"Congratulations, Michael," Johnson said. "Now, if there is no further business to conduct at this time, this board is adjourned. *Nurse!*"

A uniformed nurse entered the room with a hypodermic needle on a tray, and the board members filed out.

Outside in the hall, Michael accepted the congratulations of his fellow board members, then, when they had drifted out, he walked down the hall toward Leo Goldman's room.

Michael entered and approached the bed. Leo seemed unchanged from the day before, but his exposed left eye was closed. He opened it.

"Hi, Leo," Michael said softly.

Leo blinked rapidly.

"There was a board meeting. They chose me to succeed you."

Leo blinked rapidly again.

Michael leaned over and looked into Leo's good eye. There was intelligence there. "Leo," he said, "if you can understand me, blink once."

Leo blinked once. Leo was alive in there.

427

"I want to ask you some questions. Blink once for yes, twice for no."

Leo blinked once.

"Are you in pain?"

Leo blinked once.

"Do you want me to call the nurse?"

Leo blinked twice.

"Can you move?"

Leo blinked twice.

"Can you speak?"

Leo blinked twice.

"Do you want to see Amanda?"

Leo blinked twice.

"Do you want me to leave you alone?"

Leo blinked twice.

"I wish I could just ask you what you want," Michael said. "Don't worry, you'll get better in time."

Leo blinked twice.

Michael stared at the eye. "Don't you think you'll get better?"

Leo blinked twice.

"Leo, do you want to go on living like this?"

Leo blinked twice.

"Do you want me to do something about it?"

Leo blinked once.

Michael walked to the door and looked up and down the hallway. No one was in sight. He went back to Leo's bedside and looked around. Leo had an oxygen tube up his nose and an IV was running. If he tampered with those, somebody would notice. Gently, he lifted Leo's head and removed the pillow. He leaned over Leo.

"Is this what you want, Leo?"

Leo blinked once.

"Leo, I want to thank you for everything you've done for me."

Leo blinked once.

"I want you to know I'll see that Amanda is all right."

Leo blinked once.

"Good-bye, old friend."

Leo blinked once, and the eye filled. A tear trickled toward his ear.

Michael placed the pillow over Leo's face and pressed gently. He waited for three minutes by his watch, then he removed the pillow. He felt at Leo's neck, but couldn't find a pulse. He lifted Leo's head and placed the pillow under it, then he left the room. No one saw him leave.

For the first time since he was a little boy, Michael was fighting back tears.

CHAPTER

56

Michael stood at the podium and addressed the memorial service audience. The auditorium was packed.

"I had not known Leo Goldman as long as many of you, but I counted him as my closest friend. I have been asked to address you about Leo's professional side — Leo as filmmaker.

"Leo Goldman personified what was best in the title 'producer.' He had taste, judgment, style, an appreciation of talent of all sorts, and a keen business sense. The films Leo made as a producer were always among Centurion's best.

"But Leo was more than a producer: he was a studio head, and he operated in a manner not often seen today. He was the kind of studio head that L. B. Mayer and Jack Warner were. *He was responsible.* Leo personally analyzed and approved every project that came out of Centurion, and every movie that Centurion made reflected his taste and judgment. I think that it is possible to view every film that Centurion ever made under Leo, as I have done, and conclude that Leo Goldman never made a bad movie. Not one. And that is something that neither L.B. Mayer nor Jack Warner could have justifiably said.

"What Leo Goldman did make was hundreds of good movies, and I know that Leo would be happy to be judged by nothing other than that output. *He was responsible.*

"I have been chosen to replace Leo, but we all know that such a thing is not possible. When I was offered his place at Centurion, my first emotion was awe, followed closely by humility, when I realized what I was being asked to do. Perhaps it would be better to follow a bad studio head, because it would be easier to look better; following Leo would be very hard, because he was so good at what he did.

"But on reflection, I see that my job will be made easier because Leo did his job so well; because he made decisions, knocked heads, and, no doubt over opposition, established a standard of filmmaking that is the envy of the industry. *He was responsible.*

"My gratitude to Leo is complete. He made

it possible, first, for me to do what I do, and then for me to do what he did. If I don't do it as well, it won't be Leo's fault.

"I tell you now that I would rather work for Leo than run the studio. I would rather stand in his shadow than face the glare of solitary scrutiny, as he did.

"And if, in my examination of my own life and work, I find that I had the slightest part in driving Leo to what he finally did, I will ask God to punish me.

"I loved Leo Goldman, and I miss him. In the coming days, if I find myself in a quandary, at loggerheads with my peers, in trouble with my studio, I will ask myself, 'What would Leo Goldman have done?' And I will know what to do."

Amanda Goldman received her husband's friends and admirers at her home on Stone Canyon. Some four hundred people ate, drank, and talked of Leo Goldman and The Business.

Michael found himself besieged by new admirers congratulating him on his eulogy.

Margot Gladstone was nearby. "These people are eating out of your hand," she whispered to him when she had the opportunity. "Let's try and keep it that way."

When the crowd began to drift away,

Michael cornered Norman Geldorf and Harry Johnson, whose arm was still in its cast.

"I wanted to say this as soon as possible," he said. "I don't think we should sell to the Japanese. Not yet, anyway."

"I'm inclined to agree," Geldorf said. "With Leo gone, they'll try to knock down the price."

"Give me a chance to get established, to get some movies into production," Michael said. "Then, if selling is the right thing to do, you'll get a lot more money for the studio."

Both men nodded.

"That was a wonderful eulogy, Michael," Johnson said. "Just the right touch."

Michael was the last to leave.

"Don't go," Amanda said, clinging to him. "Stay the night."

"It's better that I go," he said. "We'll talk in a few days. See your friends, ignore me; that's the best way for a while."

"In a week I'll be on fire," she said.

"In a week you can set me afire," he replied.

Michael cloistered himself in the Malibu house for the weekend with Margot. He strode back and forth beside the pool, dictating notes for running Centurion, and Margot took them down. She cooked; they made love. There was little love in it, they both knew. They used each other to the fullest.

But in their developing relationship, Michael had found what he had never had — a confidant.

CHAPTER

57

Near the end of his first week as head of Centurion Pictures, Michael was working at his desk in what had once been Leo Goldman's office, preparing for a board meeting, when Margot Gladstone entered through the door between their adjoining offices.

"Have you heard the news this morning, or seen the papers?" she asked.

"No, neither. I haven't had time for anything but this board meeting."

She placed the *New York Times* on his desk. In the lower right-hand corner of the front page, Michael found the story:

MAFIA CHIEFTAIN DEAD AT 72

Benito Carlucci, for many years head of New York's largest Mafia family, died yesterday at the age of seventy-two, at Columbia Presbyterian Hospital, of complications of liver disease. . . .

Carlucci was convicted of a crime only once, as a young man, when he served two years in Sing Sing prison for heading a car theft ring. From the time of his release, he rose rapidly in the ranks of his criminal organization, always protected from arrest by layers of command, and at the age of only forty, he succeeded to the leadership of his Mafia family. Under his management the family took the first tentative steps toward legitimate investment, and, at the time of his death, FBI sources said that more than half the family's income derived from legitimate business, although these businesses were often operated in a fashion that flirted with illegality. . . .

Often the death of the head of a Mafia family results in a struggle for succession that is bloody, but it appears to knowledgeable observers that Carlucci, anticipating his death, mediated the succession, and arranged that the family would be run by a council, the members of which are capos of units of the family. None of the four members seems, at this time, to have the upper hand.

Services will be held tomorrow at St. Patrick's Cathedral, with the Archbishop of New York officiating.

Michael put down the paper and picked up the phone, dialing the number of a cellular phone.

"Yes?" Tommy's voice was tense.

"It's Vinnie; I just heard."

"Hold."

Michael listened as muffled orders were barked, then Tommy came back on the line.

"Sorry, Vinnie. It's been hectic around here, as you can imagine."

"I'm very sorry, Tommy; I know you loved the old man."

"I did, but he's gone, and now we've got stuff to do."

"Is everything all right?"

"Don't believe everything you read in the papers."

"When can we get together?"

"I'll try and come out there next month."

"Good. Convey my sympathy to his family."

"Of course."

Michael hung up.

"Well?" Margot asked. "What's going on?"

"He couldn't really talk," Michael said. "He'll come out here when he can, and then we'll know."

★ ★ ★

Michael called the board meeting to order. "Good afternoon, gentlemen; this will be a brief meeting. I want to bring you up to date on business, then there are two matters before the board for approval.

"Since taking charge of the studio, I have canceled the science fiction and Vietnam War projects and have written off the expenses."

There was a murmur of approval around the table.

"I have also put three pictures into production, the largest budget of which is fourteen million dollars. I expect all of them to be highly profitable.

"Naturally, there will be some personnel changes at the studio. Some of the department heads under Leo will, of course, be unhappy with working for me, and there may be some that I will be unhappy with."

Harry Johnson spoke up. "You will, of course, seek board approval of any major changes."

Michael looked at Johnson. "That concludes my update. Now I wish to bring to a vote the employment contracts for myself and Margot Gladstone. To answer your question, Harry, my proposed contract gives me full authority to hire and fire as I see fit. Do I hear a motion?"

438

"Move that the contracts be approved," a board member said.

"Second," said another.

"Any discussion?" Michael asked. "Harry?"

Johnson stood up. "Michael, first I want to say how pleased I am — and I'm sure I speak for all the board — at the way you've taken charge of the studio. Your actions on the production side are both prudent and creative, and we are all grateful." He cleared his throat. "However, there are potential problems on the business side of the studio. Some of the department heads have been in their jobs for many years and have proven their worth under Leo. All of these people have had vastly more experience than you in this business, and I, for one, am reluctant to give you the power to terminate and replace them at will."

"Thank you, Harry," Michael said. "What you say is, of course, true; some of these people have been here for a long time, and all of them are competent. All of them, however, are not happy about working for me, and unless that unhappiness can be modified in short order, I will regard such an attitude as disqualifying where these positions are concerned."

"Another thing," Johnson said. "Putting in Margot Gladstone as chief operating officer might be considered a rash act. Ms. Gladstone has been secretary to a number of high executives here, but that experience hardly qualifies her to administrate the business side of this studio."

"I understand your concern, Harry," Michael said, "but Margot knows more about how this studio works than anybody here, including me. She is highly intelligent, and I have always found her judgment to be faultless. She will, of course, report to me, and I can always overrule her actions if I disagree with them."

"A salary of a million dollars a year, plus benefits, for a woman who was recently a secretary?" Johnson asked.

"If she is qualified to be COO," Michael replied, "and I have already said I believe her to be, then her compensation package is a moderate one by industry standards."

Johnson began to speak again, but Michael held up a hand.

"Harry, I don't mean to squelch debate, but the decision before this board is a simple one: will I run this studio, or will I not? Let me be quite clear: I will accept this job only if I have the same authority that Leo had. My contract is before you; it gives me full authority. I have presented Margot Gladstone's contract to you only as a courtesy. If this board approves my contract, then my first act as CEO will be to sign Margot's contract. If this board chooses not to do so, then I can have my desk cleared out in half an hour. I think it best if I leave the meeting while you discuss this. Gentlemen, the decision is yours." Michael turned to leave.

"Michael," Johnson said.

Michael turned. "Yes?"

"I don't think it will be necessary for you to leave. I move the question."

Michael looked around the table. "All in favor?"

"Aye," the men said as one.

"Opposed?"

Silence.

"The motion is carried unanimously," Michael said. "Gentlemen, without further business, this meeting is adjourned until the next regular monthly meeting."

Michael stepped back into his office, where Margot waited for him. He walked to his desk, signed four copies of her contract, and handed her one. "You are now the chief operating officer of Centurion Pictures," he said.

Margot beamed and kissed him.

"Now," Michael said, "go fire the chief financial officer."

"Yes, sir," Margot replied.

CHAPTER

58

Michael sat in the chauffeur-driven stretch Mercedes that he had inherited from Leo Goldman and watched the Gulfstream IV jet land at Santa Monica Airport. It seemed an impossibly short runway for such a big airplane, but shortly the jet was taxiing toward where Michael waited.

Michael greeted Tommy Pro with a hug and a kiss at the bottom of the airstairs, then hustled him into the Mercedes while the chauffeur dealt with the luggage.

"That's a very nice mode of transportation," Michael said. "You can't be in too much trouble."

"Trouble?" Tommy laughed. "I should always be in this much trouble." He found the proper switch and raised the glass petition between them and the driver, who now pointed the car toward Malibu. "Can he hear us at all?" Tommy asked.

"Not at all. Leo bought a standard 600 sedan, the one with the twelve-cylinder engine, and had it stretched. He also had this compartment completely soundproofed."

Tommy fiddled with the TV. "Does this thing get CNN?"

"No, Tommy. You need cable or a satellite for CNN."

"Does it get any news at all?"

Michael leaned forward and changed the channel. "We get the network news at five o'clock out here." Tom Brokaw's image appeared on the screen.

"Good evening," the newscaster said. "Tonight, there's a new showdown with Saddam Hussein over inspections of his military installations, the president is in deep political trouble over the Iran-Contra scandal and . . ." — the picture changed to one of a dead man lying on a New York street — ". . . a generational change in a Mafia family."

Tommy heaved a deep sigh.

"What's going on?" Michael asked. "I'm not learning a hell of a lot from the newspapers."

"With any luck at all," Tommy said, "that guy lying in the street was Benny the Nose."

"Benny? Who would have the guts to whack Benny Nose?"

"You're looking at him."

"Well, I'll be damned. Tommy, bring me up to date here."

"Shhh," Tommy said, pointing at the TV.

Brokaw was back. "Early this afternoon in New York City, two Mafia capos were gunned down in the street as they left a Manhattan restaurant. These murders laid to rest the FBI theory that after the death of Benito Carlucci, power had passed to a committee of his subordinates without a struggle. Police theorize that two of the committee members had the other two rubbed out in order to consolidate their power."

"This is why I'm visiting you," Tommy said. "It's a good time to be away."

"So who's left?" Michael asked. "Who's running things?"

"Eddie and Joe Funaro are left," Tommy said, "and *I'm* running things."

"Jesus, Tommy! How'd you pull that off?"

"The old man pulled it off — him and me together. He called the four of them in and told them there was a new setup, then he told Eddie and Joe to take orders from me. Now they're running the street businesses, and I'm running everything else. They funnel the proceeds to me, and I invest legitimately."

444

"You're running *everything?*"

"Everything." Tommy looked very smug.

Michael leaned back in the seat. "So you're the Don."

Tommy grinned. "I'm the Don."

At sunset, Michael and Tommy strolled along the beach at Malibu Colony, Michael in casual California clothes and Tommy in the rolled-up trousers of his sharkskin suit and silk shirt, his necktie hanging loose. They had had dinner, talking of Tommy's new responsibilities, his new power.

"You're a very lucky man, Vinnie," Tommy said.

"Don't I know it."

"Luckier than you know."

"How do you mean?"

"If the Don had lived another twenty-four hours you'd be dead."

Michael stopped in his tracks. *"What?"*

"I held him off as long as I could, and he died."

"The old man wanted me dead?"

"You double-crossed him, Vinnie."

"Now, wait a minute, Tommy."

"Some people would say that you double-crossed me."

"Tommy . . ."

"You talked Geldorf and Johnson out of

445

selling the studio to the Japs, which means *us* and the Japs."

"It wasn't the right thing to do, Tommy. Not then."

"Why not then? I had it all set up: Geldorf and Johnson were in the bag, Goldman was dead, you were — you are — in charge."

"Tommy, listen to me. I've got a movie studio in the palm of my hand; Centurion Pictures! Do you know what that means?"

"It means one hell of a lot of money to play with," Tommy said.

"It's more than that, Tommy; I can make any movie, and I mean *any* movie, I want. I can hire any star, any director, any writer; I've got the button to the green light in my hand. I *own* the button."

"You don't own shit. You're working for a salary."

"My contract gives me the right to buy two percent of the equity a year, as long as we're profitable."

"*Two percent a year?* You're telling me that you stiffed the Don, the family, and me for *two percent a year?*"

"Tommy, I didn't stiff anybody. You're not out anything."

"The old man didn't see it that way, Vinnie, and if it hadn't been for me, you'd be feeding the fishes in the Pacific Ocean right now."

would never betray him again." Tommy looked at Michael. "That's a story you ought to remember, Vinnie."

Then Tommy turned and walked back toward the house, wading in the surf. Michael followed behind, like a puppy.

For emphasis, Tommy pointed out at the water.

"Tommy, I appreciate . . ."

"You don't appreciate nothing, Vinnie. Do you know that he actually gave me the order? He *ordered* me to whack you, and I didn't do it. The first time in my whole life I ignored an order from my Don. You don't appreciate, Vinnie; you suck at the tit, and you kick everybody else in the teeth."

"Tommy, this was my chance, don't you understand?"

"Your chance to stiff your friends?"

"My chance to run my own operation, my own life, and not be under anybody's thumb."

"That's not how you were raised, Vinnie. Shit, we're all under each other's thumbs; that's why what we have works — we all owe each other. And you thought that you could just step into Leo Goldman's shoes and not owe anybody?"

"Tommy, I owe you, I know that. I'll do anything I can to make it up to you. Just say the word; you can have whatever you want."

"You think this movie studio is some kind of toy, don't you? It's like some giant Erector Set that you get to play with and nobody else can touch, you know that? You don't recognize it for what it is, which is a machine for printing money."

"Tommy, just tell me what you want."

"I want sixty percent of the stock of Centurion Pictures. That's Harry Johnson's stock and Amanda Goldman's — her trust that Norman Geldorf runs. I'll get the rest myself."

"Tommy, if I talk them into that, I cut my own throat. I won't be in charge anymore; I'll be working for somebody else again, don't you see?"

"Vinnie, let me tell you a story. You remember Shorty?"

"Shorty? With the gimpy legs that ran errands for the Don?"

"That's the one. His legs were useless, so he sat on that little plank with the roller-skate wheels, and he pushed himself around the neighborhood, doing for the Don."

Vinnie laughed. "He could go like hell on that skateboard thing, couldn't he?"

"Sure, he could, and you know what? The Don trusted him."

"The Don trusted Shorty? I didn't know he trusted anybody."

"Very few people, but he trusted Shorty. You know why?"

"Why?"

"Did you know that once — this was before you and me were born — Shorty had the richest funeral parlor in Little Italy?"

"No, I didn't know that. How'd he end up on the skateboard?"

"The Don gave it to him, practically; loaned him the money, no interest, sent him business — a *lot* of business, if you know what I mean, and all the Don ever asked of him was that, once in a while, he would bury somebody for the Don. The Don would send him a stiff, and he would bury it, two for one, with another, legit stiff that Shorty happened to be burying anyway."

"So what happened?"

"Shorty got scared of the cops and the feds. They were sniffing around, and he got scared, and the Don sent him a stiff, and he wouldn't bury it, said he couldn't afford to take the chance, what with the cops sniffing around." Tommy stopped walking and turned to Michael. "Then one night the funeral parlor burned down. And a few days after that, men came and broke the undertaker's And that's how Eduardo Minnelli, the well and highly respected undertaker, got Shorty, the gofer."

Michael looked into Tommy's eye didn't like what he saw.

"But after that," Tommy conti Don always trusted Shorty. He with important stuff, stuff that c the Don himself up. Because h

448

449

CHAPTER

59

Michael and Amanda Goldman both reeked of cocoa butter as they stood under a hot shower, soaping each other. Amanda knelt and took him into her mouth, but he pulled her to her feet.

"Not again, no, no; I'm raw as it is."

"I can't get enough of you," she said, reaching around him and rubbing the soap into his back. They stood, kissing, until the soap had washed away, then Michael turned the shower off. He stepped out and held a terrycloth robe for her, then found one for himself.

"I feel like some eggs," he said. "Can I make you some?"

"Love some. You do that while I dry my hair."

Michael went down to the kitchen and began to work. He put some bacon on, slipped a pair of English muffins into the toaster, and whipped half a dozen eggs with a little cream while waiting for half a stick of butter to dissolve in a saucepan. He added some salt, then scrambled the eggs slowly, on the lowest possible heat, until they were fluffy and still moist, and, as Amanda came into the kitchen, he served the bacon, eggs, and muffins on large white plates.

"It smells wonderful," she said. "I didn't know you could cook."

"Almost my only dish," he said, opening a bottle of Schramsberg blanc de noirs.

"My favorite champagne," she said, sipping it. "How'd you know?"

"I've had it at your table often enough; that's where I discovered it."

She shook her hair and it fell, golden, around her shoulders. "You know something?" she asked, eating her eggs.

"What?"

"I thought I would be in some kind of shock for a while, but it's only been two weeks since Leo died, and I feel . . . liberated."

"I think a lot of people must feel that way when their other half dies. It's just that nobody wants to admit it."

"I mean, I loved Leo in my way, but I'm also glad to be free."

"Not completely free," he warned. "Remember how small a town this is. You've got to be a widow for a while."

"I don't mind that, as long as I can see you," she said.

"You can see me whenever you want," he promised. "But we have to wait a year or so before we turn up at dinner parties together."

"I can stand it if you make love to me often enough."

"How often is enough?"

She laughed. "You don't want to know."

"Let's wait until I recover before we do it again."

She placed a hand on his cheek. "I'm sorry, sweetie. I didn't mean to wear you out."

Michael took a deep breath. "Listen, we've got some business to talk."

"Okay, shoot."

"I want you to tell Geldorf that you want him to sell all the Centurion stock in the trust account."

She gaped at him. "Are you mad? I thought you wanted my backing so you could run the studio."

"Believe me, it's just the right time to sell. The Japanese are knocking on our door again, and we're in good enough shape to demand a big price."

"What about Leo's stock?"

"Tell Geldorf to sell that for you, too."

"What about the other directors?"

"When they see a majority get sold they'll get on the bandwagon fast."

She looked down at her plate for a moment. "Michael, do you remember once I told you what Leo did for me in our marriage?"

"I think so."

"I said that I could have anybody I wanted at my dinner table, remember?"

"Yes, I remember."

"Well, the reason I could do that was because my husband ran a major movie studio."

"Yes, I remember, but Leo is dead."

"But when you and I are married I want you still to run the studio."

This was the first time marriage had been mentioned, and Michael tried not to look flustered. "Don't worry, I'll still be running the studio, just under different ownership."

"But the only way I can be sure of that is by hanging on to my stock."

"But . . . at one time, before Leo died, you said you'd sell." He reached over and took her face in his hands. "Amanda, I want you to trust me on this. It's the right thing to do, believe me. The Japanese have offered me an ironclad contract."

"But they can always buy out your contract; it happens all the time in this town. They get tired of you, they want a change, they just write you a nice check and ship you out. Leo always told me that."

He was becoming irritable now. "Goddamnit, Amanda, just do as I say."

She stood up. "I think you're forgetting who you're talking to," she said, then stalked out of the house.

Michael, wearing only a robe, couldn't chase her.

Later in the afternoon, Margot came into his office.

"Michael," she said, sitting down, "I've been rereading my contract, and I find that I can be fired at any time for any reason on ninety days' notice."

Michael looked up from the script he was reading. "Margot, I've made you chief operating officer of this studio. Why would I want to fire you?"

"I know you wouldn't," she said, "because I know too much about you, but suppose something happened to you? The board could throw me right out on my arse, and I'd only have ninety days' pay to keep me."

"Margot," he said, irritated, "you've already got your pension nailed down; in such an unlikely event, you'd have what you would have had if I hadn't promoted you. That should be enough."

"It isn't enough," she said. "I'm in a whole new financial ball game, and I like it. I don't want to be in a position where I can get thrown out on my ear; can't you understand that?"

"You mean you don't want to have to rely on my word."

"If you want to put it that way, yes," Margot said.

Michael was near to losing his temper now; he was getting too much flak from women today, and he didn't like it. "Your contract remains as it is," he said. "If you don't trust me, then go fuck yourself."

Margot turned white, then she stood up. "I'm glad to know where I stand," she said coldly. Then she walked out of the room, slamming the door behind her.

Michael went back to his script, but he had trouble concentrating. Finally, he got up and opened the door that joined their offices. "Margot," he said, "I'm sorry, I . . ." He looked around the room. She was gone.

CHAPTER

60

Michael stood at the mirror and expertly tied his black silk evening tie. The phone rang, the private number that only a few people had.

"Hello?"

"It's Tommy."

He sounded unhappy, Michael thought. "Hey, Tommy, how are you?"

"Not so good. I just had a drink with Norman Geldorf."

"And?"

"He won't sell the trust's stock."

"Wait a minute, I told Amanda Goldman to tell him to sell everything, including Leo's stock."

"She didn't get the message."

"Look, Tommy, I can fix this."

"I don't think you're getting the message either, Vinnie."

"Look, she'll do whatever I tell her to; I've got her wrapped around my little finger; she thinks we're going to get married."

"Geldorf told me it was her express wish that she hang on to the stock, just so she can keep you in power at the studio."

"Tommy . . ."

"In fact, Geldorf had the distinct impression that you were playing her along, just to get her to do that."

"Tommy, that's not so; I . . ."

"Good-bye, Vinnie," Tommy said. "Or maybe I should say good-bye, Michael. That's who you are these days, isn't it?" He hung up.

"Tommy . . ." Michael crashed the phone down on the receiver. "Goddamnit!" he screamed at nobody in particular. He grabbed his dinner jacket; he was already late for an industry dinner at the Beverly Hills Hotel.

He ran down the stairs to the garage, to find the chauffeur working under the hood of the car. "What the hell?" he said.

"I'm sorry, Mr. Vincent. The starter's not getting any juice from the battery; I think there's a broken wire."

"Never mind, I'll drive myself," Michael said, getting into the Porsche.

He roared out of the garage, flashing his lights at the security guard, who got the gate up just in time, then drove down the Pacific Coast Highway, forcing himself to keep it at eighty, lest he be arrested. He was receiving an award tonight for his support of the campaign against AIDS in the Hollywood community, and he didn't want to be late for his own party.

At the predinner cocktail party he stood in line for a gin and tonic, chatting with whoever came up to him. Everybody was there this evening, the big-time players — the studio heads, talent agency heads, top actors, agents, producers. There were no more than fifty women in an audience of five hundred, he reckoned.

Margot Gladstone was one of them. She came up as he was talking with an agent and waited discreetly nearby until she could catch his eye.

"How are you, Margot? I wanted to talk to you . . ."

"That's over," she said.

He looked around and managed a smile, not wanting anyone to catch the hostility in their exchange. He took her arm. "Listen, let's talk after this; come out to the house, and . . ."

"*It's over,*" she said sharply. "The only reason I'm here is to tell you that face to face. My resignation is on your desk." She pulled her arm away from his grasp. *"All bets are off,"* she said, then she smiled. "Good-bye, Michael." She turned and made her way through the crowd.

Michael was about to go after her when an amplified voice said, "Ladies and gentlemen, please take your seats for dinner." A studio head he knew took his arm and guided him toward the head table.

Late that night, after the speeches and his acceptance of the award, Michael finally was able to disengage himself from the congratulators and get out of the ballroom. He walked out of the hotel and waited for five minutes while the Porsche was retrieved from its parking place, then, tipping the valet parker twenty dollars, he got into the car and started down the drive toward Sunset Boulevard.

He was a little drunk, he knew. It had been hot in the dining room, and a waiter had kept bringing him fresh gin and tonics. He took a few deep breaths and tried to clear his head.

Driving carefully and not too fast, Michael turned onto Sunset and headed toward the freeway that would take him to Malibu. He released the levers that held the top down and pressed the button that retracted it. The cool night air made him feel better, and the perfume from the lush gardens along Sunset made him feel happy to be in Beverly Hills.

He was right where he wanted to be, he thought. He held the reins of a great studio in his hands, and he could make any movie he wanted to. He would get square with Tommy tomorrow; this was only a little tiff between lifelong friends, and he would make it right. He would talk to Margot, too; she'd come around. He'd even give her the contract she wanted — anything to keep her happy. He needed her, after all.

A red Corvette was overtaking him on the left and, it seemed to him, crowding him a bit. Not in an aggressive mood, he gave way a little to let the sports car pass. Then, suddenly, inexplicably, the Corvette veered sharply to the right, as if to ram him.

Michael yanked hard on the wheel; he would run onto the sidewalk, if necessary, to avoid this maniac. Fortunately, there was a street to his right, and, shifting down, he turned the corner, swearing loudly. But he was still not all right. Directly in his path, two cars were stopped, side by side, taking up the whole dark street. He stood on the brake, ready to scream at these people, and, suddenly, the Corvette was beside him. Two men got out of the car and walked to either side of the open Porsche. Panicky now, Michael slammed the car into reverse, but a glance in the rearview mirror showed him another car stopped directly behind him.

"Put your hands on your head," a young voice said. An automatic pistol appeared near his head, and it was wearing a silencer.

Michael obeyed, then looked up into a face that might have been his own a few years before. He looked to his right: another such face — young, hard, free of any conscience. How could this happen to him?

"This is a robbery," the young voice said. "Let's have your wallet."

Michael slumped with relief. This was no hit; he'd already be dead if this were a contract job. He fished his wallet from his inside pocket and handed it to the young man.

"Very nice," the gunman said. "Thank you, Vinnie."

Startled, Michael looked up into the young face. "How do you . . ."

Then the young man moved the barrel of the gun from Michael's head, pointed it instead at his lap, and fired twice.

Michael screamed. His lower belly was on fire. He grabbed at his crotch, then jerked his hands back. They came away crimson with his own blood.

Michael screamed again and again. He was only vaguely aware of the cars around him roaring away, even less aware of reaching for the car phone, dialing 911.

CHAPTER

61

Michael sat at his desk, going over the budget for a film he would soon put into production. He ran through the figures, using his lifelong faculty for numbers, mentally comparing them with the figures for other, past productions, making a note here and there, indicating that the number should be discussed later with the production manager.

There was a soft knock, and Margot came through the door from her office.

"Time for the screening," she said. "Everybody's waiting for you."

Michael looked up at Margot, cool, elegant as ever. She dressed better these days on her new salary. She moved behind him.

"Shall I . . ."

He raised a hand. "No!" he barked. "I'd rather do it myself." He was more and more irritable these days, especially since there was no longer any sex to relax him, to take his mind off work. He grabbed the joystick and reversed. The chair rolled back from the desk. He moved the stick forward, and the chair rolled toward the door. Margot was there to open it for him, and he guided the chair expertly down the little ramp that had been built for him, right into the screening room.

Tommy Pro and Mr. Yamamoto turned to watch him enter.

"Hiya, Vinnie," Tommy said as Michael rolled into the place where a chair had been removed to accommodate him.

"Good morning, Tommy, Mr. Yamamoto." He made a little bow from the neck in Yamamoto's direction. How he hated the smooth little man.

"Ready?" Tommy asked.

Michael picked up the phone. "Roll it, Max."

He sat and numbly watched the film, a sorry, violent mess, riddled with car chases and shootouts, starring a kung fu expert who, until recently, had been Tommy Pro's personal trainer. Tommy was looking very trim and fit since he'd moved his operations to L.A.

The film ended and the lights went up. Yamamoto was the first to speak.

"Veddy goood, veddy goood," he said in his Oxford-accented English.

"I'm glad you liked it, Mr. Yamamoto," Michael said.

Tommy leaned over. "Vinnie, there was a car cra h I saw in the dailies — the one where the guy hits the school bus?"

"I didn't think we needed it," Michael said. "It seemed a little too much."

"I liked it," Tommy said. "Put it in."

Michael died a little more. "Of course, Tommy," he said.

CHAPTER

62

Michael straightened his desk, squared away the legal pads, scooped up the pens, and placed them in the small Acoma pot he used for a pencil holder. Satisfied that all was neat, he pushed back from the desk and lifted the heavy briefcase onto his lap, then wheeled himself across his office toward the door to the conference room for what would be his last board meeting at Centurion.

As he took his place at the center of the long table (he no longer sat at the head of the table — Tommy Provensano now occupied that seat) he felt a certain peace in knowing that his work at Centurion was nearly completed.

Certainly he felt no joy in the fact that he had publicly presided over the studio's rapid decline in the quality of its productions and the growth of its debt; he did not take it kindly that his own name was now synonymous with schlock; he felt no affection for the men — and one woman — who had sucked the very viscera from the studio that had been the pre-eminent maker of quality Hollywood films and turned it into an industry joke. Still, he felt a certain peace, knowing that it was nearly all over. He placed his briefcase on the conference table.

"Gentlemen," Tommy said, "please be seated."

The dozen men and one woman took their places at the table — Tommy Pro at the head, and Margot Gladstone to his right.

"This regular monthly meeting of the board of directors of Centurion pictures will come to order," Tommy said. "The vice-chairman of the corporation, Ms. Gladstone, will act as recorder for this meeting."

Margot gave first Tommy, then the others at the table, her warmest smile.

"This meeting," Tommy continued, "will be brief, since there is little business to conduct. We . . ."

"Mr. Chairman?" Michael said.

Tommy looked irritably in Michael's direction. "If we could just stick to the agenda," he said, and his tone brooked no argument.

"Mr. Chairman," Michael continued, despite Tommy's warning. "If I may interrupt for just a moment. The board is aware that today is our chairman's birthday, and I have been asked to say a few words and present a small gift."

Tommy looked startled, then smiled. "That is very kind of you, Michael. And may I thank all of you?"

"I will not dwell on the chairman's years," Michael said, to light laughter, "but it is well known to all of us that he has a keen interest in the weapons used in Centurion's films, so I have asked our special effects department to supply something which will be used in our forthcoming production, *Armed Force*, one that our chairman is taking a particular interest in."

Tommy leaned back in his chair and smiled broadly. "What do you have for me, Michael?"

Michael released the locks on his briefcase and opened it. Inside lay two gleaming automatic weapons and a number of accessories. Michael picked up one of the guns and began screwing a suppressor onto its barrel. "This, Tommy, is a prototype of the production model of a new automatic weapon developed by the CIA, in conjunction with the Drug Enforcement Agency. I was able to persuade the Director of Intelligence to allow us to use it in *Armed Force*." He passed the weapon down the table to Tommy, who received it gingerly.

"Is it loaded?" Tommy asked.

Michael began screwing a suppressor onto the second weapon. "Of course, Tommy — but only with ammunition formulated by Special Effects. I assure you, it would be quite safe if you raked the conference table with automatic fire." He slid back the bolt on his weapon and released it. "It cocks like so."

Tommy stood up and cocked the weapon. "I hope you don't mind, Michael, if, in light of previous events at this studio, I don't point it at anyone."

"Of course, Tommy," Michael replied. "Try that beautifully panelled wall. I assure you, it will come to no harm."

Everyone stood and backed away from the table as Tommy raised the weapon. "All right; let's pretend that all of the New York film critics are lined up against that wall." He pointed the machine gun at the wall and pressed the trigger.

The weapon exploded in Tommy's face. Pandemonium broke out in the boardroom. Some board members dived under the table, others rushed to Tommy's aid. Margot Gladstone dragged him away from the table and propped him up against a wall.

"Tommy!" she was crying, "Are you alive?"

Tommy was, indeed, alive, though his face was ruined, and he seemed able to make only croaking sounds.

"Thank you for your tender efforts on Tommy's behalf, Margot," Michael said, then he fired a short burst in her direction. Margot spun around, bounced off a wall, and fell in a heap before Tommy, who was still trying to speak.

Michael swung his weapon toward a group of directors who were now huddled in a corner of the room. "Now, Mr. Yamamoto," he said. "You may join your ancestors." He fired a long burst at the group, sweeping back and forth across the corner. The gun stopped firing, and the bolt locked. Michael reached into the briefcase for another clip, then reloaded and cocked the weapon. He swung his wheelchair back toward Tommy. "I don't want you to think that the exploding weapon was designed to kill you, Tommy," he said.

There was a hammering on the door leading into the hallway, which, as Michael knew, was always locked.

"I have kept that particular pleasure for myself."

Tommy roared something, but his words were unintelligible. One or more persons was now attempting to break down the stout mahogany door.

Michael pointed the weapon at Tommy. "On behalf of movie lovers everywhere, I give you this," he said. He fired, and Tommy's body did a little dance under the withering rain of large-caliber slugs. After a few seconds, the weapon was again out of ammunition.

Michael was reloading for the final coup when efforts to break down the door succeeded. Michael hurried, but he was not fast enough. Two uniformed security guards were emptying their weapons in his direction.

Michael felt himself fly sideways out of his wheelchair.

EPILOGUE

Michael slowly opened his eyes. He had been aware, over the past days, that heroic efforts had been made to save his life. He had been in some sort of intensive care room that was noisy and busy at all times, but now he was in a quiet place. He tried to lift his head, but the muscles would not work. He tried gripping the sides of the bed with his hands, but that didn't work either. He tried moving his toes, to no effect. In his rising panic, he tried to scream, but couldn't.

Michael spent some moments calming himself; then he swiveled his eyes around to take in as much as he could. There was a stand next to his bed that held a plastic bag of some sort of fluid; apart from that, he could only see the ceiling. He closed his eyes, and a few minutes later he dozed.

A noise awakened him; a door had opened, and now it closed. Footsteps approached his bed. Michael swiveled his eyes to try and see who it was. Amanda Goldman's face moved into his vision.

"Oh, my darling," she said, "you're awake." She moved a finger back and forth across his field of vision.

Michael's eyes followed the finger.

"You really are awake, aren't you? I've been visiting you for weeks, and they've always told me not to expect any response. Something about brain damage."

Michael's eyes widened.

"Can you hear me?" she asked. "If you can, blink once for yes and twice for no."

Michael blinked once. He could communicate! If he could communicate, then there was some way out of this!

"Can you move?" she asked.

Michael blinked twice.

"My God, you *know* me, don't you?"

Michael blinked once.

"I want you to know what's been happening," she said. "A lot of Japanese turned up at the studio, and they've been running things."

Michael closed his eyes.

"I've been taking care of your personal affairs," she said.

Michael opened his eyes again.

"My lawyers got a trust established to run your affairs, and I'm the trustee. Somebody found the will you left, naming me as beneficiary, so the court appointed me."

Michael stared at her.

Amanda sat on the bed and positioned herself so that he could see her easily. "I'm all right, I guess. Michael, there's something I want to tell you. I feel that I can confide in you more than anyone else."

Michael blinked once. He was impatient with all this talk. He had to find a way to let her know what he wanted to do.

"I've met somebody, and I've been seeing a lot of him. He's younger than I am, but that never made any difference with you and me, did it?"

Michael blinked twice. Better to humor her until he could figure out something.

"He's somebody you know, somebody you worked with," she said. "His name is Chuck Parish."

Michael's eyes opened wide again.

"You remember; you made a couple of films together. This is all real incestuous, you know, because until recently, he was living with Vanessa, your old flame. *She,* my darling, is living with Bob Hart! Can you believe it? She must be some smart cookie to have been able to winkle him out of Susan's clutches, but she did it. The divorce is the talk of the town!"

Michael blinked rapidly. This was insane.

"Chuck is sweet," she said. "Not as good as you in bed, of course, but quite all right. He doesn't seem to like to talk about you, but I knew you'd be glad I was with a friend of yours. I've taken the money in my trust that I got for my Centurion stock and formed a new production company to produce Chuck's work. He's a wonderful director and writer, as you well know, having discovered him!"

Michael closed his eyes tightly. How could he get her to shut up?

Amanda was quiet for a moment, then she wiped a tear from the corner of an eye. "You know why I'm here, don't you?"

Michael stared at her.

"I remember our conversation when Leo was in the hospital. You were right then, and I want you to know that I understand what you must be feeling about your condition. I've had a second and a third opinion, but no one gives you any hope of any sort of a recovery. I'm afraid the best you could hope for would be to be propped up in bed and pointed at a television for the rest of your life."

Michael blinked rapidly. He had to think

of some way to communicate what he wanted.

"I know what you want, my darling, because you as much as told me when Leo was ill."

Michael saw her hand go past the corner of his eye, and his head tilted up for a moment, so that he could see more of the room; then it was tilted back again.

"You changed my life," she said, and she was weeping now. "I owe you everything, but now there is only one thing I can do for you."

Michael saw something move into his field of vision, and it was white.

"Good-bye, my darling," Amanda said. "I love you."

The pillow filled his vision, and then it was dark.

Michael couldn't even blink. He fought the pillow with his mind, but it didn't work.

Suddenly it wasn't dark anymore. There was light coming from somewhere, and, miracle of miracles, he could move! He held up a hand to shield his eyes, but then it wasn't necessary. The light was kind, and it seemed to originate down a hallway or tunnel. Michael walked toward it.

Then there was a dark shape in the light — another person, and somehow he felt he knew who it was! He walked faster. It was a man, and he was walking toward Michael, his hands reaching out for him. Behind the man were other people.

Michael reached out for the man, and then he knew who he was. Onofrio Callabrese took his son's hands and held them tightly. His smile was ghastly.

Michael struggled to free himself, and then other people were around him, pulling him forward into the light. They were glad to see him, in some odd way, and he knew them all. There was a woman, and it was Carol Geraldi. She held onto him particularly. Rick Rivera was there, and — my God! It was Leo! Leo put an arm around his shoulders and hurried him forward. Benedetto and Cheech walked alongside him, and there, coming out of the light, was the lawyer, Moriarty!

Michael felt a terrible fear, and he tried to dig his heels in, but nothing could stop his progress toward the light. Inexorably they drew him into it.

Michael suddenly found that he could do more than walk. He could scream.